EMPLOYMENT LAW

D1564203

By

SAMUEL ESTREICHER
Dwight D. Opperman Professor of Law &
Director of Center for Labor and Employment Law
New York University School of Law

GILLIAN LESTER
Professor of Law
University of California at Berkeley School of Law

CONCEPTS AND INSIGHTS SERIES

FOUNDATION PRESS
75TH ANNIVERSARY

THOMSON
™
WEST

© 2008 By THOMSON/FOUNDATION PRESS
                    395 Hudson Street
                    New York, NY 10014
                    Phone Toll Free 1–877–888–1330
                    Fax (212) 367–6799
                    foundation–press.com
Printed in the United States of America
ISBN 978–1–58778–479–8

 *TEXT IS PRINTED ON 10% POST CONSUMER RECYCLED PAPER*

In memory of
Rose and David Estreicher

and

With gratitude to
Lois and Richard Lester

*

PREFACE

Not even 20 years ago, few law schools offered a course in Employment Law and few lawyers purported to practice in the field. The law of the workplace was divided into two subjects – Labor Law (the law of unions and collective bargaining) and Employment Discrimination Law (starting with Title VII of the Civil Rights Act of 1964 with accretions nearly annually as legislatures framed new anti-discrimination laws). Teachers taught in one area or the other but rarely in both. Lawyers, too, tended to divide themselves in a similar manner.

By now, Employment Law has come into its own. Perhaps in recognition of the declining strength of unions in private companies and the degree of job change and other ferment in major companies, courts are fast developing a body of employment law to complement the statutes in this area. With the ever-developing law, the practice, too, has changed. Lawyers are no longer Labor Lawyers or Civil Rights Lawyers; they are increasingly Labor and Employment Lawyers. Nomenclature is keeping pace: The plaintiff bar has organized itself as the National Employment Lawyers Association; the hoary Industrial Relations Research Association is now the Labor and Employment Research Association; and the sections of the bar in which the lawyers enroll are Sections of Labor and Employment Law. Not surprisingly, the American Law Institute has embarked for the first time on a Restatement of Employment Law.

This change is also reflected in the law schools, where Employment Law has become the essential port of entry for students interested in the workplace; those specializing in the field go on to take courses in Labor Law and Employment Discrimination and, perhaps, Employee Benefits. Employment Law is also the course that provides the overarching conceptual framework, the analytic connective tissue that enables students and instructors to fit the pieces together, to understand, for example, how the law governing union organization ties in with the background rule of employment at-will in non-union shops.

Our book seeks to provide a useful, stimulating aid for student and instructor alike as they encounter fast-paced judicial and statutory developments. We have organized the book into two parts: The first tracks the common law of the employment relationship; the second deals with statutory interventions in the historical order in which they appeared.

PREFACE

Our book is designed for both practical and theoretical minded. Each chapter, we hope, provides a clear exposition of the existing positive law, along with our commentary where appropriate. Each chapter also asks why the law intervenes at all in the particular area, but addresses the question from a perspective not unreceptive to plausible accounts of market failure in the area.

Some of the chapters appeared in print in an earlier version, and we wish to thank our coauthors and publishers for permission to reprint and modify these materials. Chapter 1 had its origin as classroom materials and then appeared as an Appendix to Cases and Materials on Employment Law 620-27 (Samuel Estreicher & Michael C. Harper eds., West/Thomson, 2004). Chapter 3 tracks some of the analysis and text in a revised version of the Council Draft of the Restatement (Third) of Employment Law (American Law Institute, 2008). Chapters 9 and 11 expand materials first published as Samuel Estreicher, Labor and Employment Law, in Fundamentals of American Law (A. Morrison ed., Oxford University Press, 1996). Finally, Chapter 13 elaborates upon Chapter 16 in Cases and Materials on Employment Discrimination and Employment Law (Samuel Estreicher & Michael C. Harper, 2d ed., West/Thomson, 2004).

* * *

This book could not have been produced without the assistance and patience of many other individuals and organization. We wish to thank, in particular, Rosetta Abraham, Ross Davidson, Michelle Illczysyn, Eileen O'Brien, Didier Reiss, Jodi Kruger, Debra Krauss, Marc Pilotin, Andrew Verriere, Daniel Dingerson, the Libraries of the NYU, UCLA and U.C. Berkeley Schools of Law; and the inspired editors at Foundation Press. Last, but not least, we acknowledge our profound debt to our mates for life, Aleta and Eric, respectively.

SAMUEL ESTREICHER
GILLIAN LESTER

March 25, 2008

SUMMARY OF CONTENTS

*

TABLE OF CONTENTS

EMPLOYMENT LAW

*

Part 1

THE NATURE OF LABOR MARKETS

Chapter 1

THE REGULATION OF LABOR MARKETS

This book deals with the body of U.S. law governing the relationship of employers and their employees that applies even though the employee works for a private company, and is not necessarily part a bargaining unit represented by a labor union or a member of a protected group under federal or state antidiscrimination statutes. We have some early chapters devoted to collective bargaining and discrimination law but they are not the focus of this book because these topics are typically covered in other texts and in other courses in the law school curriculum. There is also a historical basis for our approach. In the United States, regulation of labor markets first took the form of rules for labor organization and collective bargaining, followed by legislation in the 1960s to curb discrimination in employment decisions. Only in the 1970s did courts and legislatures begin the process of a more general regulation of employment decisions. In contrast to what might be viewed as the European model, the U.S. system starts with the assumption that market forces are ordinarily adequate to deal with problems that arise in the employment context, with the burden on those who seek regulation to show that there is some problem in the operation of labor markets that justifies intervention.

A. The Model of Competitive Labor Markets

We start with a few simple supply and demand curves to illustrate how labor markets are, in theory, supposed to work. Figure 1 illustrates the effect, under the model of perfectly competitive labor markets, of increasing the wage beyond the equilibrium wage—the wage set by the intersection of the supply and demand curves for labor. Figure 2 depicts the consequences of paying below the equilibrium wage.

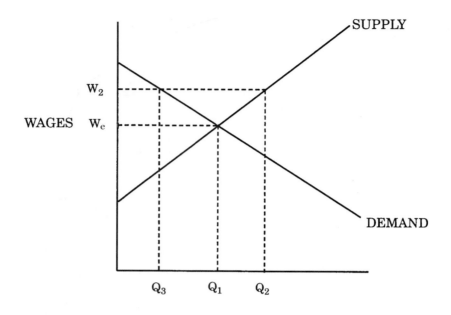

QUANTITY OF LABOR

Figure 1

Note that the supply curve for labor is upward sloping. The idea here is that the supply of labor increases at higher wages. By contrast, the demand curve for labor generally slopes downward. If capital is held constant, the value that each additional unit of labor adds (what labor economists call "the marginal product of each unit of labor") decreases as more units of labor are added. Or, put differently, if all else is held constant, the value to the employer of each additional unit of labor decreases with increased supply of labor. Consider a simple illustration: Suppose we have only one shovel and one worker. If we were to add a second worker using the same shovel at the same time, the value the second worker would add to the project would be smaller than the value the first worker added. The only way the second worker would add an equivalent or greater value is if he were using the shovel at a time when the shovel lay idle or he were a better skilled laborer.

W_e in Figure 1, at the intersection of the supply and demand curves, is the "equilibrium" or "market clearing" wage. At the equilibrium wage, the market has "cleared". The employer hires as many workers as it needs at that rate but cannot obtain qualified workers if it pays less. Employers also have no incentive to pay more than W_e. If an employer pays more, say, W_2 in Figure 1, its demand for labor falls to Q_3. There are, however, Q_2 workers available at that wage. Under perfectly competitive conditions, other firms will enter this market employing the available (unemployed) workers at wages lower than W_2. This will place pressure on the original employer who faces lower-cost competition. In time, the wage will be driven down to W_e, the equilibrium wage.

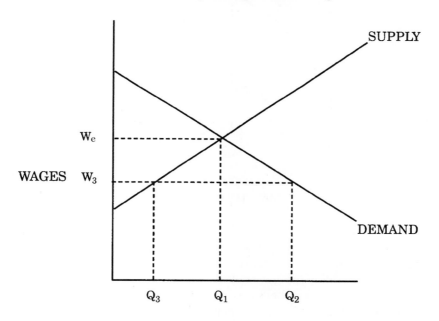

QUANTITY OF LABOR

Figure 2

Take the situation in Figure 2, where the employer pays less than the equilibrium wage, say, W_3. Such an employer gets only a Q_3 supply of workers even though it is in need of a Q_2 supply. Here, too, competition will drive the wage up to the equilibrium wage: Other firms will be able to attract workers away at a higher wage and still pay workers only their marginal product.

3

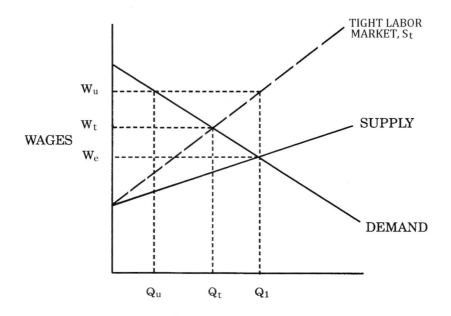

QUANTITY OF LABOR

Figure 3

Figure 3 indicates that where there is a tighter supply of labor (denoted by supply curve S_t, the equilibrium wage (here, W_t) will be higher up the demand curve; the employer will have to pay more (here W_u) to receive the same Q_1 supply of labor. The employer, however, demands fewer workers at the new equilibrium wage (only Q_t workers) and even fewer (only Q_u workers) at the wage (W_u) that would attract Q_1 workers. Because Figure 3 involves a tighter labor market than the previous figures, an increase in the effective wage (whether mandated by law or collective bargaining) from W_t to W_u involves a smaller disemployment effect than we saw in Figure 2, for only Q_1 workers are available at this wage. By contrast, in Figure 1, setting the effective wage at W_2 results in a supply of Q_2 workers but only Q_3 workers get jobs.

This is a highly stylized model that simplifies the real world. Such simplification helps economists evaluate the operation of markets that do not conform to the model. Key assumptions underlying the model are:

- *Absence of Monopoly.* There are many employers bidding for labor and many workers bidding for work. Neither firms nor workers collude with their competitors. Under this assumption, both employers and workers are "wage takers," not "wage setters"; neither has the market power unilaterally to set the equilibrium wage.

- *Absence of External Costs or Benefits.* Parties to the employment relationship bear fully the costs and recognize fully the benefits of the relationship. In other words, the costs and benefits of employment decisions are absorbed by the parties; there are no external costs (known by economists as "externalities") imposed on third parties and no external benefits gained by third parties.

- *Knowledge.* Workers are able, fairly cheaply, to calculate their contribution to the marginal product of the firm, are aware of wages and opportunities elsewhere, and can accurately assess future contingencies. Employers, too, can readily calculate their needs, workers' contributions, conditions elsewhere, and future contingencies.

- *Rationality.* Workers in this model are seeking to maximize their utility, defined for these purposes as a tradeoff between earnings and leisure; all other things being equal workers want more money to give up what leisure they presently have. Employers care only about maximizing their profits. There are no "agency costs": to the extent workers or firms operate through agents (e.g., unions or managers), the incentives of these agents are fully aligned with their principals.

- *Mobility.* Workers can costlessly change jobs, and firms can costlessly change workers.

- *Absence of Transaction Costs.* Workers and firms can costlessly write contracts to advance their respective objectives.

No real-world labor markets are competitive in this strong sense. Some markets are closer to the competitive model, in different aspects, than others. To the extent that these assumptions fail, the market may not allocate jobs, wages, income, or other resources efficiently. The case for regulation, however, requires more than simply identifying a real-world departure from these assumptions. The proponent of regulation must be able to show that regulation will address the market failure without incurring costs that outweigh the benefits of intervention. The point for the moment is to be aware of these assumptions as we explore different arguments for regulating labor markets.

5

B. Reasons for Regulation of Labor Markets

1. Redistribution

The case for employment regulation on the redistributive ratio-nale can be viewed in at least two different ways. One is to argue that there is an inherent "inequality of bargaining power" when individual workers negotiate their terms of employment with em-ployers. Because many individuals work to meet everyday necessi-ties, and lack capital to tide them over, they often do not have the same ability to search and hold out for better terms than other sellers in the marketplace. Thus, the bargains they strike are less favorable than they would be if workers did not face such pres-sures. Regulation, in the form of, say, laws mandating the provision of minimum or "living" wages, may be viewed as a way of enhanc-ing the returns to work so as to conform to some ideal of the terms that would have been reached if individuals did not have to bargain under necessitous circumstances. Social insurance may be another approach here. Historically, labor unions and benevolent associa-tions developed in part to pool resources of their members to deal with the contingencies of life such as injury or lay-offs from work. Many states, and since 1935 with the active prodding of the federal government, require employers to contribute to unemployment insurance funds out of which unemployed workers can draw both to tide them over between jobs and also arguably to enhance their bargaining leverage with new employers. Legal protection of the right of workers to form labor unions and insist on collective bargaining—a matter of federal law since the enactment of the National Labor Relations Act of 1935 (NLRA) and an earlier measure for employees in the railroad industry—can be viewed in this light, as an effort not to displace labor markets but to enable individuals to enhance their bargaining power through collective action.

A second way to view the redistributive rationale avoids any judgments about inherent inequality but seeks regulation as a means to promote social cohesion—to enhance the leverage of weaker groups so that they will have more of a stake in the society, and thus to channel conflict over the distribution of wealth into less socially destructive avenues than outright industrial warfare. This was Bismarck's stated rationale for the pioneering social insurance programs of imperial Germany, and it is also akin to the "industrial peace" justification for the NLRA.

That one can offer a rationale for regulation in these terms, of course, does not mean that the costs of such regulation disappear.

6

But it does suggest that society may legitimately pursue other objectives in addition to the most efficient allocation of goods and services.

2. Evolving Social Norms or Preference Transformation

Another argument for regulation is that it provides a means whereby society seeks to implement its value system, its notion of the fair conditions under which people may be employed. The costs, again, do not disappear, but society is willing to absorb them in the service of this larger goal by, say, paying higher prices for goods produced under fair labor conditions. Such an argument might underlie the Fair Labor Standards Act's requirement of minimum wages and payment of overtime premiums, federal and state regulations of child labor, occupational safety laws, etc. A similar argument also might be made in defense of certain discrimination laws, most notably laws requiring nontrivial costs of accommodating disabled workers or laws requiring retention of older workers.

A variant of this argument is that the law may seek to alter the values or preferences of workers and firms in order that, over time, the bargains that are reached reflect these newly instilled values. For example, occupational safety laws may create certain expectations in workers of the proper conditions for work—expectations which form a new baseline for employment contracts. Discrimination laws also may be viewed as a (largely successful) instance of preference transformation. In many situations, the claim by opponents of regulation that the costs of hiring minority or female workers would be prohibitive (e.g., due to the adverse reactions of customers or coworkers) did not materialize once the law forced virtually all firms to disregard these factors in hiring and promoting workers. In the process, social norms regarding workforce diversity evolved.

3. Correcting "Market Failure"

Yet a third rationale for regulation, one that is especially attractive to economists, is to use the instrument of law to reconstruct the market to produce the outcome that the market would have produced in the absence of market failure. Under this view, labor markets are not perfectly competitive; some forms of regulation may improve efficiency in labor markets; other forms may involve some efficiency losses but far less than suggested by the standard account. Consider again the assumptions of the standard account but with a dash of realism:

7

- *Absence of Monopoly.* In some settings, it is claimed that some firms are not wage-takers at all but really wage-setters effectively enjoying a buyer's monopoly (what is called "monopsony"). Many economists are skeptical that monopsony conditions obtain in the U.S. economy, except perhaps for isolated mining towns with one firm that is the sole employer, or a region of the country where one hospital employs all the nurses. Mandatory minimum standards, such as minimum wage and maximum hours laws, are one way to regulate monopsonistic bargaining. Laws promoting collective bargaining may be seen as a counterweight to excessive market power on the part of firms.

- *Absence of External Costs or Benefits.* Externalities are generally less important in the employment context than in other areas such as environmental regulation. However, an example relevant to the workplace setting is the costs to third parties of extended unemployment. When workers become unemployed and lose income for extended periods of time, third parties may bear costs in the form of disruptions in family and community life. Another example is occupational health. The health consequences of workplace hazards may exceed what individual workers can absorb, and society as a whole will bear some of the costs of industrial illness and disease. State provision of unemployment and health insurance may be justified on these grounds.

- *Knowledge.* Workers may have difficulty calculating the value of their contribution to the firm, especially where their contribution is part of a group effort. Despite the advent of the internet, we still do not have very good information clearinghouses informing workers of opportunities in other regions. Workers also may have difficulty learning of or understanding job hazards, the firm's future economic plans, or their own need for protection against future contingencies such as deteriorating health, poverty in old age, or a change in the value of their education and training. Employers, for their part, may have difficulty assessing the productivity of a worker, the likelihood that a worker will quit or engage in misconduct, or future contingencies such as shifts in technology, product demand and demographics.

One widely accepted way to improve the operation of labor markets is to enhance the dissemination of information about wages and employment opportunities. Federal occupational and safety laws may also require disclosure of workplace hazards that enable workers to negotiate with a better understanding of the health and safety costs of working in certain environments.

- *Rationality.* Although most firms seek to maximize profits, some employers may have a mixture of motives and objectives that deviate from pure profit maximization. This is because the firm's managers, though its agents, may have objectives that sometimes diverge from the firm's interest in maximizing profits. Managers may be insulated from competition in the market for corporate control and to that extent are freed to pursue somewhat independent objectives. Managers are human beings whose preferences and perceptions are shaped by the customs of the society in which they live. Managers may be concerned about preserving their discretionary authority even when restrictions on that authority may improve employment decision-making without detracting from profits. Workers may also demonstrate irrationality in decision-making, for example, by underestimating the risk of future hazards, or overestimating the value of future income.

- *Mobility.* Rarely can real-life workers costlessly change their jobs. Financial constraints and the inability to borrow money may make it hard to afford moving. To some extent, workers have sunk costs in their housing or have made other decisions which cannot be readily recovered. They may also have sunk costs in their jobs. In order to promote attachment to the firm, deter shirking by workers, and encourage investments by workers in firm-specific skills (skills that cannot readily be transferred to other work settings), firms may have implemented "internal labor market" policies. Such policies often use seniority rules and pension benefits to backload compensation to later stages in the worker's career or key benefits to longevity of service. Long-term workers employed under such policies cannot readily exit from the firm because they cannot capture the same compensation and benefits on the external market. Laws barring age discrimination and restricting the discharge of long-term workers might be justified as an attempt to enforce expectations under such policies. Government might also seek to promote mobility of workers by, say, reducing vesting requirements for pensions or eliminating tax incentives that promote firm provision of medical insurance. Unions similarly often seek to promote mobility within an industry by negotiating industry-wide benefits plans that are not tied to specific firms.

9

- *Absence of Transaction Costs.* Firms may seek to standardize policies for all workers in a given job classification because it is costly to negotiate individual employment contracts. Another cost may be the difficulty of confining the application of a particular employment term, e.g., a just-cause discipline system, to one worker or one sub-group of workers; as a consequence, an employer may avoid its provision altogether. A related difficulty is what economists refer to as a "collective action" problem. If one individual invests in the costly undertaking of negotiating with the employer for, say, safety standards in the workplace, other workers will enjoy the benefits of that effort without having to incur any costs, thus being able to "free ride" on the other's effort. For this reason, there may be no one worker willing to make the investment even though as a group, the workers would prefer safer working conditions. Firms, acting as coordinators of employee preferences, may provide some terms that its workers as a group prefer but will not negotiate for themselves because of this collective-action problem. One justification for labor unions is that they provide an independent mechanism for articulating employee preferences and negotiating for such collective goods.

C. Objections to Regulation

The state may intervene to regulate markets in order to achieve efficiency, or it may do so to achieve other ends, such as the redistribution of wealth, i.e., to give one party to a relationship or one or more groups a larger share of the economic rewards from their activity than they would receive in the absence of regulation.

A common objection to employment regulation is that regulation may raise the marginal cost of labor beyond its marginal contribution to the value of the firm's product or service and is therefore equivalent to an exogenous wage increase over the equilibrium wage. (Examples of regulations that have been criticized on this basis are minimum wage and hours laws, and minimum occupational safety and health laws.) Under this view, employers respond to such wage increases by reducing their hiring at the margin. They are less inclined to hire the additional worker if they have to pay more for that worker than warranted by the marginal value he adds. Workers who have and keep their jobs may benefit from the regulatory scheme. However in some cases, these workers, too, might prefer to trade away the statutory entitlements (e.g., a safer workplace or paid family leave) for other goods such as higher wages. The costs are borne by those who cannot obtain jobs and, to the extent output (either quantity or quality) is reduced to meet increased labor costs, consumers.

Those who object to a redistributive rationale for regulation also worry that it results in a kind of haphazard redistribution: the beneficiaries may end up being individuals or groups that are relatively well off, the losers may be relatively powerless consumers and unorganized workers, and very little may be taken from owners of capital. Moreover, such use of regulation may reduce social wealth more than necessary to accomplish redistributive goals. From this perspective, redistribution is best done through direct taxation and spending measures rather than regulation.

To the extent regulation increases net labor costs, proponents of regulation will seek to extend the law's reach to all firms in the market. This move, if successful, does not eliminate the costs of the regulation, such as the claimed adverse impact on workers who lose their jobs because of the increased labor costs or consumers who face higher prices or lower quality, but does tend to dilute the impact on regulated firms. The ability to generalize the costs of regulation in this manner is, of course, hampered by the ability of consumers to substitute for products produced in unregulated circumstances. For example, the phenomenon of "globalization," wherein a general reduction in the costs of transportation and communication has led to the emergence of national and international markets where consumers can learn of and purchase competitive products, is an important development here.

Many employment regulations are designed to inhibit competitive forces. This is particularly true of laws protecting the right to engage in union organization and collective bargaining or laws requiring the payment of minimum or prevailing wages. These laws seek to reduce competition from workers willing to work under conditions less favorable than the prescribed minima. Some regulations operate also to preserve the market position of existing companies by requiring new entrants to adhere to the regulatory conditions. For example, "prevailing wage" laws require governments to purchase goods and services from firms paying prevailing wages and benefits; whatever their stated rationale, such laws reduce competition among firms. Government might reexamine existing regulatory schemes, as it has in the airline and trucking industries, which may have outlived their usefulness, inhibiting competition among firms without discernible public benefit.

Laws can also serve as a barrier to information. Defamation laws, for example, may make it very difficult for employers to learn the prior history of job applicants.

11

Regulation may also have the effect of "crowding out" beneficial behavior that parties would engage in in the absence of
regulation. In this vein, it might be argued that some social welfare
policies enable firms to shift some of the costs of employment
decisions on to the larger public. For example, employers may not
be providing health insurance because they know that hospital
emergency rooms will be available to their employees.

In sum, the operation of law may serve as a barrier to, rather
than facilitator, of efficient allocation. For this reason, it is critical
to assess whether the benefits justify the costs of regulation. It is
also critically important to assess on a continuing basis whether
regulations continue to serve their intended function. If laws that
initially served to correct market failure become outmoded, they
may harm competition and efficiency without providing a counter-
vailing benefit.

D. Modes of Regulation

Regulation can take different forms:

1. *Taxing and Spending Measures*

One way to promote a social objective, say, hiring of disabled
workers, is to create direct incentives, either through tax credits or
public subsidies. Executive Order 11246, for example, imposes
affirmative action obligations on government contractors as a
means of encouraging utilization of qualified minority workers.
Such measures are likely to increase firm demand for such workers.
Government training and education programs can also improve the
supply of qualified workers to enable them to compete in markets
where the returns for work are higher. One virtue of taxing and
spending measures is that they are "on budget"; at least the direct
costs of the regulation are readily identified and those costs are
absorbed by the government. One disadvantage of such measures
may be the encouragement they provide employers to reduce pay or
benefits in the expectation that the government program will make
up the difference.

2. *"Minimum Terms" Laws or Mandates*

The Fair Labor Standards Act, child labor laws, OSHA and
discrimination laws are examples of "minimum terms" laws or
"mandates". In essence, the state is prescribing certain terms for

all employment contracts. Unlike taxing and spending measures, this form of regulation is "off budget"; the direct costs of regulation are not easily measurable and are borne, in the first instance, by employers.

3. Regulation of the Process of Bargaining

The NLRA, as mentioned, does not itself prescribe minimum terms; rather, it establishes a process of collective bargaining for workers choosing collective representation. Laws mandating certain disclosures, such as the occupational safety laws or the federal WARN legislation requiring advance notice of plant closings, may be viewed as attempts at influencing the process of negotiating employment contracts. Laws establishing waivable terms that can be bargained away by workers can also be viewed as a process-based regulation forcing parties to a relationship to divulge information that would lead to better bargains. Consider here proposals to rewrite the background assumption of employment from a waivable rule of at-will employment to a waivable rule of just-cause employment.

Chapter 2

THE EMPLOYMENT RELATIONSHIP

A. What is at Stake?

A threshold question for employment law, of course, is determining whether the firm and the individual providing services to the firm are in an employment relationship. This is especially important in dealing with statutes which typically limit their protections to "employees" and their obligations to "employers". Not all individuals who provide services to firms are employees; some may view themselves or be viewed as a matter of law as "independent contractors" who ordinarily are excluded from the scope of employment statutes. There are few exceptions, the most prominent being 42 U.S.C. § 1981 which bars racial and certain forms of ancestry discrimination in the "making of contracts".[1] There are also special laws for independent businesses, notably those establishing rights for franchisees; such laws are outside the scope of this text. We also note that many of the contract and tort principles that are the subjects of Chapters 3–5 are not limited to employment relationships.

In the usual case, individuals providing services would prefer to be treated as employees in order to come within the reach of statutory guarantees of non-discrimination, compensation for workplace injury, promised employee benefits, and the like. There are some situations where the individual may be better off being treated as an independent contractor. For example, if an individual has a tort claim against the firm, he may prefer the legal status of an independent contractor who can sue in court rather than be limited to administrative recoveries under the workers' compensation regime. Similarly, an individual who wishes to work for other clients during the engagement with the firm, or who wishes to use non-public information obtained in the course of that engagement,

---

1. See, e.g., *Danco v. Wal–Mart Stores, Inc.*, 178 F.3d 8 (1st Cir. 1999). There is also a question whether independent contractors engaged in job or wage competition with NLRA employees may enjoy a "statutory labor" exemption from the anti-trust laws, premised on their involvement in a "labor dispute" within the meaning of the Norris–LaGuardia Act, 29 U.S.C. §§ 101–115. Compare *Columbia River Assn. v. Hinton*, 315 U.S. 143, 145 (1942) (no exemp-tion: really "a dispute among businessmen over the terms of a contract for the sale of fish"), with *Home Box Office v. Directors Guild of America*, 531 F.Supp. 578, 597 (S.D.N.Y. 1982) (holding that freelance directors were common-law employees, but even if they were not, "the similarity of functions and overlap of capacities among staff and freelance directors create[] a mutuality of interest that readily justifies their bargaining collectively").

may be less likely to face implied fiduciary restrictions if he is viewed as an independent contractor rather than an employee.

B. The Nature of the Employment Relationship

There is a tendency in some of the court decisions, and in much of the academic literature, to view the question of employee status through the lens of "economic dependency"—that individuals providing services to the firm are often in an especially dependent, vulnerable state calling for the protections of the employment laws. Although this may be a fair description of many situations, it is not a good account of what lies at the core of the employment relationship. Individuals might have a great deal of leverage and could easily obtain comparable employment in the external market and yet they are still employees. In other situations, the employee and the firm are dependent on each other. Employees may have developed skills and have access to information that the firm could replicate only by costly means—training newcomers or hiring skilled employees during a period of tight labor markets. Even in settings where employees obtain "general" skills that would have value with other firms, the employees may have developed, or been trained by the firm to develop, "firm-specific" skills—knowledge of the workings of the firm, of the relations between departments, of the location of essential information, of the idiosyncrasies of equipment—that together with the input of management creates a joint value for both the firms and the employees. In these "internal labor market" settings, the relationship is plainly one of mutual dependency.

The question that needs to be asked is why firms choose to have some of the tasks required by the organization provided by employees rather than independent contractors, and why individuals agree to be employees rather than retaining their independence. From the firm's standpoint, by having these individuals inside the organization the firm gains the ability to control how their time will be utilized during the workday, and presumably this measure of control increases the value of the effort expended by the employees. Control is one mechanism for promoting alignment of incentives so that employees view their objectives while on the job as closer to the objectives of the firm; such alignment helps reduce monitoring costs for firms. Put differently, it may be more expensive for the firm to use outside vendors, even if they do not charge more for their services, because of increased costs of supervising service providers who are in business for themselves and have other clients demanding their attention. Where, however, the firm has a clearly defined, often time-sensitive, project to be completed and can count on the professional values of the outside vendors to complete the project to specifications with a minimum of supervision, the firm is less likely to use its own employees for the project. To deal with fluctuations in the business, the firm may prefer a flexible staffing arrangement whereby it supplements its regular workforce with outside vendors whom it can easily dismiss when customer orders decline.

Why does someone agree to be an employee? There is, of course, no single answer that fits every situation, but there are several factors that often inform the decision. First, the employee may prefer regularity of tenure and compensation, knowing in advance that he or she will have a job and will be paid over the course of the relationship irrespective of the fluctuating fortunes of the business. (These expectations are enhanced by the formal seniority rules of union-represented firms and the informal seniority systems used by many non-union firms.) As discussed in the first chapter, individuals may lack access to capital that will help tide them over bad times, and for this reason find employment attractive in providing a measure of security, what might be viewed as a form of self-insurance. Second, the employee may lack marketable external skills and look to a job as a means of acquiring skills that will enhance his value, hoping one day to go into business for himself. In theory, the educational system should be performing this service, but sometimes on-the-job training does a better job at imparting marketable skills. Third, in some jobs, the employee will be able to add value in his contributions to the firm that will result in higher returns over his career with that firm than he could obtain selling his skills in the external market. Here, again, we invoke the concept of the internal labor market, where the value generated by the joint efforts of the employee and the firm exceed the value the employee on his own could impart to other purchasers of his services. Finally, in the absence of a socialized system of delivering health and other insurance benefits, firms may be low-cost providers of such benefits. In part this is because firms with large workforces can provide economies of scale and also a sufficiently heterogenous population that insurers do not fear that individuals in the plan are above-average insurance risks. By contrast, sole proprietors and small companies may find it more difficult to obtain insurance and more costly when they do. Tax policy also encourages individuals to become employees because, as we will see in the chapter on employee benefits, compensation in the form of fringe benefits in qualified plans are paid for with before-tax dollars and, in the case of pension benefits, are taxed when benefits are paid out at retirement. This significant tax

16

advantage is often unavailable to individuals who are not employed by firms.

The government also has a keen interest in finding employee status. This is because only employers are required to withhold income taxes owed by employees, pay the employer portion of social security and unemployment insurance taxes, and obtain workers compensation insurance.[2]

C. Tests for Employee Status

Two tests for employee status have developed in the courts. The dominant approach is called the "common law" or "right to control" test; there is also a second test, sometimes called the "economic realities" or "economic dependency" test, that has been recognized in the case of certain statutes, most notably the Fair Labor Standards Act of 1938, 29 U.S.C. §§ 207 et seq.

1. *Common Law or "Right of Control" Test*

The control test was developed at common law not for the purpose of determining whether individuals fall within the scope of protective labor legislation, but rather for the distinct purpose of determining whether the ostensible employer should be held liable to third parties for the torts of employees committed during the course of their employment. Ordinarily, firms are not liable to third parties for the acts of independent contractors in the absence of a special contractual obligation, but they are liable for torts committed by their employees in the course of their employment. This doctrine is called "respondeat superior" liability and has its origin in the recognition that employees committing the tort are often, as a practical matter, judgment-proof. Since the harm is caused by the employee's actions in the service of the employing enterprise, the courts took the view that it is better for the firm to absorb these costs rather than leave the injured party without a remedy. The concept of control helps explain when employers should be responsible for torts committed by their agents: "A master is subject to the liability for the torts of his servants while acting in the scope of their employment."[3] This principle requires a definition of "serv-

---

2. See Rev. Rul. 87–41, 1987–1 Cum. Bull. 296, 298–99 (listing 20 factors as guides to determining whether an individual is a common-law "employee" in various tax laws).

3. RESTATEMENT (SECOND) OF AGENCY § 219(1), p. 481. A similar approach is taken in the recent RESTATEMENT (THIRD) OF AGENCY § 32.04 & comment b, pp. 139–41 (2007). In the still-pending RESTATEMENT (THIRD) OF EMPLOYMENT LAW, § 1.01(1), the drafters define an employee as an individual who "does not render the services as an independent

ant," which Section 220 of the Restatement (Second) of Agency articulates in terms of the firm's "control or right of control" of the "physical conduct" of the agent:

(1) A servant is a person employed to perform services in the affairs of another and who with respect to the physical conduct in the performance of the services is subject to the other's control or right to control.

(2) In determining whether one acting for another is a servant or an independent contractor, the following matters of fact, among others, are considered:

(a) the extent of control which, by the agreement, the master may exercise over the details of the work;

(b) whether or not the one employed is engaged in a distinct occupation or business;

(c) the kind of occupation, with reference to whether, in the locality, the work is usually done under the direction of the employer or by a specialist without supervision;

(d) the skill required in the particular occupation;

(e) whether the employer or the workman supplies the instrumentalities, tools, and the place of work for the person doing the work;

(f) the length of time for which the person is employed;

(g) the method of payment, whether by the time or by the job;

(h) whether or not the work is part of the regular business of the employer;

(i) whether or not the parties believe they are creating the relation of master and servant; and

(j) whether the principal is or is not in business.[4]

Where there is such control or right of control of such physical conduct, the agent is treated as an employee of the firm triggering the firm's vicarious liability.

The emphasis on the employer's ability to control the "physical conduct" of employees is consistent with the Restatement's focus on the issue of the employer's vicarious liability to third parties. But even the drafters of the Restatement recognize that there are

business person because the employer controls the manner and means by which the services are performed." By contrast, an independent business person "retains entrepreneurial control of the manner and means by which the services are performed...." *Id.*, § 101(2).

4. RESTATEMENT (SECOND) OF AGENCY § 220, at 485–86.

categories of undisputed employees whose physical acts can not be closely monitored by the firm. These include:

- "[S]hip captains and managers of great corporations are normally superior servants, differing only in the dignity and importance of their positions from those working under them. The rules for determining the liability of the employer for the conduct of both [these] superior servants and the humblest employees are the same; the application differs with the extent and nature of their duties."[5]

- Employees performing their duties outside of the workplace, like the "traveling salesman" who "may be ... a servant and cause the employer to be liable for negligent injuries to a customer or for negligent driving while traveling to visit prospective customers. The important distinction is between service in which the actor's physical activities and his time are surrendered to the control of the master, and service under an agreement to accomplish results or to use care and skill in accomplishing results."[6]

- Skilled employees, such as "highly skilled cooks or gardeners, who resent and even contract against interference, are normally servants if regularly employed. So, too, the skilled artisans employed by a manufacturing establishment, many of whom are specialists, with whose method of accomplishing results the employer has neither the knowledge nor the desire to interfere, are servants."[7]

Plainly, there is a tension between the inclusion of these categories in the concept of servant and the Restatement's emphasis on the master's control over the manner of doing the work as the determinative criterion of employment status. This comes out most clearly in the discussion of "fully employed but highly placed employees of a corporation, such as presidents and general managers, [who] are not less servants because they are not controlled in their day-to-day work by other human beings." The control element is supplied by "their sense of obligation to devote their time and energies to the interests of the enterprise."[8] It is perhaps for this reason that subsection 2 of § 220 includes some factors that appear to have nothing to do with control of the servant's physical activities, such as whether the individual is employed in a distinct occupation or business, the custom in the occupation or location,

5. *Id.*, Comment a. on subsection (1), at 486.

6. *Id.*, Comment e. on subsection (1), at 487–88.

7. *Id.*, Comment i. on subsection (2), at 489.

8. *Id.*, Ch. 7, Topic 2, Title B., Introductory Note, at 479.

the length of time of the engagement, the method of payment, whether the work performed is past of the employer's regular business, and the expectations of the parties to the relationship.

The Supreme Court has repeatedly held that where the statute does not define the term "employee," it is assumed that Congress intended "a common-law test" for determining employee status. The Court has framed this test as follows:

> In determining whether a hired party is an employee under the general common law of agency, we consider the hiring party's right to control the manner and means by which the product is accomplished. Among other factors relevant to this inquiry are the skill required; the source of the instrumentalities and tools; the location of the work; the duration of the relationship between the parties; whether the hiring party has the right to assign additional projects to the hired party; the extent of the hired party's discretion over when and how long to work; the method of payment; the hired party's role in hiring and paying assistants; whether the work is part of the regular business of the hiring party; whether the hiring party is in business; the provision of employee benefits; and the tax treatment of the hired party.[9]

The Court admonished, however, that "[s]ince the common-law test contains 'no shorthand formula or magic phrase that can be applied to find the answer, . . . all of the incidents of the relationship must be assessed and weighed with no one factor being decisive.' "[10]

This is the federal common law rule,[11] which the Court has insisted informs the definition of employee status in a number of federal laws, including the National Labor Relations Act,[12] the Employee Retirement Income Security Act,[13] the Social Security Act of 1948 (which explicitly refers to the common-law definition),[14] and the "work for hire" provision of Section 101 of the Copyright Act of 1976.[15] States are not obligated to follow this rule in construing

---

9. *Nationwide Mutual Insurance Co. v. Darden*, 503 U.S. 318, 323–24 (1992), quoting *Community for Creative Non–Violence v. Reid*, 490 U.S. 730, 751–52 (1989).

10. *Id.* at 324, quoting *NLRB v. United Ins. Co. of America*, 390 U.S. 254, 258 (1968).

11. It is based on "the general common law of agency, rather than the law of any particular State." *Id.* at 324 n.3, quoting *Reid*, 490 U.S. at 740.

12. See *United Ins. Co. of America*, *supra* note 10.

13. See *Darden*, *supra* note 9.

14. Social Security Act of 1948, ch. 468, § 1, 62 Stat. 438, discussed in *United States v. W.M. Webb, Inc.*, 397 U.S. 179, 183–88 (1970) (Congressional reaction to *United States v. Silk*, 331 U.S. 704 (1947)).

15. 17 U.S.C. § 101 (treating the employer as the author of works "prepared by an employee within the scope

their statutes, but are likely to follow a similar approach absent some attempt at a different definition of employee status in the particular law.

2. The "Economic Realities" or "Economic Dependency" Test

The Supreme Court, when it first confronted the definition of employee status in New Deal era laws like the National Labor Relations Act of 1935 (NLRA), the Fair Labor Standards Act of 1938 (FLSA), and the Social Security Act of 1935, was inclined to use a broader approach, that tended to de-emphasize right to control in favor of construing the term "employee" in light of the overall purposes of the law, "in the light of the mischief to be corrected and the end to be attained."[16] Congress repudiated this reading in amendments to the NLRA (by expressly including an exclusion from coverage for independent contractors and appending legislative history indicating coverage was to be read in light of the common-law definition)[17] and the Social Security Act (by expressly incorporating the common-law definition).

In one of these decisions left undisturbed by Congress, *Rutherford Food Corp. v. McComb*,[18] the Court adopted a broad reading of the term "employee" in the FLSA. In that case, the U.S. Department of Labor brought an action to enjoin Rutherford, a meat processor in Kansas City, Missouri, and Kaiser Packing Company, a slaughterhouse in Kansas City, Kansas supplying Rutherford with boned meat, from failing to pay overtime and maintain proper records with respect to their employment of meat boners. Kaiser would enter into contracts with a skilled meat boner to assemble a group of skilled boners to do the boning at the slaughterhouse. The meat boners kept their own hours and pooled their pay. A Kaiser manager would go around the boning area many times a day urging the boners "to cut all the meat off the bones". The District Court

---

of his or her employment"), construed in *Reid, supra* note 11.

16. *Silk*, 331 U.S. at 713, quoting *NLRB v. Hearst Publications, Inc.*, 322 U.S. 111, 124 (1944).

17. See Section 2(3) of the NLRA, 29 U.S.C. § 152(3); H. Rep. No. 245, 80th Cong., 1st Sess., on H.R. 3020, at 18 (1947):

In the law, there has always been a difference, and a big difference, between "employees" and "independent contractors."

"Employees" work for wages or salaries under direct supervision. "Independent contractors" undertake to do a job for a price, decide how the work will be done, usually hire others to do the work, and depend for their income not upon wages, but upon the difference between what they pay for goods, materials, and labor and what they receive for the end result, that is, upon profits.

18. 331 U.S. 722 (1947).

declined to grant the injunction sought by the Labor Department, determining that the meat boners were independent contractors. The Court of Appeals reversed, granting the requested injunction. The Supreme Court, per Justice Reed, affirmed the Court of Appeals' conclusion that the boners were not independent contractors, but remanded for further proceedings on the scope of any injunction.[19]

Justice Reed for the Court first observed that while the FLSA does not define the terms "employer" or "employee," it did (and does) contain a definition of "employ" which "includes to suffer or permit to work."[20] This definition included "many persons and working relationships which, prior to the Act, were not deemed to fall within the employer-employee category":[21] "The definition of 'employ' is broad. It evidently derives from the child labor statutes and it should be noted that this definition applies to the child labor provisions of this Act."[22] The Court determined that the boners were not independent contractors because "their work [was] a part of the integrated unit of production" as they "did a specialty job on the production line"; "[t]he premises and equipment of Kaiser were used for the work"; "[t]he group [of boners] had no business organization that could or did shift as a unit from one slaughterhouse to another"; "[t]he managing official of the plant kept close touch on the operation"; and "[w]hile profits to the boners depended upon the efficiency of their work, it was more like piecework than an enterprise that actually depended for success upon the initiative, judgment or foresight of the typical independent contractor."[23]

Rutherford remains good law in deciding questions under the FLSA. The Court, however, has declined to apply the "economic realities" test to other laws which lack a textual basis allowing coverage beyond "traditional agency law principles."[24] It is an open question, though doubtful given the Supreme Court's instructions, whether other federal laws not containing a special definition of the term "employee" can be analyzed under a broader test than the

---

19. The *Rutherford* Court decided only whether the workers in question were "employees of the operator of the Kansas plant" in question, that they "were employees of the establishment," without deciding whether they were employees of Rutherford as well as Kaiser or what the appropriate form of the injunction should be. See *id.* at 727–28, 729.

20. 52 Stat. 1060, § 3(g), codified at 29 U.S.C. § 203(g).

21. 331 U.S. at 729, quoting *Walling v. Portland Terminal Co.*, 330 U.S. 148, 150 (1947).

22. *Id.* at 728.

23. *Id.* at 729, 730.

24. *Darden*, 503 U.S. at 326 (noting the "textual asymmetry" between the FLSA and ERISA "precludes reliance on FLSA cases when construing ERISA's concept of 'employee.' ").

common-law "right to control" test. (State courts interpreting state statutes may have greater leeway.)[25]

It is unclear in what circumstances the economic-realities approach brings putative employees under statutory coverage who would be excluded as independent contractors under the common-law definition. Consider *Secretary of Labor v. Lauritzen*,[26] involving the issue whether migrant pickle pickers were employees under the FLSA or independent contractors. Families of farm workers would go to defendants' farm to pick the crop; they would be assigned plots depending on when they arrived and would receive one-half of the sales proceeds defendants received for the portion of the crop the family harvested. All planting, fertilizing, insecticide spraying, and irrigation of the crop was handled by defendants' regular employees. The court of appeals majority found the pickers were FLSA employees, relying on the "economic realities" test: "If the migrant families are pickle pickers, then they need pickles to pick in order to survive economically. The migrants clearly are dependent on the pickle business, and the defendants, for their continued employment and livelihood."[27] Judge Frank Easterbrook, concurring, suggested that the migrants were employees even under a more traditional analysis:

> The migrant workers are selling nothing but their labor. They have no physical capital and little human capital to vend. . . . The migrant workers labor on the farmer's premises, doing repetitive tasks. Payment on a piecework basis . . . would not take these workers out of the Act, any more than payment of the sales staff at a department store on commission avoids the statute. The link of the migrants' compensation to the market price of pickles is not fundamentally different from piecework compensation.[28]

3. Areas of Difficulty under the Common Law or "Right of Control" Test

As a general matter, there are many clear cases where agencies and courts have little difficulty distinguishing between employees and independent contractors under the common-law test. The situ-

25. German law extends some labor and antidiscrimination protections to "employee-like persons" who may be technically self-employed but are considered economically dependent on the users of their services; unjust dismissal law protection, however, is not offered to this group. See Wolfgang Daubler, *Work-ing People in Germany,* 21 COMP. LAB.L. & POL. J. 77 (1999).

26. 835 F.2d 1529 (7th Cir. 1987).

27. *Id.* at 1538.

28. *Id.* at 1545 (Easterbrook, J., concurring).

ations where the parties may have difficulty determining their rights and duties, and where courts are likely to be divided, include the following:

- *Off-Site Workers*. Truck drivers, taxi drivers, traveling salesmen, newspaper deliverers, home workers, and insurance claims adjusters perform their work outside the physical establishment of the firm, and sometime without physically coming to the office. In such settings, the degree of managerial supervision of their physical activities at work is likely to be minimal, and firms are likely to focus on the end product of their work (e.g., were the deliveries made on time, have customers complained about the quality of the service, has any damage occurred to the truck, have the expected number of sales or deliveries been made?). Firms may also pay these individuals in terms of the end product (e.g., commissions on sales made, on insurance claims adjusted) rather than time served. Such pay arrangements may raise difficulties or at least require adjustments under laws like the FLSA which take account of the hours of work. Also, the workers may own their own trucks or cars or rent the taxicab from owners or agents. Because the hours of work may not be closely monitored by the firm and the workers own or rent their vehicles, in theory, these workers may be able to service other clients, and may be formally permitted to do so by the firm if they get their assignments completed on a timely basis. This may suggest an opportunity for entrepreneurial activity, an important determinant of independent-contractor status. In many situations, however, this formal opportunity to act as an entrepreneur may have little basis in reality because the time required to complete their assignments or other rules of the firm, such as the required design of trucks or other instrumentalities of work, preclude work for other clients.[29]

- *Workers with Assistants*. Another area of recurring difficulty involves workers who are permitted to and actually hire their own assistants to help them with their work. (This was

29. The National Labor Relations Board has evaluated such factors in deciding the employee status of truck drivers under the NLRA. Compare *Roadway Package Systems, Inc.*, 326 N.L.R.B. 842 (1998) (finding owner-operators to be employees), with *Dial–A–Mattress*, 326 N.L.R.B. 884 (1998) (finding owner-operators to be independent contractors).

For decisions emphasizing whether putative independent contractors enjoy real entrepreneurial opportunity, see *Corporate Express Delivery Systems v. NLRB*, 292 F.3d 777 (D.C. Cir. 2002); *Desimone v. Allstate Ins. Co.*, 2000 WL 1811385 (N.D. Cal. 2000) (the latter finding independent-contractor status).

part of the fact pattern in *Rutherford* and in *NLRB v. Hearst Publications, Inc.*,[30] one of the Supreme Court decisions adopting the "economic realities" test that was later over-turned by Congress.[31]) The assistants are plainly employees of the individual who hired them, but that individual may not be in any position to undertake the obligations of an employer; the operative question is whether the assistants and the individual who hired them are also employees of the firm that benefits from their work. The hiring of assistants is one indicator of independent-contractor status but should it be determinative?

- *On-Site Workers with Broad Discretion over the Manner and Means of their Work.* A third area involves workers who come to the physical establishment of the firm—ordinarily a strong indicator of employee status—but because of their skills and professional values are not supervised by the firm with respect to how the work gets done. For example, the firm may have engaged a lawyer to take on some of the workload of a legal department that is swamped with litiga-tion. The engagement letter may specify that the lawyer is serving as an independent contractor and allow the lawyer in principle to take on other clients. The firm is interested only in results (i.e., disputes resolved) leaving it to the lawyer to exercise professional discretion; but the lawyer is given guidelines for settling cases or number of billed hours that can be devoted to a single file without additional approvals. If this lawyer were in an office of his own, agreeing to take on an important client to which he would devote the lion's share of his time, most courts would find independent-contractor status. Should the result change because the lawyer is given an office at the firm? What if the firm decides to "contract out" its entire legal department by creating "independent contractor" relationships with its former staff lawyers?

- *Dual-Capacity Workers.* Another area of continuing difficulty involves workers who perform the work of the firm but at the same are present at work in a non-employee capacity. They may be there as "salts," employees of a labor union trying to organize workers of the firm while faithfully per-forming assigned tasks for the firm. They may be there principally as students, learning on the job the skills needed

---

30. See note 16 *supra.*

31. It was also in part the fact pat-tern in *Secretary of Labor v. Lauritzen,* text accompanying notes 26–28.

to become a full-fledged teaching or medical professional or stage director. In *NLRB v. Town & County Electric, Inc.,*[32] the Supreme Court held that paid union organizers could be protected employees under the NLRA, reasoning that "moonlighting," i.e., working for two employers, was not inconsistent with employee status: "union organizing, when done for pay but during nonwork hours, would seem equivalent to simple moonlighting, a practice wholly consistent with a company's control over its workers as to their assigned duties."[33] This decision does not necessarily resolve the coverage of student workers under the NLRA because the work of union "salts" during work hours is indisputably employment in the service of the firm, whereas the work of teaching assistants or hospital interns can be characterized as "principally" for an "educational" purpose. (This is the position the current NLRB has taken, with court approval).

D.   Laws Distinguishing Among Employees

Most employment laws do not draw distinctions among employees, and, as we have seen, the common law of agency included even ship captains and the presidents of major corporations in its definition of servant. There are some situations where such lines are drawn. The most prominent example is the NLRA. Because that statute authorizes employees to engage in a form of "bounded conflict" with their firms over terms and conditions of employment, the question arises whether the owners of the firm are entitled to have their representatives excluded from the statute's reach. In its first encounter with this issue, *Packard Motor Car Co. v. NLRB,*[34] the Court held that plant foremen were statutory employees even though they exercised discretion over discipline decisions on behalf of the firm. Congress repudiated this decision in 1947, inserting into the Act an express exclusion for "supervisors".[35] In *NLRB v. Bell Aerospace Co.,*[36] the Court also read the NLRA to exclude non-supervisor "managers"—those who formulate or implement policy for the firm—from the reach of the Act, reasoning that Congress intended the employer be able to command the adherence of all of its representatives in disputes with statutory employees. It was always understood that supervisors and managers could not be in bargaining units with rank-and-file employees or make or imple-

---

32.   516 U.S. 85 (1995).
33.   *Id.* at 91.
34.   330 U.S. 485 (1947).

35.   Section 2(11) of the NLRA, 29 U.S.C. § 152(11).
36.   416 U.S. 267 (1974).

ment decisions for the firm when their own interests as employees presented a conflict of interests. The *Bell Aerospace* decision articulates a concept of "alignment of interests" between the owner and its representatives calling for exclusion from NLRA coverage even where there is no direct conflict of interest between the firm and the supervisor engaged in concerted activity.

Professional employees, who by definition exercise discretion in their work, were expressly included in the labor statute by the 1947 NLRA amendments,[37] and the Court has issued several decisions trying to work out the circumstances under which some professional employees lose coverage because they function as excluded managers[38] or supervisors.[39] In these rulings, the Court has rejected the NLRB's argument that when professionals exercise professional discretion they are not acting "in the interest" of the employer, and criticized it for being inconsistent with the agency's traditional rules in non-professional worker cases for determining supervisory or managerial status. Its most recent decision on the subject, *NLRB v. Kentucky River Community Care, Inc.*,[40] involved staff registered nurses (RNs) who in addition to their customary duties providing medical services as ordered by physicians, also served as "building supervisors" during certain shifts responsible for obtaining needed help if for some reason a shift was understaffed. The Labor Board found the RNs were not supervisors because whatever discretion they exercised did not involve "independent judgment" in the "responsible direction" of employees within the meaning of the statutory exclusion but only "ordinary professional or technical judgment in directing less-skilled employees to deliver services." The Court rejected the agency's approach, explaining that even professional judgment in directing employees is sufficiently "independent" to qualify for supervisory status, and remanded the case for a determination whether the RNs in fact functioned as excluded supervisors.[41]

Another area of live controversy involves the question whether employees who have an ownership interest in the firm are excluded from coverage under the employment laws because owners are not

---

37. See Section 2(12) of the NLRA, 29 U.S.C. § 152(12).

38. See *NLRB v. Yeshiva Univ.*, 444 U.S. 672 (1980).

39. See *NLRB v. Health Care & Retirement Corp. of Am.*, 511 U.S. 571 (1994); *NLRB v. Kentucky River Community Care, Inc.*, 532 U.S. 706 (2001).

40. See note 39 *supra*.

41. The *Kentucky River* Court offered an interesting suggestion for the agency's consideration: "Perhaps the Board could offer a limiting interpretation of the supervisory function of responsible direction by distinguishing employees who direct the manner of others' performance of discrete tasks from employees who direct other employees, as § 152(11) requires." 532 U.S. at 720.

employees. In *Clackamas Gastroenterology Associates, P.C. v. Wells*,[42] the Supreme Court confronted the issue of whether four physician-shareholders who owned a professional corporation operating as a medical clinic and constituted its board of directors were "employees" for purposes of the 15–employee threshold for covered employer status under Title I of the Americans with Disabilities Act of 1990 (ADA). The court of appeals had ruled that the physician-shareholders were statutory employees because the firm had organized itself as a corporation and, at least for tax purposes, treated the owners as employees. The corporation argued that it was the functional equivalent of a partnership and its employee-shareholders were the functional equivalent of partners and thus could not be counted as employees. The majority opinion, authored by Justice Stevens, faulted the court of appeals for failing to look to the "common-law element of control" as "the principal guidepost,"[43] even though the professional corporation was a new type of business entity that has no exact precedent in the common law. But it also disagreed with the corporation's position:

> The question whether a shareholder-director is an employee . . . cannot be answered by asking whether the shareholder-director appears to be the functional equivalent of a partner. Today there are partnerships that include hundreds of members, some of whom may well qualify as "employees" because control is concentrated in a small number of managing partners. Thus, asking whether shareholder-directors are partners—rather than asking whether they are employees—simply begs the question.[44]

The *Clackamas* Court did not decide whether the four employee-shareholders were ADA employees, remanding to the lower courts to evaluate the issue in light of "the common-law touchstone of control"[45]—presumably as articulated in the guidelines on the subject of the Equal Employment Opportunity Commission (EEOC), the federal agency responsible for ADA enforcement.[46] It

42. 538 U.S. 440 (2003).

43. *Id*. at 448.

44. *Id*. at 446.

45. *Id*. at 449.

46. The Court quoted (*id*. at 450) from the EEOC Compliance Manual § 605:00009, which refers to the following factors:

Whether the organization can hire or fire the individual or set the rules and regulations of the individual's work

Whether and, if so, to what extent the organization supervises the individual's work

Whether the individual reports to someone higher in the organization

Whether and, if so, to what extent the individual is able to influence the organization

Whether the parties intended the individual to be an employee, as expressed in written agreements or contracts

noted that some of the findings below supported the conclusion that they were not employees: "For example, they apparently control the operation of their clinic, they share the profits, and they are personally liable for malpractice claims."[47] On the other hand, the record might also support a contrary conclusion under the EEOC's standard: "For example, the record indicates that the four director-shareholders receive salaries, that they must comply with the standards established by the clinic, and they report to a personnel manager."[48]

It would seem after *Clackamas* that the form of the organization will not be decisive for determining employee status, whether for purposes of the numerical threshold for coverage or triggering the substantive obligation of legislation like the ADA[49] that does not supply its own special definition of who qualifies as an employee. Although the issue was not squarely before the Court, the decision suggests that members of large legal and accounting partnerships may well be treated as statutory employees unless their managerial responsibilities for the firm provide sufficient indicia of influence and control over firm decision-making to take them out of statutory coverage.[50] It will need to be further decided whether influence and control alone are sufficient to preclude employee status if such influence and control is not derived from a significant ownership interest.

Other than this issue of coverage of owners and partners, the discrimination laws extend protection to all employees of the firm regardless of rank or managerial responsibility. The one exception is a limited provision in the Age Discrimination in Employment Act of 1967 (ADEA) permitting the mandatory retirement at age 65 of any employee "who, for the 2–year period immediately before

---

Whether the individual shares in the profits, losses, and liabilities of the organization.

Interestingly, the Restatement (Second) of Agency § 14A, comment a, at 62 seems to go further than the EEOC position: "When one of the partners is in active management of the business or is otherwise regularly employed in the business, he is a servant of the partnership." This is also the approach of the pending Restatement (Third) of Employment Law § 103.

47. 538 U.S. at 451.

48. *Id.* at n.11.

49. The Court apparently assumed that employee status for both purposes would be governed by the same analysis. See *id.* at 447 n.6.

50. See *EEOC v. Sidley Austin Brown & Wood*, 315 F.3d 696 (7th Cir. 2002) and follow-on litigation initiated by the EEOC (former partners of a major law firm contesting their age-based mandatory retirement under the Age Discrimination in Employment Act of 1967). The opportunity of employees to become partners is treated as a working condition covered by the antidiscrimination laws. See *Hishon v. King & Spalding*, 467 U.S. 69 (1984); *Price Waterhouse v. Hopkins*, 490 U.S. 228 (1989), on remand, 737 F.Supp. 1202 (D.D.C.), affirmed, 920 F.2d 967 (D.C. Cir. 1990) (ordering admission to partnership as a remedy).

retirement, is employed in a bona fide executive or high policymaking position" and is entitled to an immediate nonforfeitable annual retirement benefit of at least $44,000.[51] This provision is narrowly construed by the EEOC to include only departments or individuals who "play a significant role in the development of corporate policy and effectively recommend the implementation thereof."[52] In one noted litigation, a senior labor counsel of a major corporation with significant supervisory authority over other attorneys, but lacking a significant role in policy-making, was held to be outside this exclusion.[53]

E.   Joint Employment

It is possible to be an employee of more than one employer, and claimants may decide to sue both employers when their immediate employer lacks the resources to pay any judgment or where the other employer effectively directs the decisions of the immediate employer.[54] The Supreme Court in *Rutherford* did not decide whether the meat processing company was in fact a joint employer of the boners, but it clearly assumed there could be a joint employment relationship depending on the circumstances.[55] Moreover, the Court has also implicitly recognized the principle of joint employment in the NLRA context.[56]

In the FLSA context which, as noted above, involves a broad statutory definition of the term "employ," the Labor Department recognizes the joint-employment principle and has brought litigation to impose individual and joint liability for failure to pay minimum wages and overtime for all work performed for all joint employers.[57] Relying on *Rutherford* and the "suffer or permit"

51.   Section 12(c)(1) of the ADEA, 29 U.S.C. § 631(c)(1).

52.   29 C.F.R. § 1625.12 (e).

53.   See *Whittlesey v. Union Carbide Corp.*, 567 F.Supp. 1320 (S.D.N.Y. 1983), affirmed, 742 F.2d 724 (2d Cir. 1984).

54.   Even in the absence of a joint employer relationship, there is some authority allowing non-employees to sue a statutory employer for *interfering* with the plaintiff's relationship with his employer. See *Sibley Memorial Hosp. v. Wilson*, 488 F.2d 1338 (D.C. Cir. 1973).

55.   Thus, for example, the Second Circuit's view in *Zheng v. Liberty Apparel Co.*, 355 F.3d 61, 70 (2d Cir. 2003), observed that *Rutherford* "held that, in certain circumstances, an entity can be a

joint employer under the FLSA even when it does not hire and fire its joint employees, directly dictate their hours, or pay them."

56.   See *Boire v. Greyhound Corp.*, 376 U.S. 473 (1964) (refusing to allow direct review of an NLRB determination that employees working for cleaning company providing services for bus terminal were employees of both their immediate employer and bus terminal because the latter determined work schedule, the number of employees and directed work performance; agency's determination was "essentially a factual issue" not dependent "solely upon construction of the statute").

57.   See 29 C.F.R. § 791.2(a).

language of the Act, the Second Circuit in *Zheng v. Liberty Apparel Company Inc.*[58] held that the following factors were to be considered in determining whether garment manufacturers ("Liberty Defendants") who hired contractors ("Contractor Corporations") to stitch and finish pieces of clothing were joint employers for FLSA purposes of the garment workers directly employed by the contractors ("the plaintiffs"):

> The factors we find pertinent in these circumstances, listed in no particular order, are (1) whether Liberty's premises and equipment were used for the plaintiffs' work; (2) whether the Contractor Corporations had a business that could or did shift as a unit from one putative joint employer to another; (3) the extent to which plaintiffs performed a discrete line-job that was integral to Liberty's process of production; (4) whether responsibility under the contracts could pass from one subcontractor to another without material changes; (5) the degree to which the Liberty Defendants or their agents supervised plaintiffs' work; and (6) whether plaintiffs worked exclusively or predominantly for the Liberty Defendants.[59]

While many of the joint-employer decisions have arisen under the FLSA, it should not be assumed that the approach of the *Zheng* court, even if a correct interpretation of the FLSA, necessarily applies to other statutes. The FLSA contains the "suffer or permit" definition of the term "employ" which formed the basis for the Supreme Court's determination in *Rutherford* than an "economic realities" test, rather than the presumably narrower common-law "right to control" test, should inform the employee-status inquiry. To the extent other laws do not contain similarly expansive language, the Court's decisions indicate that, at least as a matter of federal law, the common-law test must be used in defining who is an employee and presumably who is an employer.[60] In addition, there is an underlying, if unstated, concern in the FLSA decisions that the immediate employer operates with little capital and is likely to be an insolvent defendant; this concern may be absent or less salient in other contexts.

58.   355 F.3d 61 (2d Cir. 2003).

59.   *Id.* at 72.

60.   See, e.g., *Moreau v. Air France*, 343 F.3d 1179 (9th Cir. 2003) (finding an absence of sufficient control by the user-employer to establish joint-employer status under the Family and Medical Leave Act). Other decisions have questioned whether the contractors performed services that were an "integral" part of the user-employer's business. See, e.g., *Gonzalez–Sanchez v. International Paper Co.*, 346 F.3d 1017 (11th Cir. 2003) (contractors provided forest regeneration services for a paper company; rejecting claims under the FLSA and MIGRANT AND SEASONAL AGRICULTURAL WORKERS PROTECTION ACT, 29 U.S.C. §§ 1801 *et seq.*).

That the element of control is likely to inform the joint-employment inquiry under the federal discrimination laws is suggested by EEOC guidelines on handling issues raised by contingent workers placed by temporary employment agencies:

> A client of a temporary agency typically qualifies as an employer of the temporary worker during the job assignment, along with the agency. This is because the client usually exercises significant supervisory responsibility over the worker.... On the other hand, the client would not qualify as an employer if the staffing firm furnishes the job equipment and has the exclusive right, through on-site managers, to control the details of the work, to make or change assignments, and to terminate the workers.[61]

61. See EEOC, ENFORCEMENT GUIDANCE: APPLICATION OF EEO LAWS TO CONTINGENT WORKERS PLACED BY TEMPORARY EMPLOYMENT AGENCIES AND OTHER STAFFING FIRMS, available at www.eeoc.gov/policy/docs/conting.html.

Part 2

THE COMMON LAW OF THE EMPLOYMENT RELATIONSHIP

Chapter 3

CONTRACTUAL EXCEPTIONS TO EMPLOYMENT AT-WILL*

A. Presumption of At–Will Employment

A foundational principle of U.S. employment law is the presumption that employment is at-will: either party is free to terminate the relationship without notice or cause. Only Montana departs from this rule, having enacted a statute requiring that an employer have good cause to terminate a non-probationary employee.[1] The at-will presumption is a default rule that applies in the absence of an agreement by the parties or other enforceable promise to restrict termination. The employer's ability to terminate the relationship is also limited by a significant array of statutory laws that, for example, prohibit termination of employees for discriminatory reasons[2] or in retaliation for engaging in concerted action to improve wages and working conditions,[3] or for filing claims, giving testimony, and otherwise asserting rights under those laws.[4] It is

---

* *Authors' Note*: Much of this chapter builds on Chapter 2 of the pending RE-STATEMENT (THIRD) OF EMPLOYMENT LAW (C.D., 2007). We are grateful to the Reporters and to the American Law Institute for allowing us to use this material.

1. See MONTANA WRONGFUL DISCHARGE OF EMPLOYMENT ACT, MONT. CODE ANN. §§ 39–2–901 to–914, upheld against a state constitutional challenge for restricting judicial remedies in *Meech v. Hillhaven West, Inc.*, 238 Mont. 21, 776 P.2d 488 (1989). In 1991, the National Conference of Commissioners of Uniform State Laws approved, and circulated to the states for their consideration, a "Model Employment Termination Act"

that provided a statutory requirement of "good cause" for an employer's termination of an employee. As of December 2007, no jurisdiction has adopted the Model Act. See generally Theodore J. St. Antoine, *The Making of the Model Employment Termination Act*, 69 WASH. L. REV. 361 (1994).

2. E.g., Title VII of the Civil Rights Act of 1964, as amended, 42 U.S.C. §§ 2000e *et seq.*

3. E.g. NLRA §§ 7, 8, 29 U.S.C. §§ 157–58.

4. E.g., OSHA § 11(c), 29 U.S.C. § 660(c); 29 C.F.R. § 1977.12, sustained in *Whirlpool Corp. v. Marshall*, 445 U.S. 1 (1980).

also limited by public policy and other tort claims, discussed in Chapters 4–5. This chapter discusses the various ways, aside from collective bargaining, in which the parties may contractually override the at-will default.

Although the positive law is well settled, the normative virtues of the at-will rule continue to be debated by academic commentators.[5] Two principal justifications have been offered for the at-will rule. The first is that the presumption reflects the background assumptions of the parties to the employment contract. In other words, even if the parties did not expressly negotiate the terms of employment, the likelihood is that if they had done so (assuming full information) they would have chosen the at-will arrangement. Some studies have endeavored to support this thesis with empirical evidence, reporting for example that when asked to make comparative judgments, workers rank the importance of job security well behind other job features such as high income.[6] In addition, there is evidence that after some courts have carved out significant negotiable exceptions from the at-will rule, many employment relationships revert to the at-will default.[7] A second justification for the at-will default rule is that it reflects not so much the premises of the parties but, rather, the property rights of the employer, and for that reason any departure from that baseline should be bargained for, in the absence of a statutory or public-policy restriction.[8]

The rationale based on the efficiency of the at-will rule has been challenged by those who argue that a variety of market failures tend to interfere with workers' and employers' abilities to obtain and express accurate information about their preferences.[9] One argument is that workers may make mistakes about the actual

---

5. Compare, e.g., Richard Epstein, *In Defense of the Contract at Will*, 51 U. CHI. L. REV. 947 (1984), with PAUL C. WEILER, GOVERNING THE WORKPLACE: THE FUTURE OF LABOR AND EMPLOYMENT LAW 72–78 (1990).

6. See, e.g., Andrew P. Morriss, *Bad Data, Bad Economics and Bad Policy: Time to Fire Wrongful Discharge Law*, 74 TEX. L. REV. 1901, 1921–22 (1996).

7. See *id.*; J. Hoult Verkerke, *An Empirical Perspective on Indefinite Term Employment Contracts: Resolving the Just Cause Debate*, 1995 WIS. L. REV. 837, 839.

8. See, e.g., Keith N. Hylton, *A Theory of Minimum Contract Terms, With Implications for Labor Law*, 74 TEX. L. REV. 1741, 1752 (1996). There is some,

still inconclusive, evidence that judicial exceptions to the at-will rule raise firing costs and thus may deter new hiring. See David H. Autor, *Outsourcing at Will: The Contribution of Unjust Dismissal Doctrine to the Growth of Employment Outsourcing*, 21 J. LAB. ECON. 1 (2003) (judicial exceptions to at-will rule in 46 states explains 20% of the growth in the U.S. temporary help services industry between 1973 and 1995 and contributed 500,000 additional outsourced workers in 2000); also Max M. Schanzenbach, *Exceptions to Employment at Will: Raising Firing Costs or Enforcing Life–Cycle Contracts?* 5 AM. L. & ECON. REV. 470 (2003).

9. See generally PAUL WEILER, *supra* note 2, at 74–78.

state of the law; some writers point to survey evidence that employ-ees believe they have rights against termination without cause when in law they do not.[10] Alternatively, workers may make mis-takes about their own longer-term interests, feel reluctant to re-quest secure employment for fear that it will send a misleading signal that they are the kind of worker who especially needs it, or lack the confidence to challenge the status quo.

The at-will rule may be thought of as the default rule that operates in the absence of wrongful dismissal legislation. In most other developed countries, the rule has been displaced by statutory change protecting employees from "unfair dismissal," rather than judicial action. Typically, these laws require adjudication in special-ized tribunals outside of the civil courts and limit remedies to an established multiple of lost income (e.g., £ 75,000 in Great Brit-ain).[11] Canada's common law permits termination without cause of employees not working under a fixed-term contract if adequate notice of termination is furnished.[12]

We discuss below ways in which the at-will default rule can be contractually modified—whether by bargained-for agreement sup-ported by consideration, by employer promises that reasonably induce detrimental reliance, or by unilateral employer statements intended to govern workplace relations.

B. Agreements for a Definite Term or for an Indefinite Term Limiting Termination of Employment

1. General Principles of Contract

The at-will default rule contemplates that the parties may negotiate over the term of their relationship, including whether termination of employment requires notice or cause. Such agree-ments are governed by general principles of contract. They typically

---

10. See, e.g., Pauline T. Kim, *Bargaining with Imperfect Information: A Study of Worker Perceptions of Legal Protection in an At–Will World*, 83 CORNELL L. REV. 105 (1997).

11. See Samuel Estreicher, *Unjust Dismissal Laws: Some Cautionary Notes*, 33 AM. J. COMP. L. 310 (1985), updated in GLOBAL ISSUES IN EMPLOYMENT LAW (SAMUEL ESTREICHER & MIRIAM CHERRY eds., 2008) and GLOBAL ISSUES IN EMPLOY-MENT DISCRIMINATION LAW 147 ff. (SAMUEL ESTREICHER & BRIAN LANDSBERG eds., 2007).

12. See, e.g. *Wallace v. United Grain Growers*, [1997] 3 S.C.R. 701. In Japan, the courts first established "good faith" restrictions on termination of employ-ment by employers before 2003 legisla-tion codified those developments. See Tadahsi A, Hanami & Fumito Komiya, *Japan*, in 6 INTL. ENCYC. LAB. L. & INDUS. REL. ¶ 195, 124–25 (R. Blanpain ed.) (mo-nograph updated to November 2005).

will involve an exchange of express promises, an offer contemplating acceptance by performance, or some other promissory statement or conduct manifesting a promise by the employer to which the employee indicates assent, although no particular form of words is required.

The general contract requirement of consideration or bargained-for exchange does not necessitate mutual or identical consideration from both parties to the agreement: A single promise by the employee to work for the employer at stated terms is ordinarily sufficient to support a number of promises by the employer, including, for example, a promise to provide employment at stated terms and a promise not to terminate the relationship prior to the end of the contractual term except for good cause.

Nor is mutuality of obligation required for there to be an enforceable employment agreement. Mutuality of obligation was required in some early common law rulings; modern contract law suggests, however, that a promise is not illusory if the power to terminate is conditioned by an obligation to give notice, however brief, or on the occurrence of events beyond the promisee's control.[13] The issue arises because, even where employers agree to a "cause" limitation on discharge or other adverse employment action, employees typically do not agree to limit their prerogative to quit the job with or without cause. Indeed, even if an employee were to agree to provide cause for a voluntary termination, the general rule is that specific performance would not be available to enforce a "personal services" contract. An employer that wants to limit an employee's freedom to end the relationship does have some alternative legal avenues available. For example, depending on state law, the parties may be able to enter into an agreement prohibiting the employee from competing against the employer for some reasonable period.[14] The parties can also provide for a reasonable-notice period as a condition for entitlement to severance benefits. Under such an arrangement, the employee would be required to give advance notice of an intention to quit employment in order to receive such benefits.

2. Agreements for a Definite Term

It is well-established that if the parties specify a term of employment, the agreement will rebut the at-will presumption.

---

13. See E. ALLAN FARNSWORTH, CONTRACTS § 2.14, at 77–79 (1990); A. CORBIN, CONTRACTS, § 163 (1963). *See generally* Mark Pettit, Jr., *Modern Unilateral Contracts*, 63 B.U.L. REV. 551 (1983).

14. Restrictive covenants are discussed in Chapter 6.

This holds true even if the parties did not expressly state that "cause" is required for termination. Absent a different express undertaking in the agreement, if the employer and employee enter into a contract providing, for example, a one-year term, the employer may not dismiss the employee without cause before the term has been completed. If, by contrast, the parties enter into an agreement calling for a specified "annual salary," the at-will presumption still holds. The statement of an annual salary does not, standing alone, evidence an intention to guarantee a year's employment or otherwise overcome the presumption of at-will status.[15]

3. Agreements for an Indefinite Term Limiting Termination of Employment

Although the law here is less well settled than in the case of definite-term agreements, courts may be moving away from a traditional skepticism toward indefinite-term agreements in favor of enforcing in appropriate circumstances bargained-for agreements for an indefinite term that limit termination of employment. An indefinite-term agreement may leave open the duration of the relationship or may use vague terms like "permanent" or "career" employment. Such agreements may be enforceable if they are bargained over, typically in one-on-one dealings between the employer and employee at the time of hiring or preliminary negotiations, and there is evidence that the parties intended a "cause" limit to termination of employment by the employer. It will often be a question of fact whether the statements were merely casual comments expressing optimism about the future, or were instead intended to be binding promises of for-cause employment.

Some courts still follow the historic practice of finding oral promises of "permanent" or "lifetime" employment as per se unenforceable either for want of special consideration (independent of the employee's continuing to provide services) or mutuality of obligation (because typically the employee has not agreed to a "cause" limit on voluntary termination).[16] The modern tendency is

---

15. Georgia has a statute on the subject which states: "If a contract of employment provides that wages are payable at a stipulated period, the presumption shall arise that the hiring is for such period. . . ." O.C.G.A. § 34–7–1. That law also states that "[a]n indefinite hiring may be terminated at will by either party." *Id*. The Georgia decisions hold that mere reference to an annual salary does not require application of the state statutory presumption. *See Tipton v. Canadian Imperial Bank of Commerce*, 872 F.2d 1491, 1496–97 (11th Cir. 1989) (collecting authorities).

16. See, e.g., *Scott v. Extracorporeal, Inc.*, 545 A.2d 334 (Pa. Super. 1988) ("The promise of 'permanent' employment alone is too broad to be enforced."); *Savarese v. Pyrene Mfg. Co.*,

to evaluate indefinite-term agreements under the usual rules of contract: If the purported agreement limiting termination of employment meets the requirements of bargained-for exchange, it should be enforceable, whether it is oral or written, and for a definite or indefinite term, so long as it does not run afoul of the applicable statute of frauds.

An example is the case of *Ohanian v. Avis Rent A Car System, Inc.*[17] Ohanian, a successful regional Vice–Resident of sales for Avis in San Francisco, was recruited to become Vice–President of Sales for the Northeast region. Ohanian was reluctant to move and concerned about job security. In the course of negotiations, Ohanion asked the manager who was recruiting him about job security, and the manager told him that "[u]nless [he] screwed up badly, there is no way [he was] going to get fired . . . [he would] never get hurt here in this company." Upon receiving this assurance, Ohanian orally accepted the offer, quit his job in San Francisco and moved with his family to the northeast. He subsequently signed relocation documents stipulating that he was hired as an at-will employee. When the employer later terminated Ohanian without cause, the jury found that an employment agreement had been formed by the Avis manager's assurance (delivered in response to Ohanian's expressed concern over job security in the new job), and not by the relocation documents he later signed; and that Avis had breached the agreement. The Second Circuit affirmed, rejecting the defendant's claim on appeal that the employer's promise was too indefinite to enforce, stating that "promises of lifetime employment have long been enforced if found to be supported by sufficient consideration." The court suggested that Ohanian's relocation from San Francisco to New York was sufficient consideration.[18]

Sometimes courts use language of "implied in fact" contract to reach the same result as in *Ohanian*—indefinite-term agreements that limit termination of employment can be enforceable if they were bargained for and the parties intended to negotiate away from the at-will default rule. Sometimes the employee receives documents after he or she has moved to the new job confirming oral assurances of a "cause" limit on termination. For example, in

89 A.2d 237 (N.J. App. 1952) (such promises require specificity and independent consideration to be enforced). This skepticism over indefinite-term agreements may also influence whether a writing is required under the applicable statute of frauds. See, e.g., *McIner-* *ney v. Charter Golf, Inc.*, 680 N.E.2d 1347 (Ill. 1997) ("a writing is required for the fair enforcement of lifetime employment contracts.").

17. 779 F.2d 101 (2d Cir. 1985) (applying New York law).

18. *Id.* at 109.

Torosyan v. Boehringer Ingelheim Pharmaceuticals,[19] the defendant pharmaceutical company interviewed the plaintiff Torosyan, who was working in California, for a job as a radiochemist at their offices in Connecticut. The plaintiff told the defendant's agents that he was seeking "long-term" employment, and that he did not want to move his family from California unless the defendant could guarantee him job security. In response, one interviewer told Torosyan that if he did a good job, the defendant would "take care" of him.[20] Another interviewer told the plaintiff, "I hope you will stay forever."[21] The plaintiff later received a letter confirming the offer of employment, which stated his position, salary, and various fringe benefits, but did not mention job security. Two months later the plaintiff moved with his family to Connecticut and began work. On his first day of work, he received an employee manual that stated that the company had the right to "hire, *discharge for cause*, promote, demote, reclassify, and assign work to employees," and that under the company's "Open Door Policy" all employees had access to the company's president if dissatisfied with the resolution of a complaint by a manager.[22] Two years later, the plaintiff received an updated version of the manual that omitted any reference to "for cause" in connection with any management decisions.[23]

The plaintiff was later fired without cause. The Supreme Court of Connecticut affirmed the trial court decision that the plaintiff's employment could be terminated only for cause. As the state high court approvingly noted: "The trial court found that, in the circumstances of this case, the oral and written statements constituted promises to the plaintiff" and "that, by working for the defendant, the plaintiff accepted those promises."[24] Chief Justice Peters continued:

> Pursuant to traditional contract principles ... the default rule of employment at will can be modified by the agreement of the parties. "Accordingly, to prevail on the ... count of his complaint (that) alleged the existence of an implied agreement, the plaintiff had the burden of proving by the fair preponderance of the evidence that (the employer) had agreed either by words or conduct, to undertake (some) form of actual contract commitment to him under which he could not be terminated without cause."[25]

19. 662 A.2d 89 (Conn. 1995).

20. *Id.* at 94.

21. *Id.* at 94 n.2.

22. *Id.* at 94.

23. *Id.*

24. *Id.* at 98.

25. *Id.* at 97 (*citing Therrien v. Safeguard Mfg. Co.*, 429 A.2d 808, 809–810 (Conn. 1980)).

The case plainly involved sufficient evidence of a bargained-for agreement in the combination of the oral statements and the original terms of the employee manual. However, the state high court made special note of the fact that "[the] oral representations were material to the plaintiff's decision . . . to accept, by telephone, an offer to take a position with the defendant as a radiochemist."[26] This suggests that the oral statements alone might have been sufficient to create for-cause employment. However, suppose the employee had received the oral assurances he did, and also received an employee manual on his first day stating that in the absence of a signed agreement all employment was at-will. In such a case, perhaps it would be less reasonable to interpret the job interviewers' oral statements that the company would "take care" of him and hoped he "will stay forever" as a binding promise of indefinite career-based employment. In many cases, whether the parties intended a binding limit on termination of employment would be a question for the trier of fact, who might additionally weigh the bargaining history between the parties and any relevant policies, procedures, and practices of the employer.[27]

4. Constructive Discharge and "Wrongful Demotion"

In keeping with general principles, an employer may unilaterally alter the terms of an at-will employment contract without liability, including alterations that induce the employee to quit, so long as they do not run afoul of statutory or public-policy restrictions.[28] In some instances, an adverse employer decision may prompt a reasonable employee to quit his or her job rather than continue to work. If the employee had a statutory, public-policy, or contractual right not to be discharged in those circumstances, a court may treat the quit as if it were a dismissal under the doctrine of "constructive discharge".[29]

26. *Id.* at 94.

27. California has used the rubric of "implied-in-fact" contract doctrine to limit employer termination rights based on a "totality of the circumstances". See *Foley v. Interactive Data Corp.*, 765 P.2d 373, 388 (Cal. 1988). The California high court subsequently circumscribed the doctrine by clarifying that, at least in a group termination context, an express employer reservation of the right to discharge an employee at-will will override any promise of job security that might otherwise be implied-in-fact, and that longevity of employment, standing alone, cannot create an obligation not to discharge without cause. *Guz v. Bechtel National, Inc.*, 8 P.3d 1089, 1104 (Cal. 2000).

28. As we will discuss in Chapter 8, however, an at-will employee who quits in response to an employer's unilateral change of working conditions may in some cases be able to claim unemployment compensation benefits notwithstanding that quits are ordinarily disqualifying.

29. *See Pennsylvania State Police v. Suders*, 542 U.S. 129, 146 (2004) (to bring a Title VII claim premised on a

Nothing in contract law limits contractual modifications of the at-will default to termination of employment; in some cases the parties may have intended to curb unjustified adverse employer actions short of termination. Take the example of *Scott v. Pacific Gas & Electric Co.* (PG & E),[30] in which two engineers with senior managerial status received a 25% pay cut and were stripped of all supervisory authority. The engineers were for-cause employees and the terms of their contracts included the right to progressive discipline. The employees were not terminated and did not quit, and so the issues of wrongful termination or constructive discharge were not applicable. Nevertheless, the court found PG & E had a contractual duty not to demote without good cause and therefore the plaintiffs had cognizable claims for wrongful demotion and could recover damages.[31]

5. Statute of Frauds

If an employment agreement is oral, the statute of frauds may limit enforceability. Almost all states have a statute of frauds providing that that contracts not to be performed within one year are not enforceable unless written and signed by the party to be charged with the obligation. This means that parties could enforce an oral contract of employment for any term of one year or less, but not an oral contract of employment for, say, a two-year period.

States are divided in how they treat oral contracts for an indefinite term. If the only way to terminate a contract within one year is through breach, it does not escape invalidation under the statute of frauds. This makes sense, for if one could avoid invalidation under the statute of frauds through the possibility of breach, no contract could ever be invalidated by the statute because one can always repudiate a contract soon after incurring the obligation. A number of states analyze an indefinite-term oral contract as *capable* of performance within a one-year period, based on the possibility of its termination for reasons other than breach, such as the employer going out of business, and therefore treat it as enforceable.[32]

constructive discharge, plaintiff must show that working conditions were so intolerable that a reasonable person would have felt compelled to resign).

30. 904 P.2d 834 (Cal. 1995), *disapproved on other grounds in Guz v. Bechtel National, Inc.*, 8 P.3d 1089, n.17 (Cal. 2000).

31. *Id.* at 842. *See also Mitchell v. Connecticut General Life Ins. Co.*, 697 F.Supp. 948, 952 (E.D. Mich. 1988).

32. See, e.g., *Ohanian v. Avis Rent A Car System, Inc.*, text accompanying notes 17–18, 779 F.2d at 107 (oral promise of lifetime employment absent "just cause" held not within Statute of Frauds because contract was capable of

Other states have taken the opposite approach, holding that an indefinite oral contract is unenforceable under the statute of frauds because it is not clearly intended to be performed within one year.[33] In some cases, courts have enlisted the doctrine of promissory estoppel as a way to enforce a promise otherwise rendered unenforceable under the statute of frauds.[34]

C.   Standard of Cause

1.   Substantive Dimension

Ordinarily, when parties negotiate a definite-term agreement, either they provide in the agreement for a special payout in the event of an early termination without cause or the law assumes that a termination without cause requires payment of the contractual salary and other benefits for the duration of the term, subject to any mitigation of damages under applicable law. "Cause" in these circumstances usually refers to misconduct, other substantial malfeasance by the employee, or other material breach of the agreement, such as a failure to perform the duties of the position due to a permanent disability.[35] In some jurisdictions, it may also include the employee's gross negligence even though the conduct falls short of malfeasance. The parties are, of course, free to define in the agreement their own special understanding of what would constitute "cause" sufficient to terminate the agreement. However, absent explicit language in the agreement, cause does not include the changed economic circumstances of the employer, such as a downturn in demand for the employer's product, a fall in the employer's share price, or the sale of the business.[36] Some decisions require that the employer's stated justification be the actual reason for the termination, although the traditional rule is that the employer's motivation is irrelevant as long as adequate cause in fact existed.[37]

performance within one year since "under New York law, 'just cause' for termination may exist for reasons other than an employee's breach.").

33. See, e.g., *Graham v. Central Fidelity Bank*, 428 S.E.2d 916, 917–18 (Va. 1993).

34. See RESTATEMENT (SECOND) OF CONTRACTS § 139, at 354 (1981); also Part D of this chapter.

35. See generally RESTATEMENT (SECOND) OF AGENCY § 409(1) (requiring conduct by the agent "constitut[ing] a material breach of contract, or who,

without committing a violation of duty, fails to perform or reasonably appears unable to perform a material part of the promised service because of physical or mental disability.").

36. See, e.g., *Drake v. Geochemistry and Environmental Chemistry Research, Inc.*, 336 N.W.2d 666 (S.D. 1983); *Ryan v. Brown Motors, Inc.*, 132 N.J.L. 154, 39 A.2d 70 (N.J. 1944).

37. See, e.g., *Wilde v. Houlton Regional Hospital*, 537 A.2d 1137 (Me. 1988).

By the same token if an employer and employee have negotiated an agreement for an indefinite term that limits termination of employment, any definition of cause for termination to which the parties have expressly agreed will control. Where the agreement is silent on the question, courts will tend to find that employee misconduct, malfeasance, or material breach may constitute cause for termination, as in the case of definite-term contracts. But in addition, courts also recognize that significant changes in the economic circumstances of the employer can supply cause for termination. The explanation for this extension of the scope of cause is that it is reasonable given the potential duration of an indefinite-term contract. As stated by the court in *Ohanian*,

> Just cause can be broader than breach and here there may be just cause to dismiss without a breach. To illustrate, under the terms of the contract it would be possible that despite plaintiff's best efforts the results achieved might prove poor because of adverse business conditions. From defendant's standpoint that too would force Avis to make a change in its business strategy, perhaps reducing or closing an operation. That is, there would be just cause for plaintiff's dismissal. But if this is what occurred, it would not constitute a breach of the agreement.[38]

Although there are few cases on point, once the parties have entered into an enforceable indefinite-term agreement that limits termination of employment, it would appear inconsistent with the parties' undertaking (so construed) to allow the employer to terminate employment for purely subjective reasons, such as "lack of fit," where the employee is still adequately performing his job. In the absence of substantive grounds for dismissal available to terminate a definite-term agreement or significant changes in the firm's economic circumstances, "cause" relating to the employee's performance is ordinarily intended to include only documented poor performance.

States differ over whether dismissal of an employee hired under an indefinite "cause" agreement will stand if the employer cannot prove that the conduct justifying discharge actually occurred. The usual rule for definite-term agreement is that "cause" is an objective inquiry, not dependent on the subjective intentions of the employer.[39] At least in the content of indefinite-term agree-

---

38. *Ohanian, supra* note 17, at 108.

39. See, e.g., *Kerns, Inc. v. The Wella Corp.*, 114 F.3d 566 (6th Cir. 1997) (New York would bar inquiry into employer's motive for exercising right under the contract, and would allow consideration of after-acquired evidence of cause for terminating express distribution con-

ments, some courts have taken the view that the employer's reasonable good faith belief at the time of termination will suffice. The California Supreme Court has taken the lead in this regard in *Cotran v. Rollins Hudig Hall International, Inc.*[40] Ralph Cotran, an employee with an indefinite-term contract, was discharged for sexual harassment following an extensive internal investigation in which the employer interviewed 21 people, including several selected by the accused employee. When the case went to trial, the jury found the evidence insufficient to prove that Cotran had sexually harassed his co-workers and awarded him $1.8 million in compensatory damages for the employer's breach of contract. On appeal, the state high court analyzed whether it mattered to the employer's claim whether Cotran had in fact engaged in sexual harassment:

> The proper inquiry for the jury ... is not, "Did the employee *in fact* commit the act leading to dismissal?" It is "Was the factual basis on which the employer concluded a dischargeable act had been committed reached honestly, after an appropriate investigation and for reasons that are not arbitrary or pretextual?"[41]

And later:

> We give operative meaning to the term "good cause" in the context of implied employment contracts by defining it ... as fair and honest reasons, regulated by good faith on the part of the employer, that are not trivial, arbitrary or capricious, unrelated to business needs or goals, or pretextual.[42]

Other courts require actual cause be shown even with respect to indefinite-term agreements. The case of *Sanders v. Parker Drilling Company* is illustrative.[43] Here, Sanders and several other employees were terminated for smoking marijuana while performing their jobs on an Alaska oil rig—conduct expressly prohibited by company policy. At trial, the jury found the employer failed to prove its claim that the employees had smoked marijuana on the oil rigs,

---

tract); *McConnell v. Howard University*, 818 F.2d 58, 70 (D.C. Cir. 1987) (cause for termination of a contract with university job tenure must establish that the employee has breached the contract); *cf., Crawford Rehabilitation Services, Inc. v. Weissman*, 938 P.2d 540 (Colo. 1997) (finding after-acquired evidence of "resume fraud" provides a complete defense to claims of breach of implied contract and promissory estoppel but declining to decide whether after-acquired evidence of post-hire misconduct would be similarly analyzed).

40. 948 P.2d 412 (Cal. 1998).

41. *Id.* at 421–22.

42. *Id.* at 422. The court noted, however, that "[w]rongful termination claims founded on an explicit promise that termination will not occur except for just or good cause may call for a different standard, depending on the precise terms of the contract provision." *Id.* at 414, n.1.

43. 911 F.2d 191 (9th Cir. 1990) (applying Alaska law).

and therefore found wrongful discharge. The Ninth Circuit reversed, asserting the central question to be one of fact: "[D]id the employee do what the employer said he did?"[44] This position is in keeping with the more conventional, and, we believe, better, view of cause as an objective concept.

2. Procedural Dimension

The cause required to terminate a bilateral agreement also may have procedural dimensions, with respect to both employer and employee. The express terms of the agreement control. If those terms, for example, require the terminated employee to exhaust certain internal remedies, such as an appeal to the board of directors, those remedies ordinarily—absent proof of futility—must be reasonably exhausted before the employee may bring a lawsuit claiming that termination was not based on sufficient cause.[45] Beyond that, and even without express language in the agreement, employers are normally held to the regular and even-handed application of the grounds for terminating an employee for cause.[46]

D. Employer Promises Enforceable as a Matter of Promissory Estoppel

As a general matter, application of the doctrine of promissory estoppel in the employment context enjoys substantial judicial support.[47] Some courts, however, will not allow an oral promise otherwise enforceable under the doctrine to preclude application of the statute of frauds.[48] Where the promise in question is one of at-will employment, courts may limit the remedy to reliance damages.[49]

44. Id., at 194 (citing Touissant v. Blue Cross & Blue Shield, 292 N.W.2d 880, 896 (Mich. 1980)).

45. See, e.g., O'Brien v. New England Telephone & Telegraph, 664 N.E.2d 843 (1996).

46. This procedural-fairness principle is derived from labor arbitration precedents which may prove influential in this area.

47. See, e.g., Stewart v. Cendant Mobility Corp., 837 A.2d 736 (Conn. 2003); Helmick v. Cincinnati Word Processing, Inc., 543 N.E.2d 1212, 1217 (Ohio 1989). But see City of Midland v. O'Bryant, 18 S.W.3d 209 (Tex. 2000) (promissory estoppel cannot be used to modify at-will employment).

48. See McInerney v. Charter Golf, Inc., 680 N.E.2d 1347, 1352 (Ill. 1997); but see RESTATEMENT (SECOND) OF CONTRACTS § 139, at 354 (1981) (doctrine may be invoked to protect reliance interests arising from oral agreements otherwise barred by the statute of frauds).

49. See, e.g., Jarboe v. Landmark Community Newspapers of Indiana, Inc., 644 N.E.2d 118, 122 (Ind. 1994) (employee terminated for excessive absenteeism even though he had been assured he could stay on sick leave beyond three-month maximum could recover only for lost wages between the date of termination and the date of his medical release to return to work.). New York has adopted a particularly narrow view of

The doctrine may be of limited utility in the employment context because it requires a showing of detrimental reliance—that in making the promise the employer "should reasonably expect to induce action or forbearance" and in fact did "induce such action or forbearance" on the employee's part. Moreover, the promise "is binding if injustice can be avoided only by enforcement of the promise."[50]

The case of *Grouse v. Group Health Plan, Inc.*[51] illustrates how one court used the doctrine to grant a remedy to an employee fired from an at-will job. Grouse, a pharmacist, quit his existing job and turned down a competing job offer when offered an at-will position with Group Health. Grouse told Group Health that he would give his current employer the required two weeks' notice. The Group Health manager responsible for hiring him, Elliott, later telephoned Grouse to confirm that he had, in fact given notice to the previous employer.[52] Elliott subsequently had trouble securing positive references for Grouse. When Grouse informed Group Health he was free to begin work, they told him that they had hired someone else for the job. The Minnesota Supreme Court reversed judgment for the defendant and remanded the case for re-trial on the question of whether Grouse had a cause of action under the doctrine of promissory estoppel. The court held that although no contract between the parties existed in fact, one might be implied in law because it would be unjust not to hold Group Health to its promise of an offer of employment given Group Health's specific request that Grouse resign from his previous job in order to accept its offer. The court remanded for a new trial on damages: "Since, as the respondent points out, the prospective employment might have been terminated at any time, the measure of damages is not so much what he would have earned from respondent as what he lost in quitting the job he held and in declining one other offer of employment elsewhere."[53]

E.   Binding Employer Statements

1.   Are Statements in Employment Manuals and Handbooks Binding on the Employer?

Employers typically enter into bilateral agreements for a definite or indefinite term only with their executive employees. When

---

the doctrine in the employment setting. *See Weiner v. McGraw–Hill*, 57 N.Y.2d 458 (1982).

50. RESTATEMENT (SECOND) OF CONTRACTS, § 90 (1981).

51. 306 N.W.2d 114 (Minn. 1981).

52. *Id.* at 115.

53. *Id.* at 116.

dealing with a large number of similarly situated employees, employers tend to communicate the terms of the employment relationship through unilateral employer statements in a document such as an employee manual, personnel handbook or the like. These are usually published in a booklet, posted on a company website, or in some other way made accessible to employees. Company rules promulgated in this manner may have the effect of limiting the employer's power to terminate the employment relationship at will.[54] Rules established by unilateral statements of this kind are generally applied uniformly to all similarly situated employees and not subject to renegotiation with individual employees.

Are the policies contained in such unilateral employer statements binding on the employer? If so, what is the legal principle? Consider *Woolley v. Hoffmann–La Roche, Inc.*[55] When Richard Woolley was hired as an engineer for Hoffmann–La Roche, he was not given a written employment agreement or oral promise of job security.[56] Several weeks after he started work, he received a copy of the company Personnel Policy Manual.[57] The Hoffmann–La Roche manual was *not* distributed generally to employees, although all supervisors received it.[58]

The manual described the employees covered as "all employees of Hoffmann–La Roche."[59] A special section of the manual dealing termination contained the following statement: "It is the policy of Hoffmann–La Roche to retain to the extent consistent with company requirements, the services of all employees who perform their duties efficiently and effectively." The manual went on to define the types of termination as "layoff," "discharge due to performance," "discharge, disciplinary," "retirement" and "resignation." The manual contained no category of discharge without cause. The termination section also contained "Guidelines for discharge due to performance," which set out several preliminary steps, short of discharge, that each manager or supervisor "should consider" in cases of unsatisfactory job performance (e.g., counseling, reassignment, and so forth). A final pertinent provision stated that if the

---

54. See, e.g., *Dillon v. Champion Jogbra, Inc.*, 819 A.2d 703 (Vt. 2002); *Demasse v. ITT Corp.*, 984 P.2d 1138 (Ariz. 1999) (en banc); *O'Brien v. New England Telephone & Telegraph Co.*, 664 N.E.2d 843 (Mass. 1996); *Duldulao v. St. Mary of Nazareth Hospital Center*, 505 N.E.2d 314 (Ill. 1987); *Woolley v. Hoffmann-La Roche, Inc.*, 491 A.2d 1257 (N.J. 1985); *Thompson v. St. Regis Paper Co.*, 685 P.2d 1081 (Wash. 1984); *Toussaint v. Blue Cross & Blue Shield of Michigan*, 292 N.W.2d 880 (Mich. 1980).

55. *Woolley, supra* note 54.

56. *Id.* at 1258.

57. *Id.*

58. *Id.* at 1265.

59. *Id.* This and all remaining provisions of the manual described appear at *id.*, 1271–1273.

manager were to decide to terminate the employee, the employee should be notified of the cause for termination.

Woolley worked at Hoffmann–La Roche for nearly a decade, eventually attaining the status of Group Leader for several engineering departments before he was dismissed in connection with problems in a plant piping system that had been designed by Woolley's team.[60] In analyzing whether an employee manual like Hoffman–La Roche's could create a binding commitment of for-cause employment, the New Jersey Supreme Court endeavored to apply a unilateral contract framework. It reasoned that "the manual is an offer that seeks the formation of a unilateral contract—with the employees' bargained-for action needed to make the offer binding being their continued work when they have no obligation to continue."[61] Even an employee who was unaware of the policy could enforce the employer obligation because reliance would be irrebuttably presumed the moment the manual was distributed.[62]

Unilateral contract analysis in this context is, however, problematic. While it is true that traditional doctrine recognizes that an offer may request acceptance by performance rather than promise, enforcement ordinarily requires knowledge of the offer before completion of performance.[63] As was likely the case in *Woolley*, employees are often unaware of the contents of an employee manual or similar directive when they first accept employment, and similarly unaware of changes in these statements after they have begun employment. This is particularly true where the employer does not physically distribute a manual to all employees, but instead either gives it directly only to supervisors while making it accessible to employees in a personnel office or computer file, or provides the statements through paper leaflets or e-mail announcements to employees. Beyond this difficulty, traditional principles of consideration and bargained-for exchange rarely if ever apply because employers do not make or modify the particular promises in these unilateral statements in response to the expressed concerns of a particular prospective employee or of a particular employee threatening resignation. In addition, the doctrine of promissory estoppel would be inapplicable because of the absence in most cases of

---

60. For an insightful discussion of the case, see J. Hoult Verkerke, *The Story of* Woolley v. Hoffmann–La Roche, *in* EMPLOYMENT LAW STORIES 23–65 (SAMUEL ESTREICHER & GILLIAN LESTER EDS., 2007).

61. E.g., *Woolley, supra* note 54, at 1267.

62. *Id.* at 1268 n. 10. Woolley did not receive the policy manual (that the court

found created a binding obligation of for-cause employment) until several weeks after he commenced employment. *Id.* at 1258.

63. See RESTATEMENT (SECOND) OF CONTRACTS § 23, comment c (1981).

detrimental reliance by employees on statements contained in the employment manual or handbooks.

Other courts rest the binding effect of unilateral employer statements on concepts grounded more in equity than traditional principles of contract. When an employer announces a policy that promises certain discipline and termination procedures, and does so with the self-interested motive of receiving the benefit of improved employee attitudes, behavior, and work quality, one could say the employer ought to be estopped from later claiming its promise was illusory. This more closely describes the approach taken by the seminal Michigan Supreme Court case of *Toussaint v. Blue Cross and Blue Shield of Michigan*[64] and its progeny. An obligation created in this way will apply even to employees who do not become aware of the policy until after being hired.[65] This theory might be analogized to the federal law's well-developed "administrative agency estoppel" theory.[66] As a matter of administrative law, rules promulgated by an agency are held binding on the agency until properly modified or revoked even though no statute or regulation may have required their promulgation in the first place. By similar reasoning, unilateral employer statements that when reasonably read in context are intended to govern operational personnel decisions, should be binding on the employer until properly modified or revoked.[67]

---

64. See *Toussaint, supra* note 54, at 892–95; *Bankey v. Storer Broadcasting Co.,* 443 N.W.2d 112, 119–20 (Mich. 1989) (en banc) (on certified question from the Sixth Circuit) ("Without rejecting the applicability of unilateral contract theory in other situations, we find it inadequate [here]. We look, instead, to the analysis employed in *Toussaint* which focused on the benefit that accrues to an employer when it establishes desirable personnel policies. Under *Toussaint*, written personnel policies are not enforceable because they have been 'offered and accepted' as a unilateral contract; rather, their enforceability arises from the benefit the employer derives by establishing such policies.").

65. *Toussaint, id.,* at 892.

66. See, e.g., *Vitarelli v. Seaton,* 359 U.S. 535 (1959) (Secretary of Interior bound by regulations that he himself promulgated establishing special procedures for termination of employees for security reasons even though without such regulations he could have discharged the employee in question sum-

marily); *Service v. Dulles,* 354 U.S. 363, 379 (1957) (where Secretary of State by regulation limited his own discretion to dismiss employees in cases involving loyalty and security, the Secretary could not later contend that his discretion was unlimited); *Accardi v. Shaughnessy,* 347 U.S. 260 (1954) (regulations promulgated by Attorney General delegating to Board of Immigration Appeals the authority to exercise discretion in deportation cases have force of law and Attorney General cannot dictate the decision so long as regulations remain in force); see generally SAMUEL ESTREICHER & MICHAEL C. HARPER, CASES AND MATERIALS ON EMPLOYMENT LAW 60 n.6 (2d ed. 2004); HENRY H. PERRITT, JR., EMPLOYEE DISMISSAL LAW & PRACTICE § 4.44 (3d ed. 1982).

67. Another useful supporting analogy here may be the law on tariffs that governs entry into a field of business, the prices that may be charged, and the obligations to customers thereby incurred, even though new entrants could not be said to have agreed to those

Not all unilateral employer statements regarding the employment relationship are binding on the employer. It is often a question for the trier of fact whether a particular unilateral employer statement, or set of such statements, reasonably read in context, was intended to bind the employer. Several factors will inform this inquiry. First, the mode of dissemination may be relevant; for instance, dissemination of an employee manual limited to supervisors, without providing access for employees, may imply that it is intended only as guidance for supervisors regarding the exercise of discretionary authority rather than a statement of policy to govern the supervisor's personnel decisions. Some courts have denied enforcement altogether if a policy was distributed only to supervisors.[68] Second, a workplace culture featuring dominant reliance on bilateral agreements with employees may derogate from the significance of unilateral employer statements.

Most significant of all is whether the manual contains a statement expressly disclaiming its force as a binding obligation. Such a disclaimer may indicate that the manual is a hortatory pronouncement rather than a statement to govern the employer's operational decisions. All jurisdictions give considerable weight to the presence of a prominent disclaimer.[69] Courts disagree, however, on the precise effect it should be given. Some hold that a disclaimer renders the statements in the manual unenforceable as a matter of law.[70] Others will weigh it along with other evidence in the case, such as other employer policies and the employer's course of conduct, and leave interpretation of the parties' intent for the trier of fact. For example, questions may arise as to the clarity of the disclaimer,[71] or

terms in any meaningful sense. *See, e.g., J.I. Case Co. v. NLRB*, 321 U.S. 332, 335 (1944) (drawing analogy between collective bargaining agreement and tariffs).

68. See *Morosetti v. Louisiana Land and Exploration Co.*, 564 A.2d 151, 152 (Pa. 1989) ("The employees here . . . could show [only] an internal consideration of policy for what might be given, if and when they announced a policy for all employees. It is not sufficient to show only that they had a policy. It must be shown that they intended to offer it as a binding contract."). But see, e.g., *Nicosia v. Wakefern Food Corp.*, 643 A.2d 554, 558–59 (N.J. 1994) (fact that employer distributed manual to 300 of company's 1,500 non-union employees supported finding that manual was intended to constitute an enforceable employment contract).

69. See, e.g., *Lytle v. Malady*, 579 N.W.2d 906, 911 (Mich. 1998) (en banc); *Suter v. Harsco Corp.*, 403 S.E.2d 751 (W.Va. 1991); *Eldridge v. Evangelical Lutheran Good Samaritan* Society, 417 N.W.2d 797 (N.D. 1987); *Thompson*, 685 P.2d at 1088.

70. See, e.g., *Lytle v. Malady, supra*, at 911–13 (language in employee manual stating that "the contents of this booklet are not intended to establish, and should not be interpreted to constitute any contract between [the employer and any of its employees]" foreclosed any possibility of an employee developing an expectation of for-cause employment).

71. See, e.g., *Nicosia, supra* note 68, at 560.

the prominence of its placement.[72] Some courts have asked juries to evaluate disclaimers in light of the employer's actual practice.[73] The Wyoming Supreme Court will permit juries to disregard disclaimers in employee handbooks upon proof of detrimental reliance on representations contained in the handbook.[74]

2. Can Employers Modify or Rescind Commitments Made in Previous Unilateral Statements?

An important question dividing the courts is the legal effect of an employer's effort to revoke or modify an earlier binding unilateral statement. About half the states that have addressed the matter have held that in the absence of any express provision making a unilateral employer statement irrevocable or non-modifiable, an employer may modify or revoke it prospectively, even if the new terms are less advantageous to employees.[75] In some states, no affirmative reservation by the employer of the right to modify or revoke its unilateral statements prospectively is normally required.[76] Most courts taking this position require that the employer give advance notice of the modified statement or revocation in the same, or a substantially equivalent, manner as the original statement.[77] The new statement will then cover all employees subsequently hired, as well as those who continue their employment after appropriate notice of the modification.

This approach is not the equivalent of holding that the employer's promises contained in the original statement are "illusory" promises, for as the California Supreme Court noted in *Asmus*:

> [T]he MESP [an employer policy statement issued to employees containing an assurance of job security] was not illusory because the plaintiffs obtained the benefits of the statement while it was in effect. In other words, Pacific Bell was obligated to follow it as long as the MESP remained in effect.... As long as the MESP remained in force, Pacific Bell could not treat the contract as illusory by refusing to adhere to its terms; the

72. See, e.g., *Suter, supra* note 69, at 758.

73. See, e.g., *McGinnis v. Honeywell, Inc.*, 791 P.2d 452, 457 (N.M. 1990); *Zaccardi v. Zale Corp.*, 856 F.2d 1473, 1476–77 (10th Cir. 1988).

74. See *McDonald v. Mobil Coal Producing, Inc.*, 789 P.2d 866 (Wyo. 1990).

75. See, e.g., *Asmus v. Pacific Bell*, 999 P.2d 71 (Cal. 2000) (en banc) (on

certified question from the Ninth Circuit); *Bankey v. Storer Broadcasting Co.*, 443 N.W.2d 112 (Mich. 1989) (en banc) (on certified question from the Sixth Circuit).

76. See, e.g., *Bankey, supra* note 75, at 120.

77. E.g., *Asmus, supra* note 75, at 80 (requiring "reasonable notice to the af-

promise was not optional with the employer and was fully enforceable until terminated or modified.[78]

The rationale for permitting unilateral modification by the employer is that the prior commitment is not grounded in an agreement under ordinary contract principles or a promise enforceable as a matter of promissory estoppel. It represents a unilateral undertaking on the employer's part that is binding while in effect but that can be modified or rescinded in the same manner in which it was promulgated. Put differently, given the non-bargained origins of the original obligation, the employer intended to bound as long as it obtained operational benefits from having the policy in place; it is not reasonable to assume that an employer intended to circumscribe its operational discretion beyond that.[79] Also, from a practical perspective, permitting unilateral modification with reasonable notice avoids the administrative complexity that companies with large workforces would face if required to bilaterally negotiate future modifications with individual employees.

Roughly an equal number of states requires consideration for any modification of a unilateral statement that will reduce or eliminate favorable terms enjoyed by incumbent employees.[80] The rationale for this approach is that if one assumes that the employer policy statement gave rise to a binding obligation under traditional contract principles (consideration being either continuation of work by the employee, as the *Woolley* court reasoned, or the return benefit of an orderly, loyal, and cooperative workforce that the employer hoped its promise would invoke[81]), consideration is required to modify or revoke the original obligation, as it would be for any contract. Consideration could take the form of some new benefit to employees, detriment to the employer, or a bargained-for agreement in which the employees consent to work on the new terms henceforth.[82] Mere continuation of employment by the em-

---

fected employees"); *Bankey, supra* note 75, at 120.

78. *Asmus*, 999 P.2d at 79.

79. See, e.g., *Bankey, supra* note 75, at 119 ("When, as in the question before us, the employer changes its discharge-for-cause policy to one of employment-at-will, the employer's benefit is correspondingly extinguished, as is the rationale for the court's enforcement of the discharge-for-cause policy.").

80. See, e.g., *Doyle v. Holy Cross Hospital*, 708 N.E.2d 1140, 1144–46 (Ill. 1999); *Brodie v. General Chem. Corp.*, 934 P.2d 1263, 1268–69 (Wyo. 1997)

(holding consideration required to modify manual to restore employees to at-will status and that continued employment alone is insufficient as consideration); cf. *Demasse v. ITT Corp.*, 984 P.2d 1138, 1141 (Ariz. 1999) (on certified question from the Ninth Circuit; state high court assumed the "certified question's predicate that [the] seniority layoff promise became part of the Demasse employees' contract"); *Torosyan, supra* note 19.

81. E.g., *Brodie, supra* note 80, at 1266.

82. *Robinson v. Ada S. McKinley Community Svcs.*, 19 F.3d 359, 364 (7th Cir. 1994) (applying Illinois law).

ployees following a statement by the employer revoking earlier obligations would amount to no more than performing duties under the pre-existing contract, and thus would fail to satisfy the requirement of new consideration.

The holding of some decisions purporting to bar the employer's unilateral modification or rescission of commitments previously made in its manuals or handbooks is unclear. For example, Connecticut's position in this debate remains unsettled because the prior "cause" term in *Tarosyan* was contained in a bargained-for agreement between the employer and employee; it is therefore not surprising that the employer could not alter this agreement by a unilateral change in its employee handbook. Similarly, the Arizona high court's view in *Demasse v. ITT Corp.*[83] assumed the "certified question's predicate that [the] seniority layoff promise became part of the Demasse employees' contract." To join issue with the decisions permitting unilateral modification or decision, the employer's prior commitment would have to be predicated—not on ordinary contract principles or promissory estoppel but—on its prior unilateral promulgation.

Even in jurisdictions that permit unilateral modification or revocation of an earlier binding policy, there are some employee rights that cannot be revoked. For example, in *Dumas v. Auto Club Insurance Assn.*,[84] plaintiff employees were told when they commenced work with the company that they would receive a commission of 7% of the premiums on all policies they sold or renewed.[85] The company later modified its policy to provide a flat-rate commission. Plaintiffs challenged the application of the flat rate commission to policies they had sold while the percentage plan was still in effect. The Michigan Supreme Court acknowledged that a change in a compensation policy which affects rights or benefits already accrued may give rise to a cause of action in contract, citing as possible examples death benefits, severance pay, and profit-sharing plans. However, in this case the plaintiffs failed to demonstrate that an entitlement to commissions on renewals vested when the policies were sold.[86]

83. 984 P.2d 1138, 1141 (Ariz. 1999) (on certified question from the Ninth Circuit).

84. 473 N.W.2d 652 (Mich. 1991).

85. The facts described appear at *id.* at 654–56.

86. *Id.* at 656: "Unless otherwise provided by contract, renewal commissions or future commissions do not rest upon the sale of the original policy. Renewal contracts are separate from the originals in part requiring additional effort and consideration by salespersons in keeping policies alive."

F. Implied Duty of Good Faith and Fair Dealing

Every contract imposes on parties a non-waivable obligation to deal with the other party in good faith. The implied duty of good faith and fair dealing received early articulation in *Kirke La Shelle Co. v. Paul Armstrong Co.*: "[I]n every contract there is an implied covenant that neither party shall do anything which will have the effect of destroying or injuring the right of the other party to receive the fruits of the contract, which means that in every contract there exists an implied covenant of good faith and fair dealing."[87] This duty is inherent in the employment relationship and cannot be waived. The good-faith duty is an implied duty that needs to be read consonant with the rest of the agreement; it does not provide a basis for rewriting the substantive terms of the agreement.

In practice, the duty of good faith and fair dealing manifests itself primarily in a rule that prohibits the employer from acting opportunistically to prevent the employee from receiving a benefit he has already earned.[88] The classic illustration of this application is the case of *Fortune v. National Cash Register Co.*[89] The employer terminated an at-will salesman immediately after he secured a large order from a client within his territory. The salesman's contract specified that he would receive a bonus based on a percentage of any sales made within the territory assigned to him, whether the sale was made by him or someone else. Seventy-five percent of the applicable bonus would be paid if the territory was assigned to him when the order was placed, and the remaining 25% paid if the territory was assigned to him when the order was delivered and installed.[90] The company claimed that because the territory was no longer assigned to Fortune at the time of installation and delivery—the company having terminated Fortune by then—it did not have to pay him the final 25% of the bonus. The Supreme Judicial Court of Massachusetts upheld the trial verdict for the plaintiff, acknowledging that the employer had acted fully in accordance with its right to terminate Fortune without cause on a literal reading of the contract. However, the court held that the written contract contained an implied covenant of good faith and fair dealing, which

---

87. 188 N.E. 163, 167 (N.Y. 1933). *See also Wood v. Lucy, Lady Duff–Gordon*, 118 N.E. 214 (N.Y. 1917); RESTATEMENT (SECOND) OF CONTRACTS § 205 (1981).

88. In the context of employee benefit plans covered by ERISA, such opportunistic firings would violate the anti-

retaliation clause in § 510 of the statute, 29 U.S.C. § 1140. This section deals with a similar common-law right that applies in the context of other kinds of contractual benefits.

89. 364 N.E.2d 1251 (Mass. 1977).

90. *Id.* at 1253.

renders a termination not made in good faith a breach of the contract.[91] The court elaborated:

> Where the principal seeks to deprive the agent of all compensation by terminating the contractual relationship when the agent is on the brink of successfully completing the sale, the principal has acted in bad faith and the ensuing transaction between the principal and the buyer is to be regarded as having been accomplished by the agent. Restatement (Second) of Agency [§] 454, and Comment a (1958). The same result obtains where the principal attempts to deprive the agent of any portion of a commission due the agent. Courts have often applied this rule to prevent overreaching by employers and the forfeiture by employees of benefits almost earned by the rendering of substantial services.[92]

Note that the court did not reach this conclusion because the employer had undertaken a general obligation not to terminate the employee without cause, or because termination of employment itself was actionable. On the contrary, the employer had no such duty, only a duty to cooperate in adhering to the spirit of the bonus plan given that Mr. Fortune had performed all the service required to earn the bonus. Terminating Mr. Fortune in order to deprive him of the rest of the bonus clearly derogated from good faith.[93]

91. *Id.* at 1255–56.

92. *Id.* at 1257.

93. As the covenant is used in this context, it provides a basis for protected rights to deferred compensation, but not a basis for overturning the termination itself. See, e.g., *Wakefield v. Northern Telecom, Inc.*, 769 F.2d 109, 112 (2d Cir. 1985) (applying either New York or New Jersey law) ("Wakefield may not ... recover for his termination *per se*. However, the contract for payment of commissions creates rights distinct from the employment relation, and ... obligations derived from the covenant of good faith implicit in the commission contract may survive the termination of the employment relationship.").

Chapter 4

EMPLOYMENT TORTS

The employment relationship is fundamentally contractual in nature. The general rule is that no one is under an obligation to work for any employer, nor is any employer under an obligation to hire or retain any individual. Ordinarily, if a contract of employment or for particular compensation or terms is breached, the remedies are the usual remedies for breach of contract—giving the injured party the benefit of the contract if it had been fully performed, less whatever sums the injured employee could recover through reasonable alternative employment (or the injured employer could recover by hiring a replacement). Contract remedies seek to put the parties in the position they would have occupied absent breach, not to deter breach as such.

A. "Bad Faith Breach"

In a few areas, the law recognizes tort measures of relief for injuries arising out of a breach of contract. One such area is the cause of action for "bad faith breach" which has been recognized in many jurisdictions to deter insurance companies from taking unreasonable positions as to whether an insurance contract covers a particular claim.[1] The premise of these decisions is that once a claim has arisen, the carrier may have a strong incentive to deny coverage in arguable cases because the costs of paying the claim outweigh the costs of any litigation with the insured (who must now litigate not only the underlying dispute but also the coverage dispute with the carrier) and attendant reputational loss in the marketplace; the carrier may be relying on a practical judgment that the insured will not be able to finance a lawsuit. From the standpoint of the insured, there is no opportunity to "cover" because having incurred the insurable event he cannot purchase insurance. Tort law intervenes to discourage such opportunistic behavior. The carrier now faces tort liability, including possible punitive damages, if it lacks a reasonable good faith basis for its position. Because of the prospect of tort liability, the carrier is more likely in close cases at least to defend the insured with respect to the underlying dispute, while reserving its rights to contest coverage in later proceedings.

---

1. See, e.g., *Gruenberg v. Aetna Ins. Co.*, 510 P.2d 1032 (Cal. 1973).

For a time, the bad-faith breach tort was available in employment cases in California, based on an analogy to the relationship between an insurance company and the insured, but this position was repudiated by the state high court in *Foley v. Interactive Data Corp.*[2] The *Foley* court rejected the analogy to insurance contracts:

> [When an insurer in] bad faith refuses to pay a claim or accept a settlement offer within policy limits . . ., the insured cannot turn to the marketplace to find another insurance company willing to pay for the loss already incurred. The wrongfully terminated employee, on the other hand, can (and must, in order to mitigate damages), make reasonable efforts to seek alternative employment. . . . Moreover, the role of the employer differs from that of the "quasi-public" insurance company with whom individuals contract specifically in order to obtain protection from potential specified economic harm. The employer does not similarly "sell" protections to its employees. Nor do we find convincing the idea that the employee is necessarily seeking a different kind of financial security than those entering a typical commercial contract. . . .[3]

Most telling was the court's view that employer and employee are not in the same position of inherent conflict of interest as is characteristic of the relationship between insurer and insured once a claim has been made:

> The interests of employer and employee are most frequently in alignment. If there is a job to be done, the employer must still pay someone to do it. This is not to say there may never be a "bad motive" for discharge not otherwise covered by law. Nevertheless, in terms of abstract employment relationships as contrasted with abstract insurance relationships, there is less inherent relevant tension between the interests of employers and employees than exists between that of insurers and insureds. Thus the need to place disincentives on an employer's conduct in addition to those already imposed by law simply does not rise to the same level as that created by the conflicting interests at stake in the insurance context.[4]

The California high court clearly was of the view that unless the termination implicates a statute or public policy, the law does not seek to deter breach but, rather, to place the injured party in the position he would have enjoyed absent the breach. As such, an award of damages for lost income and benefits, less mitigation,

---

2. 765 P.2d 373 (Cal. 1988).

3. *Id.* at 396.

4. *Id.*

should suffice and is consistent with the remedies available for breach of contract generally.

Proponents of a tort remedy might argue that employment contracts are different from other contracts because individuals have non-economic interests in not suffering wrongful termination of employment and that reputational harm and other collateral costs of termination, such as uprooting family and worsening credit rating, are not likely to be captured fully in conventional recovery. In general, however, the courts have not been receptive to this type of argument, fearing perceived negative effects of "tortifying" contract disputes.

A tort remedy was recognized in *K Mart Corp. v. Ponsock,*[5] where a "tenured employee" hired under the terms of an employee handbook that promised continued employment "until retirement" and for "as long as economically possible" was discharged after nearly 10 years of service for purpose of preventing the vesting of retirement benefits. The Nevada supreme court held he could recover in tort because this was not "a mere breach of contract"; rather, "the jury could very reasonably have concluded that K Mart dismissed Ponsock for the very unworthy purpose of evading its duty to pay his retirement benefits."[6] Nevada recognizes the tort only where employers breach without justification a "contractual obligation of continued employment...."[7] The theory appears not to have picked up support in other jurisdictions.[8]

B.   Discharge or Other Discipline in Violation of Clearly Established Public Policy

1.   Common Law

One tort theory that has obtained widespread support is for discharge in violation of clearly established public policy. In a few jurisdictions, this has been extended to discipline and other adverse decisions falling short of a discharge. The tort is similar to the express anti-retaliation provisions found in employment statutes, such as anti-discrimination laws (discussed in Chapter 11), but allows a tort recovery and operates free of the procedural requirements of any particular statute.

---

5. 732 P.2d 1364 (Nev. 1987).

6. *Id.* at 1368 n.3.

7. *Sands Regent v. Valgardson,* 777 P.2d 898, 899 (Nev. 1989).

8. Moreover, as further developed in Chapter 13, federal law provides a reme-

dy in similar circumstances under § 510 of the Employee Retirement Income Security Act of 1974, 29 U.S.C. § 1140, which may preempt state law remedies for private-sector employees alleging interference with retirement plan benefits.

The theory of the tort is not so much to protect individual employees as to vindicate some external public policy directive. An early ruling is *Petermann v. International Bhd. of Teamsters*,[9] where the California appeals court held that an employee dismissed for refusing his employer's instruction to testify falsely under oath before a legislative tribunal could contest his discharge notwithstanding his status as an at-will employee: "It would be obnoxious to the interests of state and contrary to public policy and sound morality to allow an employer to discharge any employee, whether the employment be for a designated or unspecified duration, on the ground that the employee declined to commit perjury, an act specifically enjoined by statute."

For several reasons, *Petermann* presented a particularly strong case for recognizing the "public policy" claim. First, the source of the public policy was clear as it was reflected in the criminal code of the state. Second, allowing an employer to discharge an employee for refusing to perjure himself would have direct and substantial negative consequences for the public policy in ensuring truthful testimony under oath. Ordinarily, perjury is a matter for criminal prosecution, not civil actions, and the state would learn of the perjury only after the fact, if it were to learn of it at all. Third, recognition of a tort claim would not interfere with a comprehensive legislative or administrative scheme for dealing with perjury. Finally, the employee had been placed on the horns of a dilemma. The employee was subject to conflicting duties to the employer and to society. He did not merely observe illegality on his employer's part, for if he acceded to his employer's directive he would himself have become an instrumentality of the illegal conduct. Recognition of a tort cause of action would serve to bolster the resolve of an employee placed in such a dilemma to avoid perjury. As the California supreme court explained in *Tameny v. Atlantic Richfield Co.*,[10] which upheld the public-policy tort claim of an employee discharged for refusing to participate in an illegal conspiracy to fix gasoline prices: "[A]n employer's obligation to refrain from discharging an employee who refuses to commit a criminal act does not depend upon any express or implied 'promises set forth in the (employment) contract' . . . but rather reflects a duty imposed by law upon all employers in order to implement the fundamental public policies embodied in the state's penal statutes."[11]

Petermann is thus a paradigm case: (1) a source of established public policy grounded in positive law, indeed criminal law prohibi-

9. 344 P.2d 25 (Cal. App. 1959).
10. 610 P.2d 1330 (Cal. 1980).
11. *Id.* at 1335.

tions; (2) an employee confronted with the dilemma of having to choose between two conflicting duties (to the employer and to the public); (3) a clear adverse impact on public policy if employers could use their economic power to compel employees to perjure themselves; and (4) no interference with an alternative remedial scheme. As we move away from this paradigm, many courts will still recognize a tort action, but the case becomes correspondingly more difficult.

a. Source of Established Public Policy

The strongest evidence of public policy is where it is found in a statute or perhaps a provision of a state constitution. Thus, some jurisdictions have derived from state constitutional privacy guarantees a source of public policy limiting an employer's ability to subject employees to suspicionless drug testing.[12] In some cases, a well-established public policy has been recognized even if it could not be tied to a particular statute or other source of positive law. The Supreme Court of Oregon in *Nees v. Hocks*[13] held that an employer who discharged an employee for indicating she was available for jury duty violated a state public policy. The public policy was gleaned from a variety of sources including references to jury duty in the state constitution, in favor of citizens readily indicating their availability for jury duty. In *Palmateer v. International Harvester Co.*,[14] the Supreme Court of Illinois extended the citizen obligation rationale of *Nees* to include protection from employer retaliation against responding truthfully to police inquiries.

Some courts also have found in professional codes of ethics a source of established public policy, distinguishing between provisions that seek to protect public interests from those respecting internal professional interests.[15] This reflects the self-regulatory function performed by many professional associations. In the legal profession, professional codes of ethics typically become positive law through a process of review and adoption by state courts.[16] The

---

12. See, e.g., *Loder v. City of Glendale*, 927 P.2d 1200 (Cal. 1997); cf. *Luedtke v. Nabors Alaska Drilling Inc.*, 768 P.2d 1123 (Alaska 1989) (constitutional right of privacy did not extend to private action but is evidence of public policy).

13. 536 P.2d 512 (Or. 1975).

14. 421 N.E.2d 876 (Ill. 1981).

15. See *Pierce v. Ortho Pharmaceutical Corp.*, 417 A.2d 505 (N.J. 1980);

compare *Warthen v. Toms River Community Hospital*, 488 A.2d 229, 233 (N.J. App. 1985) (Code of Nurses's support for "human dignity" considerations possibly justifying refusal to dialyze a terminally ill patient held to "define[] a standard of conduct beneficial only to the individual nurse and not to the public at large.").

16. New York, not noticeably hospitable to the public-policy tort, has recognized "an implied-in-law obligation" on

process is less formal in other professions, although breach of professional standards often informs actions for professional malpractice.[17]

An open issue is whether common law decisions provide a source of public policy. Would, for example, a salesman concerned with the safety of a product he was selling be protected against discharge for complaining internally about the product? One case with such facts declined to recognize a cause of action even where the product was later withdrawn from the market, in part because the salesmen was considered to lack expertise in matters of product safety.[18] Are public-policy tort actions an appropriate avenue for resolving questions of product safety, which often depend on technical expertise and probabilistic judgments? What about questions of negligence generally? Should an employee be able to bring a public-policy claim if she is fired for reporting negligence by her employer? The answer to this depends in part on whether negligence rules are designed principally to compensate victims or are also designed to deter the underlying activity.

b.   Conflicting Duties

As *Petermann* and *Nees* illustrate, courts are likely to be receptive to the claims of employees subject to conflicting duties— the contractual duty to follow employer directives and the legal duty to not serve as an instrumentality for violating the law—and to protect employees who obey the higher duty to the public. One difficult question for the courts is whether to extend the "public policy" tort to situations where an employee is not being asked to perform an illegal act but, rather, observes an illegal act and reports the act to appropriate authorities. *Geary* and other decisions suggest a reluctance to extend the cause of action to "whistle-blowers." Some of these decisions are problematic because they do not recognize that the employee is often also being asked personally to further the illegality by certifying inappropriate results[19] or, in

an employer's part not to discipline a lawyer-employee for reasonably refusing to perform an unethical act. See *Wieder v. Skala*, 609 N.E.2d 105 (N.Y. 1992). The state high court has been unwilling to extend this cause of action to employed physicians reviewing workers' compensation claims by employees. See *Horn v. New York Times*, 790 N.E.2d 753 (N.Y. 2003).

17. See, e.g., RESTATEMENT OF THE LAW, THIRD, TORTS: LIABILITY FOR PHYSICAL HARM § 13, comment e (Proposed Final Draft No. 1, April 6, 2005).

18. See *Geary v. United States Steel Corp.*, 319 A.2d 174 (Pa. 1974).

19. See, e.g., *Murphy v. American Home Products*, 448 N.E.2d 86 (N.Y. 1983) (assistant treasurer fired for allegedly revealing to corporate officers manipulation of secret pension reserves); *Adler v. American Standard Corp.*, 830 F.2d 1303 (4th Cir. 1987) (applying Ma-

Geary's case, selling an unsafe product. Some of these decisions also tend to withhold protection from employees who make internal disclosures, seemingly preferring external reports to the media or public authorities which could be more damaging to the firm.

c.   Clear Adverse Impact on Public Policy

In *Petermann* and *Nees*, the adverse impact on public policy of withholding protection is clear—an employee likely will be coerced by his employer to lie under oath, an employee will falsely indicate unavailability for jury duty. Should the courts extend protection where employees are mistaken in their belief that they are being asked to perform an illegal act? What if Petermann had misconstrued conversations with his employer's lawyers in believing they were counseling perjury? Or if Nees mistakenly understood his employer as requiring to him to state unavailability as opposed to seeking a delay in jury service? The harm to public policy from withholding protection is attenuated because the underlying activity would not be illegal. However, the question is whether withholding protection from employees acting with a reasonable but erroneous belief would discourage employees altogether from resisting unlawful employer instructions. Most courts have held that protection should extend to reasonable and good faith, if erroneous, belief of illegality.

A number of courts have declined to extend the public policy cause of action to adverse actions short of discharge. The theory seems to be a mixture of perceived absence of necessity (employees are less likely to be deterred from refusing an unlawful assignment) and administrative concerns (getting courts too deeply involved in personnel matters).[20]

Most courts until recently have declined to extend the public-policy cause of action to intra-corporate disputes on the theory that these disputes do not implicate important public policies.[21] With the public scandals attending the unraveling of major companies like Enron, resulting in the enactment of the Sarbanes–Oxley Act of 2002, this judicial attitude may be changing.[22]

ryland law) (assistant general manager of printing division discharged for refusing to include in annual sales projections accounts obtained by alleged kickbacks).

20. But see *Trosper v. Bag 'N Save*, 734 N.W.2d 704 (Neb. 2007); *cf. Scott v. Pacific Gas & Electric Co.*, 904 P.2d 834 (Cal. 1995) (implied contractual limitation on "wrongful demotion").

21. See, e.g., *Foley v. Interactive Data Corp.*, 765 P.2d at 379–80 ("we do not find a substantial public policy prohibiting an employer from discharging an employee" for reporting relevant business information to management).

d. No Interference with an Alternative Scheme

The initial cases arose in situations where the statute giving rise to the public policy did not itself contain a private civil remedy. Thus, in *Kelsay v. Motorola, Inc.*,[23] a pioneering decision involving a discharge for filing a workers' compensation claim, the statute provided for a criminal remedy but no civil cause of action. This was also true in *Petermann*, *Tameny* and *Nees*.

The question then arises whether courts should recognize a cause of action in tort where the law establishing the public policy provides a private civil remedy. Most courts will decline to recognize a new tort in such circumstances, although a number of jurisdictions will.[24] Recognition of the cause of action is more likely where the plaintiff is not protected by the statute because he is not employed by a covered employer.

2. *Legislation*

A number of states have enacted whistleblowing or "conscientious objection" statutes. Some of these laws are limited to the public sector; others like New York's offer very narrow substantive coverage.[25] Comprehensive laws like New Jersey's[26] offer broad protection of both refusals to perform acts reasonably believed to be unlawful and whistleblowing to public bodies, and fill in most of the gaps left open by the common law. Thus, for example, the New Jersey statute covers violations of all laws, state and federal; protects internal reports of wrongdoing (even requiring them when they are not futile); and provides the full range of tort remedies, including punitive damages, plus attorney's fees.

Many federal laws regulating the workplace contain protections for refusals to perform unlawful assignments and whistleblowing.

---

22. See, e.g., *Paolella v. Browning–Ferris, Inc.*, 158 F.3d 183 (3d Cir. 1998) (applying Delaware law) (employee fired after accusing employer of fraudulently inflating client bills).

23. 384 N.E.2d 353 (Ill. 1978).

24. See, e.g., *Rojo v. Kliger*, 801 P.2d 373 (Cal. 1990) (statutory remedy does not bar public policy tort for workplace sexual harassment); *Collins v. Elkay Mining Co.*, 371 S.E.2d 46, 48 (W.Va. 1988) (failure to file charges under federal and state mine safety acts does not bar retaliatory discharge claim by coal mine foreman for refusing to falsify mine safety report).

25. N.Y. Labor Law, art. 20–C, § 740 (applying only to disclosures of wrongdoing presenting "a substantial and specific danger to public health or safety"). The law also contains an election-of-remedies provision foreclosing other state law claims. See *Pipas v. Syracuse Home Assn.*, 641 N.Y.S.2d 768 (N.Y.App. 4th Dept. 1996).

26. N.J. Stat. §§ 34:19–1 to 19–8.

The federal civil service law extends protection to disclosure of information reasonably believed to be "mismanagement, a gross waste of funds, an abuse of authority, or a substantial danger to public health or safety"; the law provides an administrative remedy but no private cause of action.[27] Prominent whistleblower provisions are also contained in the False Claims Act[28] and the Sarbanes–Oxley Act of 2002.[29]

C.   Other Tort Theories for Challenging Termination Decisions

1.   Fraud or Deceit

Aside from "public policy" and perhaps privacy claims (which are the subject of the next chapter), there are few tort theories available for challenging a termination decision. In some situations, an employee may be able to frame an employer's failure to honor promises made to induce his leaving a former place of employment as a form of misrepresentation or fraud. In one state's formulation, "[t]he elements of fraud, which give rise to the tort action for deceit, are (a) misrepresentation (false representation, concealment, or nondisclosure); (b) knowledge of falsity (or 'scienter'); (c) intent to defraud, i.e., to induce reliance [on the misrepresentation]; (d) justifiable reliance; and (e) resulting damage."[30]

Some states, like California, offer statutory protection against fraudulent inducement.[31] Despite the statutory provision, the California supreme court in *Lazar v. Superior Court*[32] allowed a tort action to proceed where the employee alleged detrimental reliance (leaving his former employment and moving from New York to California) on the employer's misrepresentation of the economic health of its business. The *Lazar* court distinguished its earlier ruling in *Hunter v. Up–Right, Inc.*,[33] involving an employer who misrepresented the nature of an impending corporate decision so as to encourage an employee's resignation:

> [W]rongful termination of employment ordinarily does not give rise to a cause of action for fraud or deceit, even if a misrepresentation is utilized to effect the termination. "[S]uch repre-

---

27. CIVIL SERVICE REFORM ACT OF 1978, as amended, 5 U.S.C. § 2301 et seq.

28. 31 U.S.C. § 3730(h).

29. 18 U.S.C. § 1514A.

30. *Lazar v. Superior Court*, 909 P.2d 981, 985 (Cal. 1996).

31. Calif. Labor Code §§ 970–72.

32. 909 P.2d 981 (Cal. 1996).

33. 864 P.2d 88 (Cal. 1993).

sentations are merely the means to the end desired by the employer, i.e., termination of employment." ...

> *Hunter* dealt with a situation atypical of the usual fraud situation, in that there the alleged perpetrator of the fraud (the defendant employer, Up–Right) was attempting to accomplish by deception something it actually had power to accomplish forthrightly—termination of the plaintiff's employment. *Hunter*'s rationale does not readily extend beyond the termination context because, in the ordinary fraud case, the alleged perpetrator of the fraud lacks the power to accomplish his objective without resort to duplicity. The effect of Up–Right's misrepresentation was simply to transform Hunter's resignation into a constructive termination.[34]

Other jurisdictions may also be receptive to situations involving relocation of employees induced by misrepresentations.[35]

2. *Wrongful Interference with Contractual Relations*

Where agents of employers secure a discharge or preclude reemployment of a former employee out of personal animosity or other personal motive, a tort action may lie against the agent for wrongful interference with contractual relations. As formulated in the Restatement, Second, of Torts § 766, the tort is quite open-ended:

> One who intentionally and improperly interferes with the performance of a contact (except a contract to marry) between another and a third person by inducing or otherwise causing the third person not to perform the contract, is subject to liability to the other for the pecuniary loss resulting to the other from the failure of the third person to perform the contract.

The tort extends to interference with prospective contractual relations and to contracts terminable at will.[36]

Some courts have been reluctant to recognize tortious interference in the employment context where the claimed interference is effected by an agent of the employer acting within the scope of his authority, not a third party.[37] Such circumstances raise the question

---

34. *Lazar*, 909 P.2d at 987.

35. See, e.g., *Sea-Land Service, Inc. v. O'Neal*, 297 S.E.2d 647 (Va. 1982).

36. See RESTATEMENT, SECOND, OF TORTS §§ 766–767.

37. See, e.g., *Becket v. Welton Becket & Assoc.*, 39 Cal.App.3d 815, 114 Cal. Rptr. 531 (1974); *Ryan v. Brooklyn Eye and Ear Hospital*, 46 A.D.2d 87, 360 N.Y.S.2d 912 (1974).

whether an employer through its agent can interfere with its own contract with the plaintiff. Other courts have held that agents can be held personally liable when they act out of a personal vendetta or other non-legitimate motives.[38]

One open question is whether the employer can be liable via respondeat superior for the acts of an agent in such circumstances. In *Cappiello v. Ragen Precision Industries, Inc.*,[39] a corporate president was successfully sued for wrongfully effecting the plaintiff's termination in order to avoid paying plaintiff accrued commissions. Although punitive damages could not be assessed against the employer itself, they could be levied against the corporate president "whom the jury found to have acted out of their own greed to procure plaintiff's commissions for their own economic benefit." And, the court held, the employer could be held vicariously liable on the facts of this case because the defendant was a high-level executive and the employer maintained a common defense with the executive.[40]

3. Intentional Infliction of Emotional Distress

The intentional infliction tort—in some jurisdictions, it is called the tort of "outrage"—offers a means of challenging not the termination itself but a particularly abusive manner of discharge or investigation leading up to it. In *Agis v. Howard Johnson Co.*,[41] a restaurant dealt with an employee theft problem by discharging waitresses in alphabetical order as a means of uncovering the offending waitress. Some jurisdictions will not recognize the tort in the absence of accompanying physical injury.[42]

The tort has been invoked as a supplementary remedy in discrimination cases, particularly those alleging sexual harassment as it provides a basis for personal liability for the employer's agents or co-workers. One question that has arisen is whether the tort is preempted by the exclusivity provision of workers' compensation laws.[43]

---

38. See, e.g., *Cappiello v. Ragen Precision Indus., Inc.*, 471 A.2d 432 (N.J. App. 1984); *Yaindl v. Ingersoll–Rand Co.*, 422 A.2d 611 (Pa. Super. 1980).

39. 471 A.2d 432 (N.J. App. 1984).

40. For an example of a statutory limit on corporate punitive damages, see Calif. Civil Code § 3294, subd. a., interpreted in *White v. Ultramar*, 981 P.2d 944 (Cal. 1999).

41. 355 N.E.2d 315 (Mass. 1976).

42. See, e.g., *Forde v. Royal's Inc.*, 537 F.Supp. 1173 (S.D.Fla. 1982) (applying Florida Law).

43. Compare, e.g., *Fermino v. Fedco, Inc.*, 872 P.2d 559 (Cal. 1994) (employer's investigative tactics amounting to false imprisonment held outside of exclusivity provision), with *Cole v. Fair Oaks Fire Protection Dist.*, 729 P.2d 743 (Cal. 1987) (firefighter's claim of hypertension resulting from harassment be-

D. Defamation

A well-established tort recognized across the U.S., defamation lies to protect the individual interest in his reputation. The elements of a plaintiffs' claim typically are (1) publication of (2) a defamatory statement, resulting in (3) damages. In most jurisdictions, the truth or falsity of the statement is not part of the plaintiff's prima facie case but has to be raised by the defendant. The defendant is also not liable if he can prove privilege.

1. Publication

Publication is a dissemination of information about an individual to third parties. As a practical matter, publication may be a difficult element for the plaintiff to prove in many cases because employers concerned about liability for defamation tend to adopt "no comment" policies, or will divulge only name, title and period of employment when responding to inquiries about former employees. Such policies may help employers avoid liability but they may also make it difficult for former employees to find new employment and disserve the public interest in having employment decisions based on accurate information about the employment records of job applicants.

Some jurisdictions recognize the concept of self-publication, which originated in the wartime case of *Colonial Stores, Inc. v. Barrett*.[44] Under the regulations of the War Manpower Commission (WPC), employers were required to furnish discharged employees with written statements of availability and employees seeking new employment were required to display these certificates to prospective employers. Barrett's employer had written on the certificate that he was fired for "improper conduct toward fellow employees," in violation of the WPC prohibition on publication of information "prejudicial to the employee in seeking new employment." Publication was satisfied by the law's requirement of self-publication.

The self-publication concept has been extended to situations involving less direct compulsion to reveal the reasons for the prior termination. In *Lewis v. Equitable Life Assur. Society*,[45] the Minnesota supreme court held that employers are subject to a defamation action if the reasons they give for a termination are defamatory (in that case, for "gross insubordination") and the employer knows or

---

cause of union activities held to be "a normal part of the employment relationship" and thus within exclusivity provision).

44. 38 S.E.2d 306 (Ga. App. 1946).

45. 389 N.W.2d 876 (Minn. 1986).

should know that the former employee will be asked by prospective employers why they were terminated and will be expected to respond truthfully to that query.[46] As this theory runs counter to the common law rule that plaintiffs should mitigate their damages, several jurisdictions have rejected the concept of mandatory self-publication in the typical employment setting.[47]

Even in jurisdictions not recognizing the concept of mandatory self-publication, publication may be found in internal communications between employees or officers of the same corporation. Some courts essentially find the publication element satisfied by evidence of such intra-corporate communications.[48] Others require that for the publication element to be satisfied, information about the plaintiff's termination must be disseminated to individuals in the company that did not have a business-related reason to receive the information.[49]

2.   *Privilege*

Assuming the defamatory statement is false, a principal issue in a defamation case will be whether the defendant issuing the statement enjoyed an absolute privilege, a qualified privilege, or no privilege at all.

a.   Absolute Privilege

An absolute privilege is likely to be limited to communications made in the context of judicial and quasi-judicial proceedings. Other legally mandated statements are generally not accorded an absolute privilege. In the securities industry, employers are required by the National Association of Securities Dealers (NASD) and other self-regulatory exchanges (SRO) to complete a Form U–5 setting forth the reasons for every termination of employment of a registered representative. In *Rosenberg v. MetLife, Inc.*,[50] responding to a

---

46. See *Downs v. Waremart, Inc.*, 926 P.2d 314 (Or. 1996); *Churchey v. Adolph Coors Co.*, 759 P.2d 1336 (Colo. 1988); *Belcher v. Little*, 315 N.W.2d 734 (Iowa 1982).

47. See *Sullivan v. Baptist Memorial Hospital*, 995 S.W.2d 569 (Tenn. 1999); *Gore v. Health–Tex, Inc.*, 567 So.2d 1307 (Ala. 1990); *Lunz v. Neuman*, 290 P.2d 697 (Wash. 1955).

48. See, e.g., *Torosyan v. Boehringer Ingelheim Pharm.*, 662 A.2d 89 (Conn.

1995); *Pirre v. Printing Developments, Inc.*, 468 F.Supp. 1028, 1041–42 (S.D.N.Y. 1979) (applying New York law); see generally RESTATEMENT, SECOND, OF TORTS § 577(1), comment (i).

49. See, e.g., *Otteni v. Hitachi America, Ltd.*, 678 F.2d 146 (11th Cir. 1982) (applying Georgia law; "communication by one corporate agent to another in the course of their duties is not publication").

50. 866 N.E.2d 439 (N.Y. 2007).

certified question from the Second Circuit, the New York high court declared that statements made on a Form U–5 should be accorded an absolute privilege because the Form was a first step in the NASD's quasi-judicial process—alerting the SRO to potential misconduct and enabling it to investigate, sanction and deter misconduct by its registered representatives. The NASD's function ultimately benefited the general investing public, which faced the potential for substantial harm if exposed to unethical brokers.

b. Qualified Privilege

Absolute privileges are rare. For statements made in the course of internal company investigations or in response to queries about the performance of former employees, only a qualified privilege is likely to be available. Such a privilege is defeated on a showing of "malice." As one court put it:

> Good faith or lack of malice does not mean lack of hostility or ill feeling; it means that "[t]he person making the statement must have reasonable grounds for believing that it is true and he must honestly believe it is a correct statement."[51]

As a practical matter, much will depend on how juries assess the reasonableness of the manner by which the employer conducted the investigation and communicated its ground for termination to the employee or prospective employer.

In recent years, legislatures have sought to encourage employers to give references by codifiying a "good faith" immunity.[52] These laws typically take the form of a presumption of the employer's good faith in providing a reference, to be rebutted on a showing of reckless, knowing or maliciously motivated disclosure of false or misleading information. This legislation would seem merely to codify the conventional qualified privilege available under common law.[53]

---

51. *Rouly v. Enserch Corp.*, 835 F.2d 1127, 1130 (5th Cir. 1988) (applying Mississippi law).

52. See, e.g., ALASKA STAT. § 9.65.10; COLO. REV. STAT. § 9-2-114; ILL. COMP. STAT. ANN. 46/10; MICH. COMP. LAWS ANN. 423.452.

53. See generally J. Hoult Verkerke, *Legal Regulation of Employment Reference Practices*, 65 U.CHI.L. REV. 115 (1998).

Chapter 5

WORKPLACE PRIVACY

This chapter presents a distinct form of labor market regulation—one intended to preserve employee interests in privacy or autonomy. Rather than simply seeking protection from employer misuse of its accepted authority, privacy rules directly challenge the very legitimacy of employer authority over aspects of the lives of employees. There is no general right of privacy in the U.S., as there is in some countries like Germany. Accordingly, this chapter is organized in terms of the source of the privacy right: constitutional law, legislation, contract, or other common law.[1]

A. Constitutional Law

Public employees receive the highest level of privacy protection because not only are they generally covered by civil service laws, and often collective bargaining contracts, but also they can invoke constitutional restrictions on government. For government employees, there are essentially two bases for privacy rights: (1) claims of physical privacy protected by the Fourth Amendment's prohibition of unreasonable search and seizure; and (2) claims of associational privacy protected by the First Amendment's guarantee of freedom of association.

1. Physical Privacy

The Fourth Amendment to the U.S. Constitution prohibits unreasonable search and seizure. An unreasonable search or seizure is one conducted without probable cause of unlawful conduct and, in some circumstances, without a warrant.

Unconstitutional seizures are not generally an issue in the employment context, although there may be circumstances where employer detention of employees accused of theft implicates the constitutional guarantee against unreasonable seizure.[2] The more likely claim is that of unconstitutional search.

---

1. For general treatments of the subject of privacy in the workplace, see MATTHEW W. FINKIN, PRIVACY IN EMPLOYMENT LAW (1995); IRA MICHAEL SHEPARD ET AL., WORKPLACE PRIVACY (2d ed. 1989); Pauline T. Kim, *Privacy Rights, Public Policy and the Employment Relationship*, 57 Ohio St. L.J. 671 (1996).

2. See *INS v. Delgado*, 466 U.S. 210, 217 (1984) (involving a "factory survey" of a workplace in search of undocumented aliens: "We reject the claim that

70

In *O'Connor v. Ortega*,[3] which involved a search of a hospital physician's office and computer after he was placed on administrative leave because of allegations of sexual harassment of two female employees and coercing employees to pay for the computer, the Supreme Court[4] announced that it would not, for Fourth Amendment purposes, equate the government's role as law enforcer and the government's role as employer. In the workplace, employees are considered to have diminished, although not non-existent, reasonable expectations of privacy, and government as employer acts for a broader range of objectives—completing the government agency's work, safeguarding government property, and resolving claims of worker misconduct toward other workers or clients of the agency. For these reasons, the Court rejected a warrant requirement:

> In our view, requiring an employer to obtain a warrant whenever the employer wished to enter an employee's office, desk, or file cabinets for a work-related purpose would seriously disrupt the routine conduct of business and would be unduly burdensome. Imposing unwieldly warrant procedures in such cases upon supervisors, who would otherwise have no reason to be familiar with such procedures, is simply unreasonable. In contrast to other circumstances in which we have required warrants, supervisors in office such as at the Hospital are hardly in the business of investigating the violation of criminal laws. Rather, work-related searches are merely incident to the primary business of the agency.[5]

The *O'Connor* Court also rejected "probable cause" as the appropriate standard for employer searches of an employee's office, finding that "special needs, beyond the normal need for law en-

the entire work force of the two factories were seized for the duration of the surveys when the INS placed agents near the exits of the factory sites. Ordinarily, when people are at work their freedom to move about has been meaningfully restricted, not by the actions of law enforcement officials but by the workers' voluntary obligations to their employers.").

3. 480 U.S. 709 (1987).

4. References in the text to the "Court" are to the plurality opinion authored by Justice O'Connor, reflecting her views and those of Chief Justice Rehnquist and Justices White and Powell. Justice Scalia concurred in the judgment, thus supplying a fifth vote. While

seemingly rejecting the plurality's government as employer vs. government as regulator distinction, Justice Scalia's justification seems as broad as the plurality's:

> The government, like any other employer, needs frequent and convenient access to its desks, offices, and file cabinets for work-related purposes. I would hold that government searches to retrieve work-related materials or to investigate violations of workplace rules—searches of the sort that are regarded as reasonable and normal in the private-employer context—do not violate the Fourth Amendment.

Id. at 732 (Scalia, J., concurring in judgment) (citations omitted).

5. *Id.* at 726.

forcement, make the ... probable-cause requirement impractica-ble"[6] in favor of a "reasonable suspicion" standard:

> ... Even when employers conduct an investigation, they have an interest substantially different from "the normal need for law enforcement." Public employers have an interest in ensuring that their agencies operate in an effective and efficient manner, and the work of these agencies inevitably suffers from the inefficiency, incompetence, mismanagement or other work-related misfeasance of its employees.... In contrast to law enforcement officials, ... public employers are not enforcers of the criminal law; instead, public employers have a direct and overriding interest in ensuring that the work of the agency is conducted in a proper and efficient manner. In our view, therefore, a probable cause requirement for searches of the type at issue here would impose intolerable burdens on public employers. The delay in correcting the employee misconduct caused by the need for probable cause rather than reasonable suspicion will be translated into tangible and often irreparable damage to the agency's work, and ultimately to the public interest.[7]

Because the Hospital had an " 'individualized suspicion' of miscon-duct by Dr. Ortega" before conducting its search, there was no need to decide in this case "whether individualized suspicion is an essential element of the standard of reasonableness that we adopt today."[8]

Under the reasoning of *O'Connor*, much turns on whether the search is being conducted by the government in its law enforcement capacity or the government as employer. If the former, traditional Fourth Amendment analysis applies; if the latter, neither a warrant nor probable cause will be required. It is not clear reasonable suspicion will always be required. Reasonable suspicion would not be needed to justify an inventory as opposed to an investigatory search. The Court also left open what standard would govern a programmatic search—where targets are determined randomly or by some other criterion like geographic location or industry that does not focus on particular individuals or firms.

Another important factor in the *O'Connor* analysis is the strength of the employee's reasonable expectation of privacy. The case involved shared space—Dr. Ortega's office was a space owned by the hospital, for which the hospital was responsible, and as to

---

6. *Id.* at 725 (quoting *New Jersey v. T.L.O.*, 469 U.S. 325, 351 (1985) (Black-mun, J., concurring)).

7. *O'Connor*, 480 U.S. at 727.

8. *Id.* at 729.

which access by other hospital employees for maintenance and security was routine. If the search had involved a personal file cabinet or private computer that Dr. Ortega had brought to the office, a search of these personal effects might call for a more demanding justification than was required in the actual case.[9]

Does an employee have a stronger privacy interest against surreptitious workplace surveillance than he or she does with respect to openly disclosed surveillance? Does the privacy interest differ or, rather, should we say that the employee has impliedly consented to the latter by continuing to work knowing of the surveillance? The decisional law is still in flux here but courts are likely to give weight to (1) whether the employees were given notice, (2) whether the employer has a legitimate business interest in maintaining the surveillance, and (3) whether the surveillance is maintained in locations and at times implicating that legitimate interest.[10]

Much of the litigation in this area has involved testing of employees for alcohol abuse or illegal drug use. In a pair of rulings that issued the same day—*Skinner v. Railway Labor Executives' Assn.*[11] and *National Treasury Employees Union v. Raab*,[12] the Supreme Court established the analytical framework for dealing with such testing under the Fourth Amendment.

In both cases, the Court conceded that a constitutional "search" had occurred. *Skinner* involved both the taking and testing of blood and urine samples from employees of federally regulated railroads involved in major accidents; *Von Raab* considered the U.S. Customs Service's taking and testing of urine samples from all employees involved in drug interdiction activities or authorized to carry firearms. The Court had long ago held a search occurs when law enforcement requires the taking of blood samples from possibly impaired motorists.[13] The taking of urine samples ordinarily involves far less of a physical intrusion but the Court recognized that these samples could be repositories of private

---

9. Consider *Gossmeyer v. McDonald*, 128 F.3d 481 (7th Cir. 1997) (upholding search of privately purchased file cabinet by employer and law enforcement officials acting on anonymous tip of employee possession of child pornography).

10. Compare *Vega-Rodriguez v. Puerto Rico Telephone Co.*, 110 F.3d 174 (1st Cir. 1997) (employees lacked a reasonable expectation of privacy against disclosed video surveillance in an open work area), with *United States v. Take-*

ta, 923 F.2d 665 (9th Cir. 1991) (defendant had a reasonable expectation of privacy against government agents' surreptitious video surveillance of an office reserved for defendant's exclusive use).

11. 489 U.S. 602 (1989).

12. 489 U.S. 656 (1989).

13. See *Schmerber v. California*, 384 U.S. 757 (1966).

information and the very act of requiring that a sample be given involved a privacy intrusion.

Following *O'Connor* and decisions involving searches of student lockers in the public school context,[14] the Court held that neither a warrant nor probable cause was required in either case. The Court explained that blood and urine tests involved limited intrusions; and that requiring a warrant was inappropriate when dealing with the government as employer. In *Skinner*, Justice Kennedy's opinion further reasoned, "the expectations of privacy of covered employees are diminished by reason of their participation in an industry that is regulated pervasively to ensure safety, a goal dependent, in substantial part, on the health and fitness of covered employees."[15] Similarly, in *Von Raab*, the privacy interests of the tested Customs employees were held diminished because of the nature of their responsibilities.

In both cases, the Court also approved testing programs that did not require the employer to have individualized suspicion of alcohol or illegal drug impairment or use. In *Skinner*, in the course of explaining the deterrent effect of the testing program, the Court emphasized the fact that the employees were involved in "safety-sensitive positions" and that the testing regulations required the occurrence of "a triggering event" like a major train accident[16]:

> By ensuring that employees in safety-sensitive positions know they will be tested upon the occurrence of a triggering event, the timing of which no employee can predict with certainty, the regulations significantly increase the deterrent effect of the administrative penalties associated with the prohibited conduct, ... concomitantly increasing the likelihood that employees will forgo using drugs or alcohol while subject to being called for duty.[17]

Although the testing program in *Von Raab* differed from the one sustained in *Skinner* because there was little evidence of drug abuse on the part of Customs personnel and there was no triggering event like a major accident, the Court reasoned that law enforcement personnel responsible for safeguarding the country's borders and authorized to use firearms necessarily enjoy a diminished expectation of privacy that does not outweigh the government interests involved:

14. *New Jersey v. T.L.O.*, 469 U.S. 325 (1985).

15. *Skinner*, 489 U.S. at 627.

16. See 49 C.F.R. § 219.201(a)(1),(3), discussed in *Skinner*, 489 U.S. at 608–13.

17. *Id.* at 629.

We hold that the suspicionless testing of employees who apply for promotion to positions directly involving the interdiction of illegal drugs, or to positions that require the incumbent to carry a firearm, is reasonable. The Government's compelling interests in preventing the promotion of drug users to positions where they might endanger the integrity of our Nation's borders or the life of the citizenry outweigh the privacy interests of those who seek promotion to these positions, who enjoy a diminished expectation of privacy by virtue of the special, and obvious, physical and ethical demands of those positions. We do not decide whether testing those who apply for promotion to positions where they would handle "classified" information is reasonable because we find the record inadequate for this purpose.[18]

The Court's opinions in *Skinner* and *Von Raab* were important signposts effectively encouraging fairly widespread testing of employees for alcohol abuse or illegal drug use. For several reasons, however, it would be a mistake to assume that testing programs can never fall short of Fourth Amendment strictures.

First, the testing programs in both cases were programmatic in the sense that employees were not tested except upon the occurrence of triggering events—in *Skinner*, the occurrence of a major train accident; in *Von Raab*, "[o]nly employees who have been tentatively accepted for promotion or transfer to one of the three categories of covered positions are tested, and applicants know at the outset that a drug test is a requirement of those positions. Employees are also notified in advance of the scheduled sample collection, thus reducing to a minimum any 'unsettling show of authority' that may be associated with unexpected intrusions on privacy."[19] In neither case was the Court authorizing a purely discretionary testing program in which the employer could pick and choose whom to test with individualized suspicion.

Second, even in the context of a programmatic testing program, the Court did not decide whether individualized suspicion would be required of government employees not involved in "safety-sensitive" jobs or requiring use of firearms or propinquity to illegal drug activity. For example, can employees be subjected to suspicionless testing because they have access to confidential information[20] or

---

18. *Van Raab*, 489 U.S. at 679.
19. *Id.* at 672, quoting *Delaware v. Prouse*, 440 U.S. 648, 657 (1979).

20. See, e.g., *NTEU v. U.S. Customs Service*, 27 F.3d 623 (D.C. Cir. 1994) (upholding testing of Customs employ-

because, as school teachers and officials, they have access to young children[21]?

Third, the Court has not addressed whether job applicants have weaker privacy interests than incumbent employees and thus can be tested for illegal drug use, without basis for suspicion or other "special needs," as part of the application process.[22]

Additionally, *Skinner* and *Von Raab* did not present issues that might arise from procedures for monitoring the giving of urine samples, ensuring an appropriate chain of custody during the testing process, and for confirming initial drug-positive results.[23]

A number of state statutes significantly regulate private employer drug testing programs. Some permit suspicionless testing only of applicants or where the employee serves in "high risk" or "safety sensitive" occupations;[24] others limit suspicionless testing to applicants.[25] All of the laws insist on certain testing and chain-of-custody safeguards.

2. Self–Incrimination

There is no viable argument that the provision of a blood or urine sample could constitute self-incrimination under the Fifth Amendment.[26] However, government employers are subject to Fifth Amendment strictures and cannot compel employees to give self-incriminatory information on penalty of their job. If immunity from subsequent prosecution is granted, an employee's refusal to answer questions closely related to a legitimate interest of the public employer may be treated as insubordination warranting dismissal or other discipline.[27]

ees with access to information about targeting of certain imports).

21. Compare *Aubrey v. School Bd. of Lafayette*, 148 F.3d 559 (5th Cir. 1998) (upholding testing of public school custodian because he interacted with school children and used dangerous equipment); *Knox Co. Educ. Assn. v. Knox Co. Bd. of Educ.*, 158 F.3d 361 (6th Cir. 1998) (upholding testing of public school teachers), with *United Teachers of New Orleans v. Orleans Parish School Bd.*, 142 F.3d 853, 857 (5th Cir. 1988) (no teacher, aide or clerical worker can be tested "absent adequate individualized suspicion of wrongful drug use").

22. See, e.g., *Willner v. Thornburgh*, 928 F.2d 1185 (D.C. Cir. 1991); *Loder v.*

City of Glendale, 927 P.2d 1200 (Cal. 1997).

23. See generally Elaine Shoben, *Test Defamation in the Workplace: False Positive Results in Attempting to Detect Lies, AIDS, or Drug Use*, 1988 U.Chi. L.F. 181; Mark A. Rothstein, *Drug Testing in the Workplace: The Challenge to Employment Relations and Employment Law*, 63 Chi.-Kent L. Rev. 683 (1987).

24. See, e.g., Conn. Gen. Stat. Ann., P.A. 87–551, L.1987.

25. See, e.g., Vt. Stat. Ann., tit. 21, §§ 511–20.

26. See *Schmerber v. California*, 384 U.S. 757 (1966).

3.   Associational Privacy

Public employees may also enjoy a degree of associational privacy both under the First Amendment and the substantive due process element of the Fifth and Fourteenth Amendments. Generally speaking, public employees cannot suffer job disadvantage because of their political views. Off-duty sexual activities and inquiry into the criminal records and associations of police officers and their relatives has resulted in mixed decisions reflecting the responsibilities of law enforcement officials.[28]

4.   State Constitutional Law

States are free to interpret their constitutions in the same way or differently from how the U.S. Supreme Court has interpreted identical or similar provisions in the U.S. Constitution. In *Loder v. City of Glendale*,[29] the California supreme court held that individualized suspicion was required under the Fourth Amendment for drug testing of incumbent employees offered a promotion but was not required under the federal or state constitutions for the testing of new hires. In addition, the privacy clauses of some state constitutions, most notably California, have been interpreted to protect employees working for private employers.[30] In some jurisdictions, the state constitution, while directly applicable only to government action, has been used as a source of public policy restricting termination decisions in the private sector.[31]

---

27. See *Gardner v. Broderick*, 392 U.S. 273, 278 (1968); *Uniformed Sanitation Men Assn. v. Commissioner of Sanitation*, 392 U.S. 280 (1968).

28. Compare, e.g., *Fraternal Order of Police, Lodge No. 5 v. City of Philadelphia*, 859 F.2d 276 (3d Cir. 1988) (sustaining background investigation into family financial status and organizational memberships of applicants for elite police anticorruption unit); *City of Sherman v. Henry*, 928 S.W.2d 464 (Tex. 1996) (rejecting substantive due process challenge to city's denial of promotion to

police officer for having committed adultery with coworker's spouse), with *Briggs v. North Muskegon Police Dept.*, 563 F.Supp. 585 (W.D. Mich. 1983), affirmed, 746 F.2d 1475 (6th Cir. 1984) (voiding dismissal of policeman for living with married woman not his wife).

29. 927 P.2d 1200 (Cal. 1997).

30. See *White v. Davis*, 533 P.2d 222 (Cal. 1975); *Hill v. National College Athletic Assn.*, 865 P.2d 633 (Cal. 1994) (en banc).

31. See Chapter 3, at 62 & n.12.

B. Legislation

Other than Massachusetts' general privacy statute,[32] legislation on both the federal and state level deals with particular investigative techniques and areas of concern.

1. *Investigative Techniques*

a. Polygraphs

Under the 1988 Employee Polygraph Protection Act,[33] "lie detector" tests, defined to include voice stress and psychological stress evaluators, are prohibited except in certain circumstances. Section 7(d) permits testing in connection with an ongoing investigation, but only if (i) administered in connection with "an ongoing investigation involving economic loss or injury to the employer's business"; (ii) the employee being tested had access to the property in question; (iii) the employer had reasonable suspicion for targeting the employee; and (iv) the employer provides a statement identifying the economic loss and the basis for individual suspicion. In addition, employers may not discipline employees for refusing to take a lie detector or because of the results of such a test "without additional supporting evidence".[34]

b. Telephone Monitoring

Under Title II of Omnibus Crime Control and Safe Streets Act of 1968, as amended by the Electronic Communications Privacy Act of 1986 (ECPA),[35] telephone communications generally cannot be intercepted. There are two important exceptions relevant in the employment context. First, if one party to the communication consents, interception is permitted.[36] Thus, either the employer or employee can tape a communication in which he is a party. (In some states, notably Maryland, even one-party consent is insufficient.) Where an employer is monitoring the telephone communications between an employee and others outside the company, the employer needs the consent of the employee, which can be implied from circumstances where the employer makes clear both the fact and manner of monitoring.[37]

---

32. See, e.g., *Cort v. Bristol–Myers Co.*, 431 N.E.2d 908 (Mass. 1982) (interpreting G.L. c.214, § 1B).

33. 29 U.S.C. §§ 2001–09.

34. Id. § 2006(d).

35. 18 U.S.C. §§ 2510–20.

36. Id. § 2511(2)(d).

37. See *Griffin v. City of Milwaukee*, 74 F.3d 824 (7th Cir. 1996).

A second exception—the "business extension" provision—exempts from the statutory prohibition of interdiction any equipment used by a telephone subscriber or user "in the ordinary course of business".[38] Where the recording instrument is provided by the telephone company, "a personal call may be intercepted in the ordinary course of business to determine its nature [i.e., is it a personal or business call] but never its contents."[39] Most courts hold that an employer needs reasonable suspicion of wrongdoing before it can eavesdrop.[40]

c.   Electronic Communication Monitoring

The ECPA amendments to Title III of the federal wiretapping law distinguish between (1) intercepting communications during their transmission, and (2) accessing previously stored communications.[41] The provisions concerning the latter are often referred to as the "Stored Communications Act" (SCA). Unlike a telephone communication, e-mail is stored in a service-provider computer until the addressee accesses the computer to retrieve and read the message. Accessing an e-mail message stored in its destination server is not an "interception" within the meaning of the ECPA because it is not acquired while being transmitted. Thus, the more restrictive provisions dealing with interception of electronic communications generally do not apply to employer monitoring of stored e-mail.[42] Under § 2701(c), moreover, the SCA's prohibition on "access" to stored communications does not apply "with respect to conduct authorized" by the service provider—a privilege which "allows service providers to do as they wish when it comes to accessing communications in electronic storage."[43] The ECPA apparently does not address retrieval of an e-mail message that already has been received. If there is any regulation here, it will be found in state law.

38. 18 U.S.C. § 2510(5)(a)(i).

39. *Watkins v. L.M. Berry*, 704 F.2d 577, 583 (11th Cir. 1983).

40. See *Briggs v. American Air Filter Co.*, 630 F.2d 414 (5th Cir. 1980); *Arias v. Mutual Central Alarm Serv., Inc.*, 182 F.R.D. 407 (S.D.N.Y. 1998).

41. 100 Stat. 1848, 18 U.S.C. §§ 2510, 2701.

42. See *Konop v. Hawaiian Airlines, Inc.*, 302 F.3d 868 (9th Cir. 2002). However, an e-mail message typically passes through a series of intermediate servers on its way to the server that is its final storage destination. The First Circuit has held that acquisition of e-mails in transient electronic storage that is intrinsic to the communication process is an "interception" of an electronic communication under the ECPA. *United States v. Councilman*, 418 F.3d 67, 79 (1st Cir.2005).

43. *Bohach v. City of Reno*, 932 F.Supp. 1232, 1236 (D.Nev. 1996).

d. Investigation of Consumer Credit Reports

The Fair Credit Reporting Act of 1970 (FCRA)[44] requires employers who decline to hire a job applicant because of the results of a credit investigation to inform the rejected applicant of the name and address of the reporting agency.[45] In addition, written authorization is required before a credit report may be requested of a job applicant or employee. Before taking adverse action on the basis of a credit report, the employer must provide the employee with a copy of the report and a written explanation of the employee's rights under the FCRA.[46] Employer concern over a Federal Trade Commission interpretation suggesting that use of outside organizations for the purpose of investigating sexual harassment charges triggered FCRA disclosure obligations to the subject of the investigation, led Congress to amend the FCRA to exclude such investigations from the definition of "consumer report".[47]

2. *Areas of Special Concern*
a. Records Privacy

The federal Privacy Act of 1974[48] grants certain rights and remedies to individuals who are the subject of records maintained by federal agencies, including the right to object to inaccurate information in such records. Some states extend the Privacy Act model to require private employers to provide employee access to personnel files and an opportunity to correct erroneous information in those files.[49] Under regulations implementing the Health Insurance Portability and Accountability Act of 1996 (HIPAA), medical information generally must be kept confidential and cannot be transmitted to third parties without written consent of the subject of the record.[50]

b. Identity Privacy

Many states also have passed laws preventing government and private companies from disclosing personal identifying information,

---

44. 15 U.S.C. §§ 1681l–1681t.

45. *Id.* § 1681m.

46. *Id.* §§ 1681b(b)(1)-(3).

47. See FAIR AND ACCURATE CREDIT TRANSACTIONS ACT OF 2003, PUB. L. NO. 108–159, 117 STAT. 1952.

48. 5 U.S.C. § 552(a).

49. See, e.g., MICH.COMP.LAWS ANN. §§ 432.501–.512.

50. See generally Kathryn L. Bakich, *Countdown to HIPAA Compliance: Understanding EDI, Privacy, and Security*, 15 BENEFITS L.J. 45 (Summer 2002). For discussion of the California medical records law, see *Pettus v. Cole*, 49 Cal. App.4th 402, 57 Cal.Rptr.2d 46 (1996).

such as social security numbers, contained in their computer systems.[51]

c.   "Legal Activity" Laws

Several states have enacted laws that protect employees from discharge or discipline for engaging off hours in lawful "recreational" activities.[52] Attempts have been made to use these laws to strike down "anti-fraternization" policies of employers that seek to bar employees from dating each other.[53]

C.   Decisional Law

Employer policies and other sources of contractual obligations can give rise to privacy claims in certain circumstances.[54] (Privacy protections can be quite extensive under collective bargaining agreements.[55]) In addition, the tort of seclusion is a well-recognized principle that has been successfully used to resist employer invasions of privacy in the workplace.[56]

---

51. See, e.g., CAL. CIV. CODE § 1798.85.

52. See, e.g., N.Y. LABOR LAW § 201–d.

53. See generally Anna M. Depaolo, *Note, Antifraternizing Polices and At-Will Employment: Counseling for a Better Relationship*, 1996 ANN. SURVEY OF AM. L. 59.

54. See, e.g., *Rulon–Miller v. IBM Corp.*, 162 Cal.App.3d 241, 208 Cal. Rptr. 524 (1984) (IBM's privacy policy used to support employee claim that ter-mination for alleged conflict of interest was pretextual).

55. See generally Edward Hertenstein, *Electronic Monitoring in the Workplace: How Arbitrators Have Ruled*, DISPUTE RESOL. J. (Fall 1997), pp. 36 ff; Denenberg & Denenberg, *Drug Testing from the Arbitrator's Perspective*, 11 NOVA L. REV. 377 (1987).

56. See, e.g., *Borse v. Piece Goods Shop, Inc.*, 963 F.2d 611, 622 (3d Cir. 1992) (applying Pennsylvania law to challenge aspects of drug testing program).

Chapter 6

INFORMATION, MOBILITY AND COMPETITION

A. Introduction

This chapter is about the ownership of information created or disseminated in the workplace. Legal restrictions on employee mobility to protect corporate information raise a number of difficult policy questions. Individuals should have the liberty to pursue their livelihoods, and yet this must be balanced against the interest of employers to protect their investments in research and development. The perceived trade-off between these policy commitments, in turn, raises highly contested theoretical and empirical questions about what allocation and form of legal constraints will optimize innovation.

Why do we need laws to protect employer investment in workplace information assets, even at the cost of restricting employee mobility? Some arguments are grounded in morality. The origins of many of the core doctrines of unfair competition law lie in the belief that it would be unjust to deprive one who has invested in research, development of goodwill, and so forth, from the fruits of that investment. The law of agency also undergirds much of the law in this area, informed by the core tenet that it is a betrayal of the duty of loyalty for an agent to compete with or reveal the confidences of the principal.

Other arguments are grounded in efficiency. The conventional economic justification for laws that allow employers to protect information is that without such protections, innovators will not receive sufficient returns on their investments, thus inhibiting optimal investment. Even assuming firms need a way to protect their investments from use or dissemination by employees, one might ask why they cannot do so simply by adjusting the price they pay for labor, rather than through the use of legal intervention and the injunctive remedies that tend to dominate enforcement in this domain. Couldn't an employer just reduce an employee's wages by an amount that corresponds to the value of information imparted? A response to this objection is that the information or customer relationships that an employer wishes to protect may be worth more than the employee has the capacity to absorb through an offsetting wage reduction.[1] The converse mechanism of paying an

---

1. Edmund Kitch, *The Law and Economics of Rights in Valuable Information*, 9 J. Leg. Stud. 683, 708 (1980).

employee to whom the firm has imparted valuable information a bonus to stay with the firm, also known as "golden handcuffs," is frequently not a viable solution either. The amount of money that the firm would have to pay to make the employee indifferent between exploiting the information elsewhere and staying might eliminate the profitability of the information entirely.[2] Moreover, if multiple employees are privy to the information, the problem multiplies accordingly—the sum of the payments required to retain each employee may very well *exceed* the value of the secret to the original employer.[3] Another non-legal possibility is modifying the production process to make the information more difficult to appropriate, e.g., fragmenting production so that no one employee knows all of the essential steps. Here, however, the costs of balkanization are obvious, and the resulting losses of production efficiency may very well outweigh any gains arising from protection of information. Hence, the conventional argument from efficiency goes, owners of information assets should be able to protect them with laws that give them property rights, as well as the ability to contractually protect the information.

There is a contrary view. Some U.S. jurisdictions (such as California) are widely thought to provide relatively weak protection to workplace-generated information.[4] A number of legal scholars have speculated that the success of Silicon Valley may be due (at

---

2. Deferred compensation schemes might also be unreliable retention devices for other reasons. *See* Peter Cappelli, The New Deal at Work: Managing the Market-Driven Workforce 185–86 (1999) (discussing the situation at IBM, in which golden handcuffs in the form of stock options collapse with a collapse in the stock price in the early 1990s, and the converse example of Microsoft, where booming stock prices in the late 1990s led some key employees whose stock options had vested to cash in their stock options and form competing start-ups).

3. Kitch, *supra* note 1.

4. *See* Cal. Bus. & Prof. Code §§ 16600–16602.5 (2006) (prohibiting non-compete covenants beyond those attached to sale of goodwill of a business, or upon dissolution of partnership or limited liability corporation). Other states restrict non-compete covenants without outlawing them entirely. *See* Ala. Code § 8–1–1 (2006); Colo. Rev. Stat. § 8–2–113 (2006); Haw. Rev. Stat.

§ 480–4(c) (2006); La. Rev. Stat. Ann. § 23:921 (2006); Mont. Code. Ann. §§ 28–2–703, –704 (2005); N.C. Gen. Stat. § 75–4 (2006); N.D. Cent. Code § 9–08–06 (2007); Okla. Stat. tit. 15, § 217 (2006). It should be noted as well that on some accounts many California firms appear to limit their exercise of even those legal rights available to them under trade secret law, whether because of California juries' reluctance to convict defendants except in the most clear-cut cases, or due to the reputational costs of bucking norms that tolerate employee mobility (norms that may have emerged as a result of the background rules pertaining to covenants). Ronald J. Gilson, *The Legal Infrastructure of High Technology Industrial Districts: Silicon Valley, Route 128, and Covenants Not to Compete* 74 N.Y.U. L. Rev. 575, 600–01 (1999); Alan Hyde, Working in Silicon Valley: Economic and Legal Analysis of a High-Velocity Labor Market 38–40 (2003).

least in part) to this legal regime. The kernel of the argument is that weak protection within high-mobility labor markets—where highly-skilled employees move easily between firms taking ideas and innovations with them—permits the rapid diffusion of information, leading to industry-wide technological gains that arguably swamp the investment disincentives that weak entitlements may engender.[5]

We do not try to resolve this debate here. As we shall see, differences of opinion on these questions influence the decisional and statutory law canvassed in this chapter. There are four major parts to this chapter. We begin with a brief review of the duty of loyalty, then move on to discuss trade secret law, the law of restrictive covenants, and finally, the legal treatment of workplace inventions.

B. Common Law Duty of Loyalty

Employment law has its roots in the law of agency, and many aspects of modern employment law doctrine still invoke principles of agency. A core principle of agency is the duty of loyalty. An agent has "a fiduciary duty to act loyally for the principal's benefit in all matters connected with the agency relationship."[6] This includes a duty not to compete with the principal for the duration of the agency relationship.[7]

Some jurisdictions distinguish between "fiduciary" and regular employees, imposing the fiduciary duty of loyalty on fiduciaries alone.[8] In such instances, fiduciary status turns on such factors as whether the employee is high-level, has sufficient authority to act for the employer, or has access to confidential information.[9] Other courts assert that all employees owe a duty of loyalty, but that the scope of the duty will depend on the nature of the employee's role

---

5. Gilson, *supra* note 4, at 608–609; HYDE, *supra* note 4, at 44.

6. RESTATEMENT (THIRD) OF AGENCY § 8.01 (2007) [hereinafter AGENCY RESTATEMENT].

7. *Id.*, § 8.04 ("Throughout the duration of an agency relationship, an agent has a duty to refrain from competing with the principal and from taking action on behalf of or otherwise assisting the principal's competitors.").

8. *E.g.*, *Modern Materials v. Advanced Tooling Specialists*, 557 N.W.2d 835, 838 (Wis. App. 1996) (finding a

duty of loyalty if an employee is a corporate officer, or if not an officer, has policy-making authority or an ability to make decisions that bind the company); *Dalton v. Camp*, 548 S.E.2d 704, 707–709 (N.C. 2001) (finding that for a fiduciary duty to exist, there must be a fiduciary relationship, and denying claim against production manager on grounds that fiduciary relation requires the fiduciary to have domination and influence on the other party, and not merely a confidential relation).

9. *Id.*

within the firm.[10] Still other courts draw no distinctions between employees for purposes of imposing the duty of loyalty.[11]

While recognizing that employees must not exploit the trust of their employer to obtain unfair advantage, agency law also tries to protect the individual employees' right to freely pursue employment and the public's interest in fostering economic competition.[12] The result is a rule that prohibits active competition by an employee prior to termination of employment, but permits an employee to prepare to compete in advance of a future separation.[13] The difficult question, of course, is when an employee's activities cross the line between preparation and outright competition. "A departing employee may not solicit his employer's customers but he may advise the customers of his intention to leave and set up a competing business."[14] In one formulation, lawful preparation becomes unfair competition when the preparatory activity "substantially hinder[s] the employer in the continuation of his business."[15] Thus, an employee need not disclose his future business plans and may even take steps to purchase a rival business as long as he does not operate the business until after separation.[16]

Many cases involve solicitation. An employee, while still employed by the employer, may not solicit customers or co-workers away from the employer.[17] Although these prohibitions are not limited to higher-level employees, such employees tend to occupy positions from which they can inflict greater harm upon the em-

---

10. *Cameco, Inc. v. Gedicke*, 724 A.2d 783, 789 (N.J. 1999) (employees occupying a position of trust and confidence owe a higher duty of loyalty than those performing low-level tasks); *Reuben C. Setliff, III, M.D., P.C. v. Stewart*, 694 N.W.2d 859, 869 (S.D. 2005) (citing *Cameco*). The court in *Dalton, supra* note 8, at 709, suggests that non-fiduciary employees may have a duty of loyalty that does not provide the basis for affirmative relief but gives the employer a defense to a claim of wrongful termination.

11. E.g., *Eckard Brandes, Inc. v. Riley*, 338 F.3d 1082, 1086 (9th Cir. 2003) (all employees, even low-level employees, have a duty of loyalty in the state of Hawaii and the cause of action may sound in either contract or tort); *Reuben C. Setliff, III, M.D., P.C. v. Stewart*, 694 N.W.2d 859, 867 (S.D. 2005) (all employees have a duty of loyalty and breach of the duty is a tort); *Williams v. Dominion Tech. Partners, LLC*, 576 S.E.2d 752

(Va. 2003) ("[U]nder the common law an employee, including an employee-at-will, owes a fiduciary duty of loyalty to his employer.").

12. *Maryland Metals, Inc. v. Metzner*, 382 A.2d 564, 568–69 (Md. 1978).

13. See AGENCY RESTATEMENT § 8. 04, which states that during the agency relationship, "an agent may take action, not otherwise wrongful, to prepare for competition following termination of the agency relationship."

14. *Cudahy Co. v. American Labs., Inc.*, 313 F.Supp. 1339, 1347 (D. Neb. 1970).

15. Id. at 1346.

16. *Maryland Metals*, 382 A.2d at 573. *See also Bancroft–Whitney Co. v. Glen*, 411 P.2d 921 (Cal. 1966).

17. See generally AGENCY RESTATEMENT § 8.04 cmt. c (an agent may not solicit customers from the principal while still employed).

ployer. Where a managerial employee acts as a "corporate pied piper" and leads away all of his employer's employees, the breach will be obvious.[18] But it may also be problematic if managers simply solicit or assist in soliciting key employees to join a competitor.[19] Solicitation of co-employees may violate the duty of loyalty even if it does not induce a breach of contract, for example, if the employees are at-will or the solicitation is unsuccessful.[20] The mere fact that co-workers jointly prepare to set up a rival business does not mean that an act of disloyalty has occurred.[21] However, if key employees leave en masse, without giving the employer an opportunity to find replacements, a court may find a breach.[22]

If a court finds a breach of the duty of loyalty, remedies include punitive and compensatory damages, injunctive relief, restitution, discharge, and disgorgement of compensation.[23] Regardless of whether the employee continued to fulfill her duties to the employer during the period of disloyalty, the employer has the right to withhold any compensation that would have been due for that period.[24] Additionally, the principal has a right to any profit earned as a result of disloyalty.[25]

C. Trade Secret Law

A trade secret is confidential information that gives a firm a competitive advantage for the very reason that it is not generally known to the public. A business might be able to protect a secret recipe, product design specifications, a marketing technique, or records of customer preferences. Misappropriation of a trade secret is a tort.[26] Trade secret law governs a significant portion of disputes

---

18. *Augat, Inc. v. Aegis, Inc.*, 565 N.E.2d 415, 420–21 (Mass. 1991).

19. See *id.* at 420 (vice president breached duty when he solicited several high-level employees to depart once new company commenced business); *Bancroft–Whitney, supra* note 16 (corporate president breach of fiduciary duty by assisting a rival company in soliciting the corporation's employees by providing a list of desirable employees and their salaries).

20. *Jet Courier Service, Inc. v. Mulei*, 771 P.2d 486, 496 (Colo. 1989).

21. See *Cudahy Co., supra* note 14 (employees joining together to form a competing business, where there is no showing of a scheme to leave employer in a position where it could not function

because of loss of key employees, not unlawful solicitation).

22. See *Bancroft–Whitney, supra* note 16.

23. AGENCY RESTATEMENT § 8.01, cmt. d.

24. See *Mulei*, 771 P.2d at 499. See generally AGENCY RESTATEMENT § 8.01, cmt. d (2).

25. AGENCY RESTATEMENT § 8.01, cmt. d.

26. See MELVIN F. JAGER, TRADE SECRETS LAW § 2:3 (2006). Trade secret law continues to have strong property overtones, especially in light of injunctive remedies available for misappropriation. *See also Ruckelshaus v. Monsanto*, 467 U.S. 986, 1002–03 (1984) (describing trade secrets as having some characteristics of property).

between employers and their former employees over ownership and use of intellectual property. Disclosure of information in the context of a confidential relationship gives rise to a duty of confidentiality which an employer may enforce through injunctive or other remedies.[27] Trade secret protection, however, does not depend on the existence of a confidential relationship.

Modern trade secret law has been influenced by the American Law Institute (ALI)'s Restatements and the Uniform Trade Secrets Act (UTSA).[28] The ALI's efforts to organize the common law principles of trade secrets appeared first in the Restatement (First) of Torts,[29] and later in the Restatement (Third) of Unfair Competition.[30] During the 1960s and 1970s, the National Conference of Commissioners on Uniform State Laws drafted a model code in response to rising concern about the uncertainty of the common law.[31] Particular areas of concern were inconsistencies in what kinds of information justified protection and what remedies ought to apply.[32] In 1985, the Commissioners promulgated the UTSA, and today all but a handful of states have legislation modeled after the UTSA.[33]

The principal intent behind the UTSA was to codify rather than amend the common law, although the Uniform Act did broaden the scope of trade secret protection in a few areas. Where earlier common law jurisprudence tended to require that a "trade secret" have been in continuous use at the time of misappropriation,[34] the UTSA dispensed with this requirement.[35] The continuous-use requirement had the effect of excluding from protection more ab-

---

27. See *Burbank Grease Svcs., L.L.C v. Sokolowski*, 717 N.W.2d 781, 797 (Wis. 2006) (holding that the fiduciary duty of loyalty includes duty not to disclose confidential information, including that which is not a trade secret); RESTATEMENT (FIRST) OF TORTS § 757 cmt. b (1939) [hereinafter FIRST TORTS RESTATEMENT]; RESTATEMENT (THIRD) OF UNFAIR COMPETITION § 41 cmt. c (1995) [hereinafter THIRD UNFAIR COMPETITION RESTATEMENT]. See also *Courtesy Temporary Svcs., Inc. v. Camacho*, 272 Cal.Rptr. 352, 359–61 (App. 1990) (noting that even if customer list was not a trade secret, unfair and deceptive practices of both current and former employees in stealing plaintiff's customers should have been enjoined as unfair trade practices under California Business and Professions Code).

28. UNIF. TRADE SECRETS ACT, 14 U.L.A. 433 (1985) [hereinafter "UTSA"].

29. FIRST TORTS RESTATEMENT § 757.

30. THIRD UNFAIR COMPETITION RESTATEMENT §§ 39–45.

31. JAGER, *supra* note 29, at app. A1.

32. *Id.*

33. Currently the only states not to have adopted the UTSA are Massachusetts, North Carolina, North Dakota, and Texas. *See id.* § 3:29. This does not mean that the law is entirely uniform. Some states have adopted the UTSA but modified certain aspects, such as the definition of a trade secret or misappropriation.

34. See FIRST TORTS RESTATEMENT § 757 cmt. b.

35. The common law has also moved away from this requirement: it does not appear in THIRD UNFAIR COMPETITION RESTATEMENT.

stract ideas that have not been reduced to practice. By dispensing with this requirement, the UTSA cast a wider net to include such things as "negative information" (information deriving from trial-and-error testing, but not leading to an end product).[36] Additionally, the UTSA included wrongful acquisition within the scope of misconduct, whereas tort law originally required subsequent use or disclosure.[37]

1. Definition of a Trade Secret

To prevail in a trade secret action, the plaintiff must prove first that it has a proprietary interest in information that qualifies as a trade secret, and second, an improper acquisition, use, or disclosure of the information by the defendant.[38] The Restatement lists six factors for determining whether a common law trade secret exists:

(1) the extent to which the information is known outside of the plaintiff's company;

(2) the extent to which the information is known to persons inside the plaintiff's company;

(3) the reasonable precautions taken by the trade secret owner to guard the secrecy of the information;

(4) the value of the information to the plaintiff;

(5) the money and effort expended in obtaining and developing the information;

(6) the time and expense required by a competitor to acquire the information.[39]

These factors are not formally assigned particular weights, but the effort of the plaintiff to keep the information secret from outsiders is especially significant.

---

36. See JAGER, *supra* note 29, § 3:35.

37. Here, too, the THIRD UNFAIR COMPETITION RESTATEMENT adapted to the changes brought about by the UTSA. UTSA § 40(a) includes acquisition of another's trade secret as a type of misappropriation.

The ECONOMIC ESPIONAGE ACT OF 1996 (EEA), 18 U.S.C. § 1832 (2006), also provides trade secret protection. Although as its title indicates, the EEA arose out of concerns about foreign economic espionage, it also criminalizes domestic trade secret theft as a matter of federal law. It carries significant criminal penalties: in addition to injunctive remedies, an individual can face fines and imprisonment, and an organization may be fined up to $5,000,000. 18 U.S.C. §§ 1832, 1836 (2006). While the Act's definition of trade secret is based on the UTSA, 18 U.S.C. § 1837, the EEA's coverage is limited to trade secrets that are in use in a product to be placed in interstate or foreign commerce. 18 U.S.C. § 1832(a) (2006). It also applies only to trade secrets pertaining to goods, not services. *Id.*

38. THIRD UNFAIR COMPETITION RESTATEMENT § 40 cmt. a.

39. FIRST TORTS RESTATEMENT § 757 cmt. b.

The UTSA defines a trade secret as:

Information, including a formula, pattern, compilation, program, device, method, technique, or process, that: (1) Derives independent economic value, actual or potential, from not being generally known to the public or to other persons who can obtain economic value from its disclosure or use; and (2) Is the subject of efforts that are reasonable under the circumstances to maintain its secrecy.[40]

Although we will use the UTSA definition as a framework for discussion, the UTSA's heavy reliance on common law doctrine means that many courts, even in jurisdictions that have adopted the UTSA, still rely on aspects of the Restatement's six-factor common-law test.

The first prong of the definition focuses on commercial advantage. The commercial-advantage requirement does not demand novelty, as patent law does.[41] It is not especially onerous, either; even modest commercial value typically suffices.[42] Although it may be difficult to prove the value of information with precision, courts are often satisfied by evidence that development or acquisition of the information required significant time and effort.[43] That said, an idea may result from sudden, spontaneous insight—a "light bulb" moment—and in such cases, the inability to prove a heavy investment in research and development is not fatal to finding that it is a trade secret.[44] Information about failed efforts at innovation—known as "negative information"—can also be valuable: after all, knowledge of the failed endeavor might save a competitor from the expense of making the same investment.[45]

The secrecy of the information is paramount. It need not be an absolute secret. If a firm must disclose the information to employees or others working closely with the firm, it will not necessarily lose protection as a result. But if information is generally known to

40. UTSA § 1.

41. ROGER M. MILGRIM, MILGRIM ON TRADE SECRETS §§ 1.08[1]–[2] (2002) (although information that is patentable will qualify as a trade secret, the reverse is not necessarily true).

42. See JAGER, supra note 29, § 3:35.

43. Ivy Mar Co. v. C.R. Seasons, Ltd., 907 F.Supp. 547, 556–57 (E.D.N.Y. 1995) (effort, time, and financial expenditure relevant to finding customer list a trade secret); Macbeth–Evans Glass Co. v. Schnelbach, 86 A. 688, 691–92 (Pa. 1913) (emphasizing the years of research and hundreds of experiments conducted by employer in holding glass-making formula to be a trade secret).

44. See, e.g., Learning Curve Toys, Inc. v. PlayWood Toys, Inc., 342 F.3d 714 (7th Cir. 2003) (lack of proof of high developmental costs does not preclude existence of a trade secret given that sometimes innovation occurs through an intuitive flash instead of a long and expensive process).

45. JAGER, supra note 29, § 5:31 (2006).

members of the trade, or is readily ascertainable through public sources, it loses protection. Courts will similarly deny trade secret status to, for example, technology generally known in the craft,[46] or customer information that is readily ascertainable.[47] So, for example, a New York court held that an investment management firm's mathematical model for determining investment strategy was not a trade secret because a financial analyst could reproduce the calculations in the program based on public disclosures by the firm.[48] Although information that is part of the public domain is not protectable, one can create a trade secret by combining publicly-known facts in a unique way. The Tenth Circuit recognized this when it reversed summary judgment against a company that claimed former employees had misappropriated its swimming curriculum.[49] The court held that even if each piece of information included in the curriculum was publicly known, the curriculum as a whole might still qualify as a trade secret.[50]

A court may also require a firm to demonstrate that it has taken reasonable steps to preserve the secrecy of the information *vis à vis* industry competitors. The firm will not be held to a standard of perfection: the UTSA requires only "efforts that are reasonable under the circumstances."[51] A firm might demonstrate sufficient efforts by showing, for example, that it has limited employee access to the information (e.g., kept it under lock and key or password-protected), built a fence or other physical barrier to public view, had employees sign confidentiality agreements, or notified those exposed to the information that it was to be kept secret.[52]

46. *Garner Tool & Die v. Laux*, 285 N.W.2d 219, 223 (Neb. 1979) (no protectable trade secret in tool and die technology because technology was generally known in the craft).

47. *Strategic Directions Group v. Bristol–Myers Squibb Co.*, 293 F.3d 1062 (8th Cir. 2002) (finding that market research questions that company presented in annual surveys, public seminars, and a copyright filing are readily ascertainable and therefore not accorded trade secret protection); *Carbonic Fire Extinguishers, Inc. v. Heath*, 547 N.E.2d 675, 677 (Ill. App. 1989) (customer information readily available in the yellow pages not a trade secret).

48. *Ashland Mgmt., Inc. v. Janien*, 624 N.E.2d 1007, 1012–13 (N.Y. 1993). *See also VFD Consulting, Inc. v. 21st Servs.*, 425 F. Supp. 2d 1037 (N.D. Cal. 2006) (actuarial material provided to defendant was readily available through public channels).

49. *Harvey Barnett, Inc. v. Shidler*, 338 F.3d 1125 (10th Cir. 2003).

50. *Id.* at 1130. *See also Minnesota Mining & Mfg. v. Pribyl*, 259 F.3d 587 (7th Cir. 2001) (protecting combination of materials in operating manuals as a trade secret).

51. UTSA § 1. *See also TouchPoint Solutions, Inc. v. Eastman Kodak Co.*, 345 F. Supp. 2d 23, 30 (D. Mass. 2004) (finding confidentiality agreement to be evidence of reasonable measures to protect secrecy even though company did not remain completely faithful to its terms).

52. *See* Robert G. Bone, *A New Look at Trade Secret Law: Doctrine in Search of Justification*, 86 CAL. L. REV. 241, 249

2.   Improper Acquisition, Use or Disclosure

Though there is no bright-line rule, improper acquisition occurs through "means which fall below the generally accepted standards of commercial morality and reasonable conduct."[53] Acquiring a secret through burglarizing a competitor's office, wiretapping a competitor's telephone, or by fraudulent means are all actionable.[54] Improper means are not limited, however, to independently tortious or criminal conduct.[55] A famous example involves a competitor of the DuPont Corporation that hired a pilot to fly over a DuPont ethanol factory and take aerial photographs of the plant's structure.[56] The defendants claimed that their actions could not be wrongful because they conducted their flight in public airspace, violated no government aviation standard, did not breach any confidential relation, and did not engage in any fraudulent or illegal conduct.[57] The Fifth Circuit disagreed, holding that although there may have been no independently unlawful act, the actions could still qualify as an improper means of discovery of trade secrets. In part, the court objected to the impropriety of free-riding on the fruits of another's investment without at least tacit permission.[58] In part, the court took umbrage at the defendants' sneaky methods: "[O]ur devotion to free wheeling industrial competition must not force us into accepting the law of the jungle as the standard morality expected in our commercial relations."[59]

Courts have broadly construed the definition of improper "use" under the UTSA and the Restatement. Generally, any action that results in either injury to the secret's owner or unjust enrichment to the defendant is wrongful.[60] Liability is not limited to circumstances where the misappropriated secret was embodied in a product marketed for sale. For example, improper usage can exist

(1998) (reviewing cases). *See also* MILGRIM, *supra* note 49, at § 1.04.

53. FIRST TORTS RESTATEMENT § 757 cmt. f.

54. *Id.*

55. THIRD UNFAIR COMPETITION RESTATEMENT, § 43 cmt. c. *But see Salton, Inc. v. Philips Domestic Appliances and Personal Care B.V.*, 391 F.3d 871, 878 (7th Cir. 2004) (stating that the common law protects a trade secret against disclosure occasioned by a breach of contract or an independent tort, such as trespass, and characterizing *E.I. duPont deNemours & Co. v. Christopher*, 431 F.2d 1012 (5th Cir. 1970), as the "arguable exception").

56. *E.I. duPont deNemours & Co.*, 431 F.2d at 1012.

57. *Id.* at 1014.

58. *Id.* at 1015 ("To obtain knowledge of a process without spending time and money to discover it independently is improper unless the holder voluntarily discloses it or fails to take reasonable precautions to ensure its secrecy.").

59. *Id.* at 1016.

60. THIRD UNFAIR COMPETITION RESTATEMENT, § 40 cmt. c.

where the knowledge is used in preliminary research for a product never brought to market.[61] Also, creation of a product that represents a modification or improvement on another's trade secret, but is still substantially derived from that information, may be actionable.[62] Nor does the information even need to relate to a tangible "product." When a former customer services manager at MAI Systems relied on his memory of the names and unique needs of MAI customers to solicit their business for his new company, he misappropriated a trade secret. The information about the unique needs of the customers was a trade secret, and the defendant's use of that information to solicit their business was improper use.[63]

It is not wrongful to discover another's trade secret through independent invention, accidental disclosure, reverse engineering, or public sources.[64] Although reverse engineering has long been recognized as lawful conduct, some software companies have recently tried to enforce mass market licenses (contractual agreements to which a software purchaser consents by clicking a box when downloading the product) that prohibit reverse-engineering of the product.[65] Whether such contracts should be enforceable is controversial and has not been definitively resolved in the courts.[66]

To be liable for improper acquisition, use, or disclosure of a trade secret, an actor must know, or have reason to know, that the information is a trade secret.[67] Constructive knowledge was at issue when Paramount Pictures hired a fellow named Bernstein based on his pitch of the concept for a new television show that in today's

---

61. See, e.g., *Telex Corp. v. International Business Machines Corp.*, 510 F.2d 894, 929 (10th Cir. 1975) (finding misappropriation in the act of hiring of employees to accelerate development of a product, even though product never made it to market); *O2 Micro Int'l Ltd. v. Monolithic Power Sys., Inc.*, 399 F. Supp. 2d 1064, 1072 (N.D. Cal. 2005) (concluding that use of trade secret information in internal research that does not lead to a final product can be improper).

62. See, e.g., *Pioneer Hi–Bred Int'l v. Holden Found. Seeds, Inc.*, 35 F.3d 1226, 1239 (8th Cir. 1994) (finding actionable misappropriation when defendant developed seeds that involved only a "slight alteration" from the plaintiff's trade secret); *Tri–Tron Int'l v. Velto*, 525 F.2d 432, 436 (9th Cir. 1975) (holding insignificant modifications immaterial). Cf. *Penalty Kick Mgmt. v. Coca Cola Co.*,

318 F.3d 1284 (11th Cir. 2003) (requiring that a beverage bottle label be "substantially derived" from the plaintiff's work for a misappropriation to succeed).

63. *MAI Systems v. Peak Computer, Inc.*, 991 F.2d 511, 521–22 (9th Cir. 1993).

64. UTSA § 1 cmt. See also *Kewanee Oil v. Bicron Corp.*, 416 U.S. 470, 476 (1974).

65. See Pamela Samuelson & Suzanne Scotchmer, *The Law and Economics of Reverse Engineering*, 111 YALE L. J. 1575, 1607–30 (2002) (discussing reverse engineering in the software context).

66. See *id.* at 1626–30.

67. THIRD UNFAIR COMPETITION RESTATEMENT § 40(b)(1)-(4); UTSA § 1(2)(i), (ii)(B).

parlance we would call reality TV.[68] The show, entitled, "Anything for the Money," involved asking contestants whether they would do outrageous things for a sum of money ("For $200 would you kiss an octopus?").[69] When Bernstein asserted that he owned rights to the idea, Paramount dispensed with its usual procedure of having its legal department confirm ownership despite its awareness that Bernstein had recently worked for the plaintiff production company as a game show developer.[70] The California Court of Appeal held there was a reasonable basis on which a jury could conclude that Paramount had actual or constructive notice that the concept belonged to the plaintiff.[71]

3. Inevitable Misappropriation

Courts have long recognized the doctrine of inevitable misappropriation as grounds for enforcing an express non-compete covenant.[72] The 1995 decision of the Seventh Circuit in *PepsiCo, Inc. v. Redmond*, however, invokes the doctrine as a basis for enjoining a former employee from working for a competitor even in the absence of a non-compete covenant.[73] *Redmond* involved a former PepsiCo marketing executive, William Redmond, who took a job at Quaker Oats. At PepsiCo the defendant had become intimately acquainted with that company's strategy to compete in the intensely competitive "sports beverage" market for 1995. Quaker appointed him vice-president in charge of Gatorade, the leading product in the sports beverage market. Redmond had not signed a restrictive covenant with PepsiCo. PepsiCo nonetheless sought to enjoin Redmond from performing his assigned duties for Quaker on the basis that he would "inevitably disclose" his intimate knowledge of PepsiCo's confidential marketing plan in his new position with Quaker.[74]

The Illinois Trade Secrets Act allows a court to enjoin the "actual or threatened misappropriation" of trade secrets.[75] Redmond had not verbally threatened to misappropriate PepsiCo's

68. *Ralph Andrews Prods., Inc. v. Paramount Pictures Corp.*, 271 Cal.Rptr. 797 (App. 1990).

69. *Id.* at 798.

70. *Id.* at 800–01. Bernstein had also failed to respond to a request from Paramount that he verify ownership.

71. *Id.*

72. *See, e.g., Eastman Kodak Co. v. Powers Film Prods., Inc.*, 189 A.D. 556,

558 (N.Y. App. Div. 1919) (enjoining former Kodak employee from working for a competitor for two years because his work for the new employer would "necessarily impart" knowledge gained from prior employer).

73. 54 F.3d 1262 (7th Cir. 1995).

74. *Id.* at 1265.

75. 765 Ill. Comp. Stat. 1065/3(a) (2006).

trade secrets. He had previously signed an express confidentiality agreement promising not to misappropriate PepsiCo's secrets. The court, however, accepted PepsiCo's argument that there was a high likelihood Redmond would breach his confidentiality agreement and disclose trade secrets because he could not help but rely on PepsiCo secrets as he developed the marketing plan for its chief competitor Quaker: "In other words, PepsiCo finds itself in the position of a coach, one of whose players has left, playbook in hand, to join the opposing team before the big game."[76] The Seventh Circuit upheld the district court's injunction prohibiting Redmond from performing any duties at Quaker for six months that involved the pricing of beverages or development of marketing or sales programs for the sale of beverages.[77]

The district court's conclusion that Redmond was likely to breach his obligation of confidentiality was influenced by the fact that Redmond had misled PepsiCo about the timing of his acceptance of Quaker's offer and the nature of his future job duties.[78] Admittedly, neither the district court nor Seventh Circuit specifically held that evidence of bad faith or misleading behavior was required. The *Redmond* decision should be read, however, in tandem with the overarching principle, which the appeals court did not purport to disturb, that a worker has a right to use his general skills, even if acquired from the employer, to compete: "One who has worked in a particular field cannot be compelled to erase from his mind all of the general skills, knowledge, and expertise acquired through his experience."[79] Courts have tried to distinguish those aspects of a worker's human capital that are trade secrets from those that are merely generalized skills and knowledge. Yet, in some contexts, it will be difficult to disentangle the two.

Redmond has been criticized for in effect imposing a covenant not to compete as a matter of law where none exists as a matter of fact.[80] Others criticisms are that the doctrine is inefficient because

---

76. *PepsiCo, Inc. v. Redmond*, 54 F.3d 1262 (7th Cir. 1995).

77. *Id*. at 1270.

78. *Id*. at 1264–65, 1270–71.

79. *ILG Indus., Inc. v. Scott*, 273 N.E.2d 393 (Ill. 1971). *See also Metro Traffic Control, Inc. v. Shadow Traffic Network*, 27 Cal.Rptr.2d 573 (App. 1994) (finding radio station unsuccessful in claiming that the quality, sound, and personality of radio anchors were trade secrets; "[A] stable of trained and talented at-will employees does not constitute an employer's trade secret.");

Smith Oil Corp. v. Viking Chem. Co., 468 N.E.2d 797, 802 (Ill. App. 1984) (holding that employer could enjoin former employees from using knowledge of customers' exact requirements for custom-blended industrial oils because they were trade secrets, but could not enjoin their use of general technical knowledge of blending and chemistry skills to develop comparable or equivalent products).

80. E.g., Elizabeth Rowe, *When Trade Secrets Become Shackles: Fairness and the Inevitable Disclosure Doctrine*, 7

it forces employers to engage in costly defensive tactics,[81] and that the remedy of injunction is too blunt an instrument to tailor to the equities of the situation.[82] At least some courts clearly share these concerns, and the Seventh Circuit's opinion may well prove to be the high water mark of the doctrine's application as a basis for barring competition by a former employee. Courts have, on the whole, been fairly conservative in granting injunctions, tending to require very specific allegations of particular trade secrets and the threat of misappropriation, sometimes imposing additional hurdles such as requiring proof of bad faith or limiting application of the doctrine to technical employment.[83] Some states reject it entirely.[84]

4. Remedies

Courts have a great deal of flexibility in fashioning remedies for misappropriation of trade secrets. The UTSA provides for injunctive relief, damages, attorney's fees, and protective measures to preserve secrecy such as a court order requiring non-disclosure by litigants.[85]

TUL. J. TECH. & INTELL. PROP. 167, 196 (2005); Sarah J. Taylor, *Fostering Economic Growth in the High–Technology Field: Washington Should Abandon its Recognition of the Inevitable Disclosure Doctrine*, 30 SEATTLE U. L. REV. 473, 499 (2007); Susan Whaley, *The Inevitable Disaster of Inevitable Disclosure*, 67 U. CIN. L. REV. 809, 842–43 (1999).

81. E.g., Alan Hyde, *The Story of PepsiCo v. Redmond, in* EMPLOYMENT LAW STORIES 117, 141 (SAMUEL ESTREICHER & GILLIAN LESTER eds., 2007); *Cf.* Gilson, *supra* note 4, at 624 (arguing that high-tech employees engaged in research and development will find it particularly difficult to avoid coming under the purview of the doctrine).

82. E.g., Jay L. Koh, *From Hoops to Hard Drives: An Accession Law Approach to the Inevitable Misappropriation of Trade Secrets*, 48 AM. U. L. REV. 271, 299–304 (1998); Lawrence Weinstein, *Revisiting the Inevitability Doctrine*, 21 AM. J. TRIAL ADVOC. 211, 226 (1997) (arguing the *PepsiCo.* injunction is overly broad, but limited in its precedential value); Gillian Lester & Eric Talley, *Trade Secrets and Mutual Investments*, USC Law School Working Paper

#00–15; Georgetown Law and Economics Research Paper No. 246406 (Oct. 2000).

83. E.g., Hyde, *supra* note 4, at 140 (courts require more specific allegations of trade secrets and threats); William Lynch Schaller, *Trade Secret Inevitable Disclosure: Substantive, Procedural & Practical Implications of an Evolving Doctrine (Part II)*, 86 J. PAT. & TRADEMARK OFF. SOC'Y 411, 428–29 (2004) (arguing courts have been parsimonious in applying inevitable disclosure doctrine); Koh, *supra* note 82, at 285–98 (discussing more stringent doctrinal approaches).

84. E.g., *Whyte v. Schlage Lock Co.*, 125 Cal. Rptr.2d 277 (App. 2002) (finding that the inevitable disclosure doctrine is inconsistent with the statutory prohibition in California on restrictive covenants, although the California Supreme Court has not directly addressed the issue). *See also Del Monte Fresh Produce Co. v. Dole Food Company, Inc.*, 148 F. Supp. 2d 1326, 1337 (S.D. Fla. 2001) (holding that Florida law has recognized threatened misappropriation but not inevitable disclosure).

85. UTSA §§ 2–5.

Once a secret is out, its value may evaporate quickly. For this reason, plaintiffs commonly seek injunctive relief in addition to damages.[86] The equitable remedy of injunction requires the plaintiff to show that his remedy at law will be inadequate, and that without an injunction he will suffer "irreparable harm."[87] Many cases, however, find irreparable harm as a matter of course when a trade secret is misappropriated.[88] The main issue dividing courts is over how long injunctive relief should last. A minority view holds that even if a trade secret eventually becomes public knowledge, one who violated a confidential relationship by misappropriating it while it was still a secret ought to be perpetually enjoined from its use.[89] This strong view emphasizes the moral harm of violating the fiduciary obligation of confidentiality and has a distinctly punitive element. Most courts have taken a different approach, also adopted by the UTSA, that an injunction should last only for the period of time that the trade secret remains a secret, or for the period of time it would have taken a competitor to reverse engineer the product.[90] This approach, also known as the "head start" approach, seeks to cabin injunctive relief to the period of time necessary to eliminate the advantage, or "head start," gained by the misappropriator through his unlawful conduct. Sensitive to the public policy in favor of employees' mobility and utilization of knowledge and skills, and yet still favoring some form of injunction so as not to "leave the faithless employee unpunished," the head-start approach strikes a compromise.[91]

86. JAGER, *supra* note 29, § 7.1. Section 2 of the UTSA, entitled "Injunctive Relief," provides that "[a]ctual or threatened misappropriation may be enjoined. Upon application to the court, an injunction shall be terminated when the trade secret has ceased to exist, but the injunction may be continued for an additional reasonable period of time in order to eliminate commercial advantage that otherwise would be derived from the misappropriation."

87. Thomas L. Casagrande, *Permanent Injunction in Trade Secret Actions: Is a Proper Understanding of the Role of the Inadequate Remedy at Law / Irreparable Harm Requirement the Key to Consistent Decisions?* 28 AIPLA Q. J. 113, 118 (2000) (reviewing origins of inadequacy and irreparable harm requirements).

88. *Id.* at 124 (noting that many cases reflexively recite that theft of a trade secret automatically inflicts irreparable harm, thus triggering injunctive remedies). These criteria may also be satisfied in cases in which no trade secret is involved, and yet the actions of the former employee are deemed to be a breach of confidence and unfair competition. JAGER, *supra* note 29, § 7.01.

89. The seminal case establishing this line of authority is *Shellmar Prods. Co. v. Allen–Qualley Co.*, 87 F.2d 104 (7th Cir. 1937) (holding that person in confidential relation with owner of trade secret who disclosed information prior to public disclosure would profit from own wrong if entitled to dissolution of injunction upon information becoming publicly known).

90. *Winston Research Corp. v. Minnesota Mining and Mfg. Co.*, 350 F.2d 134 (9th Cir. 1965); *Conmar Prods. v. Universal Slide Fastener Co.*, 172 F.2d 150 (2d Cir. 1949).

91. *Winston Research*, 350 F.2d at 142.

Despite the centrality of injunctive relief, damages still play an important role in enforcement. The wide variety of situations that may develop in trade secret litigation requires that courts be flexible in how they apply the principles of damages.[92] Damages may be awarded based on lost profits, but this will be possible only if there is some base line of past sales or other basis upon which to estimate losses with any accuracy. Damages may also take the form of an accounting for gains to the defendant based on principles of unjust enrichment.[93] The plaintiff is ordinarily entitled to the greater of these measures, although in some cases awarding both will be appropriate so long as there is no double accounting.[94] Another way to award damages, if neither lost profits nor unjust enrichment is possible, is through a "reasonable royalty" for the unauthorized use or disclosure of the trade secret.[95] This is an effort by the court to estimate the royalty the parties likely would have agreed upon if they had negotiated one. (Of course if the parties did in fact negotiate a royalty agreement, the court will seek to enforce it using ordinary principles of contract). For misappropriation that is willful and malicious, punitive damages may be available, as well as attorney's fees.[96] Attorney's fees may also be available to the defendant if a prosecution occurs in bad faith.[97]

D. Non–Compete and Other Restrictive Covenants

A covenant not to compete (also referred to as a restrictive covenant or non-compete agreement) is an agreement that an employee will not compete against the employer, or go to work for a competitor, for some specified period after termination of employ-

92. JAGER, *supra* note 29, § 7.20. Thus, for example, although damages may be based in tort or contract, courts have sometimes blurred the conceptual distinctions between them, for example, permitting damages in a breach of contract action based on the gain to the employee, rather than the loss of expected value to the employer. *See* Felix Prandl, *Damages for Misappropriation of Trade Secret*, 22 TORT & INS. L. J. 447, 448 (1987).

93. *Hoeltke v. C.M. Kemp Mfg. Co.*, 80 F.2d 912, 923 (4th Cir. 1935) (one who in breach of the confidence manufactures and sells articles embodying an invention should be held liable for the profits and damages resulting therefrom on the ground that equity will not permit one to unjustly enrich himself at the expense of another).

94. Section 3 of the UTSA makes clear that in addition to or in lieu of injunctive relief, the injured party may seek both damages for actual loss caused by misappropriation, and any unjust enrichment that is not taken into account in computing actual loss.

95. UTSA § 3(a).

96. Section 3(b) of the UTSA provides, "if willful and malicious misappropriation exists, the court may award exemplary damages in the amount not exceeding twice any award made under [the provision that allows for damages]."

97. UTSA § 4.

ment.[98] The contract typically also specifies a geographic region, and may also specify a trade or profession in which competition is prohibited. Such restrictions are generally enforceable if the employer can demonstrate that the covenant safeguards a legitimate interest and is reasonable in its scope. A small number of states, such as California, deem restrictive covenants unenforceable by statute, although most of these statutes contain exceptions.[99]

One advantage of using a restrictive covenant notwithstanding trade secret protection is that it eliminates the need for a former employee to make individualized decisions about the use of proprietary information after moving to a competitor.[100] As the discussion of inevitable disclosure made clear, general skills may be intertwined with confidential information, creating ambiguous terrain for an employee who must assess which skills and information he may use in his new employment. A bright-line contractual rule that prohibits employment with competitors obviates the need for nuanced judgments. In addition, a restrictive covenant can protect certain information assets that would not be protectable as trade secrets, such as customer relationships.

Restrictive covenants take a variety of forms. Rather than prohibiting competition altogether, a covenant might instead impose some kind of penalty in the event a former employee competes, like a sum of liquidated damages or forfeiture of stock options or pension benefits. Insofar as these also have the effect of inhibiting competition, some courts will analyze such restraints in the same way they would a non-competition covenant.[101] Other courts, how-

---

98. Restrictive covenants are also commonly used to limit competition following the sale of a business or partnership. This type of covenant is usually easier to enforce than a covenant between an employee and employer because there is less concern about inequality of bargaining power between the parties. We do not examine business or partnership covenants in this chapter.

99. See CAL. BUS. & PROF. CODE § 16600–16602.5 (exceptions include covenants attached to sale of goodwill of a business, or upon dissolution of partnership or limited liability corporation). Other state statutes that significantly limit the application of restrictive covenants include ALA. CODE § 8–1–1 (2006); COLO. REV. STAT. § 8–2–113 (2006); GA. CODE ANN. § 13–8–2,–2.1 (2006); MONT. CODE. ANN. §§ 28–2–703,–704 (2005); N.D. CENT. CODE § 9–08–06 (2005); OKLA. STAT. TIT. 15, § 217–219 (2007).

100. See Kitch, *supra* note 1, at 690–91 (arguing that the benefit of contractual protection over trade secrets law is that a contractual prohibition on mobility enables the employer to keep the former employee away from competitors in the first place). See also Paul H. Rubin & Peter Shedd, *Human Capital and Covenants Not to Compete*, 10 J. LEGAL STUD. 93, 105 (1981) (use of contractual mechanisms may be a pragmatic response to the difficulty of knowing *ex ante* whether information will be deemed a trade secret).

101. E.g., *Tatom v. Ameritech Corp.*, 305 F.3d 737, 745 (7th Cir. 2002) (finding that provision in employee stock option plan that withheld bonus and accelerated vesting of stock in the event of competition was the equivalent of a non-compete); *Anniston Urologic Assocs., P.C. v. Kline*, 689 So.2d 54, 57 (Ala.

ever, may treat such provisions more leniently as imposing only "partial restraints" that do not actually prohibit competition.

Another type of restrictive covenant does not bar competition as such but restricts the ability of the former employee to solicit the employees or customers of his or her former employer. Such provisions also require a legitimate employer purpose and reasonableness of scope and duration, but may receive wider judicial latitude because a lesser restraint is involved.

As with all contracts, consideration is required for formation of a restrictive covenant. This does not ordinarily become an issue if the covenant is entered into upon commencement of employment: the prospect of future employment is deemed sufficient consideration. Courts take differing approaches where a covenant is imposed on incumbent employees as a condition of employment. Most treat continuation of at-will employment as sufficient consideration[102] A minority of states, however, look for something more substantial: either some minimal duration of employment following the parties' signing of the covenant[103] or additional consideration that is distinct from continued employment.[104] For a time, Texas interpreted a statutory requirement that a non-compete covenant "be ancillary to or part of an otherwise enforceable agreement at the time the agreement is made" to require an enforceable agreement independent of the non-compete covenant, supported by consideration above and beyond a promise of contin-

---

1997) (finding that covenant that reduces purchase price of employee's stock options in the event of competition is a restraint on practicing profession); *BDO Seidman v. Hirshberg*, 712 N.E.2d 1220, 1222 (N.Y. 1999) (agreement requiring employee to pay monetary compensation for competing is, in purpose and effect, a form of ancillary anti-competitive agreement).

102. See, e.g., *Camco, Inc. v. Baker*, 936 P.2d 829, 832 (Nev. 1997) (adopting the "majority rule" where continued at-will employment is sufficient consideration); *Summits 7, Inc. v. Kelly*, 886 A.2d 365, 372 (Vt. 2005).

103. See, e.g., *Corroon & Black of Ill., Inc. v. Magner*, 494 N.E.2d 785, 791–92 (Ill. App. 1986) (finding that because employee had been employed for a "substantial" period after signing a non-compete, in this case four years, there was sufficient consideration to support

the agreement); *Mattison v. Johnston*, 730 P.2d 286, 289 (Ariz. App. 1986) (finding when covenant imposed after start of employment, continuation of employment for a substantial period, and not mere continued employment, is sufficient consideration). Note that the courts in these cases are simply looking at the fact of post-covenant employment, not for an *ex ante* promise of continued employment.

104. See, e.g., *National Recruiters, Inc. v. Cashman*, 323 N.W.2d 736, 740 (Minn. 1982) (where covenant not ancillary to initial hiring agreement, it can be sustained only if supported by independent consideration beyond continued employment); *Poole v. Incentives Unlimited, Inc.*, 548 S.E.2d 207, 208 (S.C. 2001) (requiring additional consideration beyond continued at-will employment in order to enforce non-compete covenant).

ued at-will employment.[105] In a later decision, however, the Texas high court significantly diluted any ancillarity requirement.[106]

1. Legitimate Interests

A non-compete covenant is enforceable only if it protects a legitimate employer interest. Probably the most universally recognized legitimate interest is trade secrets.[107] This is so even in California, which statutorily prohibits covenants not to compete.[108] Customer information and relationships may also be protectable. Some customer information may be protectable simply on the basis that it is a trade secret.[109] However, even customer relationships that are not trade secrets may be protectable on grounds that they represent valuable goodwill.[110] Other legitimate interests include non-trade secret confidential information[111] and the services of employees with unique or extraordinary talents.[112]

105. See *Light v. Centel Cellular Co. of Texas*, 883 S.W.2d 642, 644–45 (Tex. 1994), construing TEX. BUS. & COM. CODE §§ 15.50–.51.

106. See *Alex Sheshunoff Management Serv. v. Johnson*, 209 S.W.3d 644, 655–56 (Tex. 2006) (holding that ancilliarity requirement has diverted courts from what should be their central focus—the inquiry into the reasonableness of restraints).

107. *Geritex Corp. v. Dermarite Indus., LLC*, 910 F.Supp. 955, 959 (S.D.N.Y. 1996) (holding that protectable employer interests include trade secrets and confidential customer lists); *Hayden's Sport Ctr., Inc. v. Johnson*, 441 N.E.2d 927, 932 (Ill. App. 1982) (requiring that employer must show injury to a legitimate business interest, such as a trade secret, separate and distinct from defendants' breach of the covenant in order to enforce a non-compete covenant).

108. See, e.g., *Loral Corp. v. Moyes*, 219 Cal.Rptr. 836, 841 (App. 1985) ("[Section 16600 of the California Business and Professions Code] invalidates provisions in employment contracts prohibiting an employee from working for a competitor after completion of his employment or imposing a penalty if he does so unless they are necessary to protect the employer's trade secrets").

109. *Ivy Mar Co., Inc. v. C.R. Seasons, Ltd.*, 907 F. Supp. 547, 556–57 (E.D.N.Y. 1995) (finding that customer list protectable as a trade secret when the names on the list not readily ascertainable, and developing the list entailed great employer effort or expenditure).

110. *Reynolds & Reynolds Co. v. Tart*, 955 F. Supp. 547, 552–53 (W.D.N.C. 1997) ("[P]rotection of customer relationships and good will against misappropriation by departing employees is well recognized as a legitimate protectable interest of the employer.") (quoting *United Labs., Inc. v. Kuykendall*, 370 S.E.2d 375, 381 (N.C. 1988)); *Terry D. Whitten, D.D.S., P.C. v. Malcolm*, 541 N.W.2d 45, 52 (Neb. 1995) (holding that employer had legitimate interest where employee had significant personal contact with employer's patients and thus the opportunity to abscond with former employer's goodwill in the form of patients).

111. *Modern Controls, Inc. v. Andreadakis*, 578 F.2d 1264, 1268 (8th Cir. 1978) (confidential information regarding company's computer hardware development, although not rising to the level of a trade secret, protectable under a covenant not to compete).

112. See, e.g., *Ticor Title Ins. v. Cohen*, 173 F.3d 63, 70 (2d Cir. 1999) (finding that title insurance salesman's relationship with clients was special, making his services unique and thus protectable); *Clooney v. WCPO Television Divi-*

As would be true of trade secret law, the general skills, knowledge and expertise an employee acquires while working for an employer, including those obtained at the employer's expense, are ordinarily not a sufficient basis for a non-compete covenant.[113] Some courts will allow employers to protect their investments in training with an appropriate non-compete agreement[114]; others insist that the training must involve transmission of trade secrets or other confidential information.[115] Even jurisdictions viewing investments in training as protectible may require "extraordinary" or "specialized" training. [116]

Discrete contracts that require an employee to reimburse the employer for clearly identified specialized training are generally enforceable.[117] Some courts have enforced such contracts even when

sion of Scripps–Howard Broad. Co., 300 N.E.2d 256 (Ohio 1973) (finding television personality's unique services provided legitimate interest); *Dallas Cowboys Football Club, Inc. v. Harris*, 348 S.W.2d 37, 45 (Tex. App. 1961) (reversing trial judge's denial of request for new trial by football club seeking to enforce restrictive covenant against football player given evidence showing that defendant possessed unique knowledge, skill and ability).

113. See *Reed, Roberts Assocs. v. Strauman*, 353 N.E.2d 590, 593 (N.Y. 1976) ("[N]o restrictions should fetter an employee's right to use to his own best advantage the skills and knowledge acquired by the overall experience of his previous employment."); *Donahue v. Permacel Tape Corp.*, 127 N.E.2d 235, 240 (Ind. 1955) ("[K]nowledge, skill and information (except trade secrets and confidential information) become a part of the employee's personal equipment. These things cannot be taken from him, although he may forget or abandon them.") (citing *Jewel Tea Co. v. Grissom*, 279 N.W. 544 (S.D. 1938)). *See also Bryceland v. Northey*, 772 P.2d 36, 40 (Ariz. App. 1989) (finding employer's instruction on being a deejay as insufficient in supporting a restrictive covenant).

114. See, e.g., FLA. STAT. § 542.335(1)(b)(5) (2007) ("extraordinary or specialized training" is a legitimate business interest); *The Cmty. Hosp. Group, Inc. v. More*, 869 A.2d 884, 897 (N.J. 2005) (finding that hospital's investment in neurosurgeon's profes-

sional development was a protectable interest); *Beckman v. Cox Broad. Corp.*, 296 S.E.2d 566 (Ga. 1982) (employer may legitimately protect investment in time and money in developing employee's skills); *Rogers v. Runfola & Assocs., Inc.*, 565 N.E.2d 540, 544 (Ohio 1991) (employer investment in time and money in equipment, facilities, support staff and training of court reporters is protectable interest).

115. *Springfield Rare Coin v. Mileham*, 620 N.E.2d 479, 486 (Ill. App. 1993) (distinguishing general training in authenticating rare coins from confidential information).

116. E.g., *Hapney v. Central Garage, Inc.*, 579 So.2d 127, 132 (Fla. Dist. Ct. App. 1991), *rev. denied*, 591 So.2d 180 (Fla. 1991), *rev'd on other grounds by Gupton v. Village Key & Saw Shop, Inc.*, 656 So.2d 475 (Fla. 1995) (employer's investment in extending air-conditioning installer and repairer's skills to include cruise control units and cellular telephones not "extraordinary" enough to justify covenant); *Brunswick Floors, Inc. v. Guest*, 506 S.E.2d 670, 673 (Ga. App. 1998) (extensive investment in training may be protectable, but minimal training in floor installation provided to plaintiff not sufficient to justify covenant not to compete within 80–mile radius for two years).

117. See COLO. REV. STAT. § 8–2–113(2)(c) (permissible to have covenant that provides for recovery of expense of educating and training an employee who

they allow the employee to "pay" for the training in the form of restricted mobility rather than cash, e.g., by promising not to work for a particular competitor, or agreeing not to leave the company, before completing some minimum period of service.[118] However, in *Brunner v. Hand Industries*,[119] the Indiana Court of Appeals refused to enforce an agreement that took such a form. While not rejecting the legitimacy of training-reimbursement contracts in general, the Indiana court objected to the singling out of employees who worked for a competitor for purposes of requiring reimbursement, the general nature of the training for which such employees were charged, and the disproportionality between the cost of the training and the amount charged.

2. Reasonable Duration and Scope

The other limitation on enforceability is that the covenant must be reasonable in duration and scope, and in general not restrict competition any more than reasonably necessary to protect the legitimate interests of the employer.[120] Courts' analysis focuses on whether the restriction is excessive in terms of duration, geographic scope, or range of activities.

Courts typically look at the interplay between the various limitations. For example, although courts will find covenants of unlimited duration unreasonable,[121] they may be more tolerant if an indefinite covenant is adequately limited on another dimension,

has served an employer for a period of less than two years).

118. See, e.g., *Milwaukee Area Joint Apprenticeship Training Comm. for Elec. Indus. v. Howell*, 67 F.3d 1333, 1339 (7th Cir. 1995) (enforcing loan agreement obligating electrician to repay cost of apprenticeship training because it did not enjoin competition generally, only recoupment of training costs if he worked for certain competitors); *Suburban Air Freight, Inc. v. Aust*, 636 N.W.2d 629 (Neb. 2001) (upholding order that pilot reimburse airline for a sliding fraction of training costs if he departed within one year of receiving training).

119. 603 N.E.2d 157, 160–61 (Ind. App. 1992).

120. RESTATEMENT (SECOND) OF CONTRACTS § 188(1)(a)(b) cmts. b-d. The seminal holding on the enforceability of reasonable restraints remains the 18th Century English decision of *Mitchel v. Reynolds*, 24 Eng. Rep. 347 (Ch. 1711) (restraints on competition presumptively unenforceable, though presumption may be rebutted if restraint is reasonable).

121. E.g., *Kuehn v. Selton & Assocs., Inc.*, 530 S.E.2d 787 (Ga. App. 2000) (rejecting covenant prohibiting real estate agent from doing business with clients of former employer unreasonable because of indefinite duration); *Sermons v. Caine & Estes Ins. Agency, Inc.*, 273 S.E.2d 338 (S.C. 1980) (finding covenant prohibiting real estate agent from doing business "at any time" with clients of former employer deemed as unreasonable); *Mutual Serv. Cas. Co. v. Brass*, 625 N.W.2d 648, 654 (Wis. 2001) (finding restriction having no "specific time limitation" as overbroad).

such as geography.[122] The nature of the industry is also relevant. Although a one-year restriction on competition is considered reasonable in many contexts, it might be unreasonable in a high-technology field where the pace of change is very fast.[123]

When assessing geographic restrictions, courts evaluate whether the contract restricts the employee's activities beyond the physical area in which the employee could realistically usurp business opportunities of the former employer. Thus, a contract that prevents an employee from competing throughout the state will probably be unreasonable if the former employer's business is limited to a portion of the state.[124] Broader geographic restrictions might survive if the former employer's business operates beyond local geographic boundaries, such as in the case of an internet business.[125] And a court may permit even wider restrictions if, in the aggregate, the employee is sufficiently protected by the tailoring of other restrictions. Thus, for example, a covenant that prohibited a senior manager in the machine tooling industry from competing in all of North and South America was deemed reasonable in light of the fact that the former employer's business in fact extended into both regions and the covenant was limited in duration to six months.[126]

Courts will also scrutinize the range of vocational activities limited by a covenant. Preventing a former employee from practicing his trade or craft beyond the bounds of what he is trained to do or formerly did for the employer will likely be unreasonable.[127]

---

122. E.g., *Karpinski v. Ingrasci*, 268 N.E.2d 751, 753–54 (N.Y. 1971) (finding that covenant will not be stricken merely because it is unlimited as to time, where restraint is limited and reasonable with respect to area).

123. *EarthWeb, Inc. v. Schlack*, 71 F. Supp. 2d 299 (S.D.N.Y. 1999) (one-year restriction on employment in the area of on-line marketing of products and services to information technology professionals unreasonably long given dynamic nature of industry).

124. E.g., *Varsity Gold, Inc. v. Porzio*, 45 P.3d 352 (Ariz. 2002) (affirming trial court's finding that geographical scope encompassing Pennsylvania and contiguous states was overbroad when company's presence was limited to Pittsburgh). *See also Permacel Tape Co., supra* note 113, 127 N.E.2d at 241 (finding restriction on competition in United States and Canada as overbroad where employee's former responsibilities in

manufacturing and selling adhesive tape had been limited to northern Indiana).

125. *West Publ'g Corp. v. Stanley*, 20 I.E.R. Cas. (BNA) 1463 (D. Minn. 2004) (finding lack of geographical restriction reasonable since plaintiff was an "[i]nternet business"). *See also Intelus Corp. v. Barton*, 7 F. Supp. 2d 635, 642 (D. Md. 1998) (finding that business's broad geographical market allows for a non-compete without territorial limitations).

126. *Okuma Am. Corp. v. Bowers*, 638 S.E.2d 617, 620–21 (N.C. App. 2007).

127. E.g., *Karpinski, supra* note 122, 268 N.E.2d at 754 (finding covenant preventing oral surgeon from practicing dentistry following departure from oral surgery practice as overbroad because it extended beyond oral surgery); *Norlund v. Faust*, 675 N.E.2d 1142, 1155 (Ind. App. 1997) (allowing ophthalmologist to enjoin former employee optometrist

Much litigation surrounds the issue of client relationships and goodwill. Restraints that simply prevent an employee from dealing with former customers may be deemed reasonable, even if the geographic limitation is very broad.[128] Some decisions hold that a restriction imposed to protect client relationships need not be limited to prohibiting dealings with those clients with whom the employee had contact. Sensitive to the difficulty an employer may have in monitoring a former employee's solicitation of its customers, courts may enforce more general bans on competition as a means to protect clients if they are sufficiently limited in other respects.[129] Some states scrutinize not only the former employee's, but also the strength of the former employer's, relationship with clients asserted as the interest undergirding a non-compete provision. Illinois courts, for example, recognize a legitimate interest where customer relationships are "near-permanent," effectively limiting protectable customers to those over whom the employer has a de facto monopoly due to a long-standing relationship.[130]

Occasionally, particularly in the context of restrictions on professional services, a court may declare a restrictive covenant contrary to the public interest even if the agreement would otherwise satisfy reasonableness scrutiny. For example, courts in some states have limited the enforcement of restrictive covenants against physicians, citing the general rationale that the public has an interest in unconstrained access to doctors' services.[131] In the realm of legal

from contacting optometrists who referred patients to former employer, but could not enjoin former employee from acting as an optometrist in association with any ophthalmologist within specified counties, because the latter would prevent him from practicing his livelihood).

128. See, e.g., *Schmidl v. Cent. Laundry & Supply Co.*, 13 N.Y.S.2d 817, 824 (N.Y. Sup. Ct. 1939) (enforcing nine-month restrictive covenant prohibiting employee from soliciting any clients he brought to former employer's business); *Okuma, supra* note 126, 638 S.E.2d at 621–22.

129. See, e.g., *Chaichimansour v. Pets Are People Too, No. 2, Inc.*, 485 S.E.2d 248 (Ga. App. 1997) (upholding ban on provision of veterinary services to anyone within a limited area that that was closely tied to the geographic area in which employee had worked for former employer); *Systems and Software, Inc. v. Barnes*, 886 A.2d 762, 766

(Vt. 2005) (upholding covenant barring defendant from working for any direct competitor for six months, on basis that it would be too difficult to monitor whether defendant was using goodwill acquired from plaintiff to compete for former clients).

130. The legal test for determining a "near permanent" relationship is unresolved in the lower Illinois courts, which will either apply the "nature of the business" test or use an alternative seven-factor test. *Appelbaum v. Appelbaum*, 823 N.E.2d 1074, 1082–83 (Ill. App. 2005).

131. See, e.g., *Murfreesboro Med. Clinic, P.A. v. Udom*, 166 S.W.3d 674, 682 (Tenn. 2005) (finding that public policy and legislative intent dictate that restrictive covenants against physicians must be strictly limited). But see *Medical Specialists, Inc. v. Sleweon*, 652 N.E.2d 517 (Ind. App. 1995) ("Covenants against physicians are not *per se*

services, the American Bar Association's Model Rules of Professional Conduct prohibit attorneys from entering into an "agreement that restricts the right of a lawyer to practice after termination ... except an agreement concerning benefits upon retirement."[132] As a result, most states are hostile to restrictive covenants for attorneys, again asserting that it is in the interests of the public to have unlimited access to attorneys.[133]

3. Reason for Termination of Employment

The reason for termination of the employment relationship may be relevant when deciding whether to enforce a restrictive covenant. Some jurisdictions employ an "employee choice" doctrine where if the employee quits his former employment without cause, he is deemed to have chosen to bring himself within the noncompete covenant, which in these circumstances may be viewed with less scrutiny than would otherwise be the case.[134]

If the employer materially breaches the contract of employment, in many jurisdictions the employee may avoid enforcement of a covenant on the basis that the employer's breach serves to release the employee from reciprocal obligation.[135] Some courts refuse to enforce covenants against an employee fired without cause.[136] The rationale is that when the employer terminates the relationship the employee is arguably between a rock and a hard place: unable to

against public policy."); *Calhoun v. WHA Med. Clinic, PLLC*, 632 S.E.2d 563 (N.C. App. 2006) (finding that restrictive covenants for physicians are not *per se* unreasonable).

132. MODEL RULES OF PROF'L CONDUCT R. 5.6 (1983).

133. *Pettingell v. Morrison, Mahoney & Miller*, 687 N.E.2d 1237, 1239 (Mass. 1997) (stating that prohibition against restrictive covenants is motivated by the interests of clients, not the lawyers themselves); *Jacob v. Norris*, 607 A.2d 142, 146 (N.J. 1992) (explaining that limited availability of restrictive covenants on attorneys will serve the public interest in having a "maximum access to lawyers" and freedom of choice in selecting counsel).

134. See *Lucente v. International Bus. Machines Corp.*, 310 F.3d 243 (2d Cir. 2002) (applying New York law); *Central Monitoring Serv. v. Zakinski*, 553 N.W.2d 513, 521 (S.D. 1996) (enforc-

ing covenant not to compete without need to apply reasonableness test when employee quits or was fired for good cause).

135. E.g., *Alexander & Alexander v. Feldman*, 913 F.Supp. 1495, 1501–02 (D. Kan. 1996) (holding employer's breach of employment contract by unilaterally modifying compensation terms precluded enforcement of the contract's noncompete clause); *Matheney v. McClain*, 161 So.2d 516, 520 (Miss. 1964) (same); *Smith-Scharff Paper Co. v. Blum*, 813 S.W.2d 27, 28 (Mo. App. 1991) (same).

136. E.g., *SIFCO Indus., Inc. v. Advanced Plating Techs., Inc.*, 867 F.Supp. 155 (S.D.N.Y. 1994); *Bishop v. Lakeland Animal Hospital, P.C.*, 644 N.E.2d 33 (Ill. App. 1994). Some courts take the less categorical position that they are *more reluctant* to enforce a covenant if the employee was laid off for reasons not her fault than if she was terminated for cause. See, e.g., *Rao*, 718 F.2d at 224; *Zakinski*, 553 N.W.2d at 521.

work for the employer, but also unable to work for a competitor. In a similar vein, a court will deny enforcement if there is evidence of employer bad faith. So, for example, if an employer has tried to manipulate competition by hiring a worker for the *purpose* of terminating her after extracting an agreement not to compete, the court will refuse enforcement.[137]

In some jurisdictions, a general good faith principle may operate to foreclose enforcement of an otherwise reasonable covenant. The Seventh Circuit considered the case of a physician whose employer fired him, despite good performance, only days before he was eligible under the terms of the parties' employment contract to purchase half the shares of the corporation for one dollar.[138] Each party had the right to terminate the employment with 90 days' notice, and the employer had given such notice in a timely fashion.[139] The employment agreement also contained a restrictive covenant applicable if the employment was terminated "for any reason."[140] Thus although the employer was entitled, on a strict reading of the contract, to terminate the employee as it did and to enforce the restrictive covenant, the Seventh Circuit affirmed the district court's ruling that the employer had acted in bad faith and therefore could not enforce the restrictive covenant.[141] The court declined to choose which of two contractual theories dictated its ruling—whether the duty of good faith is an independent term, which when breached released the defendant from his reciprocal obligation under the covenant, or that the exercise of good faith is a condition precedent to enforcement of a non-compete covenant— and asserted that either way, the employer's failure to act in good faith precluded application of the restrictive covenant.[142]

4.   Remedies
a.   Judicial Modification

Courts sometimes reform an unreasonable non-compete agreement and enforce it. The risk associated with judicially modifying

137. *Hopper v. All Pet Animal Clinic, Inc.*, 861 P.2d 531, 541 (Wyo. 1993). Cf. *Rao v. Rao*, 718 F.2d 219, 223 (7th Cir. 1983) (holding that dismissal of former employee to prevent him from buying into the partnership constituted a lack of good faith and precluded enforcement of the restrictive covenant); *Central Adjustment Bureau v. Ingram*, 678 S.W.2d 28, 35 (Tenn. 1984) (stating that even if an employee is at-will, an arbitrary, capricious, or bad faith termination clearly would have a bearing on whether to enforce a non-competition covenant).

138. *Rao*, 718 F.2d at 219.

139. *Id.* at 221.

140. *Id.*

141. *Id.* at 221–23.

142. *Id.* at 223.

covenants is that employers may draft overbroad contracts, comfortable in the knowledge that if the contract is later challenged for overbreadth, the drafter can obtain enforcement in modified form. For this reason, some states categorically refuse to enforce overbroad restrictive covenants, and will not modify them.[145] Most courts, however, guard against perverse incentives by evaluating the facts for evidence of bad faith by the employer. If a covenant is grossly overbroad or other evidence suggests that the employer knowingly drafted an overbroad covenant, the court will invalidate the contract.[146]

"Blue penciling" is the judicial excision of an unreasonable term. It requires that a covenant be clearly divisible, allowing the court to sever the offending provision while leaving the rest of the contract intact.[147] It also requires that the remaining portions of the contract embody sufficient essential terms to be enforceable standing alone. Some courts are less insistent on this divisibility requirement.[148]

Some jurisdictions follow a "rule of reasonableness," which is the practice of narrowing enforcement of an overbroad covenant to only those portions that are reasonable. It allows for judicial construction of a reasonable term even if the contract is not amenable to precise excision of invalid terms. For example, a court might enforce a covenant that is reasonable in all respects except that it covers an overly broad geographic territory, by enforcing the injunction only for a lesser area.[149]

145. E.g., *Richard P. Rita Pers. Servs. Int'l, Inc. v. Kot*, 191 S.E.2d 79, 81 (Ga. 1972) (eschewing judicial modification because it would encourage employers to write overbroad covenants and "exercise an *in terrorem* effect on employees") (citing Harlan M. Blake, *Employee Covenants Not to Compete*, 73 HARV. J. L. 625 (1960)); *CAE Vanguard, Inc. v. Newman*, 518 N.W.2d 652, 655 (Neb. 1994) (finding that Nebraska adopts the "minority view" that courts will not reform covenants since doing so is equivalent to creating private agreements).

146. *B.D.O. Seidman*, 712 N.E.2d at 394 (stating that good faith of employer is relevant).

147. See, e.g., *Bridgestone/Firestone, Inc. v. Lockhart*, 5 F.Supp.2d 667, 683 (S.D. Ind. 1998) (stating that Indiana courts will strike readily severable invalid clauses to allow partial enforcement of the covenant); *Intermountain Eye and Laser Ctrs., P.L.L.C. v. Miller*, 127 P.3d 121, 131 (Idaho 2005) (court may blue-pencil if it can be done simply and accurately, but will not do a substantial re-write of the contract).

148. *B.D.O. Seidman*, 712 N.E.2d at 394 (describing prior judicial requirement of strict divisibility as discredited); *Central Adjustment Bureau*, 678 S.W.2d at 37 (describing trend away from blue-pencil doctrine due to its lack of flexibility).

149. See e.g., *Total Health Physicians, S.C. v. Barrientos*, 502 N.E.2d 1240, 1242–43 (Ill. App. 1986) (limiting the geographic area of an overbroad covenant to an area that was reasonable). See also *Orchard Container Corp. v. Orchard*, 601 S.W.2d 299, 303–04 (Mo. App. 1980) (reducing scope of non-compete agreement from 200– to 125–mile radius); *B.D.O. Seidman*, 72 N.E.2d at

b.   Injunction and Damages

For restrictive covenants, as with trade secrets, an injunction is the linchpin of enforcement.[150] Here, too, the fact that time may be very much of the essence in preventing disclosure or other harm, coupled with the potential inadequacy of damages *ex post*, often militates in favor of equitable remedies.

Damages may also be available. An award of damages does not preclude additional injunctive relief, even if the parties stipulated damages by agreement.[151] Compensation for lost profits, if measurable with certainty, may be awarded.[152] If the parties have negotiated a liquidated-damages clause, the court will enforce it assuming it meets the usual contractual requirements for enforcement of such clauses.[153] Indeed, including a liquidated-damages clause in a restrictive covenant may make it easier to enforce the covenant.[154]

E.   Choice of Law Clauses

As borders between states have become increasingly fluid for companies and the employees they recruit, choice of laws has become a significant issue in litigating trade secret and restrictive covenant cases. An employee who has signed a non-compete covenant in one state but then goes to another state will have a strong

394 (narrowing the class of clients to whom a covenant applied).

150. *O'Sullivan v. Conrad*, 358 N.E.2d 926, 929–30 (Ill. App. 1976) (finding that once there is a breach of covenant, injunctive relief follows almost as a matter of course); 25 RICHARD A. LORD, WILLISTON ON CONTRACTS § 67:104 (2007). *See also* FLA. STAT. § 542.335(j) (2001) ("The violation of an enforceable restrictive covenant creates a presumption of irreparable injury to the person seeking enforcement of a restrictive covenant.").

151. See, e.g., *Massachusetts Indem. & Life Ins. Co. v. Dresser*, 306 A.2d 213, 217 (Md. 1973) (holding that contractual specification of a remedy will not be construed as taking away a common-law remedy, including injunction, unless that result is imperatively required); *SSA Foods, Inc. v. Giannotti*, 434 N.E.2d 460, 463 (Ill. App. 1982) (recognizing that it is well established that a liquidated damages provision in a contract will not operate as a bar to an injunction

which is required to enforce a covenant not-to-compete) (citing *Bauer v. Sawyer*, 134 N.E.2d 329 (Ill. 1956)).

152. *Hopper, supra* note 137, 861 P.2d at 547–48.

153. See, e.g., *DAR & Assoc., Inc. v. Uniforce Servs.*, 37 F. Supp. 2d 192, 200–204 (E.D.N.Y. 1999) (enforcing liquidated-damages clause in case of breach of a non-compete agreement, on basis that it was a reasonable estimate of anticipated harm, and actual losses likely to result from breach were difficult to ascertain at time of contracting).

154. Paul R. Kitch, *Employee Noncompete and Nondisclosure Restrictive Covenants*, 88 ILL. B. J. 230, 232 (2000) (citing *Torrence v. Hewitt Assoc.*, 493 N.E.2d 74, 78 (Ill. App. 1986)) (noting that when enforcing a liquidated-damages clause in a restrictive covenant the absence of an injunction indicates that there was no impairment of the employee's right to work and thus no injury to the public interest).

interest in having his case decided under the law more favorable to employee interests. The law of the state of contracting will usually apply, unless it is inconsistent with the public policy of the forum state.[155] If the parties included a choice of law clause in their non-compete agreement, courts ordinarily defer to the parties' choice of the applicable law.[156] However, if application of the law selected would offend the public policy of the forum or "a state which has a materially greater interest,"—itself a notoriously slippery concept—courts may refuse to defer.[157]

The facts of *Manuel v. Convergys Corp.*[158] illustrate the critical role forum strategy may play in the course of non-compete litigation. Manuel was working for Convergys, an Ohio human resources outsourcing company, when he was offered a job with a competitor in Georgia. He had signed an agreement with Convergys agreeing not to compete, but told the hiring employer, Mellon, that he did not think his new job would violate the non-compete promise.[159] Manuel consulted an attorney and was advised that although the covenant would be invalid under Georgia law, it probably would be enforceable in Ohio. Manuel accepted the job with Mellon, but told Convergys that he was *not* going to work for a competitor and that he had *not* accepted a job with another company. He then immediately filed suit in Georgia for a declaration that his covenant not to compete was invalid. Convergys tried to enforce the non-compete in an Ohio court, and asked the Georgia district court to stay its proceedings until after the Ohio lawsuit was concluded.

The Georgia district court denied this motion based on the "first-filed" rule.[160] If two lawsuits involve overlapping issues and parties, there is a strong presumption in the federal courts in favor of allowing the lawsuit filed first to proceed.[161] The second-filed suit will be stayed until resolution of the first, or even dismissed. The Georgia district court decided the case based on Georgia law. Reasoning that Manuel was a Georgia resident, and that Georgia public policy strongly disfavors non-compete agreements, the district court found the non-compete agreement overbroad and invali-

---

155. E.g., *Application Group, Inc. v. Hunter Group, Inc.*, 72 Cal. Rptr. 2d 73 (App. 1998) (applying California law to invalidate a non-compete covenant drafted outside California by a non-California company and involving a non-California employee whom a California company sought to hire).

156. RESTATEMENT (SECOND) OF CONFLICTS OF LAW § 187.

157. RESTATEMENT (SECOND) OF CONFLICTS OF LAW § 187(2). An exception will

also be made if the law selected has no substantial relationship to the parties or the transaction and there is no other basis for the parties' choice. *Id.*

158. 430 F.3d 1132 (11th Cir. 2005).

159. *Id.* at 1134.

160. *Id.* at 1135.

161. *U.S. Fire Ins. Co. v. Goodyear Tire and Rubber Co.*, 920 F.2d 487, 488 (8th Cir. 1990).

dated it in its entirety.[162] The Eleventh Circuit affirmed, even acknowledging that Manuel had lied to Convergys about his employment with Mellon and had engaged in improper forum shopping. With respect to the deception, the court stated that "while Manuel's behavior was not exemplary, it does not rise to the level that would require us to conclude that the district court abused its discretion."[163] And as to the broader phenomenon of forum shopping, the Eleventh Circuit stated, "[w]e agree with the district court that there is nothing inequitable in Manuel seeking legal advice and later choosing to work in a state that shared his view that the [non-compete agreement] was invalid and unenforceable."[164]

Taken together, the choice of law doctrine and the first-filed rule create an incentive for parties to shop for the jurisdiction whose law is most favorable to their own interest, *and* to file there first. Hence, we have the proverbial "race to the courthouse." This prospect of warring declaratory judgments in the early stages of a trade secret or non-compete litigation means that competitive advantage may turn as much on forum strategy as it does on the substantive merits of the dispute.

F.   Employee Inventions

At common law, an invention is owned by the person who conceives it.[165] This is true even if the employee conceives something while on the job, using time, materials, and training provided by the employer: the employment relationship does not itself imply employer ownership of the employee's ideas.[166] As the U.S. Supreme Court explained in the seminal case of *United States v. Dubilier*[167]:

> The reluctance of courts to imply or infer an agreement by the employee to assign his patent is due to a recognition of the peculiar nature of his act of invention, which consists neither in finding out the laws of nature, nor in fruitful research as to

162. *Manuel*, 430 F.3d at 1139.

163. *Id.* at 1136.

164. *Id.* at 1137.

165. *Hapgood v. Hewitt*, 119 U.S. 226 (1886); RESTATEMENT (SECOND) OF AGENCY § 397 (1958); THIRD UNFAIR COMPETITION RESTATEMENT § 42 cmt. e.

166. See, e.g., *Vigitron, Inc. v. Ferguson*, 419 A.2d 1115, 1118 (N.H. 1980) ("That an employee's rendition of services in the course of his employment may have so enhanced his mechanical skill, scientific knowledge and inventive

faculties as to enable him to develop and perfect an idea into a patentable article, does not in itself give the employer any exclusive rights to inventions of the employee made during the employment."); *Cahill v. Regan*, 165 N.Y.S.2d 125, 127 (N.Y. App. Div. 1957) (finding that an invention belongs to the inventor even if the inventor is employed by another and makes the invention during such employment).

167. *United States v. Dubilier*, 289 U.S. 178, 188 (1933).

the operation of natural laws, but in discovering how those laws may be utilized or applied for some beneficial purpose, by a process, a device, or a machine. It is the result of an inventive act, the birth of an idea and its reduction to practice; the product of an original thought; a concept demonstrated to be true by practical application or embodiment in tangible form.

In most cases, however, an employer acquires some kind of claim on an employee's invention, whether ownership itself, or a license to use it. This may occur if the employee was hired to invent, contractually assigned property rights to the employer, used confidential information imparted by the employer in devising the invention, or used employer assets in conceiving or developing the idea.

It is well-established that if an employee is hired for the purpose of inventing a particular thing, or solving a particular problem, and the employee succeeds in doing so, he must assign any resulting patent to the employer.[168] This was not always the case. The idea that "hiring to invent" endowed the employer with contractual rights to the fruits of the employee's inventive activity appears to have emerged only in late nineteenth-century jurisprudence.[169]

Both express and implied assignment theories comprise the doctrinal foundation for the "hired-to-invent" rule. A court will sometimes find that when an employee is hired to invent something specific, there is an express assignment because the invention is the precise subject of the employment contract.[170]

Alternatively, a court may find an implied assignment when an employee is hired to invent.[171] When evaluating a theory of implied rather than express assignment, however, courts scrutinize the

---

168. *Id.* at 183 (reasoning that this is true because the invention is the very subject of the contract of employment). *See also Aetna–Standard Eng'g Co. v. Rowland*, 493 A.2d 1375, 1377 (Pa. App. 1985) (finding that absent an express contrary agreement, an employee must assign his invention to his employer if he was hired for the purpose of using his inventive ability to solve a specific problem or to design a certain procedure or device for the employer). This rule has been extended to independent contractors as well. *See* JAGER, *supra* note 29, § 8:1.

169. See Catherine L. Fisk, *Removing the "Fuel of Interest" from the "Fire of Genius": Law and the Employee–Inventor, 1830–1930*, 65 U. CHI. L. REV. 1127, 1167 (1998) (marking the beginning of this shift as the United States Supreme Court's 1886 decision in *Hapgood v. Hewitt*, 119 U.S. 226).

170. *Dubilier*, 289 U.S. at 187.

171. See, e.g., *Teets v. Chromally Gas Turbine Corp.*, 83 F.3d 403, 409 (Fed. Cir. 1996) (finding implied-in-fact agreement by employee to assign invention due to the fact that the employee had the direct assignment of inventing technology of the sort that the employee did in fact invent).

content of the job duties and employment agreement closely.[172] For example, in *Teets v. Chromalloy Gas Turbine Corp.*,[173] the defendant employer assigned the plaintiff Teets as chief engineer on a project to develop a turbine blade with very particular characteristics. Teets eventually developed a turbine blade meeting the specifications. When Teets later claimed he should own the patent, the employer successfully argued an implied assignment. Although Teets had signed no employment contract addressing ownership of inventive work, the Federal Circuit cited the facts that the employer had specifically tasked Teets with inventing this kind of turbine blade, Teets spent seventy percent of his time working on it using employer resources and employees, and Teets assisted the employer and acknowledged its role in developing the idea as the employer prosecuted a patent application.[174]

Where the relationship between the employee's job and the invention is less tight, courts have been less sympathetic to claims of implied assignment. Thus, when an employer claimed assignment of the patent for a "plug mill receiving table" designed by one of its design engineers, the Superior Court of Pennsylvania denied the claim because the employee had commenced employment with the company as a general staff engineer, rather than for the specific purpose of designing the table.[175]

Employers generally will seek to protect their interests by securing express assignment agreements from their employees. It is typical for firms with a research and development (R & D) orientation to ask employees likely to have contact with the firm's R & D activities to sign an invention assignment agreement giving the employer full rights to any inventions they might conceive.[176] This contractual assignment will trump default common-law property rights. Assignment agreements cover inventions conceived during the period of employment, but also quite commonly contain a "holdover" or "trailer" clause that assigns inventions materializing for a period of time after separation. The practice of using holdover clauses presumably owes to the difficulty of proving precisely when

172. See, e.g., *University Patents, Inc. v. Kligman*, 762 F.Supp. 1212, 1224–26 (E.D. Pa. 1991) (invalidating patent policy contained within a general employee handbook but not executed by individual employee).

173. See note 171 *supra.*

174. 83 F.3d at 408.

175. *Aetna–Standard Eng'g Co., supra* note 168, 493 A.2d at 1381. *See also Hewett v. Samsonite*, 507 P.2d 1119 (Colo. App. 1973) (denying invention rights to employer where employee who invented several products while employed was not hired or paid to invent and had signed no express agreement to assign although other employees of the company had signed such agreements).

176. See generally "back of the envelope sociology" HYDE, *supra* note 4 at 66; FREDRIK NEUMEYER, THE EMPLOYEE INVENTOR IN THE UNITED STATES: R & D POLICIES, LAW, AND PRACTICE (1971).

an inventive idea is conceived, as well as the quite real possibility that the development of an idea might have it origins in the employer's workplace milieu, and yet its actual conception may not occur until later.[177]

As with any contract, formation of an assignment agreement requires consideration. Although employment may be sufficient consideration,[178] some decisions require independent consideration when an assignment is sought from incumbent employees.[179] Aside from review for possible unconscionability,[180] in parallel fashion with the regulation of restrictive covenants, courts may limit the scope of invention assignment agreements, especially holdover clauses.[181] As an example, one court held that to be enforceable, an agreement must be limited in scope so as to protect an employer's legitimate interest while neither being "unduly harsh or oppressive" on the employee nor harming the public interest.[182] Courts may consider the type of work that the employee is engaged in relative to the type of invention being assigned;[183] the relation between the invention and the employer's business;[184] and the duration of the assignment.[185]

Another route by which an employer may lay claim to an employee's invention in the absence of an express agreement is through the duty of confidentiality. If an employee-inventor holds a

177. *Dorr-Oliver, Inc. v. United States*, 432 F.2d 447, 452 (Ct. Cl. 1970).

178. See, e.g., *Cubic Corp. v. Marty*, 229 Cal.Rptr. 828, 833 (App. 1986) (holding employment as consideration for an assignment agreement where the employment was conditional upon signing the agreement and later raise and promotion were the result of inventions).

179. See, e.g., *Hewett*, 507 P.2d at 1121.

180. See, e.g., *Cubic Corp.*, 229 Cal. Rptr. at 834 (finding a contract of adhesion not unconscionable where the employment relationship included inventive duties, thus providing compensation for such assignments through wages).

181. See THIRD UNFAIR COMPETITION RESTATEMENT § 42 cmt. g.

182. *Ingersoll–Rand Co. v. Ciavatta*, 542 A.2d 879, 887 (N.J. 1988).

183. See, e.g., *Guth v. Minnesota Mining & Mfg. Co.*, 72 F.2d 385, 388 (7th Cir. 1934) (disallowing an assignment agreement partially because agreement called for assignment of inventions relating to any business area that the employer was engaged in, not just those areas where the employee worked).

184. See, e.g., *Cubic Corp.*, 229 Cal. Rptr. at 835 (finding an assignment agreement enforceable because, in part, it was limited to those inventions that were related to the actual or anticipated business of the employer).

185. Compare *GTI Corp. v. Calhoon*, 309 F.Supp. 762, 773 (S.D. Ohio 1969) (finding a five-year holdover clause void because it restricted employee's ability to use general skill and knowledge for his own benefit), and *United Shoe Mach. Co. v. La Chapelle*, 99 N.E. 289, 293 (Mass. 1912) (denying enforcement of holdover agreement that required former employee to continue to assign for ten years after termination of employment because it represented a restraint of trade), with *Goodyear Tire & Rubber Co. v. Miller*, 22 F.2d 353 (9th Cir. 1927) (upholding employment contract that required assignment of inventions for one year following termination).

position of trust and confidence—defined as being in a position to gain intimate knowledge of the employer's business[186]—the employer may enjoin him from using an invention he conceived or developed through the use of confidential information (even information that is not a trade secret).[187] Not only may senior employees such as officers, directors or managers hold positions of trust and confidence, but so, too, might employees who have some contact with the R & D activities of the company (e.g., administrative staff charged with marketing company products).[188]

If an employee is not hired to invent, and the court finds no express or implied assignment of invention rights, the employer might still have a license to use the invention. An employer "shop right" is implied by law if the employee used the employer's time, materials, resources, or equipment to develop an invention.[189] It consists of a non-exclusive, non-transferable, irrevocable license to practice (manufacture, sell) the invention without paying royalties to the employee.[190] In the creation of an invention, there are two necessary elements: a mental concept, and the "embodiment", or implementation, of the concept. The critical area of inquiry for determining whether a shop right exists is the embodiment stage.[191] Even if the concept was developed before employment began, if the employer assisted in the embodiment stage, there can be a shop right.[192] On why an employer's investment in helping to develop an

186. *Zoecon Indus., Inc. v. American Stockman Tag Co.*, 713 F.2d 1174 (5th Cir. 1983) (finding that management personnel had "intimate knowledge of the employer's business," which implied a duty not to disclose).

187. See *supra* note 27. *See also Tlapek v. Chevron Oil Co.*, 407 F.2d 1129, 1134–35 (8th Cir. 1969) (finding that unique mineral prospecting theory conceived by employee while working for employer was confidential information that employee could not use for private gain because information was developed as a result of employer's initiative and entrusted to the employee in confidence); *Vigitron, Inc., supra* note 166, 419 A.2d at 1118 (upholding injunction against employee who developed a product while employed to invent improvements to employer's technology in the same area on basis that employee breached duty of confidentiality).

188. *Wireless Specialty Apparatus Co. v. Mica Condenser Co.*, 131 N.E. 307 (Mass. 1921) (finding that defendants involved in plaintiff's research and de-velopment activities had an implied duty of confidentiality). *See generally* JAGER, *supra* note 29, § 8:5.

189. *Vigitron, supra* note 166, 419 A.2d at 1118 ("A precondition for the application of the 'shop right' rule is that the employee not be hired for the purpose of developing the product in question.") (citing *National Dev. Co. v. Gray*, 55 N.E.2d 783 (Mass. 1944)).

190. *Dubilier*, 289 U.S. at 189.

191. See, e.g., *Kinkade v. N.Y. Ship-building Corp.*, 122 A.2d 360, 365 (N.J. 1956) (granting shop right to employer since, though employee clearly devised idea at home, implementation was done on the employer's time with its materials).

192. See, e.g., *Consolidated Vultee Aircraft Corp. v. Maurice A. Garbell, Inc.*, 204 F.2d 946, 949 (9th Cir. 1953) (allowing shop-right claim since employee used employer's materials, facilities, and time to put invention into practice, despite conceiving of the invention prior

employee's idea justifies a shop right, the Supreme Court in *Dubilier* again offers a rationale:

> Where the employment does not contemplate the exercise of inventive talent, the policy of the patent laws to stimulate invention by awarding benefits of the monopoly to the inventor and not some one else leads to a ready compromise: a shop right gives the employer an adequate share in the unanticipated boon.[193]

The employer must make a sufficient contribution, however. For example, a Missouri court found no shop right in the case of an employee who developed a novel idea for a safety device to use with elevator chairs manufactured by the employer by working during his lunch hour and using scrap materials employees were permitted to take and two small company tools.[194] Additionally, an employee can avoid a shop right by reimbursing the employer for assets used.[195]

A shop right can also be created by consent. For example, a janitor at a pecan processing plant who invented a method for removing worms from pecans at his home, using his own time and materials, granted a shop right to his employer when he freely consented to the employer's use of the invention in the factory.[196] The court made clear that an express statement of consent could create a shop right even if both the conception and reduction to practice occurred entirely on the employee's own time and using his own materials.[197]

Currently, eight states codify the common law preference of assigning inventions to employees where there is no employer contribution.[198] In these states, agreements requiring employees to assign inventions to an employer where there is no employer contribution are unenforceable.[199] However, reflecting the common

---

to actual employment); *Cahill v. Regan*, 165 N.Y.S.2d 125, 129 (App. Div. 1957) (granting of shop right but not assignment of invention after employee tells employer of idea conceived outside employment and is told to "go ahead" and use employer's facilities and assets to make physical embodiment).

193. *Dubilier*, 289 U.S. at 214.

194. *Dewey v. American Stair Glide Corp.*, 557 S.W.2d 643, 647–48 (Mo. App. 1977).

195. See, e.g., *Mechmetals Corp. v. Telex Computer Prods., Inc.*, 709 F.2d 1287, 1292 (9th Cir. 1983) (barring grant of shop right where employee com-

pensated employer for material and time used).

196. *Wommack v. Durham Pecan Co., Inc.*, 715 F.2d 962 (5th Cir. 1983).

197. *Id.* at 966.

198. See generally RESTATEMENT (SECOND) OF AGENCY § 397 (1958).

199. See CAL. LAB. CODE § 2870(a) (2007) ("Any provision in an employment agreement which provides that an employee shall assign ... any of his or her rights in an invention to his or her employer shall not apply to an invention ... developed entirely on his or her own time without using the employer's

law, these states grant employers assignment rights if the employee's invention directly relates to the employer's business or R & D activities, or if the invention comes as a result of the employee's work for the employer.[200]

As this treatment of the law of inventions has shown, there are a variety of mechanisms, contractual and equitable, by which employers may ultimately assert claims to inventions conceived by employees despite the initial proposition that he who conceives an idea owns it. Professor Robert Merges defends this ownership structure on the basis of efficiency: he argues that the default rule of employer ownership in hired-to-invent situations, as well as the widespread use and enforcement of assignment agreements, encourages investment in innovation by reducing transaction costs.[201] Because the allocation of ownership occurs at the commencement of employment, it is simpler than deals struck after an employee makes a specific invention, and it eliminates the possibility of "hold-ups" by employee-inventors.[202] If one individual, such as an employee, holds a property right in an invention that is part of a larger, multi-component process or product that a company is developing, that individual may be in a position to extort a large price from ("hold up") the manufacturer because the total market value of the end product will exceed the value of the component. The long-run consequence might be underinvestment in R & D.[203]

equipment, supplies, facilities, or trade secret information. . . ."). *See also* DEL. CODE ANN. tit. 19, § 805 (2007); 765 ILL. COMP. STAT. 1060/2 (2007); KAN. STAT. ANN. § 44–130 (2006); MINN. STAT. § 181.78 (2005); N.C. GEN. STAT. § 66–57.1 (2006); UTAH CODE ANN. § 34–39–3 (2006); WASH. REV. CODE. § 49.44.140 (2007).

200. See, e.g., CAL. LAB. CODE § 2870(a)(1)-(2) (2007).

201. Robert P. Merges, *The Law and Economics of Employee Inventions*, 13 HARV. J.L. & TECH. 1 (1999).

202. *Id.* at 12.

203. *Id.*

Part 3

STATUTORY INTERVENTIONS

Chapter 7

WORKERS' COMPENSATION LAW

It is the law in nearly every jurisdiction in the United States that employees injured while on the job can recover their medical expenses and lost income in an administrative process without proving negligence or other fault on the employer's part.[1] Heralded as a major advance in worker rights and for mitigating the harshness of industrial capitalism when first enacted in the early decades of the twentieth century, the system is now under pressure from both sides. Employers cite rising costs, some of which they attribute to fraudulent claims. Claimants criticize the system for providing compensation levels far below those available in the tort system.

A.   Origins of Workers' Compensation Legislation

The common law of the nineteenth century was not very hospitable to claims by workers injured during the course of their employment. In theory, the worker could sue his employer for negligence, but in practice such suits were stymied by the so-called "unholy trinity"—three doctrines that in almost every case prevented recovery. The first was the principle that *any* "contributory negligence" on the employee's part was a complete bar to the action.[2] Not until the middle of the last century and beyond was this doctrine replaced by the principle of "comparative negligence,"

---

1. Other sources of compensation can include paid sick leave and insurance benefits provided by the employer as well as Social Security Disability and Survivor and Medicare benefits. Social Security and Medicare pay disability benefits regardless of cause but after substantial waiting periods and only when the disabilities preclude work. In 2003, workers' compensation programs in the fifty states, the District of Columbia and the federal government paid $54.9 billion in benefits (roughly evenly divided between medical care and cash benefits); Social Security paid $70.9 billion in cash benefits to disabled workers and their dependents while Medicare paid $37.9 billion for disabled persons under age 65. See National Academy of Social Insurance, WORKERS' COMPENSATION: BENEFITS, COVERAGE, AND COSTS, 2003, pp. 1–2 (2005).

2. See, e.g., *Butterfield v. Forrester*, 11 East 60 (K.B. 1809).

i.e., that the comparative degree of fault of plaintiff and defendant should affect the measure of damages but not the issue of liability *vel non*. The second shoal was the principle of "assumption of risk": in overly hazardous occupations, the employee could not recover for reasonably foreseeable injury the risk of which he had assumed in taking the job.[3] (Economists might say that compensating pay differentials likely gave the employee greater pay and benefits than he would have obtained in less hazardous work.) Today, this concept still plays a role in tort law but with a much narrower sweep. The third barrier was the "fellow servant" doctrine: if the employee's injury was due to the negligence of a co-worker, an action might lie against the co-worker but not against the employer.[4] As a practical matter, the availability of an action against the co-worker proved of little worth because the co-worker was likely to be judgment-proof.

These hurdles to obtaining compensation for workplace injury became increasingly unacceptable in the late nineteenth and early twentieth century. Some courts began to show greater receptivity to compensation suits by holding employers liable for negligence committed by highly-placed employees who acted as representatives for the firm, such as supervisors and managers; and a few decisions started recognizing a "non-delegable" duty of employers to provide a safe workplace. The favorable experience with a workers' compensation regime in Germany during the realm of Chancellor Bismarck, the rise in power and influence of the Progressive movement, the growing militancy of the U.S. labor movement, and the realization on the part of some employer groups that the old common law barriers were being, or would soon be, dismantled, all combined to create a political environment for legislative change. And in the first two decades of the new century, nearly every state passed workers' compensation laws.

The essential features of these laws reflected a grand compromise: Workers should be able to receive fairly prompt compensation for medical expenses and injuries sustained in the course of performing work for their employer. Compensation would be forthcoming without any inquiry into fault on the employer's or anyone else's part; the only question would be whether the injury was sustained "in the course of employment". Compensation claims would be handled in a special administrative process outside of the courts, and hence the tort doctrines recognized by the courts would

3. See, e.g., *Priestly v. Fowler*, 3 M. & W. 1, 150 Reprint 1030 (1837); *Murray v. South Carolina Railroad*, 1 McMullan Law (S.C.) 385 (1841); *Far-* *well v. Boston & W.R.*, 4 Metc. (Mass.) 49 (1842).

4. *Id.*

be inapplicable. The program would be funded by an employment tax; this charge would be absorbed by the firm as the cost of doing business.

Although these laws were not universally embraced,[5] there were elements that benefited all sides. Workers would be free of the fault-based regime that often left them remediless; they would also be able to receive compensation in a prompt manner without having to navigate the complexities of the court system. Firms would enjoy the benefit of predictable liability for which they could purchase insurance or self-insure. And the larger society would be relieved of the moral dilemma of securing the fruits of a dynamic capitalism on the backs, as it were, of injured workers left to fend for themselves.

Initial judicial reaction to these laws was predictably adverse, but hostility evaporated over time. In 1908, Congress passed the Federal Employers' Liability Act (FELA)[6] providing a special tort remedy for railroad workers that ensured a higher probability of recovery than before by eliminating contributory negligence and curbing the fellow-servant doctrine as a complete defense to employer liability. (In 1920, Congress passed the Jones Act, a similar law for injured seamen.[7]) Most importantly, changes in the design of state laws and changing political climate signaled by the Wilson administration led the Supreme Court in 1917 to uphold the constitutionality of the workers' compensation laws of New York, Iowa, and Washington.[8] In short order, other states would follow suit, to the point where workers' compensation is the nearly universal approach in this country. [9]

---

5. In some quarters, organized labor preferred abolition of the common law defenses to channeling all claims into an administrative process where compensation would be administratively determined. See Office of Technology Assessment, U.S. Congress, PREVENTING ILLNESS AND INJURY IN THE WORKPLACE 207–209 (1985). See generally; Price V. Fishback & Shawn Everett Kantor, *The Adoption of Workers' Compensation in the United States*, 41 J.L. & ECON. 305 (1998); Richard A. Epstein, *The Historical Origins and Economic Structure of Workers' Compensation Law*, 16 GA.L.REV. 775 (1982); Lawrence M. Friedman & Jack Landinsky, *Social Change and the Law of Industrial Accidents*, 67 COLUM. L. REV. 50 (1967).

6. 35 Stat. 65 (1908), codified at 45 U.S.C. §§ 51–60.

7. 41 Stat. 1007 (1920), codified at 46 U.S.C. §§ 688 *et seq.* Other federal laws include ENERGY EMPLOYEES' OCCUPATIONAL ILLNESS COMPENSATION PROGRAM ACT, 42 U.S.C. §§ 7384 *et seq.* (workers in nuclear power industry); LONGSHORE AND HARBOR WORKERS' COMPENSATION ACT, 33 U.S.C. §§ 901–50 (workers in "maritime" employment); FEDERAL EMPLOYEES' COMPENSATION ACT, 5 U.S.C. §§ 8101 *et seq.* (employees of the federal government).

8. See *New York Central R.R. v. White*, 243 U.S. 188 (1917); *Hawkins v. Bleakly*, 243 U.S. 210 (1917); *Mountain Timber Co. v. Washington*, 243 U.S. 219 (1917).

9. In Texas, employers have the option of staying in the workers' compensation system or being subject to suits in the tort system. Tex. Labor Code

B. Rationale for Regulation

We will discuss in Chapter 12 the case for and against regulation promoting occupational safety and health, and will not anticipate that discussion here. In the instant context, we assume a need for regulation and the question is whether the workers' compensation system, all things considered, works as well as or better than the tort system. We assume, of course, the tort system in its present state, including widespread adoption of the comparative-negligence rule, the absence of a fellow-servant bar to recovery, and an assumption of risk doctrine that does not relieve the firm of liability for the risk of accident caused by its negligence.

Let us look, first, at workers' compensation as a compensation-delivery system. On one level, it holds a great deal of promise, for the transaction costs associated with the legal system (e.g., court fees, pre-trial discovery, attorney's fees) should be lower under workers' compensation given the no-fault framework, administrative schedules for certain injuries, and expert administrative personnel. Some estimates suggest that administrative costs of the system are high—only 60 percent of the workers' compensation premium dollar goes to the compensation, from which amounts spent on lawyers must also be deducted.[10] When compared, however, to the total costs of the litigation system (defendant and system costs in addition to attorney's fees charged by plaintiff's counsel), workers' compensation comes out favorably; indeed, some have urged use of the workers' compensation model for medical practice claims for precisely this reason.[11]

How well does the system do in replacing the income of injured workers? There are essentially four basic categories of workers' compensation claims resulting in cash benefits (other than medical benefits):

§§ 406.002, 406.034. If the employer is a "non-subscriber," the employee can recover in a civil action only by proving the employer's negligence, but shorn of the "unholy trinity" of common-law defenses. See *Werner v. Colwell*, 909 S.W.2d 866 (Tex. 1995). If the employee prevails, he can recover full tort damages, which explains why only about one-third of Texas employers are non-subscribers. See RESEARCH AND OVERSIGHT COUNCIL ON WORKERS' COMPENSATION, A STUDY OF NONSUBSCRIPTION TO THE TEXAS WORKERS' COMPENSATION SYSTEM: 2001 ESTIMATES 10, 16 (2002). For a time, it was lawful for employers to require pre-injury election by employees to be part of the employer's own compensation program even at benefit levels lower than the statutory program. See *Lawrence v. CDB Services, Inc.*, 44 S.W.3d 544 (Tex. 2001). Such pre-injury waivers are now prohibited, but the employer can still require post-injury waivers before the employer's plan will pay benefits. TEX. LABOR CODE § 406.033.

10. See INTERDEPARTMENTAL WORKERS' COMPENSATION TASK FORCE, WORKERS' COMPENSATION: IS THERE A BETTER WAY?, p. 9 (1977).

11. See PAUL C. WEILER, MEDICAL MALPRACTICE ON TRIAL (1991).

(1) "medical only" claims, usually not involving lost work time beyond the waiting period for cash benefits, and accounting for 78 percent of all cases, and 6 percent of benefits paid during 1998–2000;

(2) "temporary total disability" claims, usually involving some lost work time until healing, and accounting for 66 percent of the cases and 25 percent of benefits paid;

(3) "permanent total disability" claims, involving injuries preventing gainful employment, and accounting for 1 percent of the cases and 12 percent of benefits paid; and

(4) "permanent partial disability" claims, involving injuries considered permanent but not severe enough to preclude work, and accounting for 33 percent of the cases and 63 percent of benefits paid.[12]

Benefits for total disability are keyed to a percentage, usually two-thirds, of the worker's prior wage up to the statewide average. Typically, states provide statutory maximums for particular injuries called "scheduled benefits". Scheduled benefits differ from "non-scheduled benefits" in that the former are not contingent on actual income loss or work effort following the eligibility determination. Injuries resulting in partial disability are also handled individually. Scheduled benefits vary from state to state but draw rough—some might say, arbitrary—lines in the valuation of life and limb.[13]

One study of compensation for death from asbestos found that workers' compensation replaced 6.4 percent of total economic loss, with tort awards or settlements replacing 3.6 percent; all sources overall replaced 22.8 percent of total economic loss.[14]

A relatively recent literature survey found that the expected average weekly benefit for temporary total disability relative to the poverty level for a family of four rose from 80 percent of the poverty level in 1972 to 107 percent in 1998: "This is progress, but against a very low standard of benefit adequacy."[15] Another study, discussed in the survey, found that wage-replacement ratios for permanent partial disability claimants, as a percentage of 10–year losses, was 46 percent in New Mexico, 42 percent in Oregon, 37

12. WORKERS' COMPENSATION: BENEFITS, *supra* note 1, at 7–8.

13. See U.S. Chamber of Commerce, *2005 Analysis of Workers' Compensation Law*, Chart VII, pp. 62–65 (2005).

14. See Barry I. Castleman, ASBESTOS: MEDICAL AND LEGAL ASPECTS 796 (4th ed. 1996) (based on William G. Johnson & Edward Heler, *Compensation for Death from Asbestos*, 37 INDUS.& LAB.REL. REV. 529 (1984)).

15. H. Allen Hunt, *Benefit Adequacy for State Workers' Compensation Programs*, 65 SOCIAL SECURITY BULL. 24 (No. 4, 2003/2004).

percent in California, and 29 percent in Wisconsin: "By the two-thirds standard gross wage replacement, replacement rates for permanent partial disability compensation claims are clearly very inadequate."[16]

One reason states do not fully compensate for economic loss is that an effect of improved benefit levels may be to increase the number and frequency of claims, as employees will file more claims (preferring leisure to work, all else kept constant) and may also be less careful on the job.[17] Moreover, to the extent the system is "experience-rated," i.e., employers must pay increased premiums reflecting their claims experience, this also increases the employer's incentive to challenge borderline claims:

> [H]igher workers' compensation benefits do appear to increase the frequency-of-injury rates and workers' compensation claims, although we cannot separate out with any precision how much of the increase is "real" and how much is merely a "reporting" effect. If the system is at least partially experience rated (which it is) and labor markets are not perfectly competitive (which they probably are not), higher workers' compensation benefits should induce employers to try to prevent accidents and/or to challenge more claims. That a positive relationship between frequency and benefits is observed implies that employees' responses to higher benefits dominate, on balance, over employers' responses....
>
> Of course, the fact that increasing workers' compensation benefits does appear to increase the frequency-of-injury rates and/or workers' compensation claims does *not* imply in itself that further benefit increases are undesirable (*or* are desirable). Rather, it only tells us that there is a trade off between higher, more adequate benefits and higher injury rates and claims. Where along the trade off lines we ultimately locate will depend on policy makers' judgments about the optimal contribution of adequacy and safety.[18]

16. *Id.* at 28 & Table 1, discussing ROBERT T. REVILLE, KESLIE I. BODEN, JEFFREY E. BIDDLE & CHRISTOPHER MARDESICH, AN EVALUATION OF NEW MEXICO WORKERS' COMPENSATION PERMANENT PARTIAL DISABILITY AND RETURN TO WORK (RAND INSTITUTE FOR CIVIL JUSTICE, MR–1414–ICJ, 2001).

17. It may also reflect some skepticism over difficulties of measuring etiology and disability causation in the case of claims for permanent partial disability. See *id.* at 28 (discussing employer views); PETER S. BARTH & MICHAEL NISS, PERMANENT PARTIAL DISABILITY BENEFITS: INTERSTATE DIFFERENCES (Workers Compensation Research Institute, 1999).

18. Ronald G. Ehrenberg, *Workers' Compensation, Wages, and the Risk of Injury*, in NEW PERSPECTIVES IN WORKERS' COMPENSATION 94–95 (JOHN F. BURTON, JR., ed., 1988).

How well does the system work in reducing the risk of occupational injury? One study finds that "workers' compensation reduces worker fatality rates by almost 30 percent.... [T]here would be an additional 1,200 deaths per year on the job were it not for the financial incentives provided by workers' compensation. By, in effect, merit-rating firms based on their accident records, workers' compensation provides firms with incentives for safety that in turn result in higher levels of safety for the affected firms."[19] As the above discussion suggests, however, one cannot immediately infer from reported injury rates or claims experience whether the risk of injury is actually increasing, rather than claimants responding to improved benefit levels or eased rules of adjudication by filing more claims and the like. Research focusing on fatality rates should avoid this "reporting" effect.

C. Covered Employers and Employees

Most statutes are comprehensive in scope with few categories of exclusion. Some states exclude charitable and religious organizations from employer coverage. On the employee side, some states exclude individuals performing domestic service, agricultural workers, and casual employees.[20]

The common-law "right to control" test is typically used in deciding whether an individual providing services to the employer is an employee covered by workers' compensation or is an independent contractor presumably free to sue in tort. In close cases involving, say, owner-operators of delivery trucks expected to follow the instructions of a dispatcher,[21] or outside commission salesmen rarely required to come to the office,[22] coverage is likely to be found. An important factor pointing to coverage is whether the putative independent contractor's work is connected to the trade or business of the putative employer. Thus, for example, individuals performing routine maintenance, repair and construction work are likely to be covered, whereas those working on new production or a maintenance overhaul, requiring a shutdown, of a facility are less likely. A

---

19. W.KIP VISCUSI, RATIONAL RISK POLICY 122 (1998), reporting on MICHAEL J. MOORE & W. KIP VISCUSI, COMPENSATING MECHANISMS FOR JOB RISKS: WAGES, WORKERS' COMPENSATION, AND PRODUCT LIABILITY (1990).

20. The best general source here remains Arthur Larson, LARSON'S WORKERS' COMPENSATION LAWS, a multi-volume treatise published by Matthew Bender. The late Professor Larson taught at Duke University School of Law.

21. Compare, e.g., *Curry v. Interstate Express, Inc.*, 607 So.2d 230 (Ala.), on remand, 607 So.2d 233 (Ala. App. 1992), with *Reed v. Industrial Comm'n*, 534 P.2d 1090 (Ariz. App. 1975).

22. See, e.g., *Ware v. Industrial Comm'n*, 743 N.E.2d 579 (Ill.App. 2000); *Gordon v. New York Life Ins. Co.*, 90 N.E.2d 898 (Ill. App. 1950), motion denied, 92 N.E.2d 318 (N.Y. 1950).

second equally important, though implicit, factor is the identity of the party claiming coverage. In close cases, if the claimant is seeking coverage rather than the opportunity to sue in the tort system, coverage is more likely to be found.

Other recurring issues involve volunteer workers (who are usually covered only when they receive some compensation for the services);[23] and employees borrowed from other employers or con-tractor-employees working at the user-employer's facility, which is likely to result in secondary liability for the user-employer under the "statutory employee" provisions of many laws.[24]

D. Covered Injuries

1. Express Exclusions

Intentional Torts. Most statutes exclude intentional torts, but it should be noted that an intentional tort committed by a co-worker may still be a covered injury respecting any claim against the employer.[25] Some courts hold that the intentional-tort exclusion does not apply unless there is proof the employer "engaged in misconduct knowing it was substantially certain to cause serious injury or death...."[26]

Occupational Disease. Historically, workers' compensation laws, written to deal with "accidental" injuries, did not provide coverage for occupational disease. Disease claims raise difficult issues for the system because of the long latency period and the possible of multiple, including non-workplace, causes.[27] By now, virtually all of the states have enacted specific provisions dealing with occupational disease; typically, such provisions do not require a sudden, unexpected triggering event.[28]

Emotional Distress. The traditional rule in most jurisdictions was that an employee could not recover for an emotional injury connected with employment when the injury was not occasioned by some physical impact or the application of some form of external

---

23. See, e.g., *Humphries v. Thomas,* 422 S.E.2d 755 (Va. 1992).

24. See Larson's Workers' Compensation Laws, *supra* note 20, ch. 71.

25. See, e.g., *Hanford v. Plaza Packaging Corp.,* 811 N.E.2d 30 (N.Y. 2004).

26. *Whitaker v. Town of Scotland Neck,* 597 S.E.2d 665 (N.C. 2003); see *Zimmerman v. Valdak Corp.,* 570 N.W.2d 204 (N.D. 1997). The decisions

in this area are usefully surveyed in *Mead v. Western Slate, Inc.,* 848 A.2d 257 (Vt. 2004).

27. See Elinor P. Schroeder & Sidney A. Shapiro, *Responses to Occupational Disease: The Role of Markets, Regulation, and Information,* 72 Geo. L.J. 1231 (1984).

28. Larson's Workers Compensation Laws, *supra* note 20, ch. 52.01.

violence to the body. Some laws still expressly exclude conditions arising from emotional or mental stress.[29] Where the statutes do not contain such an exclusion, some courts are showing greater receptivity to the compensability of such claims.[30] In other jurisdictions, the courts still insist on the "physical impact" rule or require an incident or incidents "involving mental or emotional stress of an unusual or abnormal nature."[31]

Personal Animosity. Texas bars compensation for an injury "caused by an act of a third person intended to injure the employee because of reasons personal to him and not directed against him as an employee, or because of his employment."[32]

2. *"Arising out of and in the Course of Employment"*

The principal limit on coverage is the requirement, found in all of the jurisdictions, that the injury "arise out of and in the course of employment". Although usage varies among jurisdictions, the "in the course of" element refers to injuries occurring in connection with activity occurring within the time and place limits of the employment relationship; the "arise out of" element refers to the origin or cause of the injury. "An injury 'arises out of' employment when it has its origin in an employee's work-related functions and is sufficiently related to those functions to be considered part of the employee's employment contract."[33]

Most cases are fairly straightforward. Examples of difficult cases include:

29. See, e.g., *Kleinhesselink v. Chevron, U.S.A.*, 920 P.2d 108 (Mont. 1996) (effect of § 39–71–119(3), MCA).

30. See, e.g., *Carter v. General Motors Corp.*, 106 N.W.2d 105 (Mich. 1960) (benefits are payable for "incapacity to work because of a claimant's paranoid schizophrenia arising out and in the course of employment"; stress due to supervisor criticism of employee's pace of work). For a decision upholding the compensability of post-traumatic stress syndrome as either an accidental injury or an occupational disease, see *Brunell v. Wildwood Crest Police Dept.*, 822 A.2d 576 (N.J. 2003).

31. *Houser v. Bi–Lo, Inc.*, 36 S.W.3d 68 (Tenn. 2001) (denying coverage for stroke occurring after employee discovered a co-worker had ordered stock for the store resulting in receipt of an excessively large order at Christmas time). See generally Thomas S. Cook, *Workers' Compensation and Stress Claims: Remedial Intent and Restrictive Application*, 62 NOTRE DAME L. REV. 879 (1987); BUREAU OF NATIONAL AFFAIRS, STRESS IN THE WORKPLACE: COSTS, LIABILITY AND PREVENTION (1987); NATIONAL COUNCIL ON COMPENSATION INSURANCE, EMOTIONAL STRESS IN THE WORKPLACE—NEW LEGAL RIGHTS IN THE EIGHTIES (1985).

32. TEX. REV. CIV. STAT. ANN. ART. 8309, § 1; but see, e.g., *Nasser v. Security Insurance Co.*, 724 S.W.2d 17 (Tex. 1987) (restaurant employee assaulted by customer had covered claim because it was the restaurant's practice to encourage employee to be friendly with customers when they were dining alone).

33. *Horodyskyj v. Karanian*, 32 P.3d 470, 475 (Colo. 2001).

- The employer asks the employee to do work on the employer's personal residence where he is injured.[34]
- The employee takes a detour from the planned delivery route to run a personal errand and is injured by an oncoming vehicle.[35]
- Waitress suffers an assault from a customer at the restaurant.[36]
- "Horseplay" at work is tolerated by the employer.[37]

E. Potential Escape Routes from the "Exclusive" Remedy of Workers' Compensation

Because of the increasing attractiveness of the tort system, claimants often seek to bypass the workers' compensation system, with employers resisting by arguing that workers' compensation provides the exclusive remedy for their injury. Despite an express "exclusivity" provision in all of the laws, courts have been receptive to allowing tort actions in the following kinds of cases.

1. "Dual Capacity" Employer

If the employer can be found to play an additional role contributing to the claimant's injury, a suit in tort may proceed for the aggravation of the injury attributed to that second role. For example, if the employer conducts a physical examination of the employee and withholds findings that the employee had a silicosis disease resulting from his employment, an action is available for fraud; the act of conducting the examination has been held to give rise to an independent duty not covered by workers' compensation.[38]

2. Absence of a Remedy under Workers' Compensation

The exclusivity provision in some jurisdictions purports to foreclose all work-related injuries even if the particular injury is not

---

34. See, e.g., *Macchirole v. Giamboi,* 762 N.E.2d 346 (N.Y. 2001) (compensable despite employee's attempt to recover from his employer personally).

35. Cf. *Johnson v. Skelly Oil Co.,* 288 N.W.2d 493 (S.D. 1980) (compensable because employee was carrying employer's mail to deposit on his way home).

36. See note 32 *supra.*

37. See, e.g., *Prows v. Industrial Commission,* 610 P.2d 1362 (Utah 1980) (compensable unless "horseplay" is a "substantial deviation" from the course of employment).

38. See, e.g., *Millison v. E.I. du Pont de Nemours & Co.,* 501 A.2d 505 (N.J. 1985) (fraudulent concealment during medical examinations of exposure to asbestos resulting in aggravation of occupational disease not covered by workers' compensation); *Delamotte v. Unitcast Division of Midland Ross Corp.,* 411 N.E.2d 814 (Ohio App. 1978).

compensable under the statute.[39] Some courts have resisted this principle. For example, in *Smothers v. Gresham Transfer, Inc.,*[40] the employee claimed he developed an upper respiratory infection, pneumonia and bronchitis because of exposure to a chemical used by his employer in cleaning the company's trucks. He was denied compensation on the ground he failed to prove that exposure to chemicals at work was the major contributing cause of his disorder. When he later sued in tort, the trial court dismissed the action because of the exclusivity of the workers' compensation remedy. The Oregon supreme court, however, held that this application of the exclusivity provision violated the state constitution where the employee could not recover under workers' compensation.

3. Injuries Outside the "Compensation Bargain"

As the California Supreme Court stated in *Shoemaker v. Myers,*[41] "[w]here the injury is a result of conduct, whether in the form of discharge or otherwise, not seen as reasonably coming within the compensation bargain, a separate civil action may lie."[42] The underlying concept is that the exclusivity provision should be read as limited to risks that are "reasonably encompassed within the compensation bargain,"[43] and not include conduct "exceed[ing] the normal risks of the employment relationship. . . ."[44] In *Shoemaker*, statutorily authorized "whistleblower" claims were not preempted by workers' compensation.

The California courts have had difficulty working out this principle because, as the *Shoemaker* court recognized, "[e]ven if such conduct may be characterized as intentional, unfair or outrageous, it is nevertheless covered by the workers' compensation exclusivity provisions."[45]

"Public Policy" Claims. In *Gantt v. Sentry Insurance,*[46] the California high court extended the reasoning in *Shoemaker* to a

---

39. ORS 656.018(2) (1995) provides:

(2) The rights given to a subject worker ... under this chapter for injuries, diseases, symptom complexes or similar conditions arising out and in the course of employment are in lieu of any remedies they might otherwise have for such injuries ... or similar conditions against the worker's employer under other laws, common law or statute, except to the extent the worker is expressly given the right under this chapter to bring suit against the employer of the worker for an injury ... or similar condition.

40. 23 P.3d 333 (Or. 2001).

41. 801 P.2d 1054 (Cal. 1990).

42. *Id.* at 1065.

43. *Id.* at 1063.

44. *Livitsanos v. Superior Court*, 828 P.2d 1195, 1203 (Cal. 1992).

45. 801 P.2d at 1069.

46. 824 P.2d 680 (Cal. 1992).

judicially-created cause of action, holding that an employee terminated for supporting a co-worker's claim of sexual harassment stated a claim in tort for violation of public policy. Such a claim was not preempted by workers' compensation because the underlying employer conduct was deemed outside of the "compensation bargain".[47]

Sexual Harassment. By a variety of rationales, courts exclude injuries arising out sexual harassment by co-workers from workers' compensation. Colorado takes the view that such assaults are "inherently private" and thus do not "arise out of" the employment relation even though they take place during the workday at the place of employment.[48]

Defamation. In most instances, defamation claims fall outside of workers' compensation on the view that the damage to reputation causes a "proprietary" injury as distinct from a physical or mental injury, or put differently, such claims implicate an employer role distinct from its duty to provide compensation for workplace accidents.[49]

False Imprisonment. There is some authority that false imprisonment by co-workers falls outside of workers' compensation but any claim against the employer for negligence or other responsibility not itself amounting to an intentional tort is compensable only within the system.[50]

F. Challenges

Fraudulent claims bedevil the system, especially claims of "low back" injury and "repetitive stress" injuries.[51] Employer costs declined during the 1990s in part because insurance companies cut premiums to reflect higher investment returns. Since 2000, a poorer stock market performance has led to spikes in premiums, and employer costs are growing faster than cash benefits and payments for medical treatment. A number of states have passed laws to tighten evidentiary requirements and limit compensation

47. The court extended this reasoning to a public policy claim premised on the protection from disability-based discrimination found in Cal. Labor Code § 132a. See *City of Moorpark v. Superior Court of Ventura County*, 959 P.2d 445 (Cal. 1998).

48. For a good discussion, see *Horodyskyj, supra* note 33.

49. See, e.g., *Foley v. Polaroid Corp.*, 413 N.E.2d 711 (Mass. 1980).

50. See, e.g., *Meerbrey v. Marshall Field and Co.*, 564 N.E.2d 1222 (Ill. 1990).

51. See generally Martha T. McCluskey, *The Illusion of Efficiency in Workers' Compensation 'Reform'*, 50 RUTGERS L. REV. 657 (1998); Gary Schwartz, *Waste, Fraud, and Abuse in Workers' Compensation: The Recent California Experience*, 52 MD. L. REV. 983 (1993).

for particular conditions, such as mental stress and cumulative trauma disorders. Private employers, however, are reporting fewer workplace injuries that result in days away from work. This may mean either that workplaces are getting safer, these "reform" measures are discouraging claims, or some combination thereof.[52]

52. See WORKERS' COMPENSATION: BENEFITS, *supra* note 1, at 3–5.

Chapter 8

UNEMPLOYMENT INSURANCE

A. Overview

One of the most significant social reforms to emerge from the nation's experience of widespread unemployment and poverty during the Great Depression is our system of unemployment insurance (UI). Unemployment insurance provides partial, temporary wage replacement to workers who are laid off. The program, financed through a payroll tax on employers, is a major government transfer program. In 2005, UI programs paid out over $31.3 billion to 7.9 million American workers.[1]

The unemployment insurance program was established as part of the Social Security Act of 1935.[2] The initial recommendation by President Franklin Roosevelt's Committee on Economic Security, led by Secretary of Labor Francis Perkins, was to establish a mandatory national insurance system.[3] Political compromise, as well as concerns that such a program would be invalidated under the due process clauses of the Fifth and Fourteenth Amendments of the U.S. Constitution for its interference with liberty of contract, tempered the ambition of early federal legislative proposals. Senator Robert Wagner drafted the bill that would ultimately become the law and pass constitutional muster, a scheme by which the federal government created tax incentives for states to adopt their own UI programs.[4]

Unemployment insurance gives individuals protection against economic insecurity associated with sudden job (and income) loss. Because few American workers have significant savings or income from sources other than wages,[5] UI is an important way to reduce

---

1. DIVISION OF FISCAL AND ACTUARIAL SERVICES, UNITED STATES DEPARTMENT OF LABOR, UNEMPLOYMENT INSURANCE DATA SUMMARY, available at http://www.workforcesecurity.doleta.gov/unemploy/content/data_stats/datasum05/4thqtr/DataSum_2005_4.pdf [hereinafter 2005 UI DATA SUMMARY].

2. 42 U.S.C. §§ 301–1397.

3. COMMITTEE ON ECONOMIC SECURITY, SOCIAL SECURITY ADMINISTRATION, REPORT OF THE COMMITTEE ON ECONOMIC SECURITY

(1935), available at http://www.ssa.gov/history/reports/ces/ces5.html.

4. Steward Machine Co. v. Davis, 301 U.S. 548 (1937) (sustaining the constitutionality of the Social Security Act). See also Arthur Larson & Merrill G. Murray, The Development of Unemployment Insurance in the United States, 8 VAND. L. REV. 181, 187 (1955).

5. Americans are notoriously poor savers: the median 25 to 62 year-old worker has gross financial assets equal

the hardship of sudden wage interruption. Although unemployment compensation only partially replaces wages, it nevertheless reduces the net depletion of personal resources caused by unemployment. UI is also intended to have a stabilizing effect on the economy as a whole. The hardship of job loss and wage loss can extend to the families of workers who are unemployed and in the case of communities that suffer mass layoffs, affect entire communities.[6] Wage replacement also helps workers to maintain spending power, thus stabilizing the economy across cycles of economic prosperity and recession.

Another goal of UI is to help workers find jobs that fully utilize their skills and experience, thus tapping economy-wide labor power as fully as possible. Firm-level experience-rating deters employers from laying off workers in the first place. If a worker does become unemployed, weekly benefits make possible a more rigorous job search. Although there is a dispute over the optimal duration of UI benefits (some worry that too generous a scheme allows laid-off workers to opt for leisure rather than job search), a principal justification for UI benefits is that they allow a worker to hold out longer for a job matched to his skills and training rather than having to take the first job that comes along because of financial pressure.[7] Better job matches upon reemployment should maximize reemployment wages and minimize career interruptions over the longer term. UI also makes it easier for at least short-term laid-off workers to remain in the same geographical area in the event that rehiring is possible upon economic recovery. This reduces the personal and community disruption associated with economic downturns.

Despite some union provision of limited unemployment benefits to their members, private insurers have never provided unemployment insurance on a widespread basis in the United States. One explanation for this is that it is difficult for insurers to get

to less than three weeks' income. Eric Engen & Jonathan Gruber, *Unemployment Insurance and Precautionary Savings*, 47 J. MONETARY ECON. 545 (2001). Furthermore, a significant portion of the population is unable to borrow against the promise of future labor income. Stephen P. Zeldes, *Consumption and Liquidity Constraints: An Empirical Investigation*, 97 J. POL. ECON. 305 (1989).

6. See, e.g., KAN. STAT. ANN. § 44–702 (2007) (declaring that "[e]conomic insecurity, due to unemployment, is a seri-

ous menace to health, morals, and the welfare of the people"); MO. REV. STAT. § 288.020 (same); N.M. STAT. § 51–1–3 (same).

7. Specific provisions of Federal Unemployment Tax Act are consistent with this rationale. *See, e.g.*, 26 U.S.C. § 3304(a)(5)(B) (maintaining UI eligibility for workers who decline jobs where the "wages, hours, or other conditions of the work offered are substantially less favorable ... than those prevailing for similar work in the locality").

accurate information about how "risky" it is to insure a particular worker against job loss. Ordinarily, insurers charge a higher premium for people who are more likely to experience a hazard then they do for others. However, workers' employment habits (and risks) may be more variable over their life cycle than other kinds of risks that are ordinarily insured, making it difficult for insurers to predict the future. In this kind of situation, the safe strategy for the insurer is to charge everyone a flat premium matched to some estimation of average risk. But under this kind of price structure, people who pose little risk of suffering a loss will choose not to participate, and the insurer will have to raise the price for those who remain. This process can repeat itself until the price is so high that no one will be willing to pay and the market collapses. A similar informational problem that impedes private provision of wage-loss insurance is the unpredictable nature of economic recessions. Large economic shifts may lead to mass layoffs that could create a crisis of insolvency in a private insurance fund. Once again, private insurers might respond to this by charging very high premiums, but if workers cannot afford to (or their employers will not) pay such high prices, the product will not survive. Another problem for private insurers is that it may be especially difficult to monitor what economists call "moral hazard," by which the very availability of insurance encourages risk-taking behavior. Although some workers may be eager to get back to work, others may find that they prefer collecting unemployment benefits to working. Similarly, some employers may lay off employees in response to unpredictable economic shocks, while others may take advantage of the availability of UI and lay off employees simply to improve profits or share price. There are a variety of techniques that insurers can use to reduce moral hazard (and we shall see that state UI programs use a number of these techniques), but the cost of these measures may make unemployment insurance a less profitable undertaking than private insurers generally are willing to assume.

In sum, private markets have not historically provided unemployment insurance because various informational failures make it difficult for private actors to do so profitably. However, in light of the kinds of broader social concerns we have identified—protecting workers, families, and communities against the hardships associated with layoffs and sudden income loss, stabilizing consumer spending, and optimizing job matches and the economy-wide use of labor power—the state has an interest in intervening in private markets to provide for this kind of insurance.

B.   Basic Mechanics of UI Programs

1.   *Finance*

Unemployment insurance programs are based on a federal-state partnership founded on broad federal guidelines governing state-administered programs. Federal law does not require any state to establish a UI program. However, it creates strong tax incentives for doing so.

The Federal Unemployment Tax Act (FUTA) imposes a tax on every employer regardless of whether the state in which it operates has UI program.[8] As of 2008, the amount is 6% of the first $7000 in wages paid per year to each individual employed.[9] If a state creates a UI program that meets federal approval, employers will receive a credit of up to 90% of the federal tax for their contributions under the state UI law. This can effectively reduce the federal portion of the tax to as little as 0.6% of taxable wages.[10] This does not mean that employers in a state with an approved UI program will pay only 0.6% in payroll taxes to finance it. The state will impose its own payroll tax, and indeed most states have set their taxable wage base higher than the $7,000 federal minimum.[11] However, the additional money will go into a state fund to finance unemployment benefits for the workers of the employers taxed. For these reasons, there are strong incentives for states to create a federally approved UI program. By 1937, within two years of FUTA's enactment, every state in the union as well as Hawaii, Alaska and the District of Columbia, had passed federally approved legislation.[12]

State programs must meet several requirements before they will be certified by the federal government.[13] For example, revenue from each state's payroll tax must be deposited in an interest-

---

8. 26 U.S.C. § 3301 ("It is hereby imposed on every employer . . . for each calendar year an excise tax, with respect to having individuals in his employ, equal to [6.2% until the end of 2007 and 6.0% thereafter] of the total wages . . . paid by him during the calendar year with respect to employment. . . ."). Originally, the tax was 1% of the total wages of each worker.

9. 26 U.S.C. §§ 3306(b)(1), 3301 (defining "wages" as including only the first $7,000 in cash remuneration paid to an individual for their employment in a calendar year). The taxable wage base has been periodically raised by Congress

as well, although the most recent increase was in 1983.

10. 26 U.S.C. § 3302.

11. Forty-three states have a taxable wage base higher than $7,000. The state average in 2006 was $11,389. DEPARTMENT OF LABOR, UNEMPLOYMENT INSURANCE DATA SUMMARY, FIRST QUARTER 2007, *available at* http://www.workforcesecurity. doleta.gov/unemploy/content/data_stats/ datasum07/1stqtr/DataSum_2007_1.pdf.

12. Larson & Murray, *supra* note 4, at 195.

13. 26 U.S.C. § 3303.

bearing account maintained by the federal treasury and may be withdrawn by states only for the payment of benefits.[14] Additionally, the state portion of the payroll tax must be experience-rated, meaning that employers are taxed at a higher rate if they lay off more workers.[15] In addition, the Social Security Act stipulates that a state UI program will not be certified unless the state establishes a public employment office or other agency to administer UI benefits and creates procedures for merit-based selection of claims administrators, record-keeping and reporting, and a fair hearing for claimants who are denied benefits.[16] Finally, there are a variety of coverage and eligibility requirements.[17] In the remainder of Part B, we will discuss experience rating, administrative procedures, and coverage. Then, in Part C, we will turn to a detailed treatment of eligibility, which forms the basis for most litigation in the area of unemployment insurance.

2. *Experience Rating*

Experience rating is a method of taxation that charges each employer an amount related to the costs it imposes on the insurance pool.[18] Presumably, when these costs are at least partially internalized, employers will take them into account when making decisions about high-risk investment or production options that could lead to layoffs. Thus, for example, an experience-rating system reduces the incentive that would otherwise exist for firms to engage in strategic layoff cycles by repeatedly hiring workers for the minimum period necessary to achieve eligibility, and then laying them off in the expectation that UI benefits will subsidize their wages during the layoff period.[19] Under an experience-rating

---

14. *Id.* § 3304(a)(3)-(4).

15. Cf. *id.* § 3303(a)(1) (requiring state laws to only allow for a "reduced rate of contributions" on "the basis of [an employer's] experience with respect to unemployment or other factors bearing a direct relation to unemployment risk during not less than the 3 consecutive years immediately preceding the computation date").

16. 42 U.S.C § 503(a).

17. See parts B(4) & C *infra*.

18. See generally EMPLOYMENT AND TRAINING ADMINISTRATION, U.S. DEPARTMENT OF LABOR, COMPARISON OF STATE UNEMPLOYMENT LAWS: FINANCING (2006), http://www.workforcesecurity.doleta.gov/

unemploy/uilawcompar/2006/financing.pdf [hereinafter COMPARISON: FINANCING].

19. A problem recently addressed by Congress is so-called "SUTA dumping," a practice by which a business entity with a history of significant layoffs avoids liability under the state unemployment tax act (SUTA) by setting up a shell corporation with no record of layoffs and transferring all employees to that new entity in order to avoid an experience-based tax increase. The SUTA Dumping Prevention Act of 2004, Pub. L. No. 108–295, 118 Stat. 1090 (codified as amended at 42 U.S.C. §§ 503, 653), required that by 2006 all states must have in place anti-SUTA dumping legislation, including meaningful civil and criminal penalties for in-

system, such layoffs would increase the firm's rate of taxation, which would likely offset any wage savings.

The use of experience rating has been controversial since the inception of the program. Among nations with UI systems, only the United States uses an experience-rated tax to finance benefits.[20] Some initially objected to experience rating based on the worry that employers motivated to reduce costs would try to limit benefits by aggressively contesting employees' unemployment insurance claims, leading to administrative burdens on the system and the potential inhibition of meritorious claims.[21]

States use a number of different techniques for experience rating.[22] About two-thirds of states use a "reserve-ratio" formula. Under this method, employer contributions are put into a pool or "reserve" account to which payments are credited and against which benefits collected by former employees are charged. As the size of the account increases, the tax decreases according to a schedule. Most states maintain several schedules, however, so rates will depend not only on the size of the employer's account, but also on the state's total reserves, with rates decreasing as total state reserves increase.

Other less commonly used experience-rating formulas include the "benefit-ratio formula," the "benefit-wage-ratio formula," and the "payroll variation plan." Under the benefit-ratio formula, the tax rate depends exclusively on benefit payments, without taking contributions into account. Under the benefit-wage-ratio formula, the number of employees separated from each employer is multiplied by the total wages earned in the base period to determine the employer's "experience factor." The experience factor is then used in conjunction with the average state-wide duration of benefits to determine the employer's tax rate. Finally, in the payroll-variation

fractions. In California, for example, employers found guilty of SUTA dumping will face several punitive measures, including the assignment of higher unemployment insurance taxes, restrictions on the transfer of a business, and a fine against the individuals responsible for the fraudulent activity. ACT OF SEPTEMBER 28, 2004, ch. 827, 2004 Cal. Legis. Serv. 4810.

20. PEDER J. PEDERSEN & NIEIS WESTERGARD–NIELSEN, UNEMPLOYMENT: A REVIEW OF THE EVIDENCE FROM PANEL DATA, OECD ECONOMIC STUDIES NO. 20 85 (2003), available at http://www.oecd.org/dataoecd/19/50/33948388.pdf.

21. *See* ADVISORY COUNCIL ON UNEMPLOYMENT COMPENSATION, UNEMPLOYMENT INSURANCE IN THE UNITED STATES: BENEFITS, FINANCING, AND COVERAGE 73–74 (1995) (discussing Congressional debates in the 1960s on the proposed elimination of experience rating because of this concern); Joseph M. Becker, *Twenty-Five Years of Unemployment Insurance: An Experiment in Competitive Collectivism*, 75 POL. SCI. Q. 493 (1960).

22. See generally WAYNE VROMAN, U.S. DEPARTMENT OF LABOR, EXPERIENCE RATING IN UNEMPLOYMENT INSURANCE: SOME CURRENT ISSUES 6–12 (1989) (explaining how experience rating works).

plan, used only in Alaska, an employer's tax rate is based on variations in payroll, on the theory that decreasing payrolls reflect incidence of unemployment.

No method in use produces perfect experience rating. Experience rating can be described as "perfect" only when an employer is taxed exactly one dollar for every dollar of costs it imposes on the system, and "imperfect", or "partial," when the employer is taxed either more or less than one dollar for every dollar of actual costs imposed. Because all states set minimum and maximum tax rates, "low risk" firms and industries (like transportation) tend to cross-subsidize "high risk" firms and industries (like construction). State tax rates vary significantly, but minimum rates in 2005 ranged from 0% in several states to a high of 2.9% in Arizona.[23] Maximum rates ranged from 5.4% (the federally-mandated minimum) to 15.4% in Massachusetts.[24]

3. *Procedure*

When an employee is terminated or quits, she must file a claim with a public employment office or the local federal offices (if located in a territory or District of Columbia) to receive UI benefits. The claimant must supply information about her employment history and reason for termination. The employer will also be asked to submit a form stating the reasons for termination of employment. A claims examiner will assess the employee's eligibility, ability and availability for work, and reason for termination to decide whether the claimant may receive benefits.

States use different methods to determine the amount of benefits an eligible individual will receive.[25] The predominant method used for calculation, the "High–Quarter Method," takes the quarter during the previous year in which the worker had the highest earnings and divides it by thirteen (the number of weeks in a calendar quarter).[26] This amount is considered representative of a week's pay during full-time employment.[27] The benefit amount the unemployed worker receives will then depend on what percentage of wages the state chooses to replace.[28] On average, states replace

23. Comparison: Financing, *supra* note 18.

24. *Id.*

25. See Employment and Training Administration, U.S. Department of Labor, Comparison of State Unemployment Insurance Laws: Monetary Entitlement 3–9—3–12 tbl. 3–5 (2007) (listing a full account of the states' methods of calculating weekly benefits), available at http://ows.doleta.gov/unemploy/uilawcompar/2007/monetary.pdf.

26. *Id.*

27. *Id.*

28. *Id.*

50% of a worker's lost wages, up to a limit. The maximum limit is typically set at the state's overall average weekly wage. For example, suppose a worker's average weekly earnings in her highest quarter of the calendar year prior to layoff were $800 and the state replaces wages at 50% of high-quarter earnings. The worker will receive $400 per week in benefits unless it exceeds the maximum. In this state, if the maximum is determined by the state's average weekly wages and that average is $350, the hypothetical claimant's benefits will be capped at $350 per week. Because of the operation of the maximum, lower earning workers will tend to have a higher proportion of their wages replaced than higher earning workers. All states also impose a minimum benefit amount.

Another variable among state programs is the duration of benefits. First, most states require a "waiting period" before any benefits will be distributed, usually one week.[29] Fourteen states have no waiting period at all.[30] A worker will then receive unemployment benefits for some maximum period, usually twenty-six weeks.[31] While a few states established a uniform duration of twenty-six weeks for all persons receiving benefits, most states make individual determinations of benefit duration.[32] In variable-duration states, the duration of benefits is based on a formula that takes into account the worker's earnings or number of weeks worked during the year prior to layoff.[33] During periods of high unemployment, Congress has authorized periods of extended benefits. This allows workers who have exhausted conventional UI benefits to continue to receive benefits for up to 13 additional weeks.[34]

In the event a claim is denied, the claimant can appeal the decision within the agency.[35] The claimant has between five and thirty days from the date of denial of benefits, depending on state law, to file an appeal.[36] Most states provide a second appeals stage if

29. *Id.* at 3–14—3–15 tbl. 3–7.

30. *Id.* at 3–16 tbl. 3–8. Alabama, Connecticut, Delaware, Georgia, Iowa, Kentucky, Maryland, Michigan, Nevada, New Hampshire, New Jersey, Vermont, Wisconsin, and Wyoming have no waiting period.

31. *Id.* at 21.

32. *Id.*

33. *Id.* at 21–24. Table 3–12 shows state by state duration calculation.

34. See FEDERAL-STATE EXTENDED UN-EMPLOYMENT COMPENSATION ACT OF 1970, Pub. L. No. 91–373, 84 Stat. 695 (1970). The Act has been amended several times since its passage.

35. Cf. 42 U.S.C. § 503(a)(3) (requiring unemployment insurance programs to provide "opportunity for a fair hearing, before an impartial tribunal, for all individuals whose claims for unemployment compensation are denied").

36. See EMPLOYMENT AND TRAINING ADMINISTRATION, U.S. DEPARTMENT OF LABOR, COMPARISON OF STATE UNEMPLOYMENT INSURANCE LAWS: APPEALS 1–4 (2007), available at http://www.workforcesecurity.doleta.gov/unemploy/uilawcompar/2007/

a claimant is dissatisfied with the initial appeal ruling.[37] In approximately half of these states, the appeal goes before a final, administrative appeal board.[38]

All states permit an adversely affected party the right to judicial review following the administrative appeal process.[39] In certain states, courts exercise *de novo* review of the cases.[40] In most cases, however, courts review the case to determine whether, based on the evidence and law, the appeal board was justified in making its ruling.[41] From this point, decisions are appealed within the state judicial system as any other appeal would be.

4.   Coverage

Nearly 90 percent of American workers are covered by UI.[42] As mentioned, FUTA requires every employer to pay a payroll tax on the wages of those whom it employs. Coverage is limited in two principal ways. First, some entities that hire workers fall outside the definition of "employer". FUTA defines "employer" as an entity that has at least one employee for at least one day in each of 20 weeks during the year, and pays wages of at least $1500 in any calendar quarter of the year.[43] FUTA has special rules for defining "employer" in certain areas of commerce. For example, one who has paid $1000 in cash wages for household domestic services during any quarter in the current or previous year falls within the definition of "employer".[44] On the other side of the spectrum, a hiring entity does not meet the definition of employer with respect to agricultural labor until it has paid $20,000 in wages during a

appeals.pdf [hereinafter COMPARISON: APPEALS].

37. See *id.* Only four jurisdictions lack a second stage of appeals: the District of Columbia, Hawaii, Minnesota, and Nebraska. In these states, those seeking review of an appeal must go directly to the appropriate judicial body.

38. E.g., CAL. UNEMP. INS. § 1224; DEL. CODE. ANN. tit. 19, § 3318(b); N.M. STAT. § 51–1–8(H). See also COMPARISON: APPEALS, *supra* note 36, at 7–2.

39. COMPARISON: APPEALS, *supra* note 36, at 7–4.

40. E.g., TEX. LAB. CODE ANN. § 212.202 (2007); *General Motors Corp. v. California Unemployment Ins. Appeals Bd.*, 61 Cal. Rptr. 483, 486 (App.

1967) (finding that California courts will review unemployment board decisions de novo); *Robinson v. Commissioner of Labor*, 675 N.W.2d 683, 685 (Neb. 2004) (conducting *de novo* review of unemployment benefit provision).

41. E.g., WASH. REV. CODE § 34.05.570(3) (courts in Washington conduct "error of law" review); *Robinson v. Unemployment Sec. Bd. of Review*, 434 A.2d 293, 295 (Conn. 1980) (finding that courts in Connecticut do not try appeals de novo).

42. 86.2 percent of workers were covered in 2005. Calculations are based on data available in the 2005 UI DATA SUMMARY, *supra*, note 1.

43. 26 U.S.C. § 3306(a)(1).

44. *Id.* § 3306(a)(3).

calendar year.[45] Opponents argue that this exception leaves farm workers inadequately protected.[46] A handful of states provide more generous coverage to farm workers.[47]

Another limitation on coverage is the definitions of "employment" and "employee." FUTA exempts from taxation wages connected with certain types of employment (e.g., service performed in the employ of certain religious, charitable, or educational organizations).[48] However, it specifically requires that some of these federally tax-exempted areas of employment—labor performed for state and local governments, nonprofit organizations, and Indian tribes—*must* be covered under state law.[49] Coverage is extended to federal employment under two programs: Unemployment Compensation for Federal Civilian Employees (UCFE) and Unemployment Compensation for Ex–Service members (UCX). Railway workers, as well, are covered by a special program administered by the Railway Retirement Board.

FUTA uses the common-law definition of employee, although states may adopt a more generous test for coverage.[50] More than half the states have adopted some variation on the so-called "ABC" test, developed originally for Wisconsin's 1935 unemployment insurance law. Under the ABC test, service is considered employment, and the worker an employee, unless all three of the following criteria are met: (A) the worker is free from control or direction in the performance of the work under the contract of service and in fact; (B) the service is performed either outside the usual course of the business for which it is performed or is performed outside of all places of business of the enterprise for which it is performed; and (C) the individual is customarily engaged in an independent trade, occupation, profession, or business.[51] Requiring all three of these

---

45. *Id.* § 3306(a)(2)(A)-(B).

46. See Laurence E. Norton II & Marc Linder, *Down and Out in Weslaco, Texas and Washington, D.C.: Race-Based Discrimination Against Farm Workers Under Federal Unemployment Insurance*, 29 U. MICH. J.L. REFORM 177, 180–81 (1996).

47. California, D.C., Florida, Minnesota, New York, Rhode Island, and Texas. *See generally* EMPLOYMENT AND TRAINING ADMINISTRATION, U.S. DEPARTMENT OF LABOR, COMPARISON OF STATE UNEMPLOYMENT LAWS: COVERAGE 1–4 tbls. 1–3 (2006), available at http://www.workforcesecurity.doleta.gov/unemploy/uilaw

compar/2006/coverage.pdf   [hereinafter COMPARISON: COVERAGE].

48. 26 U.S.C. § 3306(c)(8).

49. 26 U.S.C. § 3304(a)(6)(A).

50. 26 U.S.C. § 3306(i).

51. See, e.g., *Fleece on Earth v. Department of Employment & Training*, 923 A.2d 594, 597 (Vt. 2007) (referring to the "ABC test" in the Vermont statutes); *Express Bus, Inc. v. Employment Sec. Comm'n*, 157 P.3d 1180, 1182 (Okla. 2007) (referring to an Oklahoma statute as the "ABC test," which "presumes the existence of an employer-employee relationship between the parties unless ... specific exemptions are shown").

elements of independence to be satisfied before a worker will be considered an independent contractor means that in practice, the ABC formulation produces broader coverage than the common-law test, which uses a "totality of the circumstances" assessment of employer control.[52]

C. Eligibility

Despite broad coverage provisions under FUTA and state laws, only about one-third of unemployed workers actually receive benefits.[53] The reason for this is that even if a worker is covered, he or she may not be eligible for benefits.

Although FUTA imposes very few eligibility limitations, state programs have fairly elaborate eligibility rules, all sharing several basic characteristics.[54] To receive benefits a worker must have established a sufficient attachment to the workforce prior to unemployment, called "monetary" eligibility.[55] In addition, the worker must satisfy the requirements of "nonmonetary" eligibility: The worker must be unemployed involuntarily for reasons that are not deemed disqualifying (such as misconduct),[56] and in most states must continue actively searching for work while receiving benefits.[57]

Recipiency, i.e., the extent to which unemployed workers receive UI benefits, has declined by approximately forty percent since the 1950s.[58] One possible explanation for this is that during the 1980s, state governments tightened eligibility standards to improve the solvency of their UI programs.[59] However, increased wages

52. See *Fleece on Earth*, 923 A.2d at 598 ("This Court has consistently held that the statutory scheme at issue here is broader than the common law master-servant relation, and it draws into its sweep workers who might be independent contractors under the common law.").

53. In 2005, the recipiency rate was 36%. See 2005 UI DATA SUMMARY, *supra* note 1.

54. FUTA regulates eligibility mainly by *prohibiting* certain bases for denial of eligibility, e.g., on the basis of pregnancy, or if the worker refuses to accept a job that comes available due to a labor dispute, etc. See U.S.C. § 3304(5)–(14).

55. See, e.g., LA. REV. STAT. ANN. § 23:1600(5); ME. REV. STAT. ANN. tit. 26, § 1192(5); OR. REV. STAT. § 657.150(2)(a).

56. See, e.g., FLA. STAT. § 443.101(1)(a); NEV. REV. STAT. § 612.385; WASH. REV. CODE § 50.20.060.

57. See, e.g., ALA. CODE § 25–4–77(a)(5); CAL. UNEMP. INS. CODE § 1253; MISS. CODE. ANN. § 75–5–511(a)(ii); 43 PA. CONS. STAT. § 813.

58. Laurie J. Bassi & Daniel P. McMurrer, *Coverage and Recipiency: Trends and Effects, in* UNEMPLOYMENT INSURANCE IN THE UNITED STATES: ANALYSIS OF POLICY ISSUES 51, 64 (Christopher J. O'Leary & Stephen A. Wandner eds., 1997) (citing data on the degree of decline in recipiency).

59. See, e.g., ADVISORY COUNCIL ON UNEMPLOYMENT COMPENSATION, DEFINING FEDERAL AND STATE ROLES IN UNEMPLOYMENT INSURANCE 43, 48–51 (1996). For a discussion of the trust fund insolvency crisis of

during this period may have offset increased earning requirements, netting a trivial effect on recipiency.[60] Another potential explanation for declining recipiency is the growing failure on the part of unemployed (even eligible) workers to apply for benefits. In recent years, only about half of workers who become unemployed have applied for benefits.[61] The drop in applications may be attributable to the decline in unions, which raise members' awareness of their entitlement to benefits and help with applications;[62] or the rise in two-earner families, which has spurred a corresponding decline in the need or tendency among some workers to apply for UI benefits upon becoming unemployed.[63] There has also been a shift in economic demand, from stable manufacturing industries that employ workers in traditional, stable jobs with strong workforce attachment, to less stable service-oriented industries that employ more part-time, temporary and short-term workers.[64] In ways that will become apparent in the discussion below, workers in intermittent or part-time employment are less likely to be able to meet UI eligibility requirements. Finally, the changing demographics of the workforce have influenced recipiency.[65] The influx of women and

the 1980s, see WAYNE VROMAN, UNEMPLOYMENT INSURANCE AND TRUST FUND ADEQUACY IN THE 1990s 1–7 (1990).

60. See Rebecca M. Blank & David E. Card, *Recent Trends in Insured and Uninsured Unemployment: Is There an Explanation?*, 106 Q. J. ECON. 1157, 1188–89 (1991) (finding increased wages offset increased earnings requirements between 1977 and 1987); WAYNE VROMAN, U.S. DEPARTMENT OF LABOR, UNEMPLOYMENT INSURANCE, WELFARE, AND FEDERAL-STATE FISCAL INTERRELATIONS (1996) (finding no relationship between changes in recipiency and state-level restrictions on monetary eligibility standards in either 1967–1980, or 1981–1994). *See also* Bassi & McMurrer, *supra* note 58, at 69–70 (reviewing empirical controversies on relationship between tightened state eligibility standards and UI recipiency in the 1980s).

61. See Wayne Vroman, *An Introduction to Unemployment and Unemployment Insurance*, THE URBAN INSTITUTE: ASSESSING THE NEW FEDERALISM, Oct. 2005, at 4 (in 2004, only 17.8 million of 32.4 million newly unemployed people filed for benefits); Stephen A. Wandner & Andrew Stettner, *Why are Many Jobless Workers Not Applying for Benefits?*, MONTHLY LAB. REV. (June 2000), p. 21

(finding based on two surveys in the early 1990s that more than half of the unemployed do not file for benefits—either because they believe they are ineligible, or because they are optimistic about finding a job).

62. Blank & Card, *supra* note 60, argue that most of the decline is explained by a shift in the unemployed population from states with high, to states with low, "takeup rates"—rates of application for benefits by eligible unemployed workers. The most significant factor affecting state take-up rates, in turn, is the state's rate of unionization.

63. Daniel P. McMurrer & Amy B. Chasanov, *Trends in Unemployment Insurance Benefits*, MONTHLY LAB. REV. (Sept. 1995), p. 35 (noting the plausibility of this explanation, although empirical research has not addressed the issue).

64. See GARY BURTLESS WITH DAVID SAKS, THE DECLINE IN INSURED UNEMPLOYMENT DURING THE 1980s 17 (1984) (changed composition of the workforce explained much of the drop in recipiency before 1980).

65. For example, among adults (25 and older), unemployed part-time workers are about half as likely (18.8 per-

younger workers into the workforce during the 1960s and 1970s meant that the traditional recipients of UI, men of prime working age with relatively stable jobs, became a smaller percentage of the unemployed.[66]

The remainder of this section contains a general overview of the two main kinds of eligibility, monetary and nonmonetary, as well as a discussion of selected areas of interest or controversy.

1. Monetary Eligibility

Monetary eligibility rules determine which workers have sufficient workforce attachment to qualify for benefits. In part, the attachment criterion seeks to exclude routine consumption of unemployment benefits as a supplement to employment earnings.[67] UI is intended, as with private insurance, as protection against an unexpected, atypical event—in this case, job loss. States use earnings or hours (or some combination of the two) as a means of measuring attachment. Workers who tend to be excluded on monetary eligibility grounds are new entrants to the workforce, people returning to the workforce after an extended absence, or workers who work part-time or intermittently or who have low aggregate earnings. The first two exclusions—new entrants and returners—are relatively uncontroversial. The exclusion of employees with low or irregular wages or hours, however, has drawn criticism that we will discuss later.

Most states use some minimum threshold of earnings or hours worked during a "base period" as a surrogate for attachment. The base period is usually the first four of the five most recent quarters preceding application for benefits. Monetary requirements in most states are modest, with the median (in 2006) being $1,950 in earnings during the base period.[68] A minimum wage worker who worked 40 hours per week would need to work about 9.5 weeks in a year under a base period earnings requirement of $1,950. Only

cent) as unemployed workers as a whole (36.6 percent) to receive UI benefits, and the gap is even greater for younger workers. WAYNE VROMAN, U.S. DEPARTMENT OF LABOR, LABOR MARKET CHANGES AND UNEMPLOYMENT INSURANCE BENEFIT AVAILABILITY 36 tbl. 3 (1998) (1996 figures).

66. See Burtless, *supra* note 64 at 99.

67. See Nicholas Barr, *Economic Theory and the Welfare State: A Survey and Interpretation*, 30 J. ECON. LITERATURE 741, 768 (1992).

68. Contrast Hawaii, which requires only $130 in earnings during the base period in order to qualify for the minimum weekly benefit with Washington, which requires $3,502. See EMPLOYMENT AND TRAINING ADMINISTRATION, U.S. DEPARTMENT OF LABOR, COMPARISON OF STATE UNEMPLOYMENT LAWS: MONETARY ENTITLEMENT (2006) 3-4-3-6 tbl. 3.3, available at http://www.workforcesecurity.doleta.gov/unemploy/uilawcompar/2006/monetary.pdf [hereinafter COMPARISON: MONETARY ENTITLEMENT].

twelve states would require a minimum wage worker to work more than 13 weeks in the year to be eligible.[69]

The method for determining the base period significantly influences the eligibility of workers with irregular wages or hours. The insertion of a one quarter "lag period"—the fifth quarter—historically gave state eligibility officers time to collect the relevant earnings or hours data from employers and tabulate eligibility.[70] The insertion of the lag, though, as well as the accident of the timing of application, may arbitrarily render some workers ineligible. Exclusion of fifth-quarter earnings is not likely to affect eligibility of full-time workers with long histories of employment. For workers with irregular schedules, however, the insertion of the lag period might produce a situation in which a worker with low earnings in the first of five quarters is excluded, while another worker with identical total earnings over the five quarters but whose fifth quarter was low will be eligible.

Many states have automated their reporting and processing procedures in the past twenty years, making the insertion of a lag period unnecessary. Concern about arbitrary exclusion of workers with irregular attachment to the workforce has led a number of states in recent years to adopt more lenient criteria through the use of an "alternative base period" (ABP).[71] If an applicant is deemed ineligible using the traditional base period, the ABP typically allows the worker to use the last four completed quarters instead.

The proxy a state selects to estimate workforce attachment also affects recipiency. Workers with few earnings or hours are less likely to be eligible than workers with high earnings or hours. In theory, this is consistent with the aim of the UI system to include only workers with substantial workforce attachment. Some have argued for more generous attachment thresholds.[72] But even accepting existing thresholds, the use of earnings as a proxy for attachment—the criterion used by most states—can lead to exclusions that are difficult to defend. A minimum-wage worker qualifies for

---

69. *Id.*

70. See WAYNE VROMAN, U.S. DEPARTMENT OF LABOR, THE ALTERNATIVE BASE PERIOD IN UNEMPLOYMENT INSURANCE: FINAL REPORT 4 (1995) (describing the history of the "first four" base period method).

71. In 1995, at least seven states had adopted an ABP (Maine, Massachusetts, New York, Ohio, Rhode Island, Vermont, and Washington). *See* VROMAN, *supra* note 52, at 4. By 2006, ten more had

done so (Connecticut, Georgia, Hawaii, Michigan, New Hampshire, New Jersey, New Mexico, North Carolina, Oklahoma, Virginia, and Wisconsin). COMPARISON: MONETARY ENTITLEMENT, *supra* note 68, 3–2–3–3 tbl. 3.2.

72. See, e.g., Deborah Maranville, *Changing Economy Changing Lives: Unemployment Insurance and the Contingent Workplace*, 4 BOST. PUB. INT'L L.J. 291, 303–04 (1995) (advocating reduction of attachment thresholds).

benefits in all states so long as he works full-time and full-year. Similarly, a half-time (20–hour per week) worker qualifies for benefits in all states so long as he works for the full year at, say, $8.00 an hour (which exceeds the minimum wage). But a half-time worker who earns the minimum wage will be disqualified in most states.[73] If the purpose of the UI program is to award benefits based on attachment to the workforce, eligibility should be linked directly to hours worked, rather than earnings, or at least offer a choice between the two.

2. Nonmonetary Eligibility

The other major criterion of eligibility turns on the worker's reason for separation from employment. Workers who voluntarily leave a job without "good cause" or who are discharged for "misconduct" are disqualified.[74] Workers must also be able, available, and actively seeking work. These limits on benefits purport to reduce workers' incentive to cause, or fail to avoid, unemployment, otherwise known as "moral hazard."

a. Voluntary Quits and "Good Cause"

Workers who voluntarily leave their employment without good cause are typically disqualified from receiving benefits for the duration of their unemployment spell, and once re-employed must work some period of time to regain eligibility.[75]

UI eligibility focuses on the employee (did the employee have good cause to leave the employer?). Good cause is generally defined as a reason "related to" or "attributable to" work. Courts have

---

73. A 1994 study showed that someone working two days per week year-round (approximately 800 hours), earning $8.00 per hour, would qualify for benefits in all but 2 states. The same worker, if earning only the minimum wage (then $4.25 per hour), would fail to qualify in 29 states. ADVISORY COUNCIL ON UNEMPLOYMENT COMP., UNEMPLOYMENT INSURANCE IN THE UNITED STATES: BENEFITS, FINANCING, & COVERAGE 93 (1995) [hereinafter ACUC SECOND ANNUAL REPORT].

74. See, e.g., ARIZ. REV. STAT. ANN. § 23–775(1) (2007); CAL. UNEMP. INS. CODE § 1256 (2007); FLA. STAT. § 443.101(1)(a) (2007); NEV. REV. STAT. § 612.385 (2007); WASH. REV. CODE § 50.20.060 (2007).

75. See, e.g., ARIZ. REV. STAT. ANN. § 23–775(1) (requiring an individual who voluntarily terminated without cause to "earn[] wages in an amount equivalent to five times the individual's weekly benefit amount"); DEL. CODE ANN. tit. 19, § 3314(1) (disqualifying individuals who leave voluntarily without good cause until the individual has worked four subsequent weeks and earned more than four times her weekly benefit amount); 820 ILL. COMP. STAT. 405/601(A) (requiring four calendar weeks of employment at earnings greater than or equal to the currently weekly benefit amount before restoring an individual's eligibility).

found "good cause" for a quit to be hazardous working conditions, a transfer to unsuitable work, or the employer's unilateral decision to change working conditions such as wages, hours, etc.[76] Most states also recognize a limited range of additional reasons, such as sexual harassment, compulsory retirement, leaving to accept other work (where the new job unexpectedly falls through), illness, moving to follow a spouse, and joining the armed forces.[77]

b. Misconduct

A worker may be disqualified from benefits if fired for "misconduct".[78] Disqualification usually lasts for the duration of unemployment, although in some states it is a fixed number of weeks (the idea being that a worker should be disqualified only for the period of time that it would take to find new employment, and that unemployment spells longer than this are not fully the fault of the worker).[79] In some states, the period of disqualification varies according to the severity of the misconduct.[80]

76. See, e.g., *Banks v. Elledge*, 535 So.2d 808 (La. App. 1988) (finding new work schedule imposed by employer as "good cause" for employee to terminate employment); *In re Perkins*, 681 N.Y.S.2d 383 (N.Y. App. Div. 1998) (finding that voluntary termination resulting from threats to personal safety supported entitlement to unemployment benefits); *Isabelle v. Department of Employment & Training*, 554 A.2d 660 (Vt. 1988) (finding substantial reduction in hours and loss of benefits as "good cause").

77. See, e.g. GA. CODE ANN. § 34–8–194 (2007) (providing that leaving employment to accompany a spouse receiving a military reassignment suffices as a good cause); HAW. REV. STAT. § 383–30(1) (2007) (excusing unemployment due to labor dispute that employee was not involved in); MASS. GEN. LAWS ch. 151A, § 25(e) (2007) (prohibiting disqualification where employee voluntarily switched in good faith to another job, but new employer could not fulfill employment obligation). *See generally* EMPLOYMENT AND TRAINING ADMINISTRATION, U.S. DEPARTMENT OF LABOR, COMPARISON OF STATE UNEMPLOYMENT LAWS: NONMONETARY ELIGIBILITY (2006) 5–1–5–2 tbl. 5–2, available at http://www.workforcesecurity.

doleta.gov/unemploy/uilawcompar/2006/nonmonetary.pdf [hereinafter COMPARISON: NONMONETARY ELIGIBILITY].

78. See, e.g., Mo. REV. STAT. § 288.040 (2007); N.H. REV. STAT. ANN. § 282–A:35 (2007) ("An unemployed individual who has been discharged for arson, sabotage, felony, assault which causes bodily injury, criminal threatening, or dishonesty connected with his or her work, shall suffer the loss of all wage credits earned prior to the date of such dismissal."); N.C. GEN. STAT. § 96–14(2) (2007); 43 PA. CONS. STAT. § 802(e) (2007).

79. See generally COMPARISON: NONMONETARY ELIGIBILITY, *supra* note 77, at 5–9–5–15.

80. See, e.g., ALA. CODE § 25–4–78 (3) (2007) (providing longer disqualification period for discharges based on criminal activity, sabotage, or the use of illegal drugs); FLA. STAT. § 443.101 (2007) (providing discretion to administrative body in determining length of disqualification period based on seriousness of misconduct); S.C. CODE ANN. § 41–35–120 (requiring commission to determine length of ineligibility based on "seriousness of cause of discharge").

145

Misconduct must generally be "willful" (or result from persistent negligence) to disqualify a claimant from benefits. Definition of willfulness varies by state. Some states have statutory definitions, whereas others rely on case law.[81] Inability to perform the requirements of the job, unless involving extreme carelessness or repeated negligence, generally does not disqualify. For this reason, conduct that might justify a termination under anti-discrimination or wrongful termination law would not necessarily disqualify a terminated employee from receiving UI benefits. Although each state follows its own precedent, the 1941 opinion of the Wisconsin Supreme Court in *Boynton Cab v. Neubeck* has been influential. The court stated as follows:

> [T]he intended meaning of the term "misconduct" ... is limited to conduct evidencing such wilful or wanton disregard of an employer's interests as is found in deliberate violations or disregard of standards of behavior which the employer has the right to expect of his employee, or in carelessness or negligence of such degree or recurrence as to manifest equal culpability, wrongful intent or evil design, or to show an intentional and substantial disregard of the employer's interests or of the employee's duties and obligations to his employer. On the other hand, mere inefficiency, unsatisfactory conduct, failure in good performance as the result of inability or incapacity, inadvertencies or ordinary negligence in isolated instances, or good-faith errors in judgment or discretion are not to be deemed "misconduct" within the meaning of the statute.[82]

Commonly recognized examples of disqualifying misconduct include serious violations of company rules,[83] insubordination,[84]

---

81. See, e.g., ARIZ. REV. STAT. ANN. § 23–619.01 (defining "willful or negligent misconduct" with various examples); *Davis v. Department of Indus. Relations*, 465 So.2d 1140, 1142 (Ala. App. 1984) (judicially defining misconduct as both "continued failure of an employee to perform his job in a manner which previous performance indicates is contrary to his experience and ability" or "deliberate, willful, or wanton disregard of an employer's interests").

82. 296 N.W. 636, 640 (Wis. 1941).

83. See *In the Matter of the Claim of Hawkins*, 678 N.Y.S.2d 703 (App. Div. 1998) (claimant's knowing violation of employer's policy governing employee purchases constituted disqualifying mis-

conduct, where violation was detrimental to employer's interest).

84. See *Public Util. Comm'n v. Tillotson*, 150 P.3d 1083 (Or. App. 2007) (claimant's repeated refusal to meet with supervisor to discuss her job performance and refusal to sign resulting reprimand constituted misconduct, defined in Oregon administrative rules as "a willful or wantonly negligent disregard of an employer's interest"); *McClinton v. Mississippi Dep't of Employment Sec.*, 949 So.2d 805 (Miss. App. 2006) (continued complaints about rudeness to co-workers after employer counseled against it, disobeying instructions from superior on how to treat a subordinate, and repeated refusal to comply with hospital emergency room proce-

misstatements on a job application,[85] refusal to perform assigned work,[86] and repeated absences.[87] Perhaps using the UI system as a "back door" way to regulate workplace drug use, a number of states also expressly disqualify employees whose reason for separation is avoidance of or testing positive on a drug test.[88] Many states also disqualify workers whose separation from employment is due to a labor dispute, although some states exempt certain kinds of labor disputes, for example, lockouts.[89] Many states impose a longer period of disqualification for "gross misconduct," such as a crime or felony.[90]

A significant controversy is whether separations from employment associated with childbearing and family care should be treated as voluntary, personal, choices and thus outside the scope of "unexpected" and involuntary job loss contemplated by UI programs.[91] The U.S. Supreme Court has spoken on the matter more than once, first by striking down a Utah statute that excluded pregnant women from eligibility for unemployment benefits for a period extending from 12 weeks before the expected due date until

dures collectively constituted insubordination justifying denial of unemployment benefits).

85. See *In re Dockal*, 824 N.Y.S.2d 777 (App. Div. 2006) (truck driver who falsely stated in employment application that he had no prior traffic violations, convictions, or accidents disqualified for misconduct).

86. See *Ottomeyer v. Whelan Sec. Co.*, 202 S.W.3d 88 (Mo. App. 2006) (failure of security guard at international airport to check identification of aircraft tug operator entering his checkpoint constituted negligence in such degree as to show an intentional and substantial disregard of his duties amounting to willful misconduct, where area of employment required a higher than normal duty of care).

87. See *Mason v. Load King Mfg. Co.*, 758 So.2d 649 (Fla. 2000) (established pattern of excessive absenteeism and tardiness sufficient to constitute misconduct); *see also Clark County Sch. Dist. v. Bundley*, 148 P.3d 750 (Nev. 2006) (clear pattern of unauthorized absenteeism can constitute disqualifying misconduct).

88. E.g., ALA. CODE § 25–4–78(3); ARIZ. REV. STAT. ANN. § 23–619.01(3); KAN.

STAT. ANN. § 44–706(b)(2) (2005); OKLA. STAT. ANN. TIT. 40 § 2–406.1 (denying benefits to workers fired for refusing to submit to a drug or alcohol test). For examples of states that deny benefits to workers for testing positive, see, *e.g.*, ALA. CODE § 25–4–78; COLO. REV. STAT. ANN. § 8–73–108(5)(e)(IX.5); FLA. STAT. § 443.101(1)(d) (2004); KAN. STAT. ANN. § 44–706(b)(2) (2005).

89. See James K. Bradley & Daniel R. Schuckers, *Toward a Unified Theory of Unemployment Compensation Eligibility for Replaced Striking Employees*, 61 U. PITT. L. REV. 499 (2000) (discussing theories underlying statutes governing eligibility for striking workers); ROBERT HUTCHENS ET AL., STRIKERS AND SUBSIDIES: THE INFLUENCE OF GOVERNMENT TRANSFER PROGRAMS ON STRIKE ACTIVITY (1989) (discussing the circumstances under which striking and other organized labor activity may disqualify workers).

90. See, e.g., D.C. CODE § 51–110(b)(1)–(b)(2) (2007); MD. CODE. ANN. LAB. & EMPL. §§ 8–1002–8–1003 (2007); MONT. CODE ANN. § 39–51–2303 (2007).

91. See generally David S. Rosettenstein, *Unemployment Benefits and Family Policy in the United States*, 20 FAM. L.Q. 393, 398–403 (1986).

a date 6 weeks post-partum.[92] The Court held that the law violated the due process clause of the Fourteenth Amendment because of its conclusive presumption that pregnant women were incapable of work during the period immediately surrounding childbirth.[93] The following year, Congress amended FUTA in § 3304(a)(12) to expressly prohibit the denial of benefits "solely on the basis of pregnancy."[94]

A decade later, the Supreme Court again addressed the exclusion of pregnant women, this time in regard to a Missouri law. The challenged law disqualified claimants for unemployment benefits who left work "voluntarily without good cause attributable to" their work or employer.[95] Although neutral in its application, the law had the effect of disqualifying workers who quit due to pregnancy.[96] The petitioner argued that the law violated FUTA § 3304(a)(12). The Court held that Congress intended only to prohibit states from singling out pregnancy for unfavorable treatment and that the law in question, a neutral rule that incidentally disqualified pregnant workers as part of a larger group (employees who quit their jobs for reasons not attributable to work or their employer), did not violate FUTA.[97] The Court resisted the invitation to interpret § 3304(a)(12) as encompassing a "disparate impact" conception of discrimination as well as prohibiting direct discrimination.[98]

In a similar vein, an employee who quits her job due to a conflict between her work schedule and a family obligation such as childcare will typically forgo benefits because these are deemed to be personal, rather than work-related, reasons. In some instances this is true even when the employer precipitated the conflict by unilaterally changing work rules.[99] Interestingly, if the same employee refuses to comply with the new rule and is fired for doing so, most jurisdictions decline to treat the employee's behavior as the

---

92. *Turner v. Department of Employment Security*, 423 U.S. 44 (1975).

93. *Id.* at 46.

94. 26 U.S.C. § 3304(a)(12).

95. *Wimberly v. Labor & Indus. Relations Comm'n of Mo.*, 479 U.S. 511 (1987).

96. Cf. *Bussmann Mfg. Co. v. Industrial Comm'n, Div. of Employment Sec.*, 335 S.W.2d 456, 461 (Mo. App. 1960) (ruling against a pregnant claimant and holding that "the purpose of the Employment Security Act is to provide the compulsory setting aside of an unemployment reserve to be used for the benefit of persons unemployed through no volition of their own").

97. *Wimberly*, 479 U.S. at 521.

98. For criticism, see Mark R. Brown, *A Case for Pregnancy–Based Unemployment Insurance*, 29 U. Mich. J.L. Reform 41, 45–54 (1996).

99. See Amy Chasanov, *Clarifying Conditions for Nonmonetary Eligibility in the Unemployment Insurance System*, 29 U. Mich J.L. Reform 89, 108 tbl. 4 (1996) (reporting that 13 states categorically deny benefits if a worker quits due to a change in work circumstances).

sort of willful misconduct that justifies disqualification from benefits.[100]

It is not clear that these divergent results can be reconciled, and this inconsistency, along with a more general concern that the UI system fails adequately to accommodate work-family conflict, has led reformers to advocate making quits related to pregnancy and work-family conflict good cause for separation from work.[101] There are significant normative questions whether a state-mandated tax-and-transfer program ought to subsidize pregnancy- and family-related job interruptions, and whether UI programs would be a suitable device for doing so.[102]

Related to work-family conflict, unemployment laws historically have made no special exceptions for domestic violence-related job separations. For example, a worker who quit her job in an effort to escape her abuser would be deemed to have voluntarily quit. In a similar vein, a worker repeatedly absent from work as a result of domestic violence or whose abuser harassed her at work and disrupted the work environment might be fired for misconduct and disqualified. Recent years have seen increasing legislative recognition of a link between domestic violence and unemployment.[103] In 1996, Maine became the first state to pass a law to include domestic violence within the scope of good cause.[104] The Maine statute, in part, provides that a claimant may not be disqualified if "the leaving was necessary to protect the claimant from domestic abuse and the claimant made all reasonable efforts to preserve the em-

100. Martin H. Malin, *Unemployment Compensation in a Time of Increasing Work–Family Conflicts*, 29 U. Mich. J.L. Reform 131, 138 (1996).

101. See, e.g., Brown, *supra* note 98, at 69–73 (pregnancy-related separations should be exempted from "voluntary" quits); Karen Syma Czapanskiy, *Unemployment Insurance Reform for Moms*, 44 Santa Clara L. Rev. 1093 (2004); Michael J. Graetz & Jerry L. Mashaw, True Security: Rethinking American Social Insurance 79 (1999) (pregnancy-related quits should be treated as a type of temporary disability, triggering UI benefits); Malin, *supra* note 100, at 169–71 (burden should be on employer to demonstrate it could not accommodate an employee with work-family conflict).

102. For discussion of these controversies, *see* Gillian Lester, *Unemployment Insurance and Wealth Redistrib-*

ution, 49 UCLA L. Rev. 335, 384–88 (2001); Gillian Lester, *A Defense of Paid Family Leave*, 28 Harv. J.L. & Gender 1, 67–70 (2005) (defending state provision of wage replacement for workers who interrupt work for pregnancy or family care and assessing the advantages and disadvantages of doing so through the unemployment insurance programs).

103. Rebecca Smith, Richard W. McHugh, & Robin R. Runge, *Unemployment Insurance and Domestic Violence: Learning from Our Experiences*, 1 Seattle J. Soc. Just. 503, 505 (2002) (reviewing studies showing a relationship between domestic violence and unemployment).

104. Me. Rev. Stat. Ann. tit. 26, § 1193(1)(A)(4) (2007). *See also* Cal. Unemp. Ins. Code § 1256 (2007); Del. Code Ann. tit 19, § 3314 (2007); Wyo. Stat. Ann. § 27–3–311(a)(i)(C) (2007).

ployment.''[105] As of 2006, 29 states had enacted similar legislation.[106] The new laws attempt, in various ways, to exempt job separations due to domestic violence from disqualification.

c. "Able and Available"

As a condition of continuing to receive benefits, claimants generally must be "able and available" for, as well as actively seeking, re-employment. All states require claimants to register at regional employment offices, which monitor recipients' search effort. This usually involves periodic meetings with UI staff and submission of a weekly record of contacts with prospective employers. The number of states with active search requirements has grown steadily since the inception of UI, presumably premised on the belief that these measures reduce UI recipiency.[107]

The "ability" criterion pertains to temporary illnesses and disabilities. Most states suspend eligibility if a worker cannot work because of temporary disability.[108] Long-term disabled workers generally will already be disqualified because they lack a history of attachment.[109]

Recipients of benefits must also be "available" for work, within limits. A worker unavailable for suitable work usually loses benefits until she becomes available again. FUTA requires states to allow claimants to refuse work with wages, hours, or other conditions

105. ME. REV. STAT. ANN. tit. 26, § 1193(1)(A)(4) (2007).

106. Arizona, California, Colorado, Connecticut, Delaware, District of Columbia, Illinois, Indiana, Kansas, Maine, Massachusetts, Minnesota, Montana, Nebraska, New Hampshire, New Jersey, New Mexico, New York, North Carolina, Oklahoma, Oregon, Rhode Island, South Carolina, South Dakota, Texas, Vermont, Washington, Wisconsin, Wyoming. *See* LEGAL MOMENTUM, STATE LAW GUIDE: UNEMPLOYMENT INSURANCE BENEFITS (2006), available at http://www.legalmomentum.org/issues/vio/ui.pdf (last visited Jun. 11, 2007).

107. SAUL J. BLAUSTEIN ET AL., UNEMPLOYMENT INSURANCE IN THE UNITED STATES 287 (1993) (reporting that the number of states requiring explicit statements of work search activities has grown from 15 in 1948, to 30 in 1971, to 40 in 1990). For a summary of research on search requirements, supporting the general conclusion that intensified requirements reduce UI recipiency levels, see Bruce D. Meyer, *Lessons from the U.S. Unemployment Insurance Experiments*, 33 J. ECON. LITERATURE 91, 112–21 (1995).

108. Suspension resulting from temporary disability typically occurs because of compensation from a temporary disability fund. *See, e.g.*, CONN. GEN. STAT. § 31–236 (2007); GA. CODE ANN. § 34–8–194(5)(B) (2007); LA. REV. STAT. ANN. § 23:1601 (2007). *But see* COLO. REV. STAT. § 8–73–110(5) (2007) (maintaining eligibility for those receiving temporary disability benefits, but reducing UI benefit amount by temporary disability benefit amount).

109. *See* Patricia M. Anderson, *Continuing Eligibility: Current Labor Market Attachment, in* UNEMPLOYMENT INSURANCE IN THE UNITED STATES: ANALYSIS OF POLICY ISSUES 125, 126 (Christopher J. O'Leary & Stephen A. Wandner eds., 1997) (surveying the ability requirements across states).

that are substantially less favorable than those prevailing for similar work in the locality.[110] Most state laws expand on this minimum by specifying various criteria for judging the suitability of a work offer. These typically include the claimant's prior experience, training and earnings, the job's distance from claimant's place of residence, risk to the claimant, the claimant's health, safety and morals, prospects for securing local work in customary occupation, and length of unemployment.[111] A handful of states require claimants to be available only for work in their usual occupation or for work compatible with their prior training or experience.[112]

Workers who attend school while searching for work raise a tricky problem. Quitting work to attend school is ordinarily seen as a voluntary quit.[113] But when a claimant enrolls in school following a non-voluntary work separation, it may be difficult to determine whether the claimant is available for work but happens to be attending school, or instead is primarily a student whose school obligations will interfere with the ability to accept employment.[114]

d. Refusal of Employment Opportunities

The availability requirement includes the duty actively to search for work with reasonable diligence. Absent evidence of sufficient effort, a worker may be disqualified. A worker who refuses suitable employment opportunities not only loses benefits, but may forgo future benefits until she "earns them back" with

110. 26 U.S.C. § 3304(a)(5)(B).

111. See, e.g., CAL. UNEMP. INS. CODE § 1258 (requiring that "the degree of risk involved to the individual's health, safety, and morals, his physical fitness and prior training, his experience and prior earnings, his length of unemployment and prospects for securing local work in his customary occupation, and the distance of the available work from his residence, and such other factors as would influence a reasonably prudent person in the individual's circumstances" be included in determining "suitable work"). See also COMPARISON: NONMONETARY ELIGIBILITY, *supra* note 47, at 5–26.

112. See COMPARISON: NONMONETARY ELIGIBILITY, *supra* note 77, at 5–26. See also ALA. CODE § 25–4–78(5)(a)(1) (2007); CAL. UNEMP. INS. CODE § 1258 (2007); FLA.

STAT. § 443.101(2)(a) (2007); 820 ILL. COMP. STAT. 405/603 (2007).

113. See generally COMPARISON: NONMONETARY ELIGIBILITY, *supra* note 7, at, 5–31–5–33 tbl. 5–31 (summarizing state rules on treatment of students). Some states have programs that allow workers to collect benefits while enrolled in a career training program that meets specified parameters. See, e.g., N.Y. LAB. LAW § 599(a)(1) (2007) (a worker will not be disqualified from benefits if regularly attending a career training program approved by the New York Labor Commissioner for purposes of upgrading claimant's existing skills).

114. See, e.g., *McCoy v. Board of Review, Dep't of Labor*, 885 A.2d 453 (N.J. App. Div. 2005) (former health aide denied unemployment benefits because she enrolled as full-time student at a college and did not make herself available for an uninterrupted work day).

more work.[115] FUTA requires only that a claimant not be denied benefits for refusing a job because of a strike, because it pays less than the prevailing wage, or because it requires membership in a company union or prohibits membership in a "bona fide" labor union.[116] State law typically requires acceptance of "suitable" employment offers absent "good cause."[117]

The question of whether a worker has refused a suitable offer entails a case-by-case inquiry. Thus, for example, adjudicators generally will not penalize a worker who walks past a "help wanted" sign on the street without inquiring, but may well penalize a worker who refuses a clear job offer that specifies wages and terms, or one who implicitly sabotages the search process by placing undue restrictions on which jobs he will accept.[118] Many states also disqualify claimants whose search is limited to part-time work.[119] Where part-time workers are eligible, they must usually have a history of part-time work prior to separation.[120] Termination of employment with a temporary help agency upon completion of an assignment is usually considered a voluntary, rather than involuntary, separation if the employee turns down subsequent temporary assignments from the same agency.[121]

Conflict between work assignments and religious beliefs has also been a subject of extensive litigation. The free exercise clause of the First Amendment prevents denial of state benefits to individuals on the basis of their religious beliefs. Employers have been unsuccessful in denying benefits to employees who quit their jobs for religious reasons, or were fired due to insubordination stemming from a religious conviction. In *Sherbert v. Verner*,[122] a member

115. See COMPARISON: NONMONETARY ELIGIBILITY, *supra* note 77, at 5–28–5–30 tbl. 5–11 (surveying penalties used by each state for refusals of suitable work).

116. 26 U.S.C. § 3304(a)(5).

117. See, e.g., CAL. UNEMP. INS. CODE § 1257 ("An individual is . . . disqualified for unemployment benefits if . . . (b) He or she, without good cause, refused to accept suitable employment when offered to him or her, or failed to apply for suitable employment when notified by a public employment office.").

118. See, e.g., *Swaby v. Unemployment Ins. Appeals Bd.*, 149 Cal.Rptr. 336 (App. 1978) (seasonal farm worker who restricted his search to three trips to the union hiring hall for one local grower was disqualified because self-imposed restrictions unreasonably excluded all other forms of labor in any locality and any other field harvesting work within a reasonable radius of his residence); *Orum v. Department of Employment Econ. Dev.*, 2006 WL 539353 (Minn. App. 2006) (former realtor disqualified because he chose to wait for former employer to recall him rather than searching for alternative jobs that might interfere with the possibility of recall).

119. COMPARISON: NONMONETARY ELIGIBILITY, *supra* note 77, at 5–22–5–25 tbl. 5–10 (summarizing state laws on part-time employment restrictions).

120. *Id.*

121. *Id.* at 5–6–5–7 tbl. 5–3 (summarizing state laws on temporary help job refusals).

122. 374 U.S. 398 (1963).

of the Seventh–Day Adventist Church was discharged because she would not work on Saturday, the day of rest prescribed by her faith. The state disqualified her from benefits on the basis that by restricting her availability in this way, she had failed, without "good cause," to accept suitable work when offered. The U.S. Supreme Court held that the state's determination violated the Free Exercise clause because the worker's ineligibility for benefits derived solely from the practice of her religion, and the "pressure upon her to forego [the practice of her religion] was unmistakable."[123] The Court has extended this reasoning to instances in which not all members of a particular religious faith agree that the work in question would be prohibited,[124] and also where the worker based his refusal on his Christian beliefs in general, rather than a tenet of any particular religious creed.[125] However, the Court upheld denial of benefits to two drug counselors who were fired for using peyote, a controlled substance they were prohibited from using under Oregon state law, even though they used it as part of a religious ritual.[126] The Court held that the individuals' religious beliefs did not excuse their compliance with an otherwise valid law prohibiting their conduct.[127]

123. *Id.*, at 404.

124. *Thomas v. Review Bd.*, 450 U.S. 707, 708 (1981). *See also Hobbie v. Unemployment Appeals Comm'n*, 480 U.S. 136 (1987) (holding that denial of benefits following discharge resulting from refusal to work on Sabbath violated free exercise clause of First Amendment).

125. *Frazee v. Illinois Dep't of Employment Sec.*, 489 U.S. 829 (1989) (claimant professing that his Christian beliefs forbade him from working Sundays, but not claiming that his membership in any particular sect forbade what his job required, was able to invoke protection of the Free Exercise Clause because he had a sincere belief that reli-

gion required him to refrain from the work in question).

126. *Employment Div., Dep't of Human Resources of Or. v. Smith*, 494 U.S. 872 (1990).

127. *Id.* at 878. Congress passed the Religious Freedom Restoration Act (RFRA) in direct response to *Smith*. RFRA explicitly reaffirmed the strict scrutiny test provided by *Sherbert* in cases where a person's religious exercise is "substantially burdened by government." 42 U.S.C. § 2000bb. However, RFRA was found to exceed Congress' powers to regulate state authority, and therefore unconstitutional under *City of Boerne v. Flores*, 521 U.S. 507 (1997).

Chapter 9

COLLECTIVE ORGANIZATION AND COLLECTIVE BARGAINING LAW

Although once the fountainhead of American employment law, union organizing and collective bargaining have receded in importance with the decline of union representation in private firms from 35 percent of the workforce in 1954 to under 10 percent today. Labor law remains important for several reasons. First, unions are still quite strong in manufacturing, transportation and certain service occupations. In government offices, unions represent nearly half of all public workers. Second, the "threat effect" of unionization—the risk non-union firms face that they may become unionized—often informs the pay and benefits they provide to their workers so that, in a sense, collective bargaining influences indirectly terms and conditions in the non-union sector. Third, much of U.S. employment law is built on the model of the labor laws; central concepts like "discrimination" and virtually all remedial principles are derived from those laws. Finally, organized labor is the principal political force in our country seeking the enactment and strengthening of protective employment laws.

A. Rationale for Regulation

The principal labor law is the National Labor Relations Act of 1935 (NLRA or Wagner Act).[1] The NLRA applies to all employers in private industries "affecting commerce," with the exception of the railroad and airlines industries. Labor relations in the latter industries are regulated by the Railway Labor Act of 1926 (RLA).[2] Both the NLRA and RLA broadly preempt all state regulation of labor relations in the industries they cover.[3] The states have enacted "mini Wagner Acts" for industries not regulated by federal law, and public sector labor relations laws for the employees of state and local governments. The federal government has a separate labor relations statute for its employees.

Congress gave two reasons for enacting the NLRA—at least one that is avowedly redistributive. The first was to improve the

1. 29 U.S.C. §§ 151–169.

2. 45 U.S.C. §§ 151–188.

3. Canada, by contrast, allows the provinces plenary authority over labor relations; the federal government regulates a limited set of industries considered to have a nationwide scope, such as transportation and communications.

154

bargaining power of workers so as to stabilize wages and bolster their purchasing power:

> The inequality of bargaining power between employees who do not possess full freedom of association or actual liberty of contract, and employers who are organized in the corporate or other forms of ownership association substantially burdens and affects the flow of commerce, and tends to aggravate recurrent business depressions, by depressing wage rates and the purchasing power of wage earners in industry and by preventing the stabilization of competitive wage rates and working conditions.[4]

The second stated objective was to "remov[e] certain recognized sources of industrial strife and unrest, by encouraging practices fundamental to the friendly adjustment of industrial disputes . . . , and by restoring equality of bargaining power between employers and employees."[5]

Section 7 of the NLRA establishes the basic rights of all covered employees: "the right to self-organization, to form, join, or assist labor organizations, to bargain collectively through representatives of their own choosing, and to engage in other concerted activities for the purpose of other mutual aid or protection. . . ."[6] The Taft–Hartley amendments of 1947, reflecting public concerns with the growing strength of unions and the strike wave of 1946, added that "employees shall also have the right to refrain from any or all of such activities. . . ."

Under the original 1935 law, only employers could violate the Act; under the 1947 and 1959 amendments, union unfair labor practices were added. (Some state "mini" Wagner Acts like New York's still provide only for employer violations.) The employer unfair labor practices (ULPs) violative of § 8(a) are:

> (1) to interfere with, restrain, or coerce employees in the exercise of the rights guaranteed in section 7;

> (2) to dominate or interfere with the formation or administration of any labor organizations or contribute financial or other support to it . . . ;

> (3) by discrimination in regard to hire or tenure of employment or any term or condition of employment to encourage or discourage membership in any labor organization . . . ;

4. Section 1 of the NLRA, 29 U.S.C. § 151.

5. *Id.*

6. Section 7 of the NLRA, *id.* § 157.

(4) to discharge or otherwise discriminate against an employee because he has filed charges or given testimony under this Act;

(5) to refuse to bargaining collectively with the representatives of his employees, subject to the provisions of 9(a).[7]

The union unfair labor practices violative of § 8(b) largely mirror the employer ULPs, but with the addition of a ban on secondary boycotts and jurisdictional strikes over work assignments in § 8(b)(4), a ban on "hot cargo" clauses in § 8(e) (agreements with firms allowing boycotts of goods from employers with whom the union has a dispute), and a qualified ban on recognitional and organizational picketing in § 8(b)(7).

B.   Basic Premises

The American labor relations system differs from its European counterparts in a number of ways. First, the system is based on an adversarial model. In most cases, unions obtain bargaining rights in elections administered by a federal agency. In such elections, management has a right to, and often does, speak out in opposition to the union.[8] Other than agreements to recognize independent unions that demonstrate majority support, companies may play no role in initiating or supporting "labor organizations," a term that is broadly defined to include any mechanism by which employees "deal with" their employer on terms and conditions of employment.[9] The labor laws are based on a fundamental division of interest between labor and management: unions can seek bargaining authority on behalf of non-managerial and non-supervisory workers, but manag-

---

7. 29 U.S.C. § 158(a).

8. Under Section 8(c) of the NLRA, id. § 158(c), the expression of views cannot constitute nor be evidence of an unfair labor practice, unless such expression contains a promise of benefit or threat of reprisal. A like rule applies under the Railway Labor Act. On comparative labor law, see generally SAMUEL ESTREICHER, GLOBAL ISSUES IN LABOR LAW (2007).

9. See Section 2(5) of the NLRA, 29 U.S.C. § 152(5), for the definition of "labor organization". Employer interference with or domination of such organizations is barred by Section 8(a)(2), 29 U.S.C. § 158(a)(2). The lead NLRB deci-

sion is *Electromation, Inc.*, 309 N.L.R.B. 990 (1992), enforced, 35 F.3d 1148 (7th Cir. 1994), where the employer in advance of any union organizing drive established "action committees" to deal with absenteeism, smoking in the workplace, and other topics. The key statutory term is "dealing with" in the Section 2(5) definition, which the Supreme Court in *NLRB v. Cabot Carbon Co.*, 360 U.S. 203 (1959), held does not require written agreements with the labor organization to trigger Section 8(a)(2) scrutiny. See generally Samuel Estreicher, *Employee Involvement and the "Company Union" Prohibition: The Case for Partial Repeal of § 8(a)(2) of the NLRA*, 69 N.Y.U.L. REV. 101 (1994).

ers and supervisors are deemed representatives of the firm who have no right to form unions or insist on collective bargaining.[10] The scope of bargaining also reflects this division between spheres of influence: the parties must bargain over wages, hours and working conditions, but decisions involving the disposition of assets and the strategic position of the firm, including plant closings, are deemed to be part of management's realm of unilateral action. Management must bargain over the effects of such decisions but not the decisions themselves.[11]

Secondly, collective bargaining is highly decentralized. Unions acquire bargaining authority on a plant-by-plant basis, often within a subgroup of workers in the plant. Unlike the German, French and Swedish systems, regional bargaining between labor federations and multi-employer organizations in the United States are exceptional; multi-employer bargaining units are formed only by consent and in many industries they have unraveled. Coalition bargaining among unions representing different units of the same employer can occur only with the employer's consent. Unions attempt to maintain "pattern" settlements across firms competing in the same product market, but are finding this increasingly difficult in the face of a growing non-union sector and the competitive pressures of global markets.

Thirdly, unions are predominantly multi-employer organizations representing employees of competing firms. Unlike Japan's enterprise unions, employee associations representing only the employees of a particular firm are rare are in the United States, and tend over time to affiliate with national labor organizations that are members of the central labor federation, the American Federation of Labor—Congress of Industrial Organizations (AFL–CIO).[12] Enterprise-based works councils—found in most continental European countries—are non-existent in the United States. American unions typically negotiate agreements with single companies, often applicable only to a particular facility.

10. The statutory exclusion of supervisors is contained in Section 2(11) of the NLRA, 29 U.S.C. § 152(11). The Supreme Court recognized an implied exclusion for "managerial" employees in *NLRB v. Bell Aerospace Co.*, 416 U.S. 267 (1974). Faculty at institutions of higher education are considered "managerial" employees if they play a role in the formulation or administration of educational policy for their employers. See

NLRB v. Yeshiva University, 444 U.S. 672 (1980).

11. See *First National Maintenance Corp. v. NLRB,* 452 U.S. 666 (1981).

12. A number of unions have left the AFL–CIO to form a rival coalition called "Change to Win". See generally Samuel Estreicher, *Disunity within the House of Labor: Change to Win or to Stay the Course?,* 27 J. Labor Res. 505 (Fall 2006)

The fact that American unions are multi-employer associations makes it difficult for firms to share non-public financial information with their unions, and to secure terms at variance with the national bargaining goals of the union.

Finally, American unions are institutionally insecure. The unions' vulnerability comes from the fact they face a growing non-union sector and are subject to various legal mechanisms that are designed to ensure union responsiveness to the rank-and-file employees. The latter include decertification elections; the employer's ability to test the union's continued majority support by withdrawing recognition; duty of fair representation suits brought by employees complaining of the union's representation in the grievance procedure or collective bargaining; the rights of non-union members to seek rebates of union dues used for non-collective bargaining purposes; and union democracy requirements for the conduct of internal union election and union discipline. As a result of these pressures, union leaders must be politically attuned to the preferences of median voters within bargaining units—typically, long-service workers who are protected from lay-off by seniority rules.

C. Administrative Procedures

Government agencies are central to the administration of the federal labor laws. In the case of the NLRA, the National Labor Relations Board (NLRB) has exclusive authority over the representation procedures and unfair labor practice provisions of the NLRA. Courts come into the picture in judicial review of final NLRB orders in unfair labor practice cases and suits to enforce collective bargaining agreements.[13] In the case of the RLA, the National Mediation Board (NMB) conducts representation elections and mediates labor disputes.

Under the NLRA, charges of unfair labor practices (ULPs) are filed with regional offices of the NLRB. If, after investigation, the charges are believed to be meritorious, the General Counsel (an independent official whose nomination is subject to Senate confirmation) issues a complaint on the government's behalf. An adversarial, trial-type proceeding is conducted before an administrative law judge (ALJ), who hears the testimony and reviews the evidence, and makes initial findings of fact and conclusions of law. If no appeal is taken, the ALJ's determination becomes the ruling of the agency. If a party appeals, the NLRB considers the record and

13. See SECTION 301 OF THE LABOR MANAGEMENT RELATIONS ACT, 29 U.S.C. § 185(a), a product of 1947 amendment to the NLRA. There is also a private right of action under Section 30, id. § 187, for victims of union secondary boycotts.

158

briefs and, on rare occasions, hears oral arguments. The final decision of the NLRB is reviewable in the federal courts of appeals. The reviewing court must uphold the agency's decisions if its findings of fact are supported by "substantial evidence" on the record "considered as a whole" and its rulings of law are in conformity with the NLRA.[14] The NLRB also has authority to fill in gaps in the statutory scheme subject to "arbitrary and capricious" review.[15]

By contrast, under the RLA, the NMB's adjudicative authority is limited to representational disputes; the parties go directly to the federal district court to enforce other statutory obligations. The NMB also has a mediation role that the NLRB was not given.

In contrast to the laws of most other countries, both statutes are based on the principle of exclusivity (only the representatives chosen by a majority of the employees in a unit may bargain, to the exclusion of individual employees or representatives of a minority); a legally mandated duty to bargain (both the exclusive bargaining representative and the employer are legally obligated to bargain in "good faith"); free collective bargaining (after exhaustion of the duty to bargain, the parties are free to press their disagreements in the form of strikes and lock-outs); and arbitration of disputes arising under collective bargaining agreements (if the parties have agreed to arbitration).

D.   Protected Concerted Activity

Section 7 protects "concerted" activity, i.e., by two or more employees, in support of wages, hours and working conditions. The right to engage in concerted activity is not limited to members of a union and, indeed, a primary purpose is to protect unorganized workers engaged in "self-organization". The right is also not limited to "reasonable" demands. Even if, for example, the employer is doing all it can to fix a plant's air conditioning system, the employees are protected in their decision to engage in collective activity to protest inadequacies in the air conditioning, even if by walking out

---

14. See *Universal Camera Corp. v. NLRB*, 340 U.S. 474 (1951). This relatively deferential standard also applies to "mixed" questions of law and fact, where the NLRB must use the appropriate legal standard but its application of that standard to a given set of facts is subject only to "substantial evidence" review. See *NLRB v. United Insurance Co.*, 390 U.S. 254 (1968). Where the statute is open on the particular question, the NLRB's statutory interpretation is also entitled to deference under *Chevron U.S.A., Inc. v. NRDC, Inc.*, 467 U.S. 837 (1984).

15. See *Allentown Mack Sales & Servs., Inc. v. NLRB*, 522 U.S. 359 (1998).

they cause some harm to the employer's business.[16] The NLRB will withhold protection, however, where employees use means that violate federal law or non-preempted state criminal or tort law, such as physically taking over the plant[17] or destroying machinery. The Board will also deny protection where employees engage in conduct inconsistent with the agency's conception of the rules of the "bounded conflict," such as placards disparaging the employer's product without making clear there is an underlying labor dispute,[18] leaving molten iron in a cupola as the strike begins,[19] or engaging in work slowdowns;[20] such activities are unprotected but not unlawful.[21]

The fact that activity is protected means that the employer cannot retaliate against employees for engaging in such activity; such retaliation would violate § 8(a)(3). However, the employer is permitted to take certain non-retaliatory actions to protect its business, such as closing the plant, locking out protesting workers, or (as we shall see) hiring replacements for employees on strike.

Modes of Proof. The principal mode of proof is to show that the employer acted with a retaliatory motive, i.e., the employee's protected activity played at least a "motivating" role. If the NLRB's General Counsel makes this showing, the agency permits the employer a complete defense if it can show it would have made the same decision even without regard to the protected activity.[22] The Board, with court approval, has ruled that some activity is inherently discriminatory in violation of § 8(a)(3)—for example, offering replacements for strikers 20 years of additional seniority as a means of keeping the plant open.[23]

The second mode of proof is a consideration of the impact of the employer's conduct on the willingness or ability of employees to exercise their Section 7 rights, balanced against the employer's legitimate interests. The NLRB, with court approval, has used this approach principally in dealing with the issue of access to the

---

16. See *NLRB v. Washington Alum. Co.*, 370 U.S. 9 (1962).

17. See *NLRB v. Fansteel Mettalurgical Corp.*, 306 U.S. 240 (1939).

18. See *NLRB v. Local 1229, IBEW*, 346 U.S. 464 (1953); *Sierra Publishing Co. v. NLRB*, 889 F.2d 210, 216 (9th Cir. 1989).

19. See *NLRB v. Marshall Car Wheel & Foundry Co.*, 218 F.2d 409 (5th Cir. 1955).

20. See *Elk Lumber Co.*, 91 N.L.R.B. 333 (1950).

21. See *NLRB v. Insurance Agents' Intl. Union*, 361 U.S. 477 (1960).

22. See *NLRB v. Transportation Management Corp.*, 462 U.S. 393 (1983).

23. See *NLRB v. Erie Resistor Corp.*, 373 U.S. 221 (1963). Despite the language of intent, these cases are really about the detrimental impact of such activity on Section 7 rights. See Samuel Estreicher, *Strikers and Replacements*, 3 LAB. LAW. 897 (1987).

employer's property. An employer presumptively violates the Act if it bars employees from engaging in solicitation during their non-work time or engaging in distributions in nonwork areas.[24] (Distribution is distinguished from solicitation because of littering issues.) Special exceptions have been recognized for customer-access areas of department stores[25] and patient-access areas of hospitals.[26] This presumption does not apply to access by nonemployees (including nonemployee union organizers) because they are not Section 7 rights holders. Access by nonemployees requires a much stronger showing that employees cannot be reached by other means.[27]

E. Selection of Exclusive Bargaining Representative

Although "members only" unionism is permissible under both the NLRA and the RLA, unions typically seek exclusive bargaining status either by securing voluntary recognition from the employer upon a showing of majority support, or petitioning the NLRB or the NMB to hold a secret-ballot representation election. Such petitions require a preliminary showing of interest (the NLRB requires that 30 percent of the employees in an appropriate unit sign cards requesting a representation election[28]). The agency conducts a hearing to resolve contested issues, if any, concerning the scope of the bargaining unit, eligibility of voters, etc., and then schedules an election to determine if a majority of employees desire union representation. (The NLRB requires that a majority of employees voting affirmatively select union representation; the NMB requires that a majority of the eligible electorate cast valid ballots.) After the election is held, the agency considers challenges based on the conduct of the election campaign. If the petitioning union was selected by a majority of the employees, and the agency has rejected challenges to the conduct of the campaign, the agency certifies the union as the exclusive bargaining representative.

In the election campaign, the employer is permitted to voice its opposition to unionism in general and to the particular union. The employer may not, however, discharge or discipline employees because of their support of the union, engage in threats of reprisal, or change the terms and conditions of work for the purpose of affect-

24. See *Republic Aviation Corp. v. NLRB*, 324 U.S. 793 (1945).

25. See, e.g., *Gayfers Dept. Store*, 324 N.L.R.B. 1246, 1250 (1997).

26. See *NLRB v. Baptist Hospital*, 442 U.S. 773 (1979); *Beth Israel Hospital v. NLRB*, 437 U.S. 483 (1978).

27. See *Lechmere, Inc. v. NLRB*, 502 U.S. 527 (1992).

28. This is an administrative requirement; Section 9(c)(1)(A) requires only a "substantial number" of employees seeking a collective representative. 29 U.S.C.§ 159(c)(1)(A).

ing the election outcome.[29] Such conduct would provide grounds for setting aside the election (if the majority of employees voted "no union")[30] or holding the employer to have engaged in unfair labor practices. Under the NLRA, if employers are guilty of egregious unfair labor practices that so mar the environment that a fair rerun election cannot be held, the NLRB may order the employer to bargain with a union that previously demonstrated majority support on the basis of authorization cards signed by a majority of the unit.[31]

F. The Process of Collective Bargaining

Under the NLRA, once the union has been certified, the parties are under a duty to meet and confer at reasonable times and engage in "good faith" bargaining. There is no legal obligation, however, to make concessions or reach agreements.[32] The duty to bargain is limited to "wages, hours and other terms and conditions of employment." These are considered "mandatory" subjects over which the parties must bargain (and provide information to substantiate bargaining positions[33]) and are free to press their disagreements to the point of "impasse," i.e., bargaining deadlock. Hard bargaining—insistence on positions on mandatory subjects—is not inconsistent with good-faith bargaining. The Court has even permitted employers to insist on "management functions" clauses that would assign to management discretionary authority over certain mandatory subjects, such as discipline and work schedules, as long the employer otherwise engaged in a sincere attempt to resolve differences with the union.[34]

---

29. See *NLRB v. Exchange Parts Co.,* 375 U.S. 405 (1964). Unions generally can promise benefits without violation Section 8(b)(1)(A) because they cannot implement such promises without the employer's agreement. They may not, however, offer immediate financial inducements to employees as a means of securing their support. See *NLRB v. Savair Mfg. Co.,* 414 U.S. 270 (1973).

30. The NLRB also asserts the authority to refuse to certify the results of elections where conduct of either party mars "laboratory conditions" even if falling short of an NLRA violation. See *General Shoe Corp.,* 77 N.L.R.B. 124 (1948). Although the agency has oscillated back and forth, its present view is that it will not invoke this doctrine in dealing with last-minute, even material,

misrepresentations. See *Midland National Life Insur. Co.,* 263 N.L.R.B. 127 (1982).

31. See *NLRB v. Gissel Packing Co.,* 395 U.S. 575 (1969).

32. See Section 8(d) of the Act, 29 U.S.C. § 158(d); *H.K. Porter Co. v. NLRB,* 397 U.S. 99 (1970).

33. See *NLRB v. Truitt Mfg. Co.,* 351 U.S. 149 (1956). Pleas of "competitive conditions" do not constitute a plea of "inability to pay" triggering the *Truitt* obligation. See, e.g., *Nielsen Lithographing Co.,* 305 N.L.R.B. 697 (1991), enforced sub nom. *Graphic Communications Intl. Union, Local 508 v. NLRB,* 977 F.2d 1168 (7th Cir. 1992).

34. See *NLRB v. American National Insurance Co.,* 343 U.S. 395 (1952).

Bargaining is not required over subjects like plant closings, advertising budgets, and capital investments that are considered to lie within the realm of "entrepreneurial control"; subjects that affect the union's relationship with its members such as strike and contract ratification votes; or subjects that alter the established framework of negotiations, such as proposals to bargain with coalitions of unions or to submit disagreements over the content of labor contracts to arbitration. These are considered "permissive" subjects over which the parties have no duty to bargain and may not be a basis for deadlock over mandatory subjects.[35]

Good-faith bargaining does require that certain procedures be followed. One is the *Truitt* duty to exchange relevant information and substantiate bargaining positions. Another is the requirement that the employer not change any terms and conditions of employment, even after a collective bargaining agreement has expired, until the employer has bargained to impasse over the proposed change; the employer may not implement more favorable terms than it was willing to offer the union at the bargaining table.[36]

During the hiatus period between collective bargaining agreements, the terms of the expired contract dealing with mandatory subjects define the operational status quo—to change any of those subjects, the party must bargain in good faith to impasse. Not all provisions of the expired contract, however, carry over because some, like the union's right to strike, the check-off and union security clauses, and the arbitration clause are considered "contract-dependent" terms requiring an agreement between the parties. Note that even though the arbitration clause does not carry over, the duty to process grievances does and there may be an obligation to arbitrate grievances that arose before the contract expired.[37]

If the parties have reached an "impasse" over mandatory subjects, the NLRA permits resort to self-help after notice is given to the Federal Mediation and Conciliation Service (FMCS) and applicable state agencies and a 60–day "cooling off" period has expired. The employer may lock-out its employees[38] and/or unilaterally implement its final offer to the union. The union may exercise

35. See *NLRB v. Wooster Division of Borg–Warner Corp.*, 356 U.S. 342 (1958).

36. See *NLRB v. Katz*, 369 U.S. 736 (1962); *Litton Financial Printing Div. v. NLRB*, 501 U.S. 190 (1991).

37. See *Litton Financial; Nolde Bros., Inc. v. Bakery Workers*, 430 U.S. 243 (1977).

38. See *American Ship Building Co. v. NLRB*, 380 U.S. 300 (1965). This case involved a post-impasse lockout, but the NLRB moved away from an impasse requirement for lockouts. See *Darling & Co.*, 171 N.L.R.B. 801 (1968), enforced sub nom. *Lane v. NLRB*, 418 F.2d 1208 (D.C. Cir. 1969).

its right to strike, which is legally protected. Although the employer may not discharge striking workers, it can, in the interest of maintaining operations, hire permanent replacements even without a showing that it could not maintain operations by other means.[39] Even if permanent replacements have been hired, however, strikers remain "employees" and have preferential rights to job openings as they occur, once the strikers have offered unconditionally to return to work.[40] Under Section 9(c)(3), they can vote in NLRB representation elections for one year from the commencement of the strike.[41] If the strike is in protest over the employer's unfair labor practices, the employer may not hire permanent replacements and returning strikers will displace replacement workers.[42] Also, if an employer resorts to a lock-out, locked-out employees may not be permanently replaced.[43] Settlement agreements between the company and the striking union sometimes provide for restoring strikers to their jobs even if this means "bumping" replacement workers.[44]

Although at least since the late 1930s, employers have had the right to hire permanent replacements as a means of staying in business, the decade of the 1980s witnessed a significant increase in the use of this bargaining tactic. Bills were pending in Congress for several years to outlaw the hiring of permanent replacements, but none was enacted into law.

The framework for collective bargaining in the railroad and airline industries resembles that of the NLRA but differs in at least two important respects. First, bargaining occurs on a carrier-wide (in airlines) or system-wide (in rail) basis; the NMB will generally

---

39. See *NLRB v. Mackay Radio & Telegraph Co.,* 304 U.S. 333 (1938). *See generally* Samuel Estreicher, *Collective Bargaining or "Collective Begging"?: Reflections on Antistrike Breaker Legislation,* 93 MICH. L. REV. 577 (1994).

40. *NLRB v. Fleetwood Trailer Co.,* 389 U.S. 375 (1967); *Laidlaw Corp.,* 171 N.L.R.B. 1366 (1968), enforced, 414 F.2d 99 (7th Cir. 1969).

41. 29 U.S.C. § 159(c)(3). The NLRB's position is that even where permanent replacements have been hired for strikers, they are not presumed to oppose the union. The union, therefore, retains its majority position unless the employer affirmatively shows that the union has lost the support of a majority of employees in the bargaining unit (counting for this purpose cross-overs, replacements and strikers (for up to the one-year period)). See *NLRB v. Curtin*

Matheson Scientific, Inc., 494 U.S. 775 (1990).

42. There is even some question whether the union can agree to waive its right to engage in an unfair labor practice strike, at least concerning employer violations that go to the essence of the relationship between the union and the employer, e.g., an employer's unlawful recognition of a rival union. See *Mastro Plastics Corp. v. NLRB,* 350 U.S. 270 (1956).

43. But see *Johns–Manville Prods. Corp. v. NLRB,* 557 F.2d 1126 (5th Cir. 1977) (lockout and hiring of permanent replacements justified by employees' in-plant sabotage).

44. Ousted replacements may have a contract or tort claim against the employer. See *Belknap, Inc. v. Hale,* 463 U.S. 491 (1983).

certify only carrier-wide units for particular crafts or classes of workers.[45] Second, there are substantial statutory impediments to changing agreements. The parties to a collective bargaining agreement are under a statutory duty "to exert every reasonable effort to make and maintain agreements".[46] A party commences the process of seeking changes in agreements by serving the other side with what is called a "Section 6 notice" containing its proposals. The parties are then obligated to engage in direct negotiations. If no agreement is reached, either party may request mediation by the NMB, or the agency can intervene on its own. The NMB has the authority to prolong bargaining (virtually free of judicial review), as long it believes further talks may be productive. As a practical matter, the NMB determines when the parties are at an impasse by making an offer of binding arbitration of the dispute; if the offer is refused, the agency declares that its mediation efforts have failed. The parties are then obligated to maintain the status quo for 30 days, in order to permit the President to establish an emergency board. If the President does not do so, the parties are free to engage in a strike or lock-out to pressure the other side. Emergency boards are common in rail disputes, but have seldom been appointed in airline disputes since the 1960s.

G.   Administering the Labor Agreement

A collective bargaining agreement is of necessity a general document that cannot contain rules for all disputes that might develop. For this reason, some mechanism is needed to resolve disputes arising under the agreement. Such disputes often involve discharges and other terms of discipline challenged by the union under the "just cause" provisions of the labor agreement, or disagreements over the meaning of particular terms governing seniority, overtime assignments, and use of subcontractors. The preferred mechanism under U.S. labor law for resolving such "rights" disputes is a contractual grievance machinery involving, in the first instance, stages of negotiations between union and management representatives, and, should disagreements persist, arbitration before a neutral arbiter. Typically, unions agree not to strike over "rights" disputes during the life of the agreement, in exchange for which employers agree to "final and binding" grievance arbitration. A limited implied duty not to strike over grievances subject to arbitration has been recognized.[47]

---

45. The statute speaks in terms of "any craft or class of employees of such carrier," § 3, Second of the RLA, 45 U.S.C. § 153, Second.

46. Section 2, First of the RLA, 45 U.S.C. § 152, First.

47. See *Local 174, Teamsters v. Lucas Flour Co.*, 369 U.S. 95 (1962).

Arbitrators are chosen by the parties. Some agreements provide for regular resort to the same arbitrator or a panel of arbitrators. More commonly, arbitrators are selected on an ad hoc basis from rosters compiled by either the Federal Mediation and Conciliation Services, the state labor relations agency, or the American Arbitration Association, a private organization providing arbitration services. Under the RLA, the parties are required to establish boards of adjustment to hear grievances (in rail, the statute establishes an industry-wide grievance apparatus, the National Railroad Adjustment Board). Hearings before arbitrators are considered more informal, quicker, and less costly than proceedings in court. Although some unions (like the International Association of Machinists, AFL–CIO) continue to use non-lawyer staff in arbitrations, the process is becoming increasingly judicialized, and reliance on lawyers is now common. The arbitrator's award is considered a "final and binding" resolution, with the legal grounds for challenging an award quite limited. Absent bias, an indefinite award, or a strong showing that the arbitrator clearly exceeded his or her authority under the contract, the court must enforce the award.

In three rulings issued the same day in 1960[48]—the so-called *"Steelworkers* Trilogy"—the Supreme Court established rules strongly supportive of labor arbitration. The Court announced a "presumption of arbitrability" under which any facially plausible claim of a contract violation within the scope of the arbitration clause of the agreement—even if of dubious merit—is presumed arbitrable, absent clear evidence in the agreement that the parties intended to exclude a particular subject from the promise to arbitrate. The Supreme Court also made clear that, since the parties bargained for their own special dispute-resolver and contract-interpreter, the courts may not set aside an award absent clear proof that the arbitrator strayed beyond his or her contractual authority. Even where an award is claimed to be inconsistent with "public policy", the Court has insisted that in order to overturn an award, the award must be in direct conflict with other "laws and legal precedents", rather than simply in tension with an assessment of "general considerations of supposed public interests." The Court has left open whether the only basis for refusing to enforce an

48. See *United Steelworkers of America v. American Mfg. Co.,* 363 U.S. 564 (1960); *United Steelworkers of America v. Warrior & Gulf Navigation Co.,* 363 U.S. 574 (1960); *United Steelworkers of America v. Enterprise Wheel & Car Corp.,* 363 U.S. 593 (1960).

award on "public policy" grounds is when the arbitrator requires conduct that the employer on its own could not lawfully engage in.[49]

There can be situations where a challenge to an employer's decision, such as a discharge, can be framed both as a breach of the collective bargaining agreement as well as an unfair labor practice under the NLRA. The NLRB's policy in such cases is to require the union, which is the exclusive representative of employees for all claims under the labor contract, to exhaust the contractual grievance procedure before the agency will exercise its statutory jurisdiction. After completion of the grievance procedure, the agency will generally defer to the results of the labor arbitration if the statutory claim involves the same facts as the contractual claim, and the arbitration award is not "clearly repugnant" to the policies of the labor law.[50]

H. Individual Rights and the Collective Agreement

Once the employees have selected an exclusive bargaining representative, their ability to negotiate individual employment contracts is severely curtailed—unless the collective agreement allows individual bargaining (common only in the sports and entertainment industries).[51] Workers also may be discharged if they engage in concerted action to compel bargaining with groups other than the exclusive representative.[52]

Concerning disputes arising under the labor agreement, individual workers file grievances with their union representatives. The union ultimately controls which grievances are taken up through the process to arbitration. If a grievance is taken to arbitration, the arbitrator's award will generally be preclusive of any court action by the employee against his or her employer for breach of contract. Even if a grievance is not taken to arbitration, its resolution by the contractual process is "final and binding" and precludes a court action.

There are two exceptions to the preclusive effect of the contractual dispute resolution process. The first is where the employee convinces a court that the union breached its duty of fair representation. The exclusive representative, as a matter of law, is under a

---

49. See *Eastern Assoc. Coal Corp. v. United Mine Workers, Dist. 17,* 531 U.S. 57 (2000); *United Paperworkers Int'l Union v. Misco, Inc.,* 484 U.S. 29 (1987).

50. *Olin Corp.,* 268 N.L.R.B. 573 (1984); *United Technologies Corp.,* 268 N.L.R.B. 557 (1984).

51. See *J.I. Case v. NLRB,* 321 U.S. 332 (1944).

52. See *Emporium Capwell Co. v. Western Addition Community Organization,* 420 U.S. 50 (1975).

duty to fairly represent all employees in the bargaining unit.[53] If a breach of this duty is shown, a court action for breach of contract against the employer may proceed.[54] The second exception is where the employee's claim is based on a public law creating individual rights not waivable by the collective bargaining representative, such as Title VII of the Civil Rights Act of 1964 or other anti-discrimination laws.[55]

I. Union Democracy

Federal labor law does not require workers to become members of labor unions even in firms where unions are the exclusive bargaining agency.[56] Indeed, the law prohibits "closed shops," i.e., agreements requiring workers to become union members as a condition of being hired for a position.[57] However, "union shop" clauses are lawful (except in states which have enacted "right to work" laws barring such provisions[58]). Under a typical union-shop clause, the employer is permitted to hire whomever it wishes, but the individual hired must within 30 days pay dues that cover the costs of collective representation. Although the NLRA uses language of "membership," which may confuse many employees, their only obligation under a union-shop clause is to pay their share of the costs of collective representation, rather than to join the union as such.[59]

Of relevance to individuals who are union members (and most represented employees become members by virtue of a union-shop clause), the federal Labor–Management Reporting and Disclosure

---

53. See *Steele v. Louisville & Nashville R.R.*, 323 U.S. 192 (1944).

54. See *Hines v. Anchor Motor Freight, Inc.*, 424 U.S. 554 (1976); *Vaca v. Sipes*, 386 U.S. 171 (1967).

55. *Alexander v. Gardner–Denver Co.*, 415 U.S. 36 (1974). The Court has held that although the "presumption of arbitrability" does not apply to arbitration, pursuant to collective bargaining agreements, of individual non–NLRA statutory rights, it has left open the question whether unions can negotiate express waivers of the right of represented employees to pursue their individual statutory claims in court. See *Wright v. Universal Maritime Servs.*, 525 U.S. 70 (1998). This issue will be decided by the Supreme Court in *14 Penn Plaza, LLC v. Pyett*, No. 07–581.

56. See *NLRB v. General Motors Corp.*, 373 U.S. 734 (1963).

57. Prior to the 1947 Taft–Hartley amendments, the closed shop was lawful. Section 8(a)(3), as amended, limits union security agreements to those which require as a condition of employment "membership" after the thirtieth day of employment. (This means that the obligation to pay dues does not arise until after the thirtieth day of employment.) Section 8(b)(2) bars union from denying "membership" to employees on grounds other than the "failure to tender the periodic dues and the initiation fees uniformly required as a condition of acquiring or retaining membership." 29 U.S.C. §§ 158(a)(3), (b)(2).

58. See Section 14(b) of the NLRA, 29 U.S.C. § 164(b).

59. See note 56 *supra*; *Marquez v. Screen Actors Guild, Inc.*, 525 U.S. 33 (1998).

Act of 1959 (LMRDA or "Landrum–Griffin Act")[60] establishes rules of internal union democracy. Under the LMRDA, union members have enforceable rights of free speech at union meetings and to run for union office free of unreasonable restrictions in fairly conducted elections. Section 8(b)(1)(A) of the NLRA also limits the bases on which unions can discipline their members, and ensures minimum standards of fairness in any union disciplinary proceedings. Union members can be subject to fines but cannot lose their jobs because of a violation of internal union rules.[61] They also have the right to resign their union membership even in the midst of a strike, irrespective of limits on resignation in the union constitution.[62]

J. Labor Law and Business Change

As a general matter, companies seeking to merge with other firms or to sell all or part of their assets are under no duty to bargain over the decision itself, although there is a duty to bargain over the "effects" of the decisions. "Effects" bargaining must be in time to permit meaningful bargaining, but can take place after the decision is made. Subjects of effects bargaining include severance pay, relocation benefits, and the like.

There may, however, be restrictions in the labor agreement requiring the employer to secure a purchaser who will assume the obligations of the unexpired agreements. Such restrictions are enforceable in arbitration, and unions may seek court injunctions to preserve the status quo pending arbitration.[63]

In mergers and sales of stock, the surviving entity or purchaser will generally be held to assume the obligation to bargain with the union and to comply with the terms of the unexpired labor agreement. In unusual circumstances, it may be possible to argue that employment conditions with the surviving entity or stock purchaser will so radically alter the preexisting employment relationship that the union cannot be considered any longer to be the exclusive representative of the workers in an appropriate unit.[64]

60. 29 U.S.C. §§ 401–531. Some provisions of the 1959 legislation also amended the NLRA.

61. See *NLRB v. Allis–Chalmers Mfg. Co.*, 388 U.S. 175 (1967); *Scofield v. NLRB*, 394 U.S. 423 (1969).

62. See *Pattern Markers' League of North America v. NLRB*, 473 U.S. 95 (1985).

63. See *Howard Johns Co. v. Hotel and Restaurant Employees*, 417 U.S. 249, 258 n.3 (1974); e.g., *Local Lodge No. 1266, Intl. Assn. of Machinists v. Panoramic Corp.*, 668 F.2d 276 (7th Cir. 1981). See generally Samuel Estreicher *Successorship Obligations*, in LABOR LAW AND BUSINESS CHANGE: THEORETICAL AND TRANSACTIONAL PERSPECTIVES ch. 4 (SAMUEL ESTREICHER & DANIEL G. COLLINS eds. 1988).

64. Compare *John Wiley & Sons, Inc. v. Livingston*, 376 U.S. 543 (1964).

In the case of asset purchases, however, the purchaser's obligations are substantially relaxed. The purchaser is free to hire an entirely independent work-force, absent proof of refusal to hire the seller's workers because of their union status.[65] The purchaser is under no obligation to assume the predecessor's labor contract—unless possibly if it hires substantially all of the predecessor's employees without predicating offers on changes in terms and conditions and without making substantial changes in the operation.[66] The purchaser is also under no obligation to bargain with the predecessor's union unless a majority of the purchaser's employees come from the ranks of the predecessor's workforce. This determination is made at the time the purchaser hires a "substantial and representative" complement, rather than the later point when its "full" complement has been hired.[67] However, a purchaser who buys a business with knowledge of the seller's unremedied unfair labor practices is subject to the NLRB's remedial authority.[68]

Special procedures govern an employer's attempt through a Chapter 11 bankruptcy petition to alter the terms of extant collective bargaining agreements.[69]

---

65. See *NLRB v. Burns International Security Servs., Inc.*, 406 U.S. 272 (1972).

66. See *id.* at 294–95 ("there will be instances in which it is perfectly clear that the new employer plans to retain all of the employees in the unit and in which it will be appropriate to have him initially consult with the employees' bargaining representative before he fixes terms.").

67. See *Fall River Dyeing & Finishing Corp. v. NLRB*, 482 U.S. 27 (1987).

68. See *Golden State Bottling Co., Inc. v. NLRB*, 414 U.S. 168 (1973).

69. See 11 U.S.C. § 1113.

Chapter 10

WAGE AND HOUR REGULATION

A. History

Both state and federal governments have laws regulating wages and hours of work. The centerpiece of federal legislation is the Fair Labor Standards Act of 1938 (FLSA).[1] The FLSA establishes unwaivable minimum standards for wages, hours of work, and child labor.

The FLSA grew out of a movement by organized labor and other groups beginning in the mid–19th century to reduce work time. Proponents of the "short hours movement" lobbied for the reduction of work hours to help reduce worker fatigue, combat sweatshop working conditions, and give wage workers more time to pursue personal activities.[2] They also sought to combat unemployment, with shorter work hours holding the promise of spreading work among a greater number of workers.

Attempts by Congress and state legislatures to shorten the workday or the workweek were stymied in the courts. Most famously, in *Lochner v. New York*,[3] the U.S. Supreme Court struck down state legislation limiting bakers' hours of work to 10 hours per day or 60 hours per week as an interference with freedom of contract and unconstitutional infringement of liberty under the Fourteenth Amendment. By the New Deal era, judicial sentiment began to shift, perhaps beginning with the Supreme Court's decision in *West Coast Hotel v. Parrish*.[4] In that case, the Court upheld a Washington state law imposing a minimum wage for women and minors as a measure necessary to prevent exploitation of workers lacking the bargaining power to demand a living wage themselves.[5] The FLSA was enacted during this more receptive judicial environment.

B. Basic Requirements of the Statute

1. Minimum Wage

Unless a state has established a higher minimum, employees are entitled under the FLSA to receive at a basic minimum wage

---

1. 29 U.S.C. §§ 201 *et. seq.*

2. See generally, DAVID R. ROEDIGER & PHILIP SHELDON FONER, OUR OWN TIME: A HISTORY OF AMERICAN LABOR AND THE WORKING DAY (1989).

3. 198 U.S. 45 (1905).

4. 300 U.S. 379 (1937).

5. *Id.* at 399.

171

per hour of work.[6] In 2007, Congress passed a law to increase the minimum wage in increments, over a two-year period, to $7.25 per hour.[7] If the employee is paid hourly, it is usually fairly simple to tell whether he or she is receiving the statutory minimum. If an employee is salaried, or paid by commission or piece-rates (i.e., according to the quantity of production), one must divide the worker's straight-time wages by the number of hours worked during a given workweek to determine the hourly rate paid. The "workweek"—7 consecutive days, or 168 hours—is the key unit of measurement under the FLSA. The statute aims to guarantee workers a basic minimum wage—every workweek. As such, an employer that pays less than the minimum wage for a given workweek will violate the statute even if compensation averaged across many weeks or months would more than satisfy the standard.[8]

Also consistent with the goal of ensuring employees have regular, accessible income, employers ordinarily must pay wages in cash or negotiable instrument "free and clear".[9] This privileging of cash-in-hand over other forms of compensation is not absolute—for example, with employees' consent, employers may consider the reasonable value of board, lodging, or other similar facilities provided to employees as "wages".[10] But it certainly constrains some employer pay practices, such as making deductions from employees' wages to pay for uniforms, tools, costs of breakage, or cash register shortages if the deduction would reduce the employee's pay below

---

6. This was the minimum wage as of 2007. 29 U.S.C. § 206 (a). More than half of the states have a higher minimum. *See* U.S. Department of Labor, Employment Standards Administration Wage and Hour Division, MINIMUM WAGE LAWS IN THE UNITED STATES—JULY 24 2007 (available at *http://www.dol.gov/esa/minwage/america.htm*). The FLSA does not preempt such state laws; in effect employers must comply with the higher minimum wage. *See* 29 U.S.C. § 218 (a).

7. FAIR MINIMUM WAGE AND TAX RELIEF ACT OF 2007 (P.L. 110–28, Title VIII, Subtitle A). Section 8102 of the Act amends the FLSA to increase the federal minimum wage to: (1) $5.85 an hour on July 24, 2007; (2) $6.55 an hour on July 24, 2008; and (3) $7.25 an hour on July 24, 2009.

8. Special exceptions from the standard minimum wage are provided for tipped employees, who may be paid as little as $2.13 per hour, as long as the tips make up the difference between their hourly wage and the statutory minimum wage (see generally, 29 U.S.C. § 203 (n), (t)), and youths under 20 years of age who may be paid a subminimum "opportunity wage" of $4.25 per hour during their first 90 consecutive days of employment (29 U.S.C. § 206 (g)).

9. 29 C.F.R. §§ 531.27, 531.35.

10. 29 U.S.C. § 203 (m). Board, lodging, or other facilities count as wages only if they are customarily furnished by the employer to the employees. *Id.*

the statutory minimum.[11] State wage payment laws further limit the employer's ability to make deductions from employee pay.

2.   Overtime Premium

Unless they are exempt from the overtime requirement, employees are to receive one and one-half times their "regular rate" of pay for any hours worked over forty in a workweek.[12] The regular rate is an hourly rate typically determined by dividing an employee's total compensation for a workweek by the total number of hours worked during that week.[13]

The regular rate for non-exempt salaried employees is treated slightly differently. It is computed by dividing the weekly salary by the number of hours the salary is intended to compensate.[14] The employee who works more hours is entitled to receive her regular rate for all hours in excess of the intended number of hours and overtime of one-half times the regular rate for all hours worked in excess of forty.[15]

The basic method for calculating overtime sounds simple enough, but it can be surprisingly complex, with dramatic consequences for employer liability. Two central questions we will address in later sections are *what counts as pay* for purposes of determining the regular rate, and *what counts as work* for purposes of determining whether an employee has worked more than 40 hours in one workweek.

3.   Child Labor Restrictions

The FLSA restricts certain child labor by establishing minimum ages for most kinds of work. The purpose of these restrictions

---

11.   DEPARTMENT OF LABOR, EMPLOYMENT STANDARDS ADMINISTRATION WAGE AND HOUR DIVISION, FACT SHEET #16: DEDUCTIONS FROM WAGES FOR UNIFORMS AND OTHER FACILITIES UNDER THE FAIR LABOR STANDARDS ACT (FLSA), available at *http://dol.gov/esa/regs/compliance/whd/printpage.asp?REF=whdfs16.htm*.

12.   29 U.S.C. § 207(a)(1); 29 C.F.R. §§ 778.110 *et seq.*

13.   29 C.F.R. § 778.109.

14.   29 C.F.R. § 778.113. The regulation gives the following example: "If an employee is hired at a salary of $182.70 and if it is understood that this salary is compensation for a regular workweek of 35 hours, the employee's regular rate of pay is $182.70 divided by 35 hours."

15.   See *id.* If, however, there is a clear mutual understanding between the employer and employee that the salary is compensation for all hours worked in a workweek regardless of the number of hours, the regular rate is determined by dividing the weekly salary by the total number of hours worked in the week. The employee is entitled to an additional one-half times the regular rate for all hours worked over forty in the workweek. 29 C.F.R. § 778.114. This is often referred to as the "fluctuating workweek" method of computation because the regular rate could change each workweek based on the number of hours actually worked. The regular rate as determined by this method must be no less than the minimum wage.

is to protect children's educational opportunities and prevent them from working in jobs detrimental to their health and well being.[16] Signaling the special importance of the child labor laws, the FLSA contains the additional enforcement mechanism of a "hot goods" provision: it is unlawful to ship goods produced in an establishment that uses prohibited child labor.[17] Many states have additional child labor restrictions.[18]

Sixteen is the minimum age for most work.[19] However, children aged fourteen to sixteen may work in certain establishments, such as offices, retailers, food services, and gas stations, provided that such work does not interfere with their schooling.[20] The FLSA also bars those younger than eighteen from engaging in "hazardous" kinds of work,[21] such as manufacturing, mining, logging and roofing.[22] There are certain kinds of work, however, that children of any age can perform such as delivering newspapers, performing in movies, television or theatrical productions, and, subject to certain limitations, working for their parents.[23] In addition, by the age of sixteen, children may perform any farm job.[24] Furthermore, as long as they have their parents' written consent, children of *any* age may work outside of school hours in non-hazardous jobs on farms owned or operated by their parents or on farms not covered by minimum wage requirements.[25]

16. U.S. D*EPARTMENT OF* L*ABOR*, O*FFICE OF THE* A*SSISTANT* S*ECRETARY FOR* P*OLICY*, E*MPLOYMENT* L*AW* G*UIDE*: C*HILD* L*ABOR* (N*ONAGRICULTURAL* W*ORK*), available at http://dol.gov/asp/programs/guide/childlbr.htm.

17. 29 U.S.C. § 212(a).

18. U.S. D*EPARTMENT OF* L*ABOR*, Y*OUTH & *L*ABOR*: S*TATE* L*ABOR* L*AW*, at http://www.dol.gov/dol/topic/youthlabor/agerequirements.htm. See also U.S. D*EPARTMENT OF* L*ABOR*, E*MPLOYMENT* S*TANDARDS* A*DMINISTRATION* W*AGE AND* H*OUR* D*IVISION*, S*ELECTED* S*TATE* C*HILD* L*ABOR* S*TANDARDS* A*FFECTING* M*INORS* U*NDER* 18 *IN* N*ON-FARM* E*MPLOYMENT AS OF* January 1, 2007, at http://www.dol.gov/esa/programs/whd/state/nonfarm.htm.

19. 29 U.S.C. § 203(*l*).

20. *Id.*; 29 C.F.R. § 570.34. Children 14–16 may work at certain jobs provided that they work outside school hours, no more than forty hours a week when school is not in session, no more than eighteen hours a week when school is in session, no more than eight hours a day when school is not is session, and no more than three hours a day when school is in session. Such children are also prohibited from working between 7:00 a.m. and 7:00 p.m. except during the summer (June 1 through Labor Day) when the evening hour is extended to 9:00 p.m. There are exemptions from these requirements for children at least fourteen years old who are involved with certain activities incident to professional sporting events. See 29 C.F.R. § 570.35.

21. 29 U.S.C. § 203(*l*).

22. 29 C.F.R. §§ 570.50–570.68.

23. 29 CFR §§ 570.123–570.126.

24. 29 C.F.R. 575.1. For criticism of the farm labor exemptions from child labor laws, *see, e.g.,* Davin C. Curtiss, *The Fair Labor Standards Act and Child Labor in Agriculture*, 20 J. C*ORP.* L. 303, 308–309 (1995).

25. *Id.*

4. Anti–Retaliation

The FLSA prohibits employer retaliation against an employee for filing a complaint or testifying in a proceeding under the FLSA—what is often termed a participation clause.[26] The FLSA does not, however, contain an express opposition clause,[27] raising the question whether employees are protected for complaining internally about wage-hour violations. Although most federal courts will find internal complaints protected,[28] some courts have held that an employee is protected only if retaliated against for filing a formal complaint to the Department of Labor or a court.[29] Another issue dividing the courts is whether employees may recover punitive damages in addition to statutory remedies for a retaliation claim.[30]

C. Rationale for Regulation

Recall from Chapter 1 our discussion of the standard economic objections to regulation. The arguments against minimum wage laws follow these same lines. Minimum wage laws have costs:

- Faced with increased costs imposed by the minimum wage requirement, employers may respond by laying off workers, employing them for fewer hours, slowing hiring, or reducing the wages of workers who are not covered by minimum wage laws.

26. 29 U.S.C. § 215 (a) (3); 29 U.S.C. § 216 (b).

27. Under Title VII of the Civil Rights Act of 1964, by contrast, employees are protected from retaliation by "oppos[ing] any practice made an unlawful employment practice" by the statute § 704(a), 42 U.S.C. § 2000e-3. See Chapter 11 for a discussion of anti-retaliation clauses in federal employment statutes.

28. See, *Valerio v. Putnam Associates Inc.*, 173 F.3d 35, 41–44 (1st Cir. 1999); *EEOC v. Romeo Community Schools*, 976 F.2d 985, 989–90 (6th Cir. 1992), *Conner v. Schnuck Markets, Inc.*, 121 F.3d 1390, 1394 (10th Cir. 1997), *EEOC v. White and Son Enterprises*, 881 F.2d 1006, 1011 (11th Cir. 1989).

29. See, *Lambert v. Genesee Hospital*, 10 F.3d 46 (2d Cir. 1993); *Ball v. Memphis Bar–B–Q Co., Inc.*, 228 F.3d 360, 364 (4th Cir. 2000).

30. Compare *Snapp v. Unlimited Concepts, Inc.*, 208 F.3d 928, 933–939 (11th Cir. 2000) (finding that the damages provision in 29 U.S.C. § 216(b) is compensatory, not punitive in nature, and thus, punitive damages are not available for FLSA retaliation claims), with *Travis v. Gary Community Mental Health Center, Inc.*, 921 F.2d 108, 111–12 (7th Cir. 1990) (finding that the 1977 amendments to the FLSA broadened the damages provision for retaliation claims, giving the courts latitude to award punitive damages).

- Those who lose their jobs are more likely to be young, unskilled workers, with the long-run effect of reducing their accumulation of on-the-job training and labor market skills.

- Increased wage costs may be passed to consumers in the form of higher prices or lower product or service quality.

On the other hand, benefits might include:

- Increased wages for some workers.

- Ripple effects leading to increases in wages currently above the minimum wage, as employers try to maintain preexisting wage differentials between jobs.

- Higher productivity on the part of workers because the employer requires greater work effort and workers feel they have more to lose if they become unemployed.

- Some workers who lose their jobs will choose to obtain more education or training rather than remaining unemployed.

The key question is whether costs outweigh benefits. Particularly contentious is the question of how the benefits and burdens of minimum wage laws are socially distributed. For example, we might worry less if minimum wage laws reduced the employment of college-bound middle class teenagers than if they reduced employment of low-skilled adults from low-income families. We do not purport to resolve this debate here, only to point out that the social utility of minimum wage laws—and the perennial question of whether Congress ought to increase the minimum wage—remain contested terrain.[31]

The oft-articulated goal of overtime laws is to spread available work across the workforce, and give workers some relief from the pressure to work long hours. To illustrate why overtime laws might, in theory, further this objective, consider an employer, Acme, which needs 60 hours of work performed in one week. Acme can hire Sarah to do all of that work, but if it does so, it will need to pay Sarah overtime equal to one-half her hourly rate for the hours she works in excess of 40. Acme must pay ($10 x .5 x 20) = $100 in overtime pay. Sarah's total compensation will be ($10 x 60) = $600

---

31. Some empirical evidence suggests limited disemployment effects from modest, phased-in increases in the minimum wage. See DAVID METCALF, WHY HAS THE BRITISH NATIONAL MINIMUM WAGE HAD LITTLE OR NO IMPACT ON EMPLOYMENT? (CENTRE FOR ECONOMIC PERFORMANCE, Discussion Paper No., 781, Apr. 2007). See also DAVID CARD & ALAN KRUEGER, MYTH AND MEASUREMENT: THE NEW ECONOMICS OF THE MINIMUM WAGE (1995). For critical reviews of the Card–Krueger findings, see, David Neumark, *Raising Incomes by Mandating Higher Wages*, NBER RESEARCH SUMMARY, NBER REPORTER, Fall 2002; Daniel Shaviro, *The Minimum Wage, Earned Income Tax Credit, and Optimal Subsidy Policy*, 64 U. CHI. L. REV. 405 (1997).

plus $100, for a total of $700. If the employer, instead, decides to hire Stan to perform the final 20 hours of labor, the wage bill will be ($10 x 40) = $400 for Sarah and ($10 x 20) = $200 for Stan, for a total of $600. In theory, then, the prospect of a lower wage bill encourages Acme to distribute available labor over two workers instead of one. In the aggregate, we might expect overtime laws to reduce unemployment. In addition, the employer's decision gives Sarah more time for leisure (whether or not she wants it).

Although this simple illustration suggests that a rational employer will spread work, this will not always be the case. First, hiring additional workers means the employer must incur additional fixed costs such as investments in training and, if the workers are full-time, often health and retirement benefits. These additional costs may offset and, in any event, reduce the overtime savings from hiring additional workers. Alternatively, the employer may hire additional workers but do so on only a short-term or temporary basis rather than expanding its permanent workforce.[32]

Secondly, the illustration assumes the employer sets wages without anticipating future overtime needs. A forward-looking employer, however, may anticipate and adjust for overtime liability when setting wages in the first instance. Nothing in the FLSA prevents an employer from intentionally making this kind of adjustment, so long as the compensating differential does not produce a wage below the statutory minimum. If Acme knows that it will pay no more than $600 for a 60–hour week or work, and yet prefers to train and supervise only Sarah rather than hiring a second worker, it can simply work backwards: in this case an hourly wage of $8.57 will produce the appropriate wage bill.[33] Recent empirical evidence suggests employers indeed may have responded to overtime laws by reducing employees' hourly wages, rather than shortening the workweek and creating more jobs.[34]

D. What Counts as Compensation?

What counts as compensation for the purpose of calculating the regular rate under the FLSA can have significant implications for overtime liability.[35] Compensation includes payments for work per-

---

32. See Sharon Rabin–Margalioth, *Cross–Employee Redistribution Effects of Mandated Employee Benefits*, 20 HOFSTRA LAB. & EMP. L. J. 311 (2003).

33. Acme must pay ($8.57 x 40) = $343 for the regular hours worked, plus ($12.86 x 20) = $257 for the overtime hours worked, for a total of $600.

34. Stephen J. Trejo, *Does the Statutory Overtime Premium Discourage Long Workweeks?* 56 IND. & LAB. REL. REV. 530 (2003).

35. The statute variously uses the terms "pay," "remuneration," and "compensation" to denote the money an employer pays an employee for work

formed whether in the form of a salary, hourly rate, day rate, job rate, piece rate, commission, bonus, shift differential, tips, meals or lodging.[36] An employer that supplements hourly wages with tips, bonuses and in-kind payments, for example, might face significant unexpected overtime liability if it makes the error of calculating overtime based solely on the hourly wage.

One area where it is easy to make mistakes is bonus and commission payments. Consider again Acme and its employee Sarah, who works 60 hours in a workweek at an hourly rate of $10 per hour. Suppose Sarah also receives a bonus of $400. Depending on the type of bonus, it may count as compensation for purposes of calculating the regular rate. If the bonus is based on some aspect of Sarah's quality or quantity of work, then it counts as compensation and must be included in calculating Sarah's regular rate. If instead the bonus is *not* based on Sarah's productivity, perhaps a gift because the employer had a good year, then it does not count as compensation in calculating the regular rate.

The regulations accompanying the FLSA offer guidance by specifying what is not to be included in the regular rate. In addition to gifts of the type illustrated above that are not dependent on the quantity or quality of work, the statute also excludes payments made for occasional periods where no work is performed (e.g., vacation, holidays, sick time, jury duty), employee benefits such as insurance, retirement and profit-sharing benefits, expense reimbursements, and certain bonuses.[37] Also excluded are extra payments at a premium rate paid for working extra time or for working on weekends or holidays.[38]

E. What Counts as Work or Hours Worked?

Accurate determination of the total hours worked in workweek is critical to insure that employees are paid properly. The FLSA does not contain a definition of "work," but defines "employ" as to "suffer or permit to work."[39] Time spent by the employee working

performed; we use the term compensation in this discussion for sake of convenience.

36. See 29 C.F.R. §§ 531.60, 778.107 *et seq.* and 778.200 *et seq.*

37. Bonuses in recognition of services performed are excluded from the regular rate calculation so long as the bonus is made at the sole discretion of the employer. Bonuses paid at regular times may be deemed non-discretionary because such bonuses create an expectation that bonuses will be paid. *See McComb v. Shepard Niles Crane & Hoist*, 171 F.2d 69 (2d Cir. 1948). Accordingly, employers should exercise caution in determining that a bonus need not be counted toward "compensation" paid to an employee.

38. 29 U.S.C. § 207(e); 29 C.F.R. § 778.200.

39. 29 U.S.C. § 203(g).

on behalf of an employer at the employer's premises or another prescribed workplace is considered "work" for purposes of the FLSA, because, at such times, the employee is "suffered" or "permitted" to work.[40]

Rest periods of a short duration, typically twenty minutes or less, are counted towards hours worked.[41] Conversely, bona fide meal periods, where the employee is completely relieved from her duties, usually lasting thirty minutes or more, are excluded from hours worked.[42]

Work hours include time voluntarily worked by the employee, with or without the employer's authorization, as to which the employer is or should be aware.[43] Such "off-the-clock" work may also be done at home with the employer's actual or constructive knowledge.[44] When overtime work is unauthorized, however, an employee may have difficulty recovering because of the knowledge requirement.[45] But liability can be established in appropriate circumstances. In *Lyle v. Food Lion, Inc.*,[46] an employee worked extra hours "off the clock" in order to meet strict performance standards despite an explicit company policy against working off-the-clock. Yet the employer was charged with constructive knowledge of the overtime work in part because it had given employees keys to the store so that they could enter the premises and work before regular business hours.[47]

Time spent waiting to work, but not actively working, is counted as hours worked in certain circumstances. This issue comes up with employees who work "on call." The test of compensability is whether the employee was "engaged to wait" (work time) or waiting "to be engaged" (not work time).[48] For example, a firefighter who watches television while waiting for an alarm, a bike messenger who reads a book while waiting for an assignment, and a factory worker who chats with coworkers while waiting for equipment to be repaired, are all "engaged to wait" and must be

---

40. See 29 C.F.R. § 785.7.

41. 29 C.F.R. § 785.18.

42. 29 C.F.R. § 785.19.

43. See 29 C.F.R. § 785.11: "Work not requested but suffered or permitted is work time. For example, an employee may voluntarily continue to work at the end of the shift. He may be a pieceworker, he may desire to finish an assigned task or he may wish to correct errors, paste work tickets, prepare time reports or other records. The reason is immaterial. The employer knows or has reason to believe that he is continuing to work and the time is working time."

44. 29 C.F.R. § 785.12.

45. Davis v. Food Lion, Inc., 792 F.2d 1274, 1276 (4th Cir. 1986).

46. 954 F.2d 984 (4th Cir. 1992).

47. *Id.*, at 987.

48. 29 C.F.R. § 785.14 (citing *Skidmore v. Swift*, 323 U.S. 134 (1944)).

compensated for that waiting time.[49] If an employee is required to remain on-call at the worksite or so close to the worksite that he cannot use the time as he pleases, he must be paid for it. On the other hand, if the employee is able to use the time effectively for his own purposes, including leaving the employer's premises, the time is not considered work time.[50]

"Sleeping on the job," one may be surprised to learn, can be compensable. If an employee is required to be on duty for a shift of less than 24 hours, and given permission to sleep when not actively working, the time spent sleeping is compensable. The theory behind this requirement is that such employees are required to be on duty, and must be paid for all on-duty time.[51] On the other hand, for shifts exceeding 24 hours, the parties may contractually agree to exclude meal periods and a regularly scheduled sleeping period from hours worked. Absent such agreement, the employer must compensate the worker for all hours on duty, including meal and sleep periods. Even with such an agreement, employees must be paid for any call to duty interrupting their sleep. Typically, if an employee cannot get at least five hours of sleep, the entire time is counted as hours worked.[52]

Another area of some ambiguity is training. Time spent by an employee in training activities is compensable work unless: (1) attendance is outside of the employee's regular work hours; (2) attendance is voluntary; (3) the training is not directly related to the employee's job; and (4) the employee does not perform any productive work during the training.[53] Applying these criteria in *Dade County, Florida v. Alvarez*,[54] the Eleventh Circuit held that physical fitness training undertaken by police officers, which allowed them to meet the fitness requirements of their position, was not compensable. The court noted that the officers determined when, where and how long to exercise, indicating that their participation was voluntary, and that the exercise was not directly related to the officer's work.[55] Rather, the officers were deemed to have reaped the benefits of maintaining good physical conditioning.

Certain travel time and time spent on activities incident to actual work are regulated by the 1949 Portal-to-Portal Act amendments to the FLSA.[56] The Portal-to-Portal Act excludes time spent

49. 29 C.F.R. § 785.15.

50. 29 C.F.R. § 785.17. *See also Dinges v. St. Mary's Hospitals, Inc.*, 164 F.3d 1056, 1057–58 (7th Cir. 1999).

51. 29 C.F.R. § 785.21.

52. 29 C.F.R. § 785.22.

53. 29 C.F.R. 785.27.

54. 124 F.3d 1380, 1385 (11th Cir. 1997).

55. *Id.*

56. 29 U.S.C. §§ 251–262.

walking, riding or traveling to and from the actual place of work from compensability under the FLSA.[57] In addition, it excludes an employee's preparatory and concluding activities, unless they are integral or indispensable parts of the employee's principal activities.[58] Matters of controversy have included whether to classify as "integral or indispensable" time spent changing into and out of protective apparel,[59] walking to the place where the gear is donned and doffed,[60] and waiting in line to obtain protective gear.[61]

F. Covered Employers and Employees

Wage and hour laws apply to "employees who in any workweek [are] engaged in commerce or in the production of goods for commerce, or [are] employed in an enterprise engaged in commerce or in the production of goods for commerce."[62] Breaking this provision down into its components, coverage operates along a number of dimensions. First, the FLSA applies to a covered enterprise, i.e., a business meeting the standards for FLSA coverage. Second, the FLSA applies only to employees; independent contractors are not covered. Third, even if an enterprise does not qualify for FLSA coverage, those employees of the enterprise who are personally engaged in commerce or the production of goods for commerce will be covered. Finally, because of the "white-collar" and other specific exemptions, certain employees may be exempt from the minimum wage and/or overtime provisions of the FLSA even if they are employed by a covered enterprise.

1. Enterprise Coverage

Not all places of work qualify as an "enterprise" under the FLSA. Some entities, such as small businesses, highly localized cottage industries, and family businesses employing only family members, are exempt from the statute.[63] The existence of both individual coverage and enterprise coverage, however, means that

---

57. See 29 C.F.R. 785.34. Travel that is part of the day's work, such as from job site to job site, is counted as hours worked. 29 C.F.R. § 785.38.

58. See 29 C.F.R. §§ 785.24, 790.8(b) and (c).

59. *Steiner v. Mitchell*, 350 U.S. 247 (1956) ("donning and doffing" of required safety clothing and equipment is integral and indispensable to principal work activities).

60. *IBP, Inc. v. Alvarez*, 546 U.S. 21 (2005) (time spent walking between the locker room and the area where required protective gear is donned and doffed is integral and indispensable to principal work activities).

61. *Id.* at 41–42 (excluded from FLSA compensability). Parties may compensate such time by agreement or custom or practice. 29 U.S.C. § 254(b).

62. E.g., 29 U.S.C. § 206 (a).

63. *Id.* § 203 (s).

even if an employer falls outside the definition of a covered enterprise, some of its employees may be covered. Conversely an employee working in a covered enterprise is protected even if she is not personally "engaged in commerce".

A covered enterprise is one that has "employees who are engaged in commerce or the production of goods for commerce, or that has employees otherwise working on materials that have been moved in or produced for commerce by any person."[64] This provision has a broad sweep, including not only employees who make or sell goods for interstate commerce, but also a second tier of employees who, while not engaged in commerce themselves, handle goods or materials that someone else has moved or produced for commerce. The entity must also have a specified minimum gross volume of business (currently $500,000 annually). Given the breadth of the interpretation of "commerce" as a practical matter, enterprises that meet the dollar volume threshold will likely be covered by the FLSA.[65] Hospitals, schools and public agencies are covered regardless of the commerce test or the dollar volume requirement.[66]

In addition, coverage is determined on an "enterprise"-wide basis. All of the related activities of an entity comprise the "enterprise" for FLSA purposes. More specifically, an enterprise includes "the related activities performed (either through unified operation or common control) by any person or persons for a common business purpose, and includes all such activities whether performed in one or more establishments or by one or more corporate or organizational units...."[67] Accordingly, multiple establishments of a single business are aggregated for determining whether the business meets the dollar volume test for coverage under the FLSA.

2. *Employee Coverage*

a. Employee vs. Independent Contractor

The FLSA applies to employees only, not to independent contractors, trainees or volunteers. The FLSA defines "employee" as "any individual employed by an employer."[68] An "employer" is

---

64. Id. § 203 (s) (1) (A) (i).

65. See D*EPARTMENT OF* L*ABOR,* E*MPLOY-MENT* S*TANDARDS* A*DMINISTRATION* W*AGE AND* H*OUR* D*IVISION,* F*ACT* S*HEET* #14: C*OVERAGE* U*NDER THE* F*AIR* L*ABOR* S*TANDARDS* A*CT* (FLSA), available at *http://dol.gov/ess/ regs/compliance/whd/printpage.asp?*

REF=whdfs14.htm (suggesting that covered enterprises are those with at least two employees and which do at least $5000,000 a year in business.).

66. 29 U.S.C. § 203 (s)(1) (B).

67. 29 U.S.C. § 203 (r)(1).

68. 29 U.S.C. § 203 (e)(1).

"any person acting directly or indirectly in the interest of an employer in relation to an employee."[69] Finally, to "employ" is "to suffer or permit to work."[70] Through this triumvirate of terms, Congress intended to sweep within the statutory scheme a somewhat broader swath of workers and workplaces than the common law or other protective statutes had previously covered.[71]

Whatever Congress' intent, judicial interpretation settled on the "economic realities" test, which asks whether the worker, regardless of how the parties have contractually labeled the relationship, is economically dependent upon the business for which he or she works. In Chapter 1, we discussed the doctrinal challenges as well as social implications of using the economic realities test to determine who is an employee for purposes of statutory coverage.

b.   Employees Personally Engaged In Interstate Commerce

Assuming a worker is an employee, even if she does not work for a covered enterprise, she will be covered by the FLSA if her work involves interstate commerce or the production of goods for commerce. The term "engaged in commerce" means *interstate* trade, commerce, transportation, transmission, or communication.[72] The term embraces goods as well as services and acts that facilitate the movement of commerce by providing raw materials or facilities (e.g., fuel, storage) used to make or operate instrumentalities of commerce that have crossed or will cross state lines.[73] Accordingly, employees meet the interstate-commerce requirement if their work involves handling goods that cross state lines or using channels of interstate commerce, including using the telephone or mail to communicate with individuals out of state.[74] In practice, therefore, the scope of the commerce requirement is extremely broad. It excludes only truly local operations that use local materials and have a local market.

---

69. 29 U.S.C. § 203 (d).

70. 29 U.S.C. § 203 (g).

71. See *Rutherford Food Corp. v. McComb*, 331 U.S. 722, 729 (1947) (holding that the "suffer or permit to work" language of the FLSA includes "many persons and working relationships which, prior to the Act, were not deemed to fall within the employer-employee category."). *See also* Chapter 2, *supra*, discussing the "economic realities" test

for determining employee status under FLSA.

72. 29 U.S.C. § 203 (b).

73. 29 U.S.C. § 203 (i), (j).

74. *See* DEPARTMENT OF LABOR, EMPLOYMENT STANDARDS ADMINISTRATION WAGE AND HOUR DIVISION, FACT SHEET #14: COVERAGE UNDER THE FAIR LABOR STANDARDS ACT (FLSA), available at http://dol.gov/ess/regs/compliance/whd/printpage.asp?REF=whdfs14.htm.

3. Exemptions

Although a worker must be an employee to receive the benefits of the statute, merely being an employee is not sufficient. Many employees are excluded from the FLSA because they fall within one or more *exempt* categories. To choose just some among numerous examples, casual babysitters, personal care workers, many white collar employees, and certain employees of amusement parks, fisheries, small farms, and newspapers are exempt from both minimum wage and overtime requirements.[75] Seamen, news announcers and editors in less populated areas, car and boat salespeople, certain kinds of agricultural workers, certain commissioned employees of retail or service establishments, taxi drivers and foster parents are among those exempted from overtime requirements.[76]

In 2004, the Department of Labor revised its longstanding regulations regarding the white-collar exemptions.[77] The white-collar exemptions exempt executive, administrative and professional employees from both overtime and minimum wage requirements. To fall within the white-collar exemptions, employees must meet both a salary-basis test and a duties test. The salary test is similar for each of the exemptions and requires that employees be paid a fixed salary of no less that $455 a week, not including board, lodging or other facilities.[78] Employees are paid a fixed salary when they are paid on a weekly, or less frequent basis, a predetermined amount which is not subject to reduction based on the quality or quantity of work performed.[79] Employees must be paid their full salary for any week in which they perform work even if some time is lost due to operational requirements of the business, availability

75. See generally, 29 U.S.C. § 213 (a) for these and other exemptions.

76. See generally, 29 U.S.C. § 213 (b) for these and other exemptions.

77. Section 13(a)(1) of the FLSA, 29 U.S.C. § 213(a)(1); Defining and Delimiting the Exemptions for Executive, Administrative, Professional, Outside Sales and Computer Employees; Final Rule, 69 Fed. Reg. 22260 (April 23, 2004) (revising 29 C.F.R. part 541).

78. 29 C.F.R. §§ 541.600, 541.606. Doctors, attorneys and certain teachers need not meet the salary test to qualify for exemption. 29 C.F.R. § 541.600(e). Additionally, this amount may be paid on a fee basis to administrative and pro-fessional employees but not to executive employees.

79. 29 C.F.R. § 541.602(a). In addition to a fixed salary, employers may pay employees additional sums such as bonuses, commissions, profit sharing and even overtime without losing the exemption, provided that the employee is guaranteed no less than $455 each week paid on a salary basis. 29 C.F.R. § 541.604(a). Also, under certain limited circumstances, an employee may be paid on an hourly, daily, shift or fee basis without losing the exemption. 29 C.F.R. §§ 541.604(b), 541.605.

of work, jury or witness duty or military leave.[80] Employers may, however, make deductions for full-day absences taken as a result of (1) an employee's personal reasons, such as vacation or personal days; (2) sickness or disability, so long as the time off is in accordance with a bona fide plan, policy of practice of providing compensation for illness or disability; and (3) disciplinary suspensions imposed in good faith for violation of workplace conduct rules imposed pursuant to a written policy applicable to all employees.[81] In addition, employers may make full-day deductions as a penalty imposed in good faith for violation of safety rules of major significance.[82] If employees are subject to improper dedications from pay, employers may lose the ability to treat the affected employees as overtime-exempt employees.[83]

The duties test varies depending on the type of exemption claimed. To fall within the executive exemption: (1) an employee's primary duty must be the management of the business in which she works or a customarily recognized department or subdivision within the business; (2) the employee must "customarily and regularly" direct the work of two or more other full-time employees; and (3) the employee must have the authority to hire or fire other employees or to make authoritative recommendations as to the status of other employees.[84] An administrative employee is one whose primary duty is "the performance of office or non-manual work directly related to the management or general business operations of the employer or the employer's customers" and involves the "exercise of discretion and independent judgment with respect to matters of significance."[85] Professional employees can be those whose primary duty requires either advanced knowledge "in a field of science or learning customarily acquired by a prolonged course of specialized intellectual instruction" or "invention, imagination, originality or talent in a recognized field or artistic or creative endeavor."[86] These duties tests are satisfied by looking at an employee's specific and particular job responsibilities. Job titles are not determinative of exempt status.[87]

---

80. 29 C.F.R. § 541.602(a) and (b)(3). However, employers may offset any amount received for the week by an employee as jury or witness fees or military pay against the salary due for that week.

81. 29 U.S.C. § 541.602(b)(1), (2) and (5).

82. 29 U.S.C. § 541.602(b)(4).

83. 29 C.F.R. § 541.603. See Auer v. Robbins, 519 U.S. 452 (1997) (agreeing with the Department of Labor that there must be an "actual practice" or "significant likelihood" of such deductions to fail the salary-basis test).

84. 29 C.F.R. §§ 541.100(a), 541.104.

85. 29 C.F.R. § 541.200(a).

86. 29 C.F.R. § 541.300(a).

87. See 29 C.F.R. § 541.2.

Under the 2004 interpretive regulations, these tests are relaxed for employees whose total annual compensation is $100,000 or more, excluding board, lodging and other facilities, and who perform office or non-manual work. Such highly compensated employees are exempt if their compensation includes "at least $455 per week paid on a salary or fee basis and if they customarily and regularly" perform (rather than have as their primary duty) any one or more of the exempt responsibilities specified in the duties tests for executive, administrative or professional employees.[88]

Other white-collar exemptions from the overtime requirements are computer employees, provided they meet certain compensation and duties tests, and "outside sales employees" (sales people who travel to their customers rather than working out of their employer's or home offices), regardless of their compensation.[89]

4. Other Exclusions from Coverage

Certain kinds of trainees and volunteers are deemed not to be employees.[90] Some interesting controversies have cropped up with respect to religious organizations and workfare programs. One case involved a Christian organization that used "associates," mainly "recovering drug addicts, derelicts, or criminals," to staff various endeavors of the organization in exchange for food, clothing, shelter, and other benefits.[91] The activities included retail clothing stores, hog farms, and electrical companies. The Secretary of Labor brought suit and at trial the associates testified that they performed the work as volunteers for religious reasons and did not seek monetary compensation. The Supreme Court held that the "associates were 'entirely dependent on the Foundation for long periods, in some cases several years' "—justifying the trial court's finding that they "must have expected to receive in-kind benefits— and expected them in exchange for their services. . . . "[92]

More recently, the Ninth Circuit considered the case of an individual who had been assigned a full-time job repairing furniture donated to the Salvation Army as part of a "work therapy" pro-

---

88. 29 C.F.R. § 541.601(a), (b)(1) and (d).

89. 29 C.F.R. §§ 541.500, 541.502.

90. 29 U.S.C. §§ 203 (e)(4) and (5), 214; *Tony and Susan Alamo Foundation v. Secretary of Labor*, 471 U.S. 290, 295 (1985) ("An individual who, 'without promise or expectation of compensation, but solely for his personal purpose or pleasure, worked in activities carried on by other persons either for their pleasure or profit,' is outside the sweep of the Act. *Walling v. Portland Terminal Co.*, 330 U.S. 148, 152, 67 S.Ct. 639, 641, 91 L.Ed. 809 (1947).").

91. *Tony and Susan Alamo Foundation v. Secretary of Labor*, 471 U.S. 290 (1985).

92. *Id.* at 301.

gram run by the organization.[93] In addition to work therapy, participants in the program received room, board, clothing, a small weekly stipend, and spiritual guidance for a period of up to six months. The court affirmed dismissal of the plaintiff's claim, distinguishing it from *Alamo* on the ground that "Williams's relationship with the Salvation Army was solely rehabilitative" and he did not depend on the Salvation Army in the same manner as the "volunteers" in *Alamo*.[94] Important factors were that Williams signed an express statement that he was a beneficiary and not employee of program, and that Williams was required to turn over to the Salvation Army his welfare benefits, including food stamps, to offset the cost of the benefits he received, thus reinforcing the parties' express understanding.[95]

Another challenging question is how participants in government "workfare" programs ought to be classified.[96] In *Colon v. City of New York*,[97] the Second Circuit reversed a district court ruling that participants in a mandatory welfare work program were not employees for purpose of Title VII. The Court held that if the plaintiffs could prove the facts alleged—that they received cash payments and certain benefits such as childcare, and did useful work—they would establish employee status.[98] By contrast, the Tenth Circuit ruled that workfare recipients did not qualify as employees under the FLSA because the workfare program was part of an overall educational experience whose goal was assistance, not employment.[99]

a. Administrative Enforcement

The Department of Labor, through its Wage–Hour Division, is responsible for administering and enforcing the FLSA.[100] The Wage–Hour Division conducts inspections of workplaces to monitor workplace compliance with the substantive provisions of the statute and regulations as well as various record-keeping requirements. Most inspections are triggered by an employee complaint, although the Department may act on its own initiative as well. Resource constraints have hampered administrative enforcement of the statute.[101]

---

93. *Williams v. Strickland*, 87 F.3d 1064 (1996).

94. *Id.* at 1067.

95. *Id.*

96. 29 U.S.C. § 203 (e) (4) (A).

97. 359 F.3d 83 (2004).

98. *Id.*, at 97.

99. *Johns v. Stewart*, 57 F.3d 1544 (10th Cir. 1995).

100. 29 U.S.C. § 204.

101. See Eugene Scalia, *Inspection and Enforcement Strategies at the U.S. Department of Labor*, 7 U. PA. J. LAB. & EMP. 529, 530–34 (2005).

There are several paths to enforcement under the FLSA. First, the Secretary of Labor may initiate an action on behalf of all affected employees to recover unpaid wages and overtime compensation.[102] The monetary recovery for a successful claim may include an additional, equal, amount of liquidated damages.[103] Additionally, the Secretary may pursue civil fines of up to $10,000 for violations of the child labor provisions, and $1,000 for each repeat or willful violation of the wage or overtime provisions.[104] The Secretary may also pursue injunctive remedies to prevent future violations of wage, overtime, retaliation, child labor, or record keeping provisions.[105] Employers may be subject to criminal prosecution for willful violations of the FLSA, including not only the minimum wage, overtime and child labor provisions of the Act but also for retaliation, failure to maintain required records, falsification of records and certain other of the Act's prohibitions.[106] An employer may be fined up to $10,000 or imprisoned up to six months.[107] The parties may settle their claims, but it has been held that if they do so without the involvement of the Secretary of Labor or without a lawsuit having been filed, the employees' consent will not operate to bar any claim under the Act.[108]

b. Private Enforcement

If the Secretary of Labor has not initiated an action seeking to hasten payment of unpaid compensation or obtain equitable relief, an employee may sue the employer directly for unpaid wages and overtime, plus an equal amount in liquidated damages.[109] A prevailing plaintiff is entitled to attorney's fees and costs. Private actions can also be brought in a representative capacity on behalf of employees who are "similarly situated"; unlike traditional opt-out class actions, individuals are bound by any judgment (and can have the benefit of the statute of limitations being tolled) only if they affirmatively opt-in to the representative action.[110]

G. State Wage Payment Laws

State laws regulate payment of wages in a variety of ways. For example, states commonly regulate the form of payment,[111] pay

102. 29 U.S.C. § 216(c).

103. *Id.*

104. 29 U.S.C. § 216 (e); 29 C.F.R. § 579.5 (a).

105. 29 U.S.C. § 217.

106. 29 U.S.C. §§ 215(a)(3), 216(a).

107. 29 U.S.C. § 216 (a).

108. *Lynn's Food Stores, Inc. v. United States*, 679 F.2d 1350, 1353–54 (11th Cir. 1982) (holding that settlement of back wage claims under the FLSA may proceed only pursuant to § 216(c) or 216(b) of the Act).

109. 29 U.S.C. § 216 (b), (c).

110. 29 U.S.C. § 216 (b).

periods,[112] wage payments after separation from employment,[113] assignment of wages,[114] deductions from wages,[115] and garnishment of wages.[116] The rationale for wage-payment laws is to protect employees from overreaching by employers based on doubtful judgments that the employee owes a debt. The concern is that employers might use their position of control over wage disbursements opportunistically to engage in self-help, thus forcing an employee who contests an employer's position to incur the costs of bring a legal action in order to recover wages owed. These laws sometimes paint with a broad brush. For example, in *Beckwith v. United Parcel Service*,[117] an employee who had been terminated for gross negligence resulting in financial losses to the employer offered to pay back the losses, using a payroll deduction arrangement, in exchange for reinstatement.[118] Eighteen months after the employee was reinstated on these terms, he successfully sued for disgorgement of all funds withheld to that point, claiming the use of a payroll deduction for this purpose violated Maine's wage payment law.[119] The First Circuit upheld judgment for the plaintiff, arguing that although the statute did not bar *all* voluntary agreements by which an employee might compensate an employer for loss, it clearly intended to prohibit such repayment by payroll deduction. The court explained:

111. See, e.g., MICH. COMP. LAWS ANN. § 408.476(1) (requiring employer to pay employees by cash, negotiable instrument, direct deposit into the employee's bank account, or issuance of a payroll debit card).

112. See. e.g., MASS. GEN. LAWS ANN. ch. 149, § 148 (requiring employer to pay employees weekly or bi-weekly, within six or seven days of the end of the pay period in which wages were earned, but with special rules for certain employees such as casual and white collar employees).

113. NEV. REV. STAT. §§ 608.020–608.040 (requiring immediate payment of an employee who is discharged, payment on next regular payday or within seven days of an employee who resigns or quits, and penalties for employer failure to comply).

114. See, e.g., MD. COM. LAW CODE ANN. §§ 15–302–15–305 (rendering any assignment of wages invalid unless approved in writing by assignor that is notarized and filed with county clerk,

limiting duration of assignment agreements, and other provisions).

115. See, e.g., OR. REV. STAT. §§ 652.610–652.615 (requiring itemization of all deductions and prohibiting deductions from pay except as required by law, authorized by employee and for the employee's benefit, and several other enumerated purposes).

116. NEB. REV. STAT. § 25–1558 (limiting amount of wages that may be garnished except in certain circumstances).

117. 889 F.2d 344 (1st Cir. 1989).

118. *Id.*, at 345.

119. The relevant provision, 26 M.R.S.A. § 629, stated, "No person, firm, or corporation shall require or permit any person as a condition of securing or retaining employment to work without monetary compensation or when having an agreement, verbal, written or implied that a part of such compensation should be returned to the person, firm or corporation for any reason other than for payment of a loan, debt, or advance made to the person . . .".

The legislature undoubtedly viewed the payroll deduction as harmful and unfair because it deprives the worker of wages earned before he has had a chance to decide on a given payday how best to allocate his available resources. ... In addition, if funds are withheld automatically, the employee who seeks to challenge a particular deduction—for example, because he thinks the debt is already repaid—would nevertheless first lose access to his money.... [120]

Beckwith illustrates the trade-off between legislation designed to prevent coercion of employees and flexibility in the private ordering of compensation arrangements: it seems legitimate to restrict employers from engaging in self-help at their own discretion, and yet absent the payroll deduction agreement in *Beckwith*, the employer might not have been willing to reinstate the employee.

120. *Beckwith*, 889 F.2d at 348–349.

Chapter 11

EMPLOYMENT DISCRIMINATION LAW

A. Rationale for Regulation

Our employment discrimination laws, and the central role they play in the overall framework of rules governing employment decisions, are a product of history. This history includes—for African–Americans, the legacy of slavery and postbellum official and private discrimination until the country began seriously to address these issues in the 1960s; for women, obstacles presented by official and private policies to restrict women to certain jobs and a continued pattern of gender pay differentials; for Hispanics and other immigrant groups, language and national origin barriers.

There are two central vantage points from which to consider the economic progress, or lack thereof, of racial or other disadvantaged minorities: (1) supply-side and (2) demand-side explanations.

1. Supply–Side Explanations

Supply side phenomena may partially explain why some groups have had more difficulty than others in achieving economic progress. To the extent workers are poorly educated, lack requisite skills or are poorly motivated, they will not be able to compete with better educated, skilled, or motivated workers and will tend to occupy jobs that offer relatively low wages and few opportunities for advancement. These supply-side factors may be at least partially the product of past or current discrimination. Employment discrimination law can play a role in counteracting supply-side factors: To the extent minority group workers do not make investments in their own human capital because of discriminatory barriers, eliminating or lowering those barriers should improve their incentives for all workers to improve their skills and education.

2. Demand–Side Explanations

Demand-side phenomena, such as the discriminatory preferences of employers, coworkers and customers, are another aspect of the problem. In an influential early work, Nobel Laureate Gary Becker of the University of Chicago posited that in a society that tolerates racial discrimination, white workers will insist on a premium to work with blacks. Under this assumption, the wage of white workers will equal the wage of black workers plus a factor, D, equal to the "market cost of discrimination", which acts as a tax on hiring and promoting black workers. Firms will seek to avoid the higher costs due to white workers' racial preferences by (i) either segregating their workforces internally, or (ii) paying blacks less than comparable whites.[1]

Becker's work was a response to the central difficulty standard economic theory has in accounting for the persistence of racial discrimination in labor markets. If firms are profit-maximizers and managers are faithful agents of the firm, it is difficult to understand why new firms do not emerge to take advantage of the availability of qualified black workers who are willing to work at lower wages than white workers. Kenneth Arrow, another Nobel Laureate in economics, attempted to explain the persistence of discrimination in terms of the "personnel investment" of firms.[2] A firm that has made the decision to hire an all-white workforce will invest in the human capital of those workers, which in turn will reduce the firm's willingness to make future job offers to minority workers in which it has made no such investment. Ultimately, any comprehensive explanation needs to take account of the broader social forces that sustain discriminatory preferences despite obvious efficiency advantages in disallowing them.[3]

3. Role of Anti–Discrimination Law

A principal rationale of Title VII and other anti-discrimination laws—in particular, their prohibition of intentional discrimination—is that discriminatory preferences of firms or coworkers themselves detract from efficiency in labor markets because such preferences add nothing to the productive process and in fact serve artificially to raise the cost of white (or other privileged) labor. Hence, by penalizing discriminatory preferences the law can reduce the demand for discrimination and, in the process, expand access to qualified, previously discriminated-against workers. Put differently, anti-discrimination laws can help labor markets function more

1. GARY S. BECKER, THE ECONOMICS OF DISCRIMINATION (1971).

2. KENNETH J. ARROW, MODELS OF JOB DISCRIMINATION, from RACIAL DISCRIMINATION IN ECONOMIC LIFE, ch. 2 (A.H. PASCAL ed. 1972).

3. Other explanations the reader might wish to consult include Michael Piore and Peter Doeringer's "segmented labor market" theory in their influential book, INTERNAL LABOR MARKETS AND MANPOWER ANALYSIS (1971); Michael Reich's "divide and conquer" theory in RACIAL INEQUALITY: A POLITICAL-ECONOMIC ANALYSIS (1981); and Nobel Laureate George Akerlof's "caste-system" account, in AN ECONOMIC THEORIST'S BOOK OF TALES, ch.3 (1984).

competitively by removing the advantages privileged workers enjoyed under discrimination and increasing the returns to work for previously disadvantaged workers. (This discussion ignores error costs and administrative costs attendant to any regulatory intervention.)

B. Title VII

The central federal statute addressing employment discrimination is Title VII of the Civil Rights Act of 1964,[4] which was amended by the Civil Rights Act of 1991 to provide additional protections for claimants of discrimination. The law was passed in response to a civil rights movement in the 1960s of African–Americans and others protesting racial segregation. The law covers all employers, private and public, with 15 or more employees, and prohibits discrimination on account of race, color, religion, national origin, and sex. The law prohibits two forms of discrimination: "disparate treatment," or intentional, discrimination and "disparate impact" discrimination.

Most cases litigated under Title VII and other anti-discrimination laws involve individual disparate treatment claims, usually in the context of a failure to promote or discharge decision.[5] Because direct evidence of intentional discrimination is often lacking, the courts allow claimants to mount a case through circumstantial evidence.[6] In general, the plaintiff is accorded a relatively modest burden to establish a "prima facie" case. In a discharge case, the plaintiff alleging race (or other prohibited) bias is required to show (1) he is a member of a Title VII (or other statutorily) protected class; (2) he was qualified for the job he held; (3) he was terminated; and (4) that his replacement is of a different race (or other impermissible ground) than the plaintiff, or there is some other basis (such as comparator or statistical evidence) for inferring discriminatory intent. Unlike a failure to hire case, where qualification may be at issue, in a discharge case most courts hold that the plaintiff need not show he was performing the job satisfactorily at the time of the discharge; often whether performance difficulties

---

4. 42 U.S.C. § 2000e *et seq.* Another federal law barring racial and certain forms of ancestry discrimination is 42 U.S.C. § 1981, a product of the Civil Rights Act of 1866.

5. Title VII also authorizes a "pattern or practice" or systemic disparate treatment challenge which uses different proof mechanisms that rely more on statistical evidence than most individual disparate treatment cases. See *Teamsters v. United States*, 431 U.S. 324 (1977); *Hazelwood School Dist. v. United States*, 433 U.S. 299 (1977).

6. See *McDonnell Douglas Corp. v. Green*, 411 U.S. 792 (1973); *Texas Dept. of Community Affairs v. Burdine*, 450 U.S. 248 (1981); *St. Mary's Honor Center v. Hicks*, 509 U.S. 502 (1993).

motivate the discharge rather than race (or other prohibited ground) is the principal issue in the case. After the plaintiff's prima facie showing is made, a burden of production—rather than persuasion—shifts to the employer to "articulate" a legitimate motive for the decision. The plaintiff then shoulders the burden of proving discriminatory intent—either by showing that the legitimate reason was not in fact the real reason for the decision but was a "pretext" for a discriminatory motive, or some other basis for inferring intentional discrimination. The Supreme Court has made clear that if the trier of fact believes that the employer's asserted reason is not the real reason motivating the complained-of decision, the trier of fact may enter a verdict for the plaintiff, provided the trier also finds that asserted reason was a pretext for a discriminatory motive.[7]

Title VII also authorizes challenges to neutral practices that have a disproportionate adverse effect on members of a statutorily protected group. This is called the "disparate impact" theory of discrimination. If an employer is unable to show "business necessity" for practices that have a disparate impact on protected groups, a violation is found even where there is no evidence of intentional discrimination. The rationale for regulation here is that such practices reduce employment opportunities for protected groups without advancing important goals of the firm; hence, regulation can "costlessly" improve economic opportunities for previously disadvantaged groups. Utilizing the disparate-impact theory plaintiffs have successfully overturned practices in particular circumstances such as aptitude tests[8] and height and weight requirements.[9] Although there was some question whether the "disparate impact" approach could be used to challenge subjective hiring and promotion practices,[10] such doubts have been laid to rest as a result of the Civil Rights Act of 1991.[11]

Express authorization of disparate-impact challenges is found in § 703(k) of Title VII, as amended by the 1991 law. Section 703(k)(1)(B)(i) provides that the plaintiff must show that a "particular" employment practice causes a disparate impact, "except that

---

7. See *Reeves v. Sanderson Plumbing Products, Inc.,* 530 U.S. 133 (2000).

8. See *Griggs v. Duke Power Co.,* 401 U.S. 424 (1971); *Albemarle Paper Co. v. Moody,* 422 U.S. 405 (1975).

9. See *Dothard v. Rawlinson,* 433 U.S. 321 (1977).

10. The Supreme Court's decision in *Watson v. Fort Worth Bank and Trust,* 487 U.S. 977 (1988), permitted such challenges, but its ruling a year later in *Wards Cove Packing Co. v. Atonio,* 490 U.S. 642 (1989), appeared to circumscribe the disparate-impact theory *of* discrimination altogether. The 1991 amendments restored the holding in *Watson.*

11. 42 U.S.C. § 2000e(k).

if the complaining party can demonstrate to the court that the elements of a respondent's decision-making process are not capable of separation for analysis, the decisionmaking process may be analyzed as one employment practice."

Title VII has been interpreted not to reach sexual orientation discrimination against gay and lesbian individuals,[12] although a growing number of state and local laws prohibit such discrimination.[13] If, however, an employer discriminates against employees because of gender-linked stereotypes, e.g., a male is disadvantaged because of "feminine" traits, such a practice could constitute gender discrimination in violation of Title VII.[14]

Title VII also prohibits discrimination on account of national origin, which can be challenged on both intentional and disparate impact theories.[15] It does not reach, however, discrimination on account of citizenship status. Section 102 of the Immigration Reform and Control Act of 1986 (IRCA)[16] prohibits such discrimination against any "intending citizen" (either a resident alien or an alien seeking legalization under IRCA's amnesty program or lawfully admitted under the refugee and asylum provisions of federal immigration law). IRCA reaches only intentional citizenship status discrimination, and does not authorize a disparate-impact challenge.

C. Gender Discrimination

Gender discrimination, i.e., discrimination between men and women, is outlawed by Title VII. Like racial discrimination, gender discrimination, which can be challenged by both men and women, is viewed as unfair to individuals, creating obstacles to equal opportunity, and as unnecessary, if not harmful, to a productive economy. Gender discrimination includes the use of stereotypes that result in different standards of job performance and demeanor for women than for men,[17] the making of unwanted sexual offers and other

---

12. See, e.g. *DeSantis v. Pacific Tel. & Tel. Co.*, 608 F.2d 327 (9th Cir. 1979); *Smith v. Liberty Mutual Ins. Co.*, 569 F.2d 325 (5th Cir. 1978).

13. See, e.g., CAL. LAB. CODE §§ 1101, 1102, 1102.1; CONN. GEN. STAT. §§ 46a–60, 46a-81a; HAW. REV. STAT. §§ 378 et seq.; MASS. GEN. L. ch. 151b, §§ 3(6), 4; MINN. STAT. § 363.01; N.J. REV. STAT. §§ 10:5–4, 10:5–5, 10:5–12 ; VT. STAT. ANN. tit. 21, § 495(a); WIS. STAT. ANN. §§ 111.31–.395; D.C. CODE ANN. §§ – 2501, 1–2503, 1–2512.

14. Case law here builds on the Supreme Court's holdings in *Price Waterhouse v. Hopkins*, 490 U.S. 228 (1989); *Oncale v. Sundowner Offshore Services, Inc.*, 523 U.S. 75 (1998), that intentional discrimination prohibited by Title VII includes discrimination based on gender stereotyping.

15. See *Espinoza v. Farah Mfg. Co.*, 414 U.S. 86 (1973).

16. 8 U.S.C. § 1324b.

17. See *Price Waterhouse v. Hopkins*, 490 U.S. 228 (1989).

sexual harassment as a condition for obtaining a job, promotion or raise, or resulting in a workplace environment that treats women differently than men.[18] Since 1978, Title VII also requires employers to treat pregnancy on the same terms as they would any other disability under their benefit plans.

Employers are permitted a limited defense to show that the use of sex in employment decisions is a "bona fide occupational qualification" (BFOQ). This BFOQ defense is narrowly interpreted to shield only those practices implicating the firm's "business essence", such as hiring women as cocktail waitresses in a "Playboy Club" or persons of Chinese national origin to preserve a sense of authenticity in a restaurant that serves Chinese food. The BFOQ defense is not available to permit an airline to hire women only as flight attendants, even where this caters to customer preferences,[19] or to exclude women who might become pregnant from jobs whose conditions might endanger an unborn child,[20] except perhaps in rare circumstances where female employees nearing their due date are unable to perform their job duties.[21]

In the Equal Pay Act of 1963,[22] formally amending the Fair Labor Standards Act of 1938, Congress established the principle that men and women must receive equal pay for "equal work on jobs the performance of which requires equal skill, effort, and responsibility, and which are performed under similar working conditions. . . ." Title VII prohibits intentional sex-based discrimination in compensation and benefits,[23] including the use of gender-based actuarial classifications in pension and insurance plans.[24] However, neither the Equal Pay Act nor Title VII authorizes what is called a "comparable worth" challenge, under which the employer would have to provide equal pay for different jobs that are deemed to be of 'comparable worth' in some objective sense.[25]

18. See *Meritor Savings Bank, FSB v. Vinson*, 477 U.S. 57 (1986); *Harris v. Forklift Systems, Inc.*, 510 U.S. 17, (1993).

19. See, e.g. *Diaz v. Pan American World Airways*, 442 F.2d 385 (5th Cir. 1971).

20. See *International Union, UAW v. Johnson Controls, Inc.*, 499 U.S. 187 (1991).

21. See, e.g., *Levin v. Delta Air Lines*, 730 F.2d 994 (5th Cir. 1984).

22. 29 U.S.C. §§ 206(d), 216–17.

23. See *County of Washington v. Gunther*, 452 U.S. 161 (1981).

24. See *Arizona Governing Committee v. Norris*, 463 U.S. 1073 (1983); *Los Angeles Dept. of Water & Power v. Manhart*, 435 U.S. 702 (1978).

25. See, e.g., *American Federation of State, County, and Municipal Employees, AFL–CIO v. Washington*, 770 F.2d 1401 (9th Cir. 1985). See generally Paul C. Weiler, *The Wages of Sex: The Uses and Limits of Comparable Worth*, 99 HARV. L. REV. 1728 (1986). Compare SAMUEL ESTREICHER & BRIAN LANDSBERG, GLOBAL ISSUES IN EMPLOYMENT DISCRIMINATION LAW (2008) (comparative-worth claims in Canada and abroad).

D. Religious Discrimination

Title VII also prohibits discrimination on account of religion. The statutory prohibition extends beyond intentional discrimination to include employer refusals to extend "reasonable accommodation" to the religious practices of employees. Employees assigned to work on days of religious observance have a qualified right to request that the employer readjust their work schedules to accommodate their religious practices. However, the required level of accommodation does not entail disturbing the seniority or contractual rights of other employees.[26]

E. Age Discrimination

By virtue of the Age Discrimination in Employment Act of 1967 (ADEA), the anti-discrimination principle also applies to employees over the age of 40 complaining of age-based discrimination. (In some states like New Jersey, individuals below the age of 40 are also protected against age bias.) Federal law protects against discrimination in favor of younger workers but does not prohibit discrimination in favor of older workers.[27]

This statute presents difficulties not present in Title VII because age-based rules may promote legitimate employer objectives (as in the design of retirement benefit plans), and increasing age may be associated with legitimate employer considerations, such as years out of school and declining performance levels.

ADEA recognizes both intentional and disparate impact discrimination claims, although under the latter theory, employers have an affirmative defense. Thus, for example, a claimant might prove that an employer policy that used a criterion correlated with age, such as years of service, had a disproportionately adverse affect on older workers.[28] Under § 4(f)(1), the employer is permitted to use "reasonable factors other than age" (RFOA) even where the factor may have a disparate impact on older workers. Thus, for example, a municipal plan to raise police salaries to bring them in line in surrounding area police forces did not violate ADEA even though less senior police officers tended to receive a higher percentage improvement in their salaries than more senior officers. Such a plan was justified by the RFOA defense: "the City's decision to grant a larger raise to lower echelon employees for the purpose of bringing salaries in line with that of surrounding police forces was

---

26. See *Trans World Airlines v. Hardison*, 432 U.S. 63 (1977).

27. See *General Dynamics Land Sys., Inc. v. Cline*, 540 U.S. 581 (2004).

28. See *Hazen Paper Co. v. Biggins*, 507 U.S. 604 (1993).

a decision based on a 'reasonable factor other than age' that responded to the City's legitimate goal of retaining police officers."[29] The RFOA allowance is broader than the "business necessity" defense allowed employers in a Title VII disparate-impact challenge.

For employers covered by the ADEA, mandatory retirement is generally unlawful. (In Japan, by contrast, mandatory retirement rules are lawful.) A narrow exception (Section 12(c)(1) of ADEA) permits mandatory retirement at age 65 or later of employees who are entitled to a non-forfeitable annual retirement benefit of $44,000 or more and who, for 2 years prior to retirement, were "employed in a bona fide executive or high policy-making position."[30] In a case resulting in a $200,000 verdict, a corporation's chief labor counsel (with supervisory authority over the firm's labor lawyers) was held not to be a "bona fide executive" or in a "high policymaking position" within the meaning of this exemption.[31]

A common practice of employers seeking to reduce the size of their workforce is to establish incentive programs, such as enhanced early retirement benefits, to encourage employees to retire voluntarily. Such programs are lawful provided they do not confer more valuable benefits on younger workers while withholding such benefits from older workers. Employers have also attempted to trade specially enhanced severance packages in return for agreements to waive ADEA claims. Such waiver agreements are lawful provided they are "knowing and voluntary". Under the Older Workers Benefit Protection Act of 1990 (OWBPA),[32] Congress stipulated minimum requirements for such agreements.[33]

---

29. See *Smith v. City of Jackson,* 544 U.S. 228, 242 (2005).

30. 29 U.S.C. § 631(c)(1).

31. See *Whittlesey v. Union Carbide Corp.,* 567 F.Supp. 1320 (S.D.N.Y. 1983), *affirmed,* 742 F.2d 724 (2d Cir. 1984). See generally the EEOC's interpretation of the exemption in 29 C.F.R. § 1625.12.

32. Pub. L. No. 101–433, Oct. 16, 1990, 104 Stat. 978 *et seq.,* amending, inter alia, Section 7 of ADEA.

33. For individual agreements, Congress requires a written agreement expressly waiving ADEA rights or claims (but not claims or rights arising after the agreement); additional consideration for the waiver; written advice from the employer to consult with an attorney; a 21–day waiting period to consider the agreement; and a 7–day period to revoke the agreement. For agreements "requested in connection with an exit incentive or other employment termination program offered to a group of employees", Congress requires a longer waiting period (45 days instead of 21 days). In addition, employers must disclose any eligibility factors for individuals covered by the program and "the job titles and ages of all individuals eligible or selected for the program" and the ages of all individuals "in the same job classification or organizational unit" who were not selected for the program. OWBPA also requires that age-based distinctions in benefit plans generally conform to an equal-contribution or equal-cost rule. See 29 U.S.C. § 626(f).

F. Disability Discrimination

The anti-discrimination principle also applies to discrimination against individuals with disabilities. Like race discrimination, adverse treatment of individuals on account of disability or handicap violates norms of fairness, reduces opportunities for disadvantaged groups, and may reflect uninformed stereotypes about the limits of disabled workers.

Although some state laws barred handicap discrimination prior to the enactment of the Americans With Disabilities Act of 1990 (ADA),[34] only federal sector employers and government contractors were under a duty, as a matter of federal law, not to discriminate against otherwise qualified employees on account of their disability. With the passage of the ADA, all private and public employers with 15 or more employees are barred from disability-based discrimination. (Thus, ADA's coverage is coextensive with that of Title VII.) ADA represents an extensive regulation of the workplace. The statute bars both intentional and disparate-impact discrimination. All employment standards having an adverse impact on individuals with disabilities must be "job-related and consistent with business necessity." Employers may also not require medical examinations prior to making offers of employment (except for tests for illegal drug use); post-offer examinations must be job-related and follow strict rules of confidentiality.

In a departure from the equal-treatment rule of most other employment discrimination laws, the ADA also imposes affirmative obligations on employers by requiring them to provide "reasonable accommodation" of "qualified individuals with a disability". The reasonable-accommodation duty may in particular circumstances include "making existing facilities used by employees readily accessible to and usable" by individuals with disabilities and "job restructuring, part-time or modified work schedules, reassignment to a vacant position, acquisition or modification of equipment or devices, appropriate adjustment or modifications of examinations, training materials or policies, the provision of qualified readers or interpreters, and other similar accommodations for individuals with disabilities."[35] The rationale for this reasonable accommodation duty is twofold. First, it is hoped that some of the costs anticipated in employing disabled individuals will turn out to be minimal, and employers will then reassess the desirability of hiring such individuals in the future. Secondly, it has been argued the statute seeks to advance a social norm of "mainstreaming" disabled individuals,

---

34. 42 U.S.C. §§ 12101 *et seq.*   **35.** 42 U.S.C. § 12111(9).

whether or not the costs of accommodation exceed the value of the job as measured by the salary it commands.

The reasonable-accommodation duty is not limitless. In one case, Robert Barnett, a former US Airways baggage handler from San Francisco, injured his back while on the job. At his doctor's suggestion, Barnett was reassigned to the mail room. The company later told Barnett that, according to company policy, he would have to give up that job to make room for another employee who had more seniority. The Supreme Court held that the duty did not require an employer to ignore seniority rights of employees. The Court has rejected the view that all accommodations are "reasonable" as long as they are effective, i.e., permit the claimant to perform the essential functions of the job.[36] Rather, the proposed accommodation must not only be effective but must also be "reasonable" in light of the costs it imposes on the employer or coworkers. Employers can show that the proposed accommodation is not "reasonable" or entails an "undue hardship"—a term defined in the statute as "an action requiring significant difficulty or expense, when considered in light of certain factors, such as the cost of the accommodation; the overall financial resources of the facility in question; the overall financial resources of the employing entity; and the type of operation of the covered entity."[37]

A good deal of litigation has occurred over whether claimants fall within the ADA's protective class. The term "disability" means an individual with "a physical or mental impairment that substantially limits one or more of the major life activities of such individual", or an individual with "a record of such impairment", or an individual who is erroneously "regarded as having such an impairment".[38] Individuals with contagious diseases, including individuals who test positive for the HIV virus, are protected by the ADA[39] However, employers may maintain requirements that an individual not pose "a direct threat to the health or safety of other individuals in the workplace," or to the individual himself.[40] Individuals "currently engaged in the illegal use of drugs" are excluded from the protected class of "qualified individuals with a disability". Such exclusion does not extend, however, to individuals who have successfully completed a supervised drug rehabilitation program, are currently in such a program and not engaged in drug use, or are

---

36. See *US Airways, Inc. v. Barnett,* 535 U.S. 391 (2002).

37. 42 U.S.C. § 12111(10).

38. 42 U.S.C. § 12102(2).

39. See *Bragdon v. Abbott,* 524 U.S. 624 (1998) (dentist required to treat pa-

tient infected with HIV in his office under ADA's public accommodation title).

40. See *Chevron v. Echazabal,* 536 U.S. 73 (2002).

"erroneously regarded as engaging in" illegal use of drugs. The ADA does not exclude current alcoholics from coverage, although employers may hold alcoholics (as well as drug users) to the same job standards as applied to other employees.

An employer's benefit plans may not treat individuals with disabilities differently than other employees. However, the statute does not prohibit insurers or health care organizations that administer benefit plans from "underwriting risks, classifying risks, or administering such risks that are based on or not inconsistent with State law"—or self-insured employers making similar risk classification decisions—provided that such decisions are "not used as a subterfuge to evade the purposes" of the ADA.[41] A June 1993 administrative guidance from the Equal Employment Opportunity Commission (EEOC), the federal agency that administers the ADA, interpreted this provision to allow universal, nondisease-specific restrictions on coverage, such as limits on "mental/nervous" conditions or "eye care", blanket exclusion of preexisting conditions, or caps on annual benefits for the treatment of any physical condition. But disease-specific provisions must be justified "by legitimate actuarial data, or by actual or reasonably anticipated experience", and must treat conditions with "comparable actuarial data and/or experience" in the same fashion.[42]

G. Retaliation

Virtually every antidiscrimination law also contains a provision prohibiting employer retaliation for filing claims or giving testimony in proceedings under the statute.[43] Section 704(a) of Title VII contains such a "participation" clause but it also contains an "opposition" clause protecting individuals who oppose practices they reasonably believe to be unlawful under the statute. Protection under the participation clause tends to be absolute because the employee is using the formal processes provided by the law, and the employer has ample means to defend itself by resisting the claim on the merits. Because Title VII's opposition clause extends to conduct outside those formal processes, the courts have grafted onto the clause a requirement, derived from analogous precedent under the NLRA, that the employee use reasonable means of opposition.

---

41. 42 U.S.C. § 12201(c).

42. See EEOC INTERIM ENFORCEMENT GUIDANCE ON THE APPLICATION OF THE ADA TO DISABILITY-BASED DISTINCTIONS IN EMPLOYER-PROVIDED HEALTH INSURANCE (June 8, 1993).

43. Job applicants and former employees are typically protected under these retaliation provisions even when their terms seem to cover only incumbent employees. See *Robinson v. Shell Oil Co.*, 519 U.S. 337 (1997) (interpreting § 704(a) of Title VII).

Unreasonable opposition may be found where an employee's persistent internal complaints undermine the ability of the employer to perform its functions.[44] Most retaliation provisions do not privilege employees to refuse to perform work assignments, although the U.S. Department of Labor has issued an OSHA regulation, sustained by the Supreme Court, permitting refusal to perform assignments reasonably perceived as threatening imminent harm to safety.[45]

The Supreme Court has made clear that an employee is protected against retaliation even if the employee does not suffer some official change in his employment status but, rather, is subjected to an undesirable work assignment within his job classification or harassment by supervisors or coworkers. The Court further stated that actionable retaliation can include negative treatment outside of the workplace, provided the treatment was serious enough to be likely to deter other employees from engaging in protected activity.[46]

H. Administrative Process and Remedies

A Title VII, ADEA or ADA claimant must first file a charge with a federal agency, the Equal Employment Opportunity Commission (EEOC), or the state agency with similar responsibilities. The administrative agency then investigates the charge and has the option of filing suit on behalf of the claimant. If the EEOC declines to proceed further, the agency issues a "right to sue" letter and the Title VII claimant may go to court; the agency's disposition cannot block a private lawsuit unless the agency agrees to sue on the claimant's behalf.

If a violation is found, the court may award back-pay and reinstatement, or front-pay in lieu of reinstatement, to put the employee in the position he or she would have been in had the discrimination not occurred. (In one celebrated case, a female employee of a major accounting firm, who was discriminatorily denied a partnership promotion, was awarded partnership status as a remedy[47]). As a result of the 1991 amendments, jury trials are available in Title VII actions challenging intentional discrimination, and plaintiffs may seek compensatory damages for future economic loss and non-economic loss (such as damages for 'pain and suffer-

---

44. See, e.g., *Hochstadt v. Worcester Foundation,* 545 F.2d 222 (1st Cir. 1976).

45. See *Whirlpool Corp. v. Marshall, Secretary of Labor,* 445 U.S. 1 (1980).

46. See *Burlington Northern & Santa Fe Ry. Co. v. White,* 548 U.S. 53 (2006).

47. *Hopkins v. Price Waterhouse,* 920 F.2d 967 (D.C. Cir. 1990).

ing') as well as punitive damages.[48] Such damages are, however, capped at levels ranging from $50,000 to $300,000 depending on the size of the defendant's workforce. This cap does not apply to equitable relief under § 706(g) of Title VII, the provision authorizing back-pay and front-pay in lieu of reinstatement.[49]

Class actions have figured significantly in Title VII litigation. Under Rule 23 of the Federal Rules of Civil Procedure, class actions seeking predominantly equitable relief (which typically includes back-pay) need not provide opt-out rights but courts often require them. Where damages are sought as well as equitable relief, most courts require that the plaintiffs provide notice and opt-out rights.[50] By contrast, ADEA and the EPA utilize the enforcement procedures of the FLSA and permit only "opt-in" collective actions; individuals are bound only to the extent they have affirmatively consented to representation.[51]

Similar remedies are provided under ADEA. Jury trials are available in ADEA actions, which authorize back-pay and reinstatement or front-pay in lieu of reinstatement as customary remedies. Punitive and compensatory damages are not authorized, but economic losses are doubled in cases involving "willful" violations— where the employer "knew or showed reckless disregard for the matter of whether its conduct was prohibited by the ADEA."[52]

---

48. On the issue of employer liability for punitive damages, see *Kolstad v. American Dental Assn.*, 527 U.S. 526 (1999).

49. See *Pollard v. E.I. du Pont de Nemours & Co.*, 532 U.S. 843 (2001).

50. See, e.g., *Jefferson v. Ingersoll International, Inc.*, 195 F.3d 894 (7th Cir. 1999).

51. 29 U.S.C. § 216(b). The process of sending out court notices to potential opt-in claimants is the subject of *Hoffmann–La Roche, Inc. v. Sperling*, 493 U.S. 165 (1989).

52. See *Trans World Airlines v. Thurston*, 469 U.S. 111, 126 (1985); *Hazen Paper Co. v. Biggins*, 507 U.S. 604 (1993).

Chapter 12
OCCUPATIONAL SAFETY AND HEALTH

In 1970 Congress enacted the Occupational Safety and Health Act (OSHA or Act). There were some prior federal laws in this area,[1] but the OSHA was the first comprehensive federal regulation of the occupational safety and health practices of private industry.

A. Coverage and Regulatory Scheme

OSHA's sweep is quite broad, reaching all private employers in industries "affecting commerce"; government employment is the principal exclusion from coverage. Enforcement responsibility was lodged with the Occupational Safety and Health Administration, a unit of the Department of Labor, with adjudicative responsibility assigned to a new government agency, the Occupational Safety and Health Review Commission (OSHRC).[2] An advisory body, the National Institute for Occupational Safety and Health (NIOSH), now part of the Department of Health and Human Services, was also established. The Secretary has authority to issue occupational safety and health standards as well as enforce the "general duty" of a covered employer to provide a place of employment "free from recognized hazards that are causing or are likely to cause death or serious physical injury to his employees" (often referred to as the

---

1. These include the WALSH-HEALY PUBLIC CONTRACTS ACT OF 1936, 41 U.S.C. § 35 (setting mild standards for federal contractors), the COAL MINE SAFETY ACT OF 1952, and the MARITIME SAFETY ACT OF 1958 (which amended the Longshoremen's and HARBOR WORKERS' COMPENSATION ACT), the SERVICE CONTRACT ACT OF 1965, 41 U.S.C. § 351 *et seq.*, the METAL AND NONMETALLIC MINE SAFETY ACT OF 1966, the COAL MINE HEALTH AND SAFETY ACT OF 1969, the CONTRACT WORK HOURS AND SAFETY STANDARDS ACT OF 1969 (establishing federal standards for construction on public works), and the FEDERAL RAILWAY SAFETY ACT OF 1970 (containing standards for passenger and employee safety). In addition, in the 1947 LABOR MANAGEMENT RELATIONS ACT, which amended the NLRA, Congress provided in Section 502 that employees walking off the job because of "abnormally dangerous" conditions would not be deemed

to have engaged in a strike in violation of a contractual no-strike pledge. Under Section 4(b)(2) of OSHA, the safety and health standards promulgated under the Walsh–Healy, Service Contract, and some other laws were superseded upon the promulgation of corresponding standards pursuant to OSHA deemed by the Secretary of Labor to be "more effective". 29 U.S.C. § 653(b)(2). In 1977 Congress passed the FEDERAL MINE SAFETY AND HEALTH ACT, 30 U.S.C. §§ 801–962, which lodged enforcement with the Mine Safety and Health Act and created an independent adjudicative body, the Mine Safety and Health Review Commission (MSHRC).

2. See *Martin v. OSHRC*, 499 U.S. 144 (1991) (Secretary of Labor's policy views, as opposed to adjudicative findings of fact, control over conflicting OSHRC interpretation).

"general duty" clause).[3] The agency also has extensive authority to inspect workplaces and require recordkeeping, and can levy penalties for noncompliance.[4] Criminal prosecutions are also authorized, but this authority has been rarely invoked.

1. Covered "Workplace" and "Working Conditions"

OSHA applies "with respect to employment in a workplace...."[5] In *Frank Diehl Farms v. Secretary of Labor*,[6] the Labor Department argued that the temporary housing provided to migrant farm workers, although not a condition of employment, was directly related to the workers' employment and was a "workplace" subject to OSHA standards. The Eleventh Circuit disagreed, reasoning that the agency's authority was limited to "the place where work is performed,"[7] and does not encompass a residence or "any employer provided device or facility"[8] that is not itself a condition of employment: "In order for coverage under the Act to be properly extended to a particular area, the conditions to be regulated must fairly be considered working conditions, the safety and health hazards to be remedied occupational, and the injuries to be avoided work-related."[9] The court insisted on adherence to the agency's prior condition-of-employment interpretation: "Only if company policy or practical necessity force workers to live in employer provided housing is the degree of coercion such that the hazards of apartment living are sufficiently related to employment to come under the scope of the Act."[10] The dissenting judge countered that the employer provided housing to the migrant workers in order "to assure an available supply of labor," and hence these camps were an "intrinsic part of the 'work situation' or 'working conditions,'" even though the employer also hired workers who did not live in the camps.[11]

2. Limited Preemption of State Law

Section 18 of OSHA gives the Secretary of Labor authority to permit states to opt out of the federal law if they establish plans offering comparable protections. There are 23 approved state

---

3. 29 U.S.C. § 654(a)(1).

4. As discussed below, the Department of Labor lacks the resources to hold inspections for more than a very small percentage of U.S. workplaces.

5. 29 U.S.C. § 663(a).

6. 696 F.2d 1325 (11th Cir. 1983).

7. *Id.* at 1331.

8. *Id.* at 1332.

9. *Id.*

10. *Id.* at 1333.

11. *Id.* at 1334 (Johnson, J., dissenting).

plans.[12] Under Section 4(b)(1), the Act does not apply to working conditions of employees "with respect to whom other Federal agencies ... exercise statutory authority to prescribe or enforce" occupational safety or health standards.

OSHA does not, as a general matter, preempt state workers' compensation laws or occupational safety and health regulation. Under Section 4(b)(4), the Act is not to be construed "to supersede or in any manner affect any workmen's compensation law or to enlarge or diminish or affect in any other manner the common law or statutory rights, duties, or liabilities of employers and employees under any law with respect to injuries, diseases, or death of employees arising out of, or in the course of, employment."[13] However, once an occupational safety or health standard has been promulgated under OSHA, the states are barred from issuing regulations on the same subject matter, unless they are acting pursuant to an approved plan under Section 18. This preemption principle is implied from Section 18(a), which states that the Act does not prevent states from "asserting jurisdiction under State law over any occupational safety or health issue with respect to which no standard is in effect" under the federal law.

In *Gade v. National Solid Wastes Management Association*,[14] the Supreme Court considered whether Illinois laws requiring the licensing of hazardous waste crane operators were preempted by OSHA because the Labor Department had promulgated standards requiring specified training for workers and supervisors engaged in hazardous waste operations.[15] Justice O'Connor, writing for a plurality of the Court,[16] rejected the view that the Act does not preempt non-conflicting state regulations at all. "Congress expressly saved two areas from federal pre-emption,"[17] the opinion noted, referring to the Section 4(b)(4) provision quoted above and the state's ability to regulate in the absence of a federal standard under Section 18(a). In addition, the states have "the option of pre-empting federal regulation entirely"[18] by securing their plans under Section 18(b). However, Section 18(b) " 'unquestionably' pre-empts any state law or regulation that establishes an occupational health and safety standard on an issue for which OSHA has already

12. 29 U.S.C. § 667(b); see 29 C.F.R. Parts 1952–56.

13. 29 U.S.C. § 653 (a)(4).

14. 505 U.S. 88 (1992).

15. 29 C.F.R. § 1910.120.

16. Justice Kennedy, concurring, supplied the fifth vote. He agreed with the thrust of the plurality opinion, but

disagreed with the plurality's characterization of the issue as one of "implied" preemption; in his view, Section 18(b) established a rule of "express" preemption once a federal standard has issued on the subject.

17. *Id.* at 96.

18. *Id.* at 97.

promulgated a standard, unless the State has obtained the Secretary's approval for its own plan."[19] Reasoning that that "[t]he design of the statute persuades us that Congress intended to subject employees to only one set of regulations,"[20] the plurality found the Illinois measures preempted. Although "state laws of general applicability (such as laws regarding traffic safety or fire safety) that do not conflict with OSHA standards and that regulate the conduct of workers and nonworkers alike would generally not be pre-empted,"[21] the Illinois laws were "directed at workplace safety" at least in part because they required training and certification of workers engaged in hazardous waste operations; "a law directed at workplace safety is not saved from pre-emption simply because the State can demonstrate some additional effect outside of the workplace."[22] Thus, under *Gade*, the state law will be preempted, regardless of whether it seeks to promote other objectives, if it "directly, substantially, and specifically regulates occupational safety and health."[23]

Unfortunately, the Court in *Gade* did not offer a clear analysis of the relationship between the savings clause in Section 4(b)(4) and the rule of preemption under Section 18 once a federal standard has been promulgated under OSHA. Presumably, even if there is a federal standard in place, the states can still apply their workers' compensation laws and other laws "with respect to injuries, diseases, or death of employees arising out of, or in the course of, employment." The issue might come up where states seek to impose criminal penalties for workplace hazards that also violate an OSHA standard. In *People of the State of Illinois v. Chicago Magnet Wire Corp.*,[24] a decision antedating *Gade*, the Illinois Supreme Court held that the state could impose criminal penalties on a company that was alleged knowingly and recklessly to have caused the injury of 42 employees by failing to provide necessary safety precautions to avoid exposure to toxic substances that were the subject of an OSHA standard. The state high court invoked the savings clause in Section 4(b)(4) of the Act and further noted that the state's purpose was retributive justice as well as deterrence and that the purpose of Section 18 was to create "a nationwide floor of effective safety and health standards," not block the states from attaching "more stringent standards or penalties than OSHA...."[25] It is not clear whether this reasoning survives *Gade*.[26]

19. *Id.*
20. *Id.* at 99.
21. *Id.* at 107.
22. *Id.*
23. *Id.*

24. 534 N.E.2d 962 (Ill. 1989).

25. *Id.* at 967. For similar rulings, see *People v. Pymm Thermometer Corp.*, 563 N.E.2d 1 (N.Y. 1990); *People v. Hegedus*, 443 N.W.2d 127 (Mich. 1989).

In its 1997 ruling in *Industrial Truck Association, Inc. v. Henry*,[27] the Ninth Circuit held that California's Proposition 65, the Safe Drinking Water and Toxic Enforcement Act, which requires the state to publish and maintain a list of chemicals known to cause cancer, birth defects or other reproductive harms and prohibits businesses from intentionally exposing individuals to these chemicals without clear warnings, was preempted by OSHA in light of the federal Hazard Communication Standard.[28] Even though California had an approved plan,

> any portions of Proposition 65 [and accompanying regulations] not included as part of the State Plan relate to the "issue" of the [Standard] and are therefore preempted. Our conclusion is based on OSHA's definition of the term "issue" within the Hazard Communication Standard and the preemptive reach of the phrase "relating to" under [the Act and the Standard].[29]

Here, the Standard expressly stated that it "is intended to address comprehensively the issue of evaluating the potential hazards of chemicals, and communicating information concerning hazards and appropriate protective measures to employees, and to preempt any legal requirements of a state ... pertaining to this subject."[30]

In another post-*Gade* ruling, *Commonwealth v. College Pro Painters, Ltd.*,[31] the state high court ruled that the defendant could not be prosecuted for failing to post "a Massachusetts Rigging Registration Number" and for failing to have a licensed painter's rigger at the worksite because OSHA standards "addressed the same occupational health and safety issues...."

The flip-side issue is whether conflict between OSHA standards and state workers' compensation laws provides employers a defense to federal obligations because § 4(b)(4) states that OSHA is not to be interpreted "to supersede or in any manner affect any workmen's compensation law...." The prevailing view is that this provision "means only that the Act and OSHA regulations are not to be interpreted to alter the terms of any [workers' compensation] law."[32] Thus, even though the OSHA Access to Exposure and

---

26. Professor Rothstein maintains that state criminal laws generally are not preempted. See MARK A. ROTHSTEIN, OCCUPATIONAL SAFETY AND HEALTH LAW § 33, at 46–47 (1998).

27. 125 F.3d 1305 (9th Cir. 1997).

28. 29 C.F.R. § 1910.1200; the agency's authority to issue this standard was upheld in *United Steelworkers of America v. Auchter*, 763 F.2d 728 (3d Cir. 1985); *Martin v. American Cyanamid*

Co., 5 F.3d 140 (6th Cir. 1993) (sustaining authority to require manufacturers to include on shipping labels the "target organ" effects of exposure).

29. *Henry*, 125 F.2d at 1311.

30. 29 C.F.R. § 1910.1200(a)(2).

31. 640 N.E.2d 777 (Mass. 1994).

32. *General Motors Corp., Electro-Motive Div.*, 14 OSHC (BNA) 2064, 1991 OSHD (CCH) ¶ 29,240 (1991), citing

Medical Records rule,[33] giving employees access to medical and exposure records concerning them, was being invoked by employee-claimants in an Illinois workers' compensation proceeding, OSHRC ruled that the fact OSHA standards might have some "practical effect" on workers' compensation claims—here, providing employees access to information that might not be available in state proceedings—did not provide an employer defense. The Commission reasoned that "[t]he OSHA records access rule does not change the terms of either" the state workers' compensation or occupational diseases laws. Nor must state adjudicators "do anything inconsistent with the[] terms" of the state laws because of the OSHA rule.

3. *Exclusive Agency Enforcement*

The preemption issue is particularly salient here because there is no private cause of action to enforce obligations under OSHA, even with respect to the no-retaliation protections of Section 11(c).[34] Only the Secretary of Labor has authority to cite an employer for violation of a standard or violation of the general duty clause. Adjudication of citations occurs before an administrative law judge, subject to review by OSHRC. (There is no jury trial.[35]) If the Secretary disagrees with a decision by OSHRC, only she can petition for review in the courts of appeals. Employers can resist citations and seek judicial review of OSHRC decisions as an aggrieved party. Employees or their union representatives also have specified participation rights: they can petition for adoption of a standard (§ 6(b)(1)); serve on a standards advisory committee (§ 7(b)); seek judicial review if "adversely affected" by an OSHA standard (§ 6(f)); file a complaint seeking an OSHA inspection (§ 8(f)(1)); participate in an OSHA inspection of the facility (§ 8(e)); seek a writ of mandamus if the Secretary "arbitrarily or capriciously fails to seek" injunctive relief against imminent hazards "reasonably expected to cause death or serious physical harm" (§ 13(d)); elect party status in contests to citations initiated by the employer, and seek judicial review of OSHRC decisions (§ 11(a)). There is also authority permitting employees to seek judicial review of the Secretary's arbitrary and capricious refusal to issue a standard.[36]

United Steelworkers of America v. Marshall, 647 F.2d 1189, 1234–36 (D.C. Cir. 1980); *Pratico v. Portland Terminal Co.*, 783 F.2d 255, 265–67 (1st Cir. 1985).

33. 29 C.F.R. § 1910.20.

34. 29 U.S.C. § 660(c); see *Wood v. Department of Labor*, 275 F.3d 107 (D.C.

Cir. 2001) (Secretary has unreviewable discretion whether to proceed).

35. Upheld against Seventh Amendment challenge in *Atlas Roofing Co. v. OSHRC*, 430 U.S. 442 (1977).

36. See note 68 *infra*.

B.   Rationale for Regulation

In standard economic theory, the existence of risk does not itself warrant regulation because rational actors will respond to risk by insisting on higher rewards for the same activity. If labor markets are functionally efficiently, then presumably firms that present significant risks of workplace injury or illness must pay workers a premium (i.e., higher wages, better fringe benefits, better working conditions) over what qualified workers would obtain in other employment not involving risks. Firms would therefore have an incentive to reduce risks up to the point where the marginal costs of additional risk reduction exceed the hazard premium needed to obtain workers at that level of risk. Under this account, there would be no need for OSHA, especially in a world with workers' compensation.

One problem with this account is that it is costly to obtain information about the workplace health and safety records of employers. There may be no central, accessible repository of such information. Workers may have difficulty determining whether a particular instance of a workplace injury they do learn about was due to the worker's own negligence as opposed to the firm's. Diseases are especially difficult to track because of the often considerable time lag between exposure and the onset of identifiable symptoms, and some symptoms may have multiple causes not easily traced to workplace exposure. If there is asymmetrical access to information, the hazard premium may be set too low or not at all.

Some aspects of OSHA regulation may thus be justified as an attempt to correct this market failure in information. Firms are better situated to know of hidden or long-term hazards and have little incentive to explain these hazards to employees. For example, the Act's record-keeping requirements, the OSHA Access to Exposure and Medical Records rule and the agency's Hazard Communication Standard attempt to reduce this disparity in access to information between employers and employees.

OSHA requirements cannot be waived by employees or their representatives even if full information is provided. This suggests that the Act also rests on other justifications, for presumably collective bargaining agents should be able to do an acceptable job in representing employee valuations of potential safety problems.[37]

---

37.   See generally David Weil, Individual Rights and Collective Agents: The
Role of Old and New Workplace Institutions in the Regulation of Labor Markets?
(NBER Working Paper 9565, 2003).

It has been claimed that workers may not be able fully to appreciate long-term, probabilistic risks, undervaluing such risks in bargains with firms.[38] In addition, unregulated bargaining may not fully account for the external or public costs of declining worker health and safety.[39]

Like the FLSA and child labor laws, OSHA reflects a collective social judgment about standards of fairness and decency, a judgment that individuals should not be subjected to work conditions that fall below certain minimum wage and safety standards. The law, in effect, stipulates the minimum terms under which a worker may be engaged.[40]

To the extent the law covers all of the nation's employers, OSHA should create no competitive disadvantage within American product markets. If the countries with whom we compete have similar laws which are enforced with comparable efficacy, there should be no competitive disadvantage in those foreign markets. However, such laws do increase the cost of hiring workers at the margin, and hence may reduce employment levels. Moreover, within the U.S., the law may be enforced unevenly, for the government tends to inspect workplaces where employees or their representatives have lodged complaints, particularly stringent standards may have been imposed on certain industries but not others, and the "feasibility" constraint on standards may tend to shield weaker industries from the full regulatory reach.

It is difficult to determine OSHA's impact on occupational safety and health. In 2006, there were approximately 115 million employees working at 7.1 million worksites covered by the Act; the Department of Labor conducted 38,579 inspections, with state plans providing another 58,058 inspections.[41] Most inspections occur as a result of complaints from employees or their representatives or in targeted areas like construction sites. One empirical

---

38. See W. KIP VISCUSI, RISK BY CHOICE 59–67 (1983) and his *Risk Perceptions in Regulation, Tort Liability, and the Market*, 14 REGULATION (Fall 1991), pp. 50–57; Mary Loring Lyndon, *Information Economics and Chemical Toxicity: Designing Laws to Produce and Use Data*, 87 MICH.L.REV. 1795 (1989); Cass R. Sunstein, *Legal Interference with Private Preferences*, 53 U.CHI.L.REV. 1129 (1986).

39. See SUSAN ROSE-ACKERMAN, *Progressive Law and Economics—And the New Administrative Law*, 98 YALE L.J. 341, 356 (1988).

40. For a consideration of the "standard economic objection" to "minimum standards" legislation, see STEVEN L. WILLBORN, *Individual Employment Rights and the Standard Economic Objection: Theory and Empiricism*, 67 U. NEB. L. REV. 101 (1988).

41. See notes 87–88 and accompanying text.

study of the 1973–1983 period found that "OSHA's effect appears to be in the range of 1.5 to 3.6 percent of the current lost workday incidence rate [due to injuries and illnesses]. Viewed somewhat differently, OSHA prevents from 1 to 2 injuries involving at least one day of [lost] work per 1,000 workers annually."[42] Other studies find a similar small, but beneficial effect.[43]

C. Standards

Under Section 5(a) of the Act, each covered employer "shall comply with occupational safety and health standards promulgated under OSHA." Section 6 gives the Secretary of Labor authority to engage in four types of standard-setting or rule-making functions: (1) promulgation of "national consensus standards" (§ 6(a)); (2) promulgation of new or modified standards or the revocation of previous standards (§ 6 (b)); (3) the issuance of immediate "emergency temporary standards" to avert "grave danger from exposure to substances or agents determined to be toxic or physically harmful or from new hazards" (§ 6(c)); and (4) the granting of employer-sought variances from standards if the employer can show that its practices or conditions "will provide employment and places of employment which are as safe and healthful as those which would prevail if he complied with the standard" in question (§ 6(d)).

1. Setting the Standard

Shortly after the Act became effective, in order to establish a quick baseline for industry, the Secretary used his authority under Section 6(a) to adopt a series of "national consensus standards" largely derived from privately adopted, optional industry standards established by the American National Standards Institute (ANSI) and the National Fire Protection Association (NFPA). Since Section 6(a) provided only a two-year period for setting these initial standards without utilizing the Act's rule-making procedures, the Secretary may have acted without carefully reviewing each of the industry standards adopted; many of the standards were, in the words of one commentator, "trivial, outdated, and even ludicrous."[44] More-

---

42. W. Kip Viscusi, FATAL TRADEOFFS: PUBLIC & PRIVATE RESPONSIBILITIES FOR RISK 219 (1992).

43. See J.W. Ruser & R.S. Smith, *The Effect of OSHA Records–Check Inspections on Reported Occupational Injuries in Manufacturing Establishments*, 1 J. OF RISK & UNCERTAINTY 415 (No. 4,

1988); J.T. Scholz & W.B. Gray, *OSHA Enforcement and Workplace Injury: A Behavioral Approach to Risk Assessment*, 3 J. OF RISK & UNCERTAINTY 283 (No. 3, 1990).

44. Mark A. Rothstein, *OSHA After Ten Years: A Review and Some Proposed Reforms*, 34 VAND. L. REV. 71, 73–74 (1981).

over, many of these often detailed specifications were never intended by the private standards organizations to serve as mandatory rules; at most, they were recommendations as to best practices for optional implementation. The agency faced a bit of a dilemma: If it proceeded under the expedited procedure in Section 6(a), it had only two years to establish these initial standards. On the other hand, some courts held that the agency had to adopt the private standards verbatim, and could not adopt "should" standards as mandatory rules, without employing the more time-consuming rule-making procedure in Section 6(b).[45] Ultimately bowing to this judicial reaction, the agency revoked 153 "should" standards in 1984 without converting them into mandatory standards.

The principal standard-setting authority is contained in Section 6(b), which provides for a somewhat more complicated procedure for rule-making than generally required under the notice-and-comment procedures of Section 553 of the Administrative Procedure Act. The Secretary may initiate the process on her own or on the basis of information provided by "an interested person", labor or employer organizations, a nationally recognized standards-producing organization, the Secretary of Health and Human Services, or NIOSH. The Secretary may also seek the assistance of an advisory committee appointed under Section 7. After appropriate consultation, the Secretary publishes a proposed rule in the Federal Register and provides a 30–day period to submit written data or comments. If an interested person files written objections, the agency holds a hearing to consider the objections. Within 60 days after the close of the public comment period or the hearing, the Secretary can issue the rule or make a determination that a rule should not issue. Under Section 6(b)(6), an employer can apply to the Secretary for a temporary order granting a variance from a standard on the ground that it lacks the necessary personnel or equipment or needs to engage in construction in order to come under compliance.

The Act does not expressly set forth criteria for rules not dealing with toxic materials or harmful physical agents. (As we will see below, Section 3(8) does provide a definition of the term "standard".) However, under Section 6(b)(5), if the standard deals with such materials or agents, the Act states that the Secretary

> shall set the standard which most adequately assures, to the extent feasible, on the basis of the best available evidence, that no employee will suffer material impairment of health or functional capacity, even if such employee has regular exposure

---

45. See *Usery v. Kennecott Copper Corp.*, 577 F.2d 1113 (10th Cir. 1977).

to the hazard dealt with by such standard for the period of his working life.

Development of standards "under this subsection" is to be based on "research, demonstrations, experiments, and such other information as may be appropriate." In addition to "the attainment of the highest degree of health and safety protection," the Secretary is also urged to consider "the latest available scientific data" and experience under OSHA and related laws.

The Secretary's rule-making authority under Section 6 has been before the Supreme Court on two occasions. In *Industrial Union Dept. v. American Petroleum Institute* (Benzene Decision),[46] the Court struck down the agency's Benzene Standard which had called for an exposure limit of 1 part benzene per million parts of air (ppm), a reduction from the previous ANSI-based national consensus standard of 10 ppm. Benzene at very high levels of concentration (20,000 ppm or above) can cause immediate death, and persistent exposure at levels above 25–40 ppm can lead to blood deficiencies and diseases of the blood-forming organs. In a 1974 report, NIOSH noted there was a "distinct possibility" that benzene also caused leukemia; however, because all known cases had occurred at very high exposure levels, it declined to recommend a change in the 10 ppm standard.[47] Two years later, in light of intervening studies, NIOSH now recommended setting the exposure limit as low as possible. In 1977 OSHA issued an emergency standard reducing the benzene exposure limit to 1 ppm, but implementation was halted by a temporary restraining order of the Fifth Circuit. The agency then issued a proposal for a permanent standard setting the limit at 1 ppm. In its notice accompanying the proposed standard, the agency did not ask for comments on whether benzene presented a significant risk at exposures of 1 ppm or less; the notice sought comment only on whether lowering the exposure limit would be feasible. The agency explained that whenever a carcinogen was involved, its assumption was that no safe level of exposure exists in the absence of clear proof establishing such a level. "Given OSHA's cancer policy, it was in fact irrelevant whether there was any evidence at all of a leukemia risk at 10 ppm. The important point was there was no evidence that there was not some risk, however small, at that level."[48] Believing that its mandate under Section 6 was to give workers maximum protection from exposure to toxic substances, the Secretary's policy was to reduce exposure to the lowest level "feasible," that is, the level that was

46. 448 U.S. 607 (1980).
47. *Id.* at 618–19.
48. *Id.* at 624.

214

technologically achievable but would not impair the stability of the affected industries.

The agency again met with resistance in the Fifth Circuit. The court issued an order remanding the standard for further proceedings because the agency had not demonstrated that this reduction in the level of exposure would result in appreciable benefits commensurate with the costs of compliance. The court of appeals' judgment was affirmed by the Supreme Court but on somewhat different grounds.

Justice Stevens' plurality opinion agreed with the lower court that Section 3(8)'s definition of the term "standard" as one that is "reasonably necessary and appropriate to provide safe or healthful employment" was applicable to all standards, including standards dealing with toxic substances under § 6(b)(5); and the § 3(8) definition "requires the Secretary, before issuing any standard, to determine that it is reasonably necessary and appropriate to remedy a significant risk of material health impairment."[49] In the absence of this determination, there was no need to decide the further question whether § 6(b)(5) required a cost-benefit analysis.

Justice Stevens sought to assure the agency that its burden under § 3(8) would not be too onerous. This threshold determination of identifying a "significant" risk "is not a mathematical straightjacket. Some risks are plainly acceptable and others are plainly unacceptable."[50] A one in a billion risk of dying from cancer by taking a drink of chlorinated water would be negligible, while a one in a thousand risk of death from regular inhalation of gasoline vapors that are two percent benzene would pose a significant risk that the Secretary could seek to eliminate. Although the agency has "no duty to calculate the exact probability of harm, it does have an obligation to find that a significant risk is present before it can characterize a place of employment as unsafe."[51]

Justice Powell filed a concurring opinion in which he adopted the Fifth Circuit's view that a cost-benefit analysis was required. Justice Rehnquist joined in the result only, arguing that he would invalidate the first sentence of § 6(b)(5) as an unconstitutional delegation of legislative authority to an administrative agency; the agency's choice is "between setting a safe standard or setting no standard at all."

In its second encounter with Section 6 rule-making, *American Textile Manufacturers Institute, Inc. v. Donovan* (Cotton Dust Deci-

---

49. Id. at 639–40.   **51.** *Id.*
50. Id. at 655.

sion),[52] the Court upheld the agency's Cotton Dust Standard.[53] In this case, there was no issue as to whether exposure to cotton dust caused a significant risk of a "constellation of respiratory effects" known as byssinosis.[54] The only question was whether Section 6(b)(5)'s requirement of "feasibility" incorporated a cost-benefit analysis. Writing for a five-Justice majority (the four dissenters in the benzene case joined by Justice Stevens), Justice Brennan answered the question left open the year before: Without deciding whether § 3(8) contemplates some form of cost-benefit analysis, the Court held that § 6(b)(5) standards did not require the use of a cost-benefit analysis:

> ... For even if [§ 3(8)] does, Congress specifically chose in § 6(b)(5) to impose separate and additional requirements for issuance of a subcategory of occupational safety and health standards dealing with toxic materials and harmful physical agents; it required that that those standards be issued to prevent material impairment of health to the extent feasible....

> ... Agreement with [the] argument that § 3(8) imposes an additional and overriding requirement of cost-benefit analysis on the issuance of § 6(b)(5) standards would eviscerate the "to the extent feasible" requirement. Standards would inevitably be set at the level indicated by cost-benefit analysis, and not at the level specified by § 6(b)(5).[55]

The Court also left open the possibility that even if a § 6(b)(5) standard were feasible, § 3(8)'s "reasonably necessary or appropriate" language might impose additional requirements.[56]

In light of the Cotton Dust Decision's discussion of the plurality opinion in the Benzene Decision, it would seem clear that at least two aspects of the latter opinion reflect the views of a majority of the Court: (1) the applicability of the § 3(8) definition of the term "standard" to all OSHA standards, and (2) the requirement read into that definition that the agency must show that its standard will achieve a demonstrable improvement in worker safety or health.

The courts of appeals have addressed other issues concerning OSHA's standard-setting authority. These include:

---

52. 452 U.S. 490 (1981).

53. 29 C.F.R. § 1910.1043.

54. Even at the level permitted by the OSHA standard, the agency "found that the prevalence of at least Grade 1/2 byssinosis would affect 13% of all em-

ployees in the yarn manufacturing sector." 452 U.S. at 503.

55. *Id.* at 512–13.

56. See *id.* at 513 n.32.

- *Multi-Substance Standards.* The agency can engage in a "generic" rulemaking in which it sets a standard for multiple substances, as it did in the Air Contaminants Standard,[57] a revision of permissible exposure limits for 428 toxic substances. However, "OSHA has a responsibility to quantify or explain at least to some reasonable degree, the risk posed by each toxic substance regulated."[58]

- *Non-§ 6(b)(5) Standards.* The agency is entitled to deference to its judgment that grain dust in grain handling facilities is not a "harmful physical agent" under § 6(b)(5). Adopting a middle position between absolute safety protection to the extent feasible and strict cost-benefit analysis, the Fifth Circuit has held that the "reasonably necessary or appropriate" standard of § 3(8) that applies to non-§ 6(b)(5) standards requires only that the costs of the regulation be "reasonably related" to the expected benefits.[59]

- *Medical Monitoring.* Medical monitoring of employees for exposure to dust in cottonseed mills can be required even if the Secretary cannot demonstrate a significant risk of harm.[60] The agency had "rested its finding of no significant risk on 'the assurance that retention of medical surveillance will provide a backstop if that judgment is incorrect and this surveillance will protect the health of the employees.' "[61] The D.C. Circuit, per then-Judge Ruth Ginsburg, agreed, relying on dicta in the Benzene Decision suggesting that "in setting a permissible exposure level in reliance on less-than-perfect methods, OSHA would have the benefit of a backstop in the form of medical monitoring and medical testing."[62]

- *Preference for Environmental Controls vs. Respirators?* The courts have deferred to the agency's view that respirators or other protective equipment cannot substitute for feasible environmental or engineering modifications even though they are a good deal less costly. As the Court noted in the Benzene Decision, the agency takes this position in part because respirators may interfere with vision and mobility

---

57. 29 C.F.R. § 1910.1000.

58. See *AFL–CIO v. OSHA*, 965 F.2d 962, 975 (11th Cir. 1992).

59. See *National Grain & Feed Association v. OSHA*, 866 F.2d 717 (5th Cir. 1988). See generally CASS SUNSTEIN, THE COST-BENEFIT STATE: THE FUTURE OF REGULATORY PROTECTION (American Bar Assn., 2002).

60. *National Cottonseed Products Association v. Brock*, 825 F.2d 482 (D.C. Cir. 1987).

61. *Id.* at 487, quoting 50 Fed. Reg. 51,136.

62. The Court left open "what cost-benefit considerations, if any, should govern the Agency's imposition of such requirements." 448 U.S. at 657–58 & n.65.

and because workers find them uncomfortable and resist their use.[63]

- *Medical Removal and Wage Guarantees.* The Cotton Dust Decision struck down the wage-guarantee provision of the agency's standard requiring employees unable to wear respirators during the transitional period to be given an opportunity to transfer to another provision without loss of pay: "We hold that, whether or not OSHA has this underlying authority, the agency has failed to make the necessary determination or statement of reasons that its wage guarantee requirement is related to the achievement of a safe and healthful work environment."[64] The reason given for the guarantee is that otherwise employees will be reluctant to disclose health hazards for fear of loss of pay or discharge. The wage guarantee in the agency's Lead Standard was upheld in a 1980 decision of the D.C. Circuit[65]; post-*Cotton Dust* rulings have upheld interpretations of the guarantee provision in the Lead Standard to include premium payments such as production bonuses.[66]

- *"Technology–Forcing" Standards?* The agency can engage in some "technology-forcing," requiring an employer to implement technology that "looms on today's horizon," but lacks authority to impose "an affirmative duty on each employer to research and develop new technology."[67]

- *Compelling Standard Setting?* In unusual circumstances, the courts have addressed the issue of agency inaction, essentially forcing the agency to issue standards.[68]

The agency has faced considerable controversy in attempting to promulgate a standard dealing with "ergonomics," which it defines as

63. See 448 U.S. at 627 & n.24.

64. 452 U.S. at 537–38.

65. *United Steelworkers of America v. Marshall*, 647 F.2d 1189 (D.C. Cir. 1980).

66. See *United Steelworkers of America v. Schuylkill Metals Corp.*, 828 F.2d 314 (5th Cir. 1987).

67. *AFL-CIO v. Brennan*, 530 F.2d 109, 121–22 (3d Cir. 1975); *American Iron & Steel Institute v. OSHA*, 577 F.2d 825, 838 (3d Cir. 1978); see *Society of the Plastics Industry, Inc. v. OSHA*, 509 F.2d 1301 (2d Cir. 1975).

68. See *Public Citizen Health Research Group v. Chao*, 314 F.3d 143 (3d Cir. 2002) (9–year delay in adopting new standard for hexavalent chromium; court required promulgation of proposed standard pursuant to judicial timetable); *Farmworker Justice Fund, Inc. v. Brock*, 811 F.2d 613 (D.C. Cir. 1987) (ordering standard to issue after the agency had withdrawn proposed standard); *cf. United Mine Workers of Am. v. Department of Labor*, 358 F.3d 40 (D.C. Cir. 2004) (MSHA failure to provide adequate justification for withdrawing proposed rule). But see, e.g., *UAW v. Chao*, 361 F.3d 249 (3d Cir. 2004) (Secretary's failure to adopt a standard limiting exposure to metal working fluids held not to be an abuse of discretion).

the study of the design requirements of work in relation to the physical and psychological capabilities and limitations of people; that is, ergonomics seeks to fit the job to the person rather than the person to the job. The aim of the discipline is to prevent the development of occupational disorders and to reduce the potential for fatigue, error, or unsafe acts through the evaluation and design of facilities, environments, jobs, task, tools, equipment, processes, and training methods to match the capabilities of specific workers.[69]

OSHA issued a standard in 2001 near the tail end of the Clinton Administration. Extensive employer opposition, based on the perceived costs of compliance (both in required engineering changes and pay protection during periods of rest or light duty) and questions about the agency's authority to act at all in this area, led Congress to exercise its authority under the Congressional Review Act[70] to rescind the standard.[71] The Secretary has sought to address ergonomics issues under the General Duty Clause (as discussed below).

2. Securing Compliance with OSHA Standards

Under Section 5(a)(2) of the Act, each covered employer must "comply with occupational safety and health standards promulgated under" the Act. The Secretary effects compliance through its authority to investigate workplaces and act on complaints leading to citations and possible penalties under Sections 9 and 10. The Secretary's prima facie case consists of proving that

> (1) the cited standard applies, (2) there was a failure to comply with the cited standard, (3) an employee had access to the violative condition, and (4) the employer knew or should have know of the condition with the exercise of reasonable diligence.[72]

In cases involving elimination of a "hazard," the Secretary would also have to show the existence of such hazard. In these proceedings, the courts will defer to reasonable interpretation by the agency of its own standards and rules and regulations.[73]

---

69. 57 Fed. Reg. 34191, 34199 (Aug. 3, 1992) (notice of proposed rule-making).

70. Pub. L. 104–121 (1996), codified at 5 U.S.C. § 801.

71. President George W. Bush signed S.J. Res. 6 (repealing the ergonomics standard) on March 20, 2001.

See generally J. Parks, *Lessons in Politics: Initial Use of the Congressional Review Act*, 55 ADMIN. L. REV. 187, 192–95 (2003).

72. ROTHSTEIN, OCCUPATIONAL SAFETY AND HEALTH LAW, *supra* note 26, § 102, at 152.

73. See, e.g., the *Schuylkill Metals* decision cited in note 66 *supra*.

The employer can raise technological and economic feasibility as a defense in such enforcement proceedings.[74] Even though pre-enforcement judicial review of standards is provided under Section 6(f), employers can also challenge the validity of the standard's promulgation at the enforcement stage. The Eighth Circuit has ruled, however, that such challenges are limited to substantive, as opposed to procedural, grounds of invalidity;[75] other circuits disagree.[76]

Other employer defenses include that the standard is vague, the alleged violation was not within the scope of employment, or the injury was caused by unpreventable employee misconduct or concerted employee refusal to comply.[77] The courts have held, for example, that

> To establish the affirmative defense of "unforeseeable employee misconduct," an employer must prove that (1) it established work rules to prevent the violation; (2) these rules were adequately communicated to the employees; (3) it took steps to discover violations; and (4) it effectively enforced the rules when infractions were discovered.[78]

D. General Duty Clause

Even where the Secretary has not promulgated a standard on an issue, she can proceed under the "General Duty Clause." Under Section 5(a)(1) each covered employer

> shall furnish to each of his employees employment and a place of employment which are free from recognized hazards that are causing or are likely to cause death or serious physical harm to employees. . . .[79]

There is no private cause of action under the General Duty Clause; any proceedings must be brought by the agency. The employer's

---

74. See, e.g., *Atlantic & Gulf Stevedores, Inc. v. OSHRC*, 534 F.2d 541, 538 (3d Cir. 1976).

75. See *National Industrial Constructors, Inc. v. OSHRC*, 583 F.2d 1048 (8th Cir. 1978).

76. See, e.g., *Marshall v. Union Oil Co.*, 616 F.2d 1113, 1118 (9th Cir. 1980).

77. Under Section 5(b), an employee must also "comply with occupational safety and health standards and all rules, regulations, and orders issued pursuant to [the Act] which are applicable to his own actions and conduct." 29 U.S.C. § 654(b). Even though stated as an affirmative duty of employees, the circuits hold that "unforeseeable employee misconduct" is an affirmative defense to be proven by the employer. See, e.g., *D.A. Collins Construction Co., Inc. v. Secretary of Labor*, 117 F.3d 691, 695 (2d Cir. 1997).

78. 117 F.3d at 695.

79. 29 U.S.C. § 654(a)(1).

compliance with an OSHA standard is usually a defense, except when the employer is on notice that the standard is inadequate to deal with the specific hazard in its workplace.[80]

The Secretary's prima facie case consists of proving

(i) the existence of a hazard likely to cause death or serious physical harm; (ii) the employer's recognition (*i.e.*, awareness) of the hazard; (iii) the availability of feasible means to abate the hazard; and (iv) the employer's failure to implement the feasible means of abatement.[81]

The employer's violation is "willful" (relevant to any assessment of penalties) "if it is committed with intentional disregard of, or plain indifference to, the requirements of the statute."[82] As this formulation indicates, the statutory requirement that the workplace be "free" of recognized hazards means free of hazards that are "preventable" by reasonable employer diligence. A single instance of an employee mishap does not establish a violation in the absence of proof of a failure by the employer to provide reasonable precautionary measures.[83]

Employer defenses are similar to those available in cases involving failure to comply with OSHA standards. Thus, for example, "unpreventable employee misconduct" is a defense to a Section 5(a)(1) violation here, as well. However, the employer cannot simply rely on the discretion of its supervisors; the employer is effectively under an affirmative duty to instruct employees on "(1) how to recognize and avoid unsafe conditions they may encounter on the job, and (2) the regulations applicable to those hazardous conditions."[84]

Even though its attempt at issuing an ergonomics standard was stymied by Congressional action, the Secretary has relied on the General Duty Clause to cite employers for ergonomics hazards. In *Beverly Enterprises, Inc.*,[85] OSHRC ruled that low back pain caused by ergonomics lifting hazards involved a risk of serious physical harm under the Clause, as it was likely to have a signifi-

---

80. See, e.g., *UAW v. General Dynamics Land Systems Div.*, 815 F.2d 1570 (D.C. Cir. 1987).

81. *Caterpillar, Inc. v. OSHRC*, 122 F.3d 437, 440 (7th Cir. 1997) (summarizing OSHRC precedent).

82. *Id.* (finding "willful" violation when employer was aware that repairing a machine caused shooting studs and did not take precautionary measures).

83. *National Realty and Construction Co., Inc. v. OSHRC*, 489 F.2d 1257, 1265 (D.C. Cir. 1973).

84. *Superior Custom Cabinet Company, Inc.*, 18 OSHC (BNA) 1019, 1997 OSHD (CCH) ¶ 31,422 (OSHRC, 1997).

85. 19 OSHC (BNA) 1161, 2000 OSHD (CCH) ¶ 32, 227 (OSHRC, 2000); see also OSHA, EFFECTIVE ERGONOMICS: STRATEGY FOR SUCCESS, available at www. osha.gov/SLTC/ergonomics/index.html.

cant effect on employees' ability to perform their normal activities; moreover, the Secretary did not have to show a direct causal connection between the cited working conditions and the harm to be prevented. In *Matter of the Establishment Inspection of the Kelly–Springfield Tire Company*,[86] the Seventh Circuit upheld an investigation concerning possible ergonomic-based violations of the Clause.

E.   Inspections

Under Section 8(a), the Secretary has broad authority "to enter without delay and at reasonable times" any workplace "where work is performed by an employee of an employer" and "to inspect and investigate" at reasonable times and in a reasonable manner "all pertinent conditions, strictures, machines, apparatus, devices, equipment, and materials therein, and to question privately any such employer, owner, operator, agent, or employee."[87]

Given the sheer number of workplaces in the U.S. (approximately 7 million) and the limited number of OSHA and state inspectors, the agency can investigate only a small percentage of sites. In fiscal year 2006, it conducted 38,579 inspections; over half (21,504, or 55.7%) involved targeted high hazard sites and over half (22,891, or 59.3%) involved the construction industry. Another 58,058 inspections were conducted by the states.[88] Inspections flowing from complaints by employees or their representatives or reported accidents accounted for about one-fifth (7,376, or 19.1%) of the total.[89] Targeted employers are often subject to repeat inspections, but there is little evidence of any appreciable benefit after the second inspection.[90] There is also some evidence that the presence of a labor union at the workplace increases the likelihood of an OSHA inspection.[91]

86. 13 F.3d 1160, 1166 & nn. 2–3 (7th Cir. 1994).

87. 29 U.S.C. § 657(a).

88. See Dept. of Labor, *OSHA Facts– August 2007,* at www.osha.gov/as/opa/oshafacts.html.

89. *Id.*

90. See DAVID WEIL, THE IMPACT OF OSHA ENFORCEMENT ON REGULATORY COMPLIANCE IN THE U.S. CONSTRUCTION INDUSTRY (July 1999).

91. See David Weil, *Are Mandated Health and Safety Committees Substitutes or Supplements to Labor Unions?*, 52 INDUS. & LAB. REL. REV. 339 (April 1999) and his INDIVIDUAL RIGHTS AND COLLECTIVE AGENTS: THE ROLE OF OLD AND NEW WORKPLACE INSTITUTIONS IN THE REGULATION OF LABOR MARKETS? (NBER Working Paper 9565, March 2003), available at www.nber.org/papers/w9565. The GAO reported in 2000 that "[e]stablishments experiencing labor unrest [i.e., a strike or allegation of unfair labor practices] are about 6.5 times more likely to be inspected by OSHA than establishments not experiencing labor unrest (8.6 percent inspected compared with about 1.3 percent) during fiscal years 1994 through 1998"; 76 percent of the establishments experiencing such "unrest" were unionized, as compared with 24 percent of all establishments inspected

In *Marshall v. Barlow's Inc.*,[92] the Supreme Court held that the Fourth Amendment requires the agency to secure a warrant based on probable cause before it can conduct a nonconsensual inspection of a private workplace. A warrant "would provide assurances from a neutral officer that the inspection is reasonable [and] is authorized by statute." However, "probable cause in the criminal law sense is not required"[93]—only a showing of reasonable suspicion of a violation or that the inspection is part of a reasonable administrative plan. A warrant is not required where there is consent, an OSHA official observes a violation in plain view, or in emergency circumstances. The effect of the *Barlow's* ruling is to prevent the agency from showing up at a workplace unless the site has been selected as part of a reasonable inspection scheme; truly random selection by computer is permissible,[94] but a wholly discretionary selection is not.

In inspections that are not part of an administrative plan but, rather, are in response to a complaint, courts have ruled that the agency cannot act solely on the basis that a complaint has been made; it should interview the complainant and take other steps to "confirm the validity of the complaint" short of inspection of the workplace.[95] Although in a targeted or programmed inspection, the scope of the inspection can be fairly broad, the scope of an inspection based on a complaint will be determined by the reasonable allegations in the complaint.[96]

F. Protection Against Discrimination

The efficacy of the statutory scheme depends in good part on the willingness of employees or their representatives to disclose unsafe conditions to their employer and, where that is unavailing, to report the condition to the Department of Labor. Accordingly, Section 11 (c) protects employees from employer discrimination because they have filed a complaint or gave testimony "or because of the exercise by such employee on behalf of himself or others of any rights afforded by" the Act.[97] There is no private right of action

by OSHA. See GOVT. ACCOUNTING OFF., WORKER PROTECTION: OSHA INSPECTIONS AT ESTABLISHMENTS EXPERIENCING LABOR UNREST (GAO/HEHS–00–144, Aug. 2000), p. 5.

92. 436 U.S. 307 (1978).

93. *Id*. at 320.

94. See "anticipatory warrant" procedure in 29 C.F.R. § 1903.4; see, e.g.,

National Engineering & Contracting Co. v. OSHRC, 45 F.3d 476 (D.C. Cir. 1995).

95. *Kelly-Springfield Tire Co., supra* note 86, at 1166.

96. See, e.g., *Trinity Industries, Inc. v. OSHRC*, 16 F.3d 1455 (6th Cir. 1994).

97. 29 U.S.C. § 660(c).

under Section 11(c);[98] it is enforced exclusively by the Secretary who has authority to petition the federal district courts to issue an injunction and seek reinstatement with back pay.

Employees in general do not have a right to refuse a work assignment because they believe they are encountering "potential unsafe conditions at the workplace"; the usual recourse is to complain to the employer or union representative and, if dissatisfied with the response, pursue the matter with OSHA.[99] The agency, however, has established by regulation a limited right to walk off the job:

> [O]ccasions might arise when an employee is confronted with a choice between not performing assigned tasks or subjecting himself to serious injury or death from a hazardous condition at the workplace. If the employee, with no reasonable alternative, refuses in good faith to expose himself to the dangerous condition, he would be protected against subsequent discrimination. The condition causing the employee's apprehension of death or injury must be of such a nature that a reasonable person, under the circumstances then confronting the employee, would conclude that there is a real danger of health or serious injury and that there is insufficient time, due to the urgency of the situation, to eliminate the danger through resort to regular statutory enforcement channels. In addition, in such circumstances, the employee, where possible, must also have sought from his employer, and been unable to obtain, a correction of the dangerous condition.[100]

The agency's authority to promulgate this regulation was upheld by the Supreme Court in *Whirlpool Corp. v. Secretary of Labor*.[101] In that case, maintenance workers at a manufacturing plant were required to step on a wire-mesh screen approximately 20 feet above the plant floor to remove debris; the employer was in the process of installing a heavier wire in the screen when an employee fell to his death through the screen in an area where the stronger mesh was not yet in place. Two employees, Deemer and Cromwell, refused an assignment to work on a section of the old screen and were discharged. Pursuant to the quoted regulation, the Secretary sued to obtain their reinstatement, which the court of appeals ordered and the Supreme Court affirmed.[102]

98. See note 34 *supra*.

99. 29 C.F.R. § 1977.12 (b)(1).

100. 29 C.F.R. § 1977.12(b)(2).

101. 445 U.S. 1 (1980).

102. The Supreme Court noted that five years after the fatality, OSHRC affirmed the Secretary's citation of a violation of the General Duty Clause but decided to give the employer six months

G.   Conclusion

After 35 years, OSHA remains at the center of controversy. Employee and union spokespersons question the statute's efficacy, noting, in particular, the agency's limited capacity to engage in surprise inspections of workplaces and the general unwillingness of employees in non-union firms to voice complaints about unsafe working conditions.[103] Some academic commentators would urge the Secretary to be more mindful of the costs of compliance and more willing to allow use of less-costly respirators and other personal protective equipment in place of engineering controls.[104] Employers not surprisingly also complain about costs and the agency's regulatory overreaching into areas, like ergonomics, where the underlying science and causation issues remain unsettled.

The agency has faced a gargantuan task, raising the question whether Congress was wise to enact an all-industry regulatory regime rather than continue along the prior course of legislation focusing on problems in particular industries.

---

to correct the problem. *Id.* at n.4, citing *Whirlpool Corp.*, 1979 OSHD (CCH) ¶ 23,552. The Commission's order had been vacated on the ground that the agency had not shown there was a feasible alternative to the protective screen used by the employer. See *Whirlpool Corp. v. OSHRC*, 645 F.2d 1096 (D.C. Cir. 1981).

103. This has been the thrust of Professor Weil's work, see note 91 *supra*.

104. See Viscusi, *supra* note 42, at 172–73.

Chapter 13

EMPLOYEE BENEFITS LAW

A. Overview

Building on earlier efforts—notably, § 302 of the Labor Management Relations Act of 1947 (LMRA or Taft–Hartley Act) which set ground-rules for multiemployer benefit plans negotiated through collective bargaining-(often referred to as "Taft Hartley plans") and the disclosure and reporting requirements in the Welfare and Pension Plans Disclosure Act of 1958—Congress in 1974 enacted the Employee Retirement Income Security Act (ERISA).[1] Congress intervened in this area because of the perception that state laws governing contracts and pension trusts had proven incapable of protecting the pension benefits of workers who lost their jobs prior to retirement age or who learned upon retirement that their employer or the plan's trust lacked sufficient assets to satisfy its benefit obligations.[2] Although ERISA does not mandate that employers offer a pension or other benefits, related tax law requires employers to meet a number of rules for pension and welfare benefit plans as a condition of tax-advantaged treatment.

There are two basic types of ERISA pension plans: "defined contribution" (DC) plans that provide for an individual account for each participant and for benefits based solely upon the amount contributed to that account plus any income or other gain (earned by the contributions); and "defined benefit" (DB) plans which, although defined in the statute as any pension plan other than a DC plan, typically involve plans where the employer promises to pay a specific or definitely determinable benefit.[3] In addition to "employee pension benefit" plans, ERISA also regulates, in a more

---

1. Pub.L. No. 93–406, 88 Stat. 829, codified at various places in the Internal Revenue Code (Code) and at 29 U.S.C. §§ 1000 *et seq.*

2. See generally RICHARD A. IPPOLITO, PENSIONS, ECONOMICS, AND PUBLIC POLICY (1986); Nancy J. Altman & Theodore R. Marmor, *ERISA and the American Retirement Income System*, 7 AM.J. OF TAX POLICY 31 (1988).

3. DB plans traditionally have taken the form of "final average pay" plans which essentially reward long-term ser-

vice by calculating benefits on the basis of the last few years of pay before retirement. As discussed below, employer-sponsors increasingly have frozen accruals under such plans and have converted to "cash balance" plans which, while still DB plans since investment risk remains with the plan (and ultimately the employer-sponsor), do not have this "backloading" feature. DC plans also come in different forms (e.g., money purchase, profit sharing, § 401(k), employee stock ownership plans).

226

limited manner, "employee welfare benefit" plans,[4] which can cover such non-retirement benefits as health insurance, disability insurance and severance pay.[5] As discussed below, salary and other pay practices requiring no plan administration are not covered by ERISA.

The ERISA scheme is quite complicated, but in general its substantive regulations fall into three basic categories:

(i) minimum standards designed to promote non-forfeitable pension rights, such as vesting (initially, after 10 years of service, now reduced to 5 years' "cliff" vesting or 3–7 years' phased vesting as a result of 1986 tax reform legislation), benefit accrual, and minimum age and service conditions;

(ii) plan funding requirements to ensure that DB pension plans will have adequate assets to meet promised benefits; and

(iii) fiduciary standards and reporting and disclosure obligations.

Whereas pension benefit plans are subject to all three forms of regulation, welfare benefit plans are subject only to fiduciary and reporting and disclosure obligations. In other words, ERISA does not require vesting or advance funding of welfare benefits.[6]

The Department of Labor (DOL) is charged with the primary responsibility of interpreting and enforcing the labor provisions of ERISA. (The Department of the Treasury through the Internal

---

4. See 29 U.S.C. § 1002(1).

5. There are also non-ERISA employee benefit plans. The Department of Labor, for example, has stated that payroll deduction plans for individual retirement accounts are not ERISA plans, provided (i) no employer contributions are made; (ii) employee participation is voluntary; (iii) the employer permits but does not sponsor the program; and (iv) the employer receives no consideration (other than reasonable compensation for services rendered in connection with the payroll deduction process). See DOL Bull. 99–1, discussed in Interpretive Bulletin Assures Employer Payroll Deduction IRAs Are Not ERISA Plans, (BNA) Daily Labor Rep., No. 117, June 18, 1999, p. A–2; see also Judy C. Bauserman, *Allowing Employees to Choose Transportation Fringe Benefits*, 24 EMPLOYEE RELS. L.J. 123 (no. 4, Spring 1999).

6. There are also certain deferred compensation plans, known as "top hat" plans, that are subject to ERISA's enforcement provisions but exempt from substantive provisions like plan funding and fiduciary duties. A "top hat" plan is one "which is unfunded and is maintained primarily for the purpose of providing deferred compensation for a select group of management and highly compensated employees." 29 U.S.C. § 1051(2). The employer does not receive a deduction and the employee is not taxed until receipt of the deferred amount but any funds set aside to pay these benefits are subject to the claims of creditors in the event of the employer's insolvency or bankruptcy. The "rabbi trust," a commonly used mechanism, is an irrevocable trust for deferred compensation that cannot be reached by the employer but can be reached by the employer's creditors. See, e.g., *In re IT Group, Inc.*, 448 F.3d 661 (3d Cir. 2006).

Revenue Service is chiefly responsible for interpreting and enforcing the vesting, minimum participation, funding and tax law obligations of qualified plans.) In addition to agency enforcement, ERISA authorizes private rights of action. Participants or beneficiaries under ERISA plans may bring a civil action in federal court for any violation of the statute, including breach of fiduciary duties.[7] They may also seek review of benefits decisions by plan administrators.[8] In addition, individuals challenging a retaliatory discharge or other discrimination on account of their participation in benefit plans or assertion of rights under the statute have a remedy under § 510 of ERISA.[9]

Aside from ERISA, there are a few other federal laws that regulate employee benefits. The federal antidiscrimination statutes (Title VII, ADEA and the ADA) involve some regulation of employee benefits. Recent examples of other federal employee benefit laws are the Family and Medical Leave Act (FMLA) (discussed in Chapter 14) and the Worker Adjustment and Retraining Notification Act of 1988 (WARN),[10] the federal plant-closing law. In addition, the Consolidated Omnibus Budget Reconciliation Act (COBRA),[11] formally an amendment to ERISA, requires employee health care benefits plans to provide for continuation of health care coverage for 18 months (in some situations, 36 months), at the departing employee's expense; and the Health Insurance Portability and Accountability Act of 1996 (HIPAA)[12] limits exclusions for preexisting medical conditions and posits other rules to enable departing employees to qualify under the health care plans of their new employer. State laws dealing with employee benefits are generally preempted by ERISA, with the important exception of insurance laws which allows indirect regulation of insured (but not self-insured) plans; there are also a few areas, like family and medical leave and WARN, where federal law expressly permits states to enact higher levels of worker protection.

B.   Rationale for Regulation

1.   Why Do Employers Provide Pensions?

In view of the fact that neither federal nor state laws mandate pension benefits for employees, why do employers voluntarily pro-

7. 29 U.S.C. § 1132(a)(3). The Internal Revenue Code provisions are not enforceable by private suit.

8. 29 U.S.C. § 1132(a)(2) (after exhaustion of the claims procedure provided for in § 1133).

9. 29 U.S.C. § 1140.

10. 29 U.S.C. §§ 2101–2109.

11. 29 U.S.C. §§ 1161 *et seq.*

12. 29 U.S.C. § 1181.

vide such benefits? One important reason is that pension and other benefits, such as health care coverage, can be "purchased" by the employee in a tax-advantaged manner; in a sense, the government subsidizes compensation in the form of employee benefits by allowing employers to deduct from business income contributions they make to benefit plans and by not requiring employees to pay income tax on the "receipt" of such contributions (and in the case of pensions, not realizing any gains for tax purposes until retirement benefits are paid).

These tax consequences do not tell the entire story. It is also often in the employer's interest to promote long-term commitment on the part of its workforce because employees willing to make such a commitment may be higher-quality workers or workers willing to invest in job-specific skills (i.e., skills that, while helpful to the particular employer, do not increase the employee's value in the general labor market, and hence are not portable). Pension benefits, especially DB plans which often take the form of "backloading" compensation by offering benefits keyed to compensation in later, usually higher-paying years of service, help further this "bonding" of the employee to the particular employer. Indeed, until ERISA, pension benefits often did not "vest" (i.e., become non-forfeitable) until the employee became eligible to retire under the terms of the pension plan. One effect of ERISA regulation has been progressively to reduce this vesting period—thus making pension benefits more portable among jobs. As a result of 1986 tax reform legislation, the vesting rule for DB plans is now 5 years' "cliff" vesting (or 3–7 years on a phased schedule).[13] The overall effect is to reduce somewhat the "bonding" effect, although it is still the case that DB plans and other benefits encourage long-term service in the formula used to calculate payouts.

In recent years, many employers appear to be less concerned with promoting long-term commitment to the firm, or put differently, increasingly interested in attracting and retaining (for a time) high-mobility employees not likely to remain with a firm over their careers. For this reason, and perhaps also to avoid burdensome ERISA and Code regulations that apply disproportionately to DB plans, these employers have shifted to DC plans. Benefits under DC plans are portable since vesting typically occurs contemporaneously with the making of the employer's contribution; they also contain no "backloaded" future rewards for long-term employment. The

---

13. Under the PENSION PROTECTION ACT OF 2006, beginning in 2007 (later for collectively bargaining plans), participants in DC plans have to vest either under a 3–year cliff or 2–6 year graduated schedule for all non-elective contributions, not just matching contributions as under prior law.

downside, from the employees' standpoint, is that the risk of investment loss is borne entirely by employees, whereas in DB plans the risk is borne entirely by the plan (and, to some extent, by the employer-sponsor). The recent emergence of "cash balance" plans is an attempt to capture some of the portability of DC plans without shifting investment risk to employees.[14]

2. Why Regulate?

Why has the federal government chosen to regulate employee benefit plans in a manner that does not mandate the creation of plans or the provision of particular benefits but does impose fiduciary, financing, reporting and disclosure duties for pension benefit plans? There are several possible explanations.

One justification for federal law is to achieve the efficiency gains of a uniform set of rules, supplemented by an evolving federal common law under ERISA, for what are likely to be firm-wide benefit plans for multi-state companies. ERISA thus broadly preempts state laws "relating to" employee benefits to advance this interest in uniform administration of employee benefit plans.

Second, responding to abuses in some union-administered funds and well-publicized failures to honor pension commitments such as occurred in connection with the 1963 closing of the Studebaker automobile plant in South Bend, Indiana, the law seeks to shore up the credibility of pension promises. Pension promises are not simple contracts:

> On its face, the pension contract is tenuous. In exchange for lower cash wages, the firm promises workers pension payments many years in the future. Yet it can either terminate the plan at any time or fire workers prior to retirement; in either case, the firm can impose large capital losses on workers. Because of the complexity of the contract and its long-term nature, informational problems would appear to abound. And, the contract is largely implicit, making it unenforceable in the courts. Moreover, there is a potential for a lemons market; if some firms perpetrate fraud, the expected "quality" of all pensions is reduced. Pensions appear to offer a classic example of a product that could not survive in an unfettered competitive market, one that would require at least some governmental regulation to survive.[15]

14. See text accompanying 60–65 *infra.*

15. Richard A. Ippolito, *The Implicit Pension Contract: Development and New Directions*, 22 J. HUMAN RESOURCES 441,

ERISA and related Code provisions seek to "enforce" such implied promises by (i) requiring plan administrators or anyone with discretionary authority over plan assets to adhere to the terms of existing plans and to act as fiduciaries for participants and beneficiaries with respect to plan assets; (ii) reducing the service period for vesting and prohibiting strategic terminations for the purpose of defeating well-established pension benefit expectations; (iii) establishing minimum-funding requirements for DB plans; (iv) placing some restrictions on plan terminations; and (v) creating an insurer of last resort, the Pension Benefit Guarantee Corporation (PBGC), to ensure partial benefit payments to beneficiaries in the event of termination of an under-funded plan.[16]

Third, the mandatory insurance feature of ERISA may be conceived as an effort not only to protect employees in insolvent plans but also to encourage pension savings by ensuring that the "lemons" (defaulting employer-sponsors) do not drive down the willingness to invest in pensions:

> Why mandatory federal pension insurance? Prior to the mandate, private markets did not develop because of adverse selection (firms in poor financial shape are most likely to insure), asymmetric information (companies have better knowledge than insurers), and moral hazard (insured companies may underfund absent minimum financing requirements). Federal insurance pooling across risk classes overcomes some of these difficulties and might be warranted on grounds of imperfect worker knowledge and a reduction in externalities resulting from terminated pension plans....
>
> That being said, federal insurance is not without its own set of problems; in particular, adverse selection. Many firms have dropped out of the PBGC pool by phasing out their [DB] plans, instead making [DC] plans available to workers. Plans remaining with the PBGC then become more risky and require

459–60 (no. 3, summer 1987). One could question, as an initial matter, why the risk of reputational harm in the labor market is not sufficient to curb opportunistic employer behavior: employers who act to defeat expectations of plan beneficiaries may have difficulty encouraging employees to make these sorts of investments in the future. See generally John T. Addison & Barry T. Hirsch, *The Economic Effects of Employment Regulation: What Are the Limits?*, ch. 4 in

GOVERNMENT REGULATION OF THE EMPLOYMENT RELATIONSHIP 152 (BRUCE E. KAUFMAN ed., 1997).

16. The Multiemployer Pension Plan Amendments Act of 1980 (codified at 29 U.S.C. §§ 1381–1461) addresses the special withdrawal and termination issues arising in the context of pension plans covering several employers that are jointly administered by union and management trustees.

higher premiums, in turn accelerating the movement out of DB plans. . . .[17]

A fourth thread that runs through the statute is minimizing discrimination in favor of highly compensated employees. ERISA creates incentives for employers to establish pension plans offering broad coverage to employees by limiting tax-preferred status to "qualified" plans that contain certain minimum-participation requirements and are not skewed in favor of highly compensated employees. (See note 37 *infra*).

3. *Implications of the Shift to DC Plans*

DB plan coverage is on the decline, from 89 percent of medium and large firm employees in 1985 to 50 percent in 1997.[18] The move to DC plans enhances mobility of workers across firms and allows them to make their own investment decisions. Some commentators have suggested that a fear of taking on investment risks may lead many workers to make conservative, relatively low-yield often fixed-income investments, and to under-invest in equity due to the volatility of equity returns.[19] A danger from the other direction is that some employee-participants, until they experience directly stock market downturns, may be too optimistic, over-investing in equity—particularly where plans provide for investment in employer securities—and failing to pursue a diversified portfolio strategy. Under current law, employer-sponsors may have few incentives to guide employee choice, because fiduciary obligations apply when the plan "limit[s] or designat[es] investment options which are intended to constitute all or part of the investment universe" for the participant.[20]

17. Addison & Hirsch, supra note 15, at 152. The promise-enforcing rationale applies principally to DB plans, and not to DC plans where the employer "performs" its obligation by making the promised contributions.

18. Policy implications are assessed in Samuel Estreicher & Laurence Gold, *The Shift from Defined Benefit to Defined Contribution Plans*, 11 LEWIS & CLARK L. REV. 331 (2007); Olivia S. Mitchell, *New Trends in Pension Benefit and Retirement Provisions* (NBER Working Paper Series 7381, Oct. 1999), p. 19; also LIVING WITH DEFINED CONTRIBUTION PLANS (OLIVIA S. MITCHELL & SYLVESTER SCHIEBER eds., 1998).

19. See Jeffrey N. Gordon, *Employees, Pensions, and the New Economic Order*, 97 COLUM. L. REV. 1519, 1562–66 (1997) (advocating a new capital market instrument, a "pension equity collar," that would provide a guarantee of a minimum return close to the long-term average equity return in exchange for giving up or sharing returns that exceed the long-term average).

20. See Final Regulation Regarding Participant Directed Individual Retirement Accounts (ERISA Section 404(c) Plans) (Preamble), 57 Fed.Reg. 46,906, 46,924 n.27 (1982), quoted in Gordon, *supra* note 19, at 1565 n.148; see, e.g., *In re Unisys Savings Plan Litigation*, 173 F.3d 145 (3d Cir. 1999) (plan trus-

In view of the shift away from DB plans, there may be need to re-examine whether diversification requirements should apply to certain types of DC plans. In the case of DB plans, fiduciaries having discretionary authority to invest plan assets must diversify their holdings, and such plans cannot hold more than 10 percent of plan assets in the stock of the sponsor-employers (ERISA § 407(a)(2)). By contrast, 401(k) plans, a popular form of DC plan, can make express provision to hold employer stock above the 10 percent limit. And employee stock ownership plans (ESOPs), another type of DC plan designed to encourage employee ownership, are exempted from the diversification requirement and 10% cap on ownership of employer stock.[21] A common criticism of pension plan investments in employer stock is that, whatever their merits as employee motivators, they exacerbate employee risk by making both employment and retirement benefits dependent on the employer's continued solvency.[22]

The shift to DC plans has also placed increasing emphasis upon the negative effects of cash-outs when employees change employers. While in theory an individual who rolled over every DC accrual during his career into rollover individual retirement accounts (IRAs) would have a substantial retirement accumulation—assuming favorable market conditions for investments made with IRA funds—it may be forcefully argued that those most in need of such an accumulation upon retirement are those who are most likely to have taken cash-outs along the way to satisfy other cash demands (e.g., tuition, mortgage and credit-card debt). Legislation curbing

tees acted prudently in their choice of investment options). The general issues are usefully explored in *Symposium: Getting Ready for Individually Managed Pensions: A Global Perspective,* 64 BKLYN. L. REV. 739 ff. (no. 3, Fall 1998).

21. Participant-directed DC plans are also exempt from the diversification requirement.

22. See Susan J. Stabile, *Another Look at 401(k) Plan Investments in Employer Securities,* 35 JOHN MARSHALL L. REV. 539 (2002); Deborah M. Weiss, *Worker Ownership and Retirement Security,* ch. 26 in EMPLOYEE REPRESENTATION IN THE EMERGING WORKPLACE: ALTERNATIVES/SUPPLEMENTS TO COLLECTIVE BARGAINING 627–41 (SAMUEL ESTREICHER, ed. 1998).

Some countries take a different view of the merits of diversification. In Ger-

many, for example, companies may fund pensions by creating book reserves against their own retained earnings; in essence, pension promises are entirely unfunded liabilities. Pension security is provided in the form of a mandatory pension termination insurance funded by German employers and insurance carriers. The German system assumes that German managers will do a better job of investing the assets allocated to pension promises than would outside investors. See James H. Smalhout, THE UNCERTAIN RETIREMENT: SECURING PENSION PROMISES IN A WORLD OF RISK 223–30 (1996); Lothar Schruff, *Pensions and Post–Retirement Benefits by Employers in Germany,* 64 BKLYN. L. REV. 795 (1998). See generally THE ECONOMICS OF PENSIONS: PRINCIPLES, POLICIES AND INTERNATIONAL EXPERIENCE (SALVADOR VALDES-PRIETO ed. 1997).

cash-outs may, however, cause employees to be less willing to make voluntary retirement contributions.

In view of the shift away from DB plans, and evidence indicating a considerable reluctance of average and lower income individuals affirmatively to participate in DC plans, even when employers provide a match from their funds, the IRS, in a number of revenue rulings, approved automatic enrollment features in 401(k) and certain other DC plans, along with a three-percent employee contribution through payroll deductions, subject to an opportunity to opt-out of the plan.[23] The Pension Protection Act of 2006 further supports automatic enrollment by freeing 401(k) plans that use this mechanism from the nondiscrimination requirements.[24]

C. Coverage Issues

1. Covered "Plans"

Because of the tax advantages of a qualified plan, most employers have a strong incentive to take steps to ensure that they have established a plan that meets the applicable ERISA and Code requirements. In particular, if IRS requirements are not met, employers will find that contributions they make to fund employee benefits cannot be deducted from their income until benefits are actually paid out to employees.

Although ERISA offers definitions for the terms "employee pension benefit plan" and "employee welfare benefit plan" in § 3(1)-(3), the statute does not define the operative term "plan". It will not always be clear whether the employee benefit provisions of a particular employment contract are part of an ERISA-covered plan rather than merely terms of a contract governed by state law. This question often arises in the context where the employer is arguing that an employee or former employee's state law claim is preempted by ERISA, presumably to take advantage of the no-jury trial and limited damages available in ERISA actions. As will be discussed below, such a claim is preempted if it "relates to" the administration of an ERISA plan. Sometimes, the employee-claimant will be arguing for ERISA coverage in order to avoid a provision in the contract purporting to authorize forfeiture of accrued benefits if, say, the employee is fired for "cause" or the employee works

---

23. Rev. Rul. 98–30, 1998–1 CB 1273; Rev. Rul. 2000–8, 2000–1 CB 617.

24. PENSION PROTECTION ACT OF 2006, Pub.L. No. 109–280, 120 Stat. 780 (Aug. 17, 2006); Default Investment Alterna-

tives under Participant Directed Individual Account Plans, 72 Fed. Reg. 60,452 (Oct. 24, 2007) (to be codified at 26 C.F.R. pt. 2550).

for a competitor in breach of a non-compete covenant. If the benefits are considered part of an ERISA-covered employee benefit plan, forfeiture of accrued benefits would be unlawful.

Whether the case involves pension benefits or welfare benefits, the threshold question is whether a benefits arrangement unilaterally provided by an employer or set out in an employment contract is a "plan, fund, or program" covered by ERISA.[25] One guidepost is offered by *Massachusetts v. Morash*,[26] where the Court held that an employer's policy of paying employees out of company funds for unused vacation time did not constitute an ERISA plan and was subject to state regulation. Vacation payments, Justice Stevens' opinion noted, are "typically fixed, due at known times, and do not depend on contingencies outside the employee's control," and hence "present none of the risks that ERISA is intended to address."[27] Even though vacation benefits are listed in ERISA § 3(1), that reference "should be understood to include within the scope of ERISA those vacation benefit funds, analogous to other welfare benefits, in which either the employee's right to a benefit is contingent upon some future occurrence or the employee bears a risk different from his ordinary employment risk."[28]

Thus, while *Morash* makes clear that regular payroll practices are generally not ERISA plans, a fairly broad subject matter—including medical benefits, accident, disability and unemployment insurance, day care, scholarship funds, prepaid legal services, and severance pay—would seem to be potential candidates for (ERISA plans under the § 3(1) definition of welfare benefit plans and its reference to benefits described in § 302(c) of the LMRA). It still needs to be determined whether an employer's policies or practices with respect to such subjects constitute an ERISA plan. Here, a second guidepost is provided by the Eleventh Circuit in *Donovan v. Dillingham*[29]: "[A] 'plan, fund, or program' under ERISA is established if from the surrounding circumstances a reasonable person can ascertain the intended benefits, a class of beneficiaries, the source of financing, and procedures for receiving benefits."[30]

The *Dillingham* test does not yield predictable results in part because of the sheer variety of benefit plans.[31] Thus, for example,

---

25. 29 U.S.C. §§ 1002(1) and (2)(A).

26. 490 U.S. 107 (1989).

27. *Id.* at 115.

28. *Id.* at 116.

29. 688 F.2d 1367, 1373 (11th Cir. 1982) (en banc).

30. For criticism of the *Dillingham* test, see Jay Conison, *Foundations of the Common Law of Plans*, 41 DePaul L. Rev. 575, 648–49 (1992) (whether a plan exists "must be made to depend on employer representations and employee expectations, not on the benefits that may or may not be provided.").

31. For some difficult-to-reconcile results, compare, e.g., *Collins v. Ralston Purina Co.*, 147 F.3d 592, 595 (7th Cir.

the "class of beneficiaries" prong does not necessarily rule out plans covering only a single person.[32] Also because the Act does not require advance funding for welfare benefits like severance pay, the "source of funding" element may be deemed satisfied even though no trust has been established. As the Supreme Court stated in *Fort Halifax Packing Co., Inc. v. Coyne*,[33] employers "should not be able to evade the requirements of the statute merely by paying ... benefits out of general assets." The Act does require even welfare benefits plans to provide a written plan document and summary description of eligibility and claim procedures, but it is unclear whether non-compliance here will derogate from ERISA coverage. *Fort Halifax* suggests, however, that one essential component of a plan is the need for an ongoing administrative scheme. The Court held in that case that a state law requiring a one-time severance payment in the event of a plant closing was not preempted by ERISA because a one-time payment did not require the sort of ongoing administrative scheme characteristic of an ERISA plan.[34]

1998) (retention payments under change-of-control agreement held an ERISA plan because it involved "prospect of multiple payments to various managers, at different times and under different circumstances"); *Dranchak v. Akzo Nobel Inc.*, 88 F.3d 457, 459–60 (7th Cir. 1996) (negotiation of enhanced pension and severance benefits was subject to ERISA, not state contract law); *Williams v. Wright*, 927 F.2d 1540 (11th Cir. 1991) (employer's letter promising monthly payments, use of office car, and reimbursement of country club dues to induce retirement, held to be a single-participant ERISA plan), with *Velarde v. PACE Membership Warehouse, Inc.*, 105 F.3d 1313 (9th Cir. 1997) (stay-on bonus held not ERISA plan because it required no ongoing administrative scheme); *Nagy v. Riblet Products Corp.*, 79 F.3d 572, 574 (7th Cir. 1996); *Delaye v. Agripac, Inc.*, 39 F.3d 235 (9th Cir. 1994) (severance pay arrangement held not to be a plan); *James v. Fleet/Norstar Financial Group*, 992 F.2d 463 (2d Cir. 1993) (employer's offer of 60 days' pay for workers staying on after their last day of work held not to create an ERISA plan); *Wells v. General Motors Corp.*, 881 F.2d 166 (5th Cir. 1989) (collectively bargained term allowing employees to exchange seniority and rehire rights for severance pay held not be an ERISA plan); *Jervis v. Elerding*, 504 F.Supp. 606 (C.D. Cal. 1980).

32. DOL regulations envision a plan covering one or more employees as within ERISA. See, e.g., 29 C.F.R. § 2510.3–3(b) (1988) ("[A] Keogh plan under which one or more common law employees, in addition to the self-employed individuals, are participants covered under the plan, will be covered under Title I [of ERISA]."); 29 C.F.R. § 2510.3–2(d) (under some circumstances, individual retirement accounts or annuities are covered by ERISA).

33. 482 U.S. 1 (1987).

34. Because of gaps in ERISA and its preemption of state law, courts have developed "ERISA common law" as a gap-filler. See, e.g., *Noorily v. Thomas & Betts Corp.*, 188 F.3d 153 (3d Cir. 1999) (employer initially announced that employees choosing not to relocate would receive severance payments from unfunded benefit plan, but changed policy when it became clear that most of its product managers and engineers would not be relocating; plaintiffs, after this policy change, declined to transfer and sued unsuccessfully to recover once-promised severance pay).

2.   Eligible "Participants"

As is true of virtually all employment statutes, and as we have seen in connection with the *Darden* decision discussed in Chapter 2, ERISA's protections extend only to "employees" and persons with coverage or anticipated coverage under employee benefit plans (including active employee participants, retired participants, dependents and other beneficiaries). As discussed below in connection with the *Vizcaino* litigation, the law does not require an employer to provide even undisputed common-law employees with pension or welfare benefits.

If an employer does establish a plan for employees, it will have to meet certain minimum participation requirements. Otherwise eligible employees over the age of 21 must be allowed to participate in a qualified pension plan no later than after completing one year of service (two years in the case of a plan providing for 100 percent vesting after two years of service).[35] Plans can, however, effectively exclude part-time employees because a "year of service" means a 12–month period in which the employee works at least 1000 hours.[36] In addition, the Tax Reform Act of 1986 established new minimum coverage tests intended to make it more difficult for employers to exclude substantial portions of their workforce even if they wish to maintain a qualified plan only for some groups of employees.[37] Moreover, the language used in plan documents may further cabin the employer's ability to limit eligibility to particular employees while excluding others who are similarly situated.

The latter issue is well illustrated by *Vizcaino v. Microsoft Corporation*.[38] In that case, a class of individuals performing services for Microsoft sued the company and its various pension and welfare plans, including its Savings Plus Plan (SPP), an ERISA-

---

35. ERISA § 202(a), 29 U.S.C. § 1052(a).

36. ERISA § 203(b)(2)(A), 29 U.S.C. § 1053(b)(2)(A).

37. A plan is not qualified unless it satisfies either the Internal Revenue Code (IRC) § 410(b)(1)(A) test and the "ratio percentage test", or the IRC § 410(b)(2) "average benefit test". To satisfy the ratio-percentage test, the ratio of the percentage of non-highly compensated employees who benefit under the plan divided by the percentage of highly compensated employees who benefit must be at least 70 percent. The first prong of the average-benefit test requires a "reasonable" classification "established under objective business criteria"; this would "generally include specified job categories, nature of compensation (i.e., salaried or hourly), geographic location, and similar bona fide business criteria." Treas. Reg. § 1.410(b)–4. The second prong relies on the plan's ratio percentage and concentration percentage (the percentage of all employees who are not highly compensated employees). DB plans must also comply with an additional coverage test under IRC § 410(b). The term "highly compensated employee" is defined in IRC § 414(q). See generally JOHN H. LANGBEIN & BRUCE A. WOLK, PENSION AND EMPLOYEE BENEFIT LAW ch. 6 (3d ed. 2000).

38.   120 F.3d 1006 (9th Cir. 1997) (en banc).

covered plan, and sought a determination that they were entitled to participate in the plan benefits because those benefits were available, in the terms of the SPP, to "any common law employee ... who is on the United States payroll" of Microsoft. After signing agreements acknowledging they were independent contractors, the plaintiffs were hired to work on specific projects and performed a number of different functions, such as production editing, proof-reading, formatting, indexing, and testing. Often they worked alongside regular Microsoft employees and under the same supervision. However, they were not paid for their services through the payroll department, but rather submitted invoices to and were paid through the accounts payable department. An IRS audit determined that the plaintiffs were employees as to whom employment taxes should have been paid and income taxes withheld. Microsoft then offered some of the plaintiffs regular employee status and others were given the opportunity to work for a temporary employment agency supplying temporary workers to Microsoft on an as-needed basis.

With respect to the plaintiffs' claim under the SPP, the Ninth Circuit held that the benefits administrator's decision to exclude them from benefits was arbitrary and capricious in light of Microsoft's concession (made after an IRS audit) that the plaintiffs were common law employees and that their written acknowledgement of independent-contractor status when hired was without legal effect. The court sent the cases back to the plan administrator to interpret the SPP's restriction of benefits to "common law employee[s] who [are] on the United States payroll of the employer," with a strong hint that the administrator should find coverage:

> We have ... pointed out that we are dubious about the proposition that Microsoft would manipulate plan coverage by assigning recognized common law employees to its accounts payable department or to its payroll department, as it saw fit. We have our doubts that it could properly do so. But it is the terms of the SPP which control, and the plan is separate from Microsoft itself. Thus, we cannot, and will not, predict how the plan administrator, who has the primary duty of construction, will construe the terms of the SPP.[39]

Vizcaino does not stand for the proposition that freelance employees improperly misclassified as independent contractors necessarily have a right to participate in a firm's employee benefit plans. The court's remand suggests that this issue is governed by

---

39. *Id.* at 1031. The court also indicated that the plaintiffs had a viable state law contract claim to participate in a non-ERISA stock purchase plan, which was purportedly offered to all employees.

the plan documents which, in that case, apparently contained a broad inclusive definition of eligible participants—all "common law employee[s] . . . on the United States payroll of the employer". A different result likely would have obtained if the plan contained a narrower definition of eligibility.[40]

A few district courts have relied on the Code's definition of a "leased" employee to require companies to include "common law employees" on the payroll of a "leasing organization" in their pension benefit plans.[41] One way to avoid directly hiring a person is for a company to enter into a contract with a third party (the "leasing organization"), whereby the latter entity places the person on the premises of the organization that needs the services (the "recipient organization"). The leasing organization purports to be the "employer," and may even provide the "leased" employee with pension and welfare benefits. This organization retains the formal authority to hire, fire, discipline, and promote the "leased" employee, although as a practical matter the recipient organization exercises day-to-day control over the employee. Under 1992 amendments to the Code,[42] IRC § 414(n) requires the sponsor of a qualified plan using the services of "leased" employees to treat that person "as an employee of the recipient" for "anti-discrimination" testing purposes. The purpose of this provision is to ensure that employer-sponsors do not evade the non-discrimination requirements applicable to qualified plans—which typically insist on eligibility for a certain percentage of non-highly compensated employees relative to the number of highly compensated employees who will benefit under the plan (see note 37 supra)—by using "leased" employees to reduce the number of non-highly compensated employees who would be counted for purposes of the required comparison.

The courts of appeals generally have rejected the view of a few district courts that workers falling within the § 414(n) definition of "leased employees" must be treated as employee-participants in the benefit plans of the recipient organization. As the Tenth Circuit reasoned: "It is well established that ERISA does not prohibit an employer from distinguishing between groups or categories of em-

---

40. Participants have a right to information about plan benefits and procedures under ERISA. Some courts have held that this disclosure obligation is triggered by a "colorable claim" to eligibility for benefits. See, e.g., *Abraham v. Exxon Corp.*, 85 F.3d 1126, 1132 (5th Cir. 1996).

41. See *Renda v. Adam Meldrum & Anderson Co.*, 806 F.Supp. 1071, 1079–

80, 1082 (W.D.N.Y. 1992); *Bronk v. Mountain States Tel. & Tel., Inc.*, 943 F.Supp. 1317 (D.Colo. 1996), reversed, 140 F.3d 1335 (10th Cir. 1998).

42. See TAX EQUITY AND FISCAL RESPON-SIBILITY ACT OF 1982, Pub.L. No. 97–248, § 248(a), 96 Stat. 324.

ployees, providing benefits for some but not for others. . . . The [IRS] regulations purport to do no more than determine whether a plan is a qualified tax plan. Failure to meet the requirements of those regulations results in the loss of a beneficial tax status; it does not permit a court to rewrite the plan to include additional employees."[43]

D. Preventing Forfeiture of Pension Benefits

1. *Vesting Rules*

A principal objective of the ERISA and related IRC provisions is to prevent forfeiture of accrued pension benefits. The legislation seeks to accomplish this objective by a variety of mechanisms. The first, of course, is the rule on vesting of pension benefits: "cliff vesting" after five years of service (§ 203(a)(2)(A)) or graduated vesting after three to seven years (§ 203(a)(2)(B)). Cliff vesting is more common in DB than DC plans. The one-year[44] and over-age 21 waiting periods permitted under the statute affect only eligibility; the period for calculating vesting starts with the first year of service (after age 18).

An employee's right to an accrued benefit is not subject to forfeiture. IRC § 411(b) requires qualified pension plans to provide that an employee's "right to a normal retirement benefit is nonforfeitable upon the attainment of normal retirement age" (usually age 65). Thus, while non-qualified pension and all welfare benefit plans (which are not subject to any vesting requirement) can contain clauses providing for forfeiture in the event of termination of employment for "cause" or working for a competitor, such "bad boy" clauses would jeopardize the tax status of qualified pension plans.

Employers cannot effectively defeat the purpose of the vesting rule by terminating their plans without jeopardizing qualified sta-

---

43. *Bronk*, 140 F.3d at 1338–39. Accord, *MacLachlan v. ExxonMobil Corp.*, 350 F.3d 472 (5th Cir. 2003); *Clark v. E.I. Dupont De Nemours & Co.*, 105 F.3d 646 (4th Cir. 1997); *Trombetta v. Cragin Fed. Bank for Sav. Employee Stock Ownership Plan*, 102 F.3d 1435 (7th Cir. 1996); *Abraham v. Exxon Corp.*, 85 F.3d 1126 (5th Cir. 1996). See generally; Micah Berul, *Courts' Treatment of ERISA Claims Brought by Nonstandard Workers*, 29 EMPLOYEE RELS. L.J. 70 (Fall 2003); Mark Berger, *The Contingent Employee Benefits Problem*, 32 IND. L.

REV. 301 (1999) and his *Unjust Dismissal and the Contingent Worker: Restructuring Doctrine for the Restructured Employee*, 16 YALE L. & POL'Y REV. 1 (1997); Howard Pianko, *Microsoft and Its Legacy—Employers Confront "Contingent" Worker Benefit Issues*, 5 ERISA AND BENEFITS L.J. 249, 257 n.21 (1999).

44. ERISA § 202(a)(1)(B)(i), 29 U.S.C. § 1052(a)(1)(B)(i) allows a plan to require a two-year waiting period if it provides for 100 percent vesting after two years.

tus. Under IRC § 411 (d)(3), employees are entitled to the vesting of their accrued benefits, to the extent funded, in the event of the termination or partial termination of a plan. This is a subset of the non-discrimination principle in IRC § 401(a); the underlying concern is with a "pattern of abuse under the plan (such as dismissal of employees before their accrued benefits become nonforfeitable) tending to discriminate in favor of . . . highly compensated employees" or other reason to believe there has been or will be "an accrual benefits or forfeitures tending to discriminate in favor of" the highly compensated (IRC § 411(d)(1)).[45]

Responding to a spate of terminations in the 1980s of over-funded plans for the purpose of securing a reversion of residual assets to the employer, Congress placed some roadblocks in the path of such maneuvers. Reversion of a surplus is still permissible but only after "all liabilities of the plan to participants and their beneficiaries have been satisfied" (ERISA § 4044(d)(1)); typically, the employer purchases annuities from an insurance company to meet these obligations. However, the surplus recovered in this manner is taxable income to the employer, and a 50% nondeductible excise tax is levied unless a specified percentage of the surplus is used to fund a qualified replacement plan or increase benefits for participants (IRC § 4980)

2. *Minimum Funding Requirements*

A second statutory mechanism for minimizing the risk of forfeiture is the minimum funding rules requiring that money be set aside to pay for promised benefits under DB plans (ERISA §§ 301–306 & IRC § 412). Under the Pension Protection Act of 2006, new rules essentially require 100% funding of accrued benefits and give plans seven years to reach that target.

3. *Prohibition of Discharge for Attaining or Exercising Pension Rights*

A third measure for preventing forfeiture is ERISA § 510, which prohibits discharge or any form of discipline against a participant or beneficiary "for exercising any right [under an employee benefit plan or Title I of the Act] or for the purpose of

---

45. There is no comparable provision under ERISA, although decisions of plan administrators holding that a full or partial plan termination has not occurred are subject to review under the "arbitrary and capricious" standard. *See, e.g.,* *Sea Ray Employees' Stock Ownership and Profit Sharing Plan v. Robinson,* 164 F.3d 981 (6th Cir. 1999).

interfering with the attainment of any right to which such participant may become entitled under the plan [or under Title I]."[46] This provision (which is discussed further in Part G) plainly prevents employers from discharging or laying-off employees in order to prevent vesting. It also more broadly bars employers from discharging or laying-off employees in order to save pension costs. For example, in *Gavalik v. Continental Can Co.*,[47] Continental developed a so-called "liability avoidance program" in deciding which plants to close and which employees to lay-off. The program sought "to avoid triggering future vesting by placing employees who had not yet become eligible [on] layoff, and to retain those employees whose benefits had already vested."[48] The Third Circuit held that even if the company was motivated by legitimate considerations in making its selection decisions, "the desire to defeat pension eligibility was a 'determinative factor' in each of Continental's challenged actions."[49] This decision turns on the evidence plaintiffs marshaled of "specific intent" on Continental's part to interfere with pension eligibility. Presumably, if the Company had used non-benefit related factors, such as overall labor costs, in making the selection decisions, the result might have been different.[50]

4. Regulating the Rate of Accrual of Pension Benefits

Fourth, ERISA regulates the rate of accrual of pension benefits to prevent back-door erosion of the vesting principle through delayed accrual of future benefits. The accrual formulas are set out in ERISA § 204(b)(1).

5. No Cut-back of Accrued Benefits

Fifth, while it is contemplated that plans will be amended from time to time to reflect changing tax and regulatory requirements, § 204(g) of ERISA stipulates, with certain exceptions, a "no-cutback" rule for pension plans: "The accrued benefit of a participant under a plan may not be decreased by an amendment of the plan. . . ." One critical issue is the definition of an "accrued bene-

46. Section 510, 29 U.S.C. § 1140, as part of ERISA and enforceable under Title I, is limited to equitable relief. See, e.g., *Millsap v. McDonnell Douglas Corp.*, 368 F.3d 1246 (10th Cir. 2004).

47. 812 F.2d 834 (3d Cir. 1987).

48. *Id.* at 840.

49. *Id.* at 865.

50. See, e.g., *Nemeth v. Clark Equipment Co.*, 677 F.Supp. 899, 909 (W.D. Mich. 1987) ("At most, pension costs amounted to 20% of the total difference in costs between the two plants. Although this is a substantial amount, the Court finds that Clark would have made the decision to close Benton Harbor even if it had ignored the cost of the pension plan altogether.").

fit". It would include for DB plans "the individual's accrued benefit determined under the plan [and] expressed in the form of an annual benefit commenced at normal retirement age" (§ 3(23)); some decisions, relying on an IRS release, include plan-prescribed cost-of-living adjustments on the theory that an accrued benefit can be expressed in terms of a formula, and not only a promised benefit.[51] As originally enacted, the statute did not bar the reduction of early retirement benefits, but a later amendment extended the no-cutback rule to early retirement benefits or a "retirement-type" subsidy "with respect to benefits attributable to service before the amendment."[52]

The no-cutback rule does not cover reductions in future accrued benefits. A plan could be amended to reduce an accrual rate from, say, three percent of the three highest-paying years of service multiplied by the number of years of service to two percent for each year of service; this change could be applied only to the period of service following the change. ERISA § 204(h) imposes notice requirements in the event of a plan amendment working "a significant reduction in the rate of future benefit accrual...."

6. PBGC Termination Insurance

The ultimate guarantee against forfeiture is the provision of PBGC termination insurance under Title IV of ERISA. The insurance scheme applies only to single-employer DB plans[53] and is funded by an annual premium of $30 per plan participant, with a second-tier premium for terminated plans. The PBGC will guarantee only vested pension benefits, not "benefits becoming nonforfeitable solely on account of termination of a plan...."[54] The law sets a maximum guaranteeable benefit.[55] In addition, benefit increases

51. See, e.g., *Hickey v. Chicago Truck Drivers*, 980 F.2d 465 (7th Cir. 1992); *Shaw v. International Assn. of Machinists*, 563 F.Supp. 653, affirmed, 750 F.2d 1458 (9th Cir. 1985). Both decisions involved employees who retired before the attempt to eliminate the cost-of-living clause took effect; presumably, the results would have been different for employees who had accrued benefits but had not yet retired when the change went into effect.

52. ERISA § 204(g)(2)(A), 29 U.S.C. § 1054(g)(2)(A); IRC § 411(d)(6)(B)(i).

53. Termination and withdrawal rules for multiemployer plans are the

subject of the Multiemployer Pension Plan Amendments of 1980, *supra* note 16. A central feature is the requirement that employers withdrawing from such plans pay withdrawal liability so that the employers remaining in the plan not end up with a disproportionate share of the responsibility for accrued benefits of plan participants. The constitutionality of the scheme was upheld in *Connolly v. PBGC*, 475 U.S. 211 (1986).

54. ERISA § 4022(a), 29 U.S.C. § 1322(a).

55. 29 C.F.R. § 4022.22.

resulting from plan amendments adopted within five years of the termination are not paid in full, and current employees lose most benefits not yet fully earned as of the plan termination.[56]

Because of the insurance program, plan terminations are closely regulated. A DB plan may not be terminated voluntarily unless it satisfies the requirements for a "standard termination" or a "distress termination" (ERISA § 4041(a)). A standard termination, while reviewed by the PBGC (ERISA § 4041(b)), is available only where plan assets are sufficient to cover all liabilities for accrued benefits to date (including plan shutdown benefits). A distress termination occurs when plan assets are not sufficient to cover liabilities, and cannot be effected unless specified distress criteria are satisfied for each contributing employer and each member of a "controlled group" of such employers (§ 4041(c)).[57] The PBGC can also compel an involuntary plan termination (§ 4042).[58]

Employer-sponsors can take certain actions short of plan termination, such as a plan amendment effective only as to future service that reduces the rate of future accruals or decreases or eliminates ancillary benefits (such as benefits payable on death or disability). A plan amendment ending all future accruals, however, may be regarded as a partial termination triggering IRC § 411(d)(3). The PBGC carefully scrutinizes transactions that may be enagaged in for the purpose of evading liability; under § 4069, added in 1986, the agency can examine transactions occurring within five years of the plan termination.

As a practical matter, plans cannot limit the employer's obligations to its promised contributions, or the fund's obligations to the assets in the fund. This is the result of ERISA § 4022(a), which states that the PBGC "shall guarantee the payment of all nonforfeitable benefits" and the agency's determination that the full amount of benefits vested in a plan is non-forfeitable irrespective of plan language limiting the employer's or the fund's obligations.[59] The upshot is that promised accrued benefits measure the ultimate

---

56. ERISA §§ 4022(a)-(b), 29 U.S.C. §§ 1322(a)–(b), § 1301(a)(8); 29 C.F.R. §§ 4022.24–25.

57. Section 4062, 29 U.S.C. § 1362, establishes contingent liability of the employer's entire controlled group for unfunded liabilities of the terminated plan. On the controlled group issue, see, e.g., *PBGC v. Ouimet Corp.*, 630 F.2d 4 (1st Cir. 1980).

58. Voluntary terminations cannot occur if they would violate the terms of

an existing collective bargaining agreement (§ 4041(a)(3)).

59. 29 U.S.C. § 1322(a); 29 C.F.R. § 2605.6(a); see *Matter of Defoe Shipbuilding Co.*, 639 F.2d 311 (6th Cir. 1981). The *Defoe* decision assumes that the point was already decided by the Supreme Court in *Nachman Corp. v. PBGC*, 446 U.S. 359 (1980), but this may be a misreading of *Nachman*; see *id.* at 397 (Powell, J., dissenting).

obligation to plan participants, not contribution levels. The way for an employer to limit its obligation to promised contribution levels is to establish a DC plan, which requires establishment of "an individual account for each participant and for benefits based solely upon the amount contributed to the participant's account" (ERISA § 3(34)).

When a plan terminates with insufficient assets, the PBGC becomes the trustee of the plan, taking over its assets and liabilities. It then uses the plan's assets and its own funds to pay most of the remaining guaranteed benefits. The employer-sponsor and its controlled group remain liable for unfunded benefit liabilities; the PBGC ultimately has a lien in an amount up 30 percent of the collective net worth of the plan sponsor and members of its controlled group (ERISA § 408).

Note on Conversion to "Cash Balance" DB Plans

Traditional "final average pay" DB plans favor long-service workers because the retirement benefit is keyed to compensation received during the final, usually higher-paying years of employment. This feature served employer objectives to encourage long-term service. In recent years, however, greater labor market mobility has led to concerns that "final average pay" plans are not suited to employees who are unlikely to remain with the employer over the course of their careers. Moreover, the volatility of the stock market has resulted in significant fluctuations in employer funding obligations, making traditional DB plans less attractive to employer-sponsors. Presumably, in order to attract and retain high-mobility, early-career employees, as well as reduce future funding obligations, some companies have converted to "cash balance" plans. Such plans are DB plans, but differ from "final average pay" plans in that participant benefits are determined by reference to a hypothetical account balance that appears to operate much like a DC plan. A hypothetical account is established for each participant-employee, and contributions and interest are credited to the individual's hypothetical account in much the same way actual contributions and earnings would be allocated to the participant's account in a DC plan. However, unlike a DC plan, contributions and interest allocated to the participant's hypothetical account are specified by the plan document and do not depend on actual plan earnings. Thus, like a DB plan, the employer bears the investment risk in a cash balance plan, whereas individuals bear that risk in a DC plan.[60]

---

60. See Alvin D. Lurie, *Cash Balance Plans: Enigma Variations*, 85 TAX NOTES 503, Oct. 25, 1999, pgs. 507–08.

For participant-employees beginning employment or still in their early years of service with the particular employer, the transfer to a cash-balance plan is beneficial because once the eligibility period is met, the individuals enjoy fully mobile pension benefits without the "lock in" effect of "final average pay" plans. Moreover, benefits are likely to be larger for less senior workers because benefits are no longer keyed to late-career earnings. However, for participant-employees in the middle of their careers or approaching retirement, the transfer to a cash-balance plan usually will be experienced as a lowering of their expected pension benefit. For example, in September 1999, IBM's attempt to move to the cash-balance formula ignited a near-revolt of its middle-aged employees, even sparking some halting unionization efforts (an unprecedented development for this company). IBM felt compelled to promise employees 40 or older with at least 10 years of service that they could remain in the old plan.[61] Most companies converting to cash balance plans include a transitional provision, either grandfathering incumbent employees or providing enhanced credits to older workers.

Legal challenges to cash-balance plans involve claims of violations of ERISA and age discrimination rules. One argument is that "frontloaded" cash-balance plans violate ERISA § 204(b)(1)(H) & IRC § 411(b)(1)(H), and a similar provision of the Age Discrimination in Employment Act of 1967 (ADEA),[62] which provide that in a DB plan "the rate of an employee's benefit accrual" may not be reduced "because of the attainment of any age." For example, a cash balance plan using a typical level percent of pay credit (such as 4% of pay) is claimed by conversion opponents to have a rate of benefit accrual that decreases with the age of the participant; the benefit accrual decreases with age because any future interest credits (which are included in the calculation of accrued benefits) decrease as the employee-participant approaches normal retirement age. Employers would respond, however, that "the rate of benefit accrual" is not defined in the statute or regulations and any "benefit accrual" should be measured by the level pay credit; they also would rely on IRS and Treasury positions taken in 1991 rejecting the IRC § 411(b)(1)(H) argument.

---

61. See *Boomer Backlash: Controversy Besetting New Pension Plan Rise with IBM's Retreat*, Wᴀʟʟ Sᴛ. J., Sept. 20, 1999, p. A1, col. 1.

62. ERISA § 204(b)(1)(H), 29 U.S.C. § 1054(b)(1)(H); ADEA § 4(i)(1)(A)

(prohibiting in the case of a DB plan, "the cessation of an employee's benefit accrual or the reduction in rate of an employees benefit accrual, because of age"). 29 U.S.C. § 623(i)(1)(A).

Second, opponents might argue that ADEA is also violated because of the "wear away" provision commonly used in conversion to cash-balance plans. There would be no ADEA issue (other than with respect to the accrual question discussed in the preceding paragraph) if the plan simply provided for the freezing of accrued benefits plus future accruals under the cash-balance formula. The ADEA issue arises because employers more typically provide for conversion of the employee's existing accrued benefit

to an actuarially equivalent cash balance, which is frozen. The participant's benefit is then defined as the greater of this balance or the balance that would have been accrued had the cash balance plan been in effect from the beginning of the participant's participation on the original plan.

To see the age-dependent aspect of such a formula, examine the cash balances for A and B. Had the cash balance plan been in effect for their ten years of prior service, each would have a cash balance equal to $78,227, reflecting a $5,000 annual addition based on salary and 8 percent annual interest. Their frozen balances would be quite different. They each have an accrued benefit of $20,000 per year for life, payable at age 65. Assume this is actuarially equivalent to a lump sum of $162,720 at age 65. Since B is 64 when the plan is amended, B's hypothetical cash balance at that time would be this amount discounted for one year at 8 percent, or $156,667. Since this is higher than the cash balance formula, B's cash balance will be frozen at this amount for many years into the future. The wear-away means that B will accrue no new benefits under the plan until the $78,227 balance grows above $156,667.

Now let us look at A's situation. Since A is 34 when the plan is amended, his frozen cash balance would be $162,720, discounted by 31 years, or $14,972! Since this is far less than A's balance under the new formula, A would have a cash balance of $78,227 and would begin to accrue new benefits in the current year since there is no higher benefit to wear away.[63]

Hence, B would argue that simply because of his age he receives no new benefit while A does. The employer-sponsor's response here would be that the cash-balance formula is age neutral (a level pay credit), that employers should not be penalized for previously having established a plan that favored the long-service, typically older worker, and that any disparate-impact challenge under ADEA

63.   LANGBEIN & WOLK, *supra* note 37, at 481.

is foreclosed where benefits plans provide for equal contributions irrespective of age.[64]

The first court of appeals to address squarely the status of cash-balance plans under ERISA § 204(b)(1)(H)(i) found no violation. In *Cooper v. IBM Personal Pension Plan*,[65] the Seventh Circuit reasoned that (i) the "rate of an employee's benefit accrual" is not reduced on account of age when employees receive the same pay credit and the same interest credit each year irrespective of their age; (ii) the provision requires that "benefit accrual," rather than the "accrued benefit," not decrease on account of age, and "the phrase 'benefit accrual' reads most naturally as a reference to what the employer puts in (either in absolute terms or as a rate of change) while the [statutorily] defined phrase 'accrued benefit' refers to outputs after compounding [of interest]"; and (iii) the fact that the present value of the contributions to a younger employee's account is greater than the present value of the same contributions to an older worker is simply a function of the time value of money rather than age.

The controversy over cash balance plans is likely to resolved in light of the Pension Protection Act of 2006, amending ERISA to make clear that a DB plan does not discriminate on the basis of age if a participant's accrued benefit under a DB is not less than the accrued benefit of any "similarly situated" employee, defined to mean identical in every respect other than age. The measure also expressly permits the accrued benefit to be determined as the balance of a hypothetical account, in addition to the traditional final average pay basis. Conversions to cash-balance plans cannot result in a "wear-away" of previously accrued benefits, thus requiring participants to begin accruing new benefits after the conversion to be added to existing accrued benefits under the prior final average pay formula.

E. Reporting and Disclosure Obligations

The vesting rule and related protective provisions apply only to pension benefit plans. ERISA also provides for disclosure and fiduciary obligations, as well as § 510 non-interference protections, which apply to pension and welfare benefit plans alike.

Part 1 of Title I of ERISA establishes a number of reporting and disclosure requirements typically imposed on the administrator of the plan (under § 3(16), usually the person so named in the plan documents or the employer-sponsor). These include a summary

---

64. See § 4(f)(2)(B) of ADEA, 29 U.S.C. § 623(f)(2)(B).

65. 457 F.3d 636, 638 (7th Cir. 2006).

plan description (SPD), statement of benefits accrued, annual reports and periodic accounting and actuarial reports. The SPD requirement is of particular importance. The SPD is a written summary of an employee benefit plan written in a manner to be understood by the average plan participant and sufficiently accurate and comprehensive to advise participants and beneficiaries of their rights under the plan.[66] Many decisions hold that an SPD stating terms in a fashion that is more generous to claimants than that provided in plan documents is enforceable against the plan.[67]

In general, disclosure obligations, like the SPD, extend to "each participant covered under the plan" and "each beneficiary who is receiving benefits under the plan" (§ 101(a)). Often it is not contested whether an individual is a covered participant or beneficiary, but sometimes that is the very matter in issue, and the question turns on whether a claimant comes within the statutory term "participant," which includes "any employee or former employee ... who is or may become eligible to receive a benefit of any type from an employee benefit plan, or whose beneficiaries may be eligible to receive any such benefit." (§ 3(7)).

In *Firestone Tire & Rubber Co. v. Bruch*,[68] plaintiffs, former employees of Firestone hired by Occidental, the purchaser of several Firestone plants, brought a class action challenging Firestone's refusal to pay them severance benefits. As part of their lawsuit, they sought damages for Firestone's failure to provide plan information from Firestone under ERISA § 104(b)(4), which provides:

> The administrator shall, upon written request of any participant or beneficiary, furnish a copy of the latest updated summary plan description, plan description, and the latest annual report, any terminal report, the bargaining agreement, trust agreement, contract, or other instruments under which the plan is established or operated. ...

The Supreme Court, per Justice O'Connor, held that the definition of "participant" in § 3(7) also governed entitlement to disclosure under § 104(b)(4):

> In our view, the term "participant" is naturally read to mean either "employees in, or reasonably expected to be in, currently covered employment," or former employees who "have ... a reasonable expectation of returning to covered employment" or

---

66. ERISA § 102, 29 U.S.C. § 1022; see 29 C.F.R. § 2520.102.

67. See, e.g., *Burke v. Kodak Retirement Income Plan*, 336 F.3d 103 (2d Cir. 2003).

68. 489 U.S. 101 (1989).

who have "a colorable claim" to vested benefits. In order to establish that he or she "may become eligible" for benefits, a claimant must have a colorable claim that (1) he or she will prevail in a suit for benefits, or that (2) eligibility requirements will be fulfilled in the future. . . . "A former employee who has neither a reasonable expectation of returning to covered employment nor a colorable claim to vested benefits, however, simply does not fit within the [phrase] "may become eligible."[69]

Firestone narrows somewhat the administrator's obligation to provide plan information to benefits claimants by requiring this threshold showing of potential eligibility.

Although Congress's purpose in establishing the ERISA disclosure regime was in part to facilitate monitoring of fiduciary conduct by plan participants and beneficiaries,[70] the courts have not been receptive to attempts to require disclosures going beyond information about plan benefits and eligibility rules but that might facilitate the bringing of claims. In *Hughes Salaried Retirees Action Committee v. Administrator*,[71] the Ninth Circuit rejected an attempt by a group of retirees to compel the plan administrator to furnish them with a list of the names and addresses of all retired participants of the plan so they could communicate with them about Hughes's allegedly "unlawful use of excess Plan assets for the sole purpose of meeting Hughes' funding obligations" and "to gain support for their efforts to obtain increased benefits through negotiation or if required, litigation, as well as to monitor the Plan." The court rejected the argument that the requested list fell within § 101(b)(4):

[A] list of plan participants cannot possibly be considered an instrument "under which the plan is established or operated." The plain language of the statute limits the universe of documents falling within that phrase to documents similar in nature to those specifically identified, which describe the terms and conditions of the plan, as well as its administration and financial status. . . . Unlike the documents specifically listed in § 104(b)(4)—plan descriptions, annual and terminal reports,

---

69. *Id.* at 117.

70. See H.R. Rep. No. 533, 93d Cong., 1st Sess. 11 (1974) ("[T]he safeguarding effect of the fiduciary responsibility section will operate efficiently only if fiduciaries are aware that the details of their dealings will be open to inspec-

tion, and that individual participants and beneficiaries will be armed with enough information to enforce their own rights as well as the obligations owed by the fiduciary to the plan in general.").

71. 72 F.3d 686 (9th Cir. 1995) (en banc).

and bargaining and trust agreements—participants' names and addresses provide no information about the plan or benefits.[72] The court also rejected the retirees' argument that ERISA's general fiduciary duty provision (§ 404(a)(1)(A)) required disclosure because even though the requested list did not provide information about the provisions of benefits they were seeking the information in order to monitor the plan's failure to use surplus assets for the exclusive benefit of participants or beneficiaries:

> [S]ince a participant list will not provide the Retirees with any information about the Plan, we fail to see how the list, or the access to other participants that it would facilitate, will aid in monitoring the Plan's management. . . . [T]he Retirees want to use the list to solicit financial support for future litigation. Congress has provided for recovery of costs and attorneys' fees under ERISA § 502(g), 29 U.S.C. § 1132(g), and we find nothing in ERISA suggesting that Congress intended to help plan participants amass a litigation war chest by soliciting donations from other plan participants and beneficiaries.[73]

Did the court in *Hughes* give adequate weight to the organizational problems confronting participants who suspect a violation of their ERISA rights? It should be noted that unions, who might be expected to pursue such claims on behalf of participants or retirees under plans they have negotiated, represent less than 10 percent of the private-sector workforce. The problem is exacerbated for participants who are retirees because even where unions bargain on behalf of active employees, they have no right to insist on bargaining on behalf of retirees.[74] The underlying issue in cases like *Hughes* may be one of agency—that, at least in the absence of a union representative, there is no basis for assuming that the participant requesting the information sought in *Hughes* has any authority to act on behalf of other participants.[75]

F. Fiduciary Obligations

Section 404(a)(1) of ERISA imposes a duty of loyalty on a plan fiduciary "to discharge his duties with respect to the plan solely in

---

72. *Id.* at 690.

73. *Id.* at 694.

74. See *Allied Chem. & Alkali Workers v. Pittsburgh Plate Glass Co.*, 404 U.S. 157 (1971) (retirees are neither "employees" under the National Labor Relations Act, 29 U.S.C. §§ 151 *et seq.*, nor bargaining-unit members, and benefits for retirees are not a mandatory subject of collective bargaining); see also *Schneider Moving & Storage Co. v. Robbins*, 466 U.S. 364, 376 n. 22 (1984) (suggesting that unions owe no duty of fair representation to retirees).

75. Consider in this regard the special procedures for termination/modification of retiree welfare-benefits in bankruptcy reorganizations, see § 1114 of the Bankruptcy Code, 11 U.S.C. § 1114.

the interest of the participants and beneficiaries...." Four aspects of this duty are listed:

- To act "for the exclusive purpose of providing benefits to participants and their beneficiaries";

- To act "with the care, skill prudence, and diligence under the circumstances then prevailing of a prudent man acting in a like capacity";

- To diversify plan investments "unless under the circumstances it is clearly prudent not to do so"; and

- To act in accordance with plan documents and instruments to the extent they are consistent with the Act.

In addition, under § 406, fiduciaries are barred from engaging in a number of "prohibited transactions" with "a party in interest" (defined in § 3(14)). These rules are designed to prevent fiduciaries (and certain other persons) from engaging in transactions involving plan assets likely to involve a conflict of interest.

1. *Determining Fiduciary Status*

ERISA envisions there may be a number of plan fiduciaries in addition to the plan administrator. Under § 2(21)(A), a person is a "fiduciary" with respect to a plan to the extent

(i) he exercises any discretionary authority or discretionary control respecting management of such plan or exercises any authority or control respecting management or disposition of its assets;

(ii) he renders investment advice for a fee or other compensation, direct or indirect, with respect to any moneys or other property of such plan ..., or

(iii) he has any discretionary authority or discretionary responsibility in the administration of such plan. ...

Under § 402(a)(1), every plan is required to designate one or more "named" fiduciaries who will have "authority to control and manage the operation and administration of the plan." The employer-sponsor is permitted to designate the named fiduciary (§ 402(a)(2)). A plan may also delegate responsibility over the investment of plan assets to "one or more investment managers" (defined in § 3(38)) appointed by the named fiduciary (§ 403(a)(2)). Because in part delegation of investment responsibility to an investment manager absolves the trustee of responsibility (§ 405(d)(1)), the selection of an investment manager is itself a fiduciary act.[76]

The touchstone of ERISA fiduciary status is discretionary authority with respect to plan administration or plan assets. Those who engage in purely administrative acts, including insurance companies retained to process claims, are not fiduciaries.[77] Nor are service providers like attorneys, accountants or actuaries unless they in fact exercise discretionary authority;[78] they do, however, come within the definition of a "party in interest" subject to the prohibited-transaction rules of § 406. Investment advisers, by contrast, are always fiduciaries under § 2(21)(A)(ii).

2. *"Dual Hat" Issues*

ERISA permits the plan sponsor, typically the employer, also to act as the plan administrator, a central fiduciary role (§ 3(16)(ii)). This pragmatic concession—otherwise, plans might face significant additional costs in hiring a separate administrative staff and employers might be reluctant to establish plans if they could not continue to influence of disposition of plan assets—raises a number of difficulties.

a.   Giving Advice to Employee Participants

In *Varity Corp. v. Howe*,[79] the Court held that Varity was acting as an ERISA "fiduciary" when it deliberately misled its employees into persuading them to work for a separately incorporated subsidiary, Massey Combines, by implying that employees' benefits would remain secure when they transferred to the subsidiary, despite Varity's awareness that Massey Combines was insolvent from the day it was created:

> To decide whether Varity's actions fall within the statutory definition of "fiduciary" acts, we must interpret the statutory terms which limit the scope of fiduciary activity to discretionary acts of plan "management" and "administration." ERISA § 3(21)(A). ... The ordinary trust law understanding of fiduciary "administration" of a trust is that to act as an administrator is to perform the duties imposed, or exercise the powers conferred by the trust documents. ... The law of trusts also

---

76. See generally Bernard M. Baum, *Trustees and Their Professionals*, 19 EMPLOYEE BENEFITS J. 7 (March 1993).

77. See, e.g., *Baker v. Big Star Div. of the Grand Union Co.*, 893 F.2d 288 (11th Cir. 1989); but see *Libbey–Owens–*

Ford Co. v. Blue Cross & Blue Shield Mutual of Ohio, 982 F.2d 1031 (6th Cir. 1993).

78. 29 C.F.R. § 2509.75–5.

79. 516 U.S. 489 (1996).

understands a trust document to implicitly confer "such powers as are necessary or appropriate for the carrying out of the purposes" of the trust. ... Conveying information about the likely future of plan benefits, thereby permitting beneficiaries to make an informed choice about continued participation, would seem to be an exercise of a power "appropriate" to carrying out an important plan purpose. After all, ERISA itself specifically requires administrators to give beneficiaries certain information about the plan. See, e.g., ERISA §§ 102, 104(b)(1), 105(a). And administrators as part of their administrative responsibilities, frequently offer beneficiaries more than the minimum information that the statute requires—for example, answering beneficiaries' questions about the meaning of the terms of a plan so that those beneficiaries can more easily obtain the plan's benefits. ...

Moreover, [the information at a critical meeting with Varity employees] came from those within the firm who had authority to communicate as fiduciaries with plan beneficiaries. Varity does not claim that it authorized only special individuals, not connected with [the documents distributed at the meeting], to speak as plan administrators. See § 402(b)(2) (a plan may describe a "procedure under the plan for the allocation of responsibilities for the operation and administration of the plan").

Finally, reasonable employees, in the circumstances found by the District Court, could have thought that Varity was communicating with them both in its capacity as employer and its capacity as plan administrator. Reasonable employees might not have distinguished consciously between the two roles. But they would have known that the employer was their plan's administrator and had expert knowledge about how their plans worked. The central conclusion ("your benefits are secure") could well have drawn strength from their awareness of that expertise, and one could reasonably believe that the employer, aware of the importance of the matter, so intended.[80]

A similar issue concerns whether the employer-plan administrator, as an ERISA fiduciary, has a duty to tell its employees that it is seriously considering a proposal to offer eligible employees early-retirement incentives. Most courts take the view that "once [the employer begins] serious consideration of a proposal to offer

---

80. Id. at 502–503. For advice to employers on how to limit liability under *Varity*, picking up on the Court's reference to § 402(b)(2), see Howard Pianko, *To Limit ERISA Liability Exposure[:] Adopt a "PAPA" ("Process and Procedure Approach")*, 1 ERISA PANEL COUNSEL 1 (no. 1, Summer 1996).

more advantageous severance benefits, information about that proposal [is] material to the retirement decisions of employees" and should be disclosed.[81] "[S]erious consideration" takes place, under these rulings, when "(1) a specific proposal (2) is being discussed for the purpose of implementation (3) by senior management with the authority to implement the change."[82]

b.   Making Benefit Determinations

Under § 503, plans are required to notify participants or beneficiaries of the denial of their claims for benefits, and to provide a "reasonable opportunity" for "a full and fair review by the appropriate named fiduciary of the decision denying the claim."[83] Although an exhaustion requirement is not specified in the statute, the courts have held that, in general, a participant or beneficiary may not bring an action under § 502(a)(1)(B) for claims under the plan unless he first has exhausted the plan's internal claims procedure, including appeals.[84] Typically, in single-employer plans, managerial employees of the employer-sponsor administer the claims procedure and make the final determinations for the plan.

In a different part of *Firestone Tire & Rubber Co. v. Bruch*, the Court held that the standard of review governing benefit denial decisions challenged under § 502(a)(1)(B) is de novo review "unless the benefit plan gives the administrator or fiduciary discretionary authority to determine eligibility for benefits or to construe the terms of the plan."[85] Soon after this decision, employer-sponsors amended their plans to lodge interpretive authority with plan administrators, thus seeking to elicit a more deferential "abuse of discretion" scrutiny from reviewing courts.[86]

When dealing with funded pension plans, the plan administrator, even though he or she may be an employee of the employer-sponsor, normally faces no serious conflict of interest in making

---

81. See, e.g., *Bins v. Exxon Company U.S.A.*, 189 F.3d 929, 931 (9th Cir. 1999).

82. *Fischer v. Philadelphia Elec. Co.*, 96 F.3d 1533, 1539 (3d Cir. 1996)

83. The requirements for a "reasonable claims procedure" are set out in 29 C.F.R. § 2560.503–1.

84. See, e.g., *Barrowclough v. Kidder, Peabody & Co.*, 752 F.2d 923 (3d Cir. 1985). Exhaustion of plan procedures is not required where such resort would be futile or the claimant has been wrongfully denied meaningful access to the claims procedures. See, e.g., *Carter v. Signode Indus., Inc.*, 688 F.Supp. 1283, later proceeding, 694 F.Supp. 493 (N.D. Ill. 1988).

85. *Firestone*, 489 U.S. at 115.

86. See, e.g., *Lowry v. Bankers Life & Casualty Retirement Plan*, 871 F.2d 522 (5th Cir. 1989) (on rehearing); *Lakey v. Remington Arms Co.*, 874 F.2d 541 (8th Cir. 1989).

benefits decisions in particular cases, unless perhaps a determination affects a large group of claimants calling into question the need for possible additional funding. In the case of unfunded benefit plans, however, every favorable decision on a claim is a call on the employer's general assets. In *Firestone* itself, the severance pay plan in issue was an unfunded plan so that money spent to pay for severance benefits was money spent by Firestone. Justice O'Connor's opinion noted, without deciding, that "if a benefit plan gives discretion to an administrator or fiduciary who is operating under a conflict of interest, that conflict must be weighed as a 'facto[r] in determining whether there is an abuse of discretion.' "[87] Accordingly, many courts have held that heightened judicial review is required when the plan administrator both administers the plans and pays the benefits.[88]

c. Amending the Plan

The Supreme Court has insisted that a sharp line be drawn between "settlor" and "fiduciary" roles, holding that when the employer amends or terminates a plan it acts as a "settlor" under trust law and should not be held to the standard of an ERISA "fiduciary". The Court first articulated this approach in *Curtiss–Wright Corp.* v. *Schoonejongen*,[89] which involved an amended welfare benefit plan. The same rule was applied in the context of an amended pension benefit plan in *Lockheed Corporation v. Spink*.[90] Lockheed had amended its DB plan for salaried employees to provide financial incentives for certain employees to retire early. Lockheed established two programs, both of which offered increased pension benefits to employees who would retire early, payable out of the plan's surplus assets. Both programs required as a condition of the receipt of benefits that participants release any employment-related claims they might have against Lockheed. Though Spink was eligible for one of the programs, he declined to participate because he did not wish to waive any ADEA or ERISA claims. He then retired, without earning any extra benefits for doing so.

The Court reversed the Ninth Circuit's ruling that the plan amendments violated ERISA § 406(a)(1)(D), 29 U.S.C. § 1106(a)(1)(D), which prohibits a fiduciary from causing a plan to

---

87. 489 U.S. at 115 (citing RESTATEMENT (SECOND) OF TRUSTS § 187, Comment d (1959)).

88. See, e.g., *Torres v. Pittston*, 346 F.3d 1324 (11th Cir. 2003).

89. 514 U.S. 73 (1995).

90. 517 U.S. 882 (1996).

engage in a transaction that transfers plan assets to a party in interest or involves the use of plan assets for the benefit of a party in interest. The Court held this was in error because to prove a § 406 violation, "a plaintiff must show that a fiduciary caused the plan to engage in the allegedly unlawful transaction," and Lockheed was acting as a settler, not a fiduciary, when it amended the plan:

> Lockheed acted not as a fiduciary but as a settlor when it amended the terms of the Plan to include the retirement programs. Thus, § 406(a)'s requirement of fiduciary status is not met. While other portions of ERISA govern plan amendments, see, e.g., 29 U.S.C. § 1054(g) (amendment generally may not decrease accrued benefits); § 1085b (if adoption of an amendment results in underfunding of a defined benefit plan, the sponsor must post security for the amount of the deficiency), the act of amending a pension plan does not trigger ERISA's fiduciary provisions.[91]

The Court also rejected the argument that that Lockheed's early retirement programs were prohibited transactions within the meaning of § 406(a)(1)(D) because the required release of employment-related claims by participants created a "significant benefit" for Lockheed:

> By Spink's admission, the employer can ask the employee to continue to work for the employer, to cross a picket line, or to retire early. The execution of a release of claims against the employer is functionally no different; like these other conditions, it is an act that the employee performs for the employer in return for benefits. . . .

> [W]hatever the precise boundaries of the prohibition in § 406(a)(1)(D), there is one use of plan assets that it cannot logically encompass: a quid pro quo between the employer and plan participants in which the plan pays out benefits to the participants pursuant to its terms. When § 406(a)(1)(D) is read in the context of the other prohibited transaction provisions, it becomes clear that the payment of benefits in exchange for the performance of some condition by the employee is not a "transaction" within the meaning of § 406(a)(1). A standard that allows some benefits agreements but not others, as Spink suggests, lacks a basis in § 406(a)(1)(D); it also would provide little guidance to lower courts and those who must comply with ERISA. We thus hold that the payment of benefits pursuant to an amended plan, regardless of what the plan requires of the

---

91. *Id.* at 891.

employee in return for those benefits, does not constitute a prohibited transaction.[92]

Can *Spink* be squared with the anti-inurement provision of § 403(c)(1), which provides that "the assets of a plan shall never inure to the benefit of any employer and shall be held for the exclusive purposes of providing benefits" to participants and their beneficiaries and defraying reasonable plan expenses (except upon a plan termination)?[93] A partial answer can be gleaned from *Hughes Aircraft Company v. Jacobson*.[94] In that case, because its pension plan was over-funded, Hughes suspended its contributions in 1987, and two years later amended the plan to provided that new participants could not contribute to the plan and would receive fewer benefits. However, existing participants could continue to contribute or opt to be treated as new participants who would not be required to make contributions. The Court held that the amendment did not affect the rights of pre-existing plan participants and that Hughes's use of the plan surplus to fund the non-contributory portion of the plan did not violate the anti-inurement provision:

> As the language of [the anti-inurement provision] makes clear, the section focuses exclusively on whether fund assets were used to pay pension benefits to plan participants, without distinguishing either between benefits for new and old employees under one or more benefit structures of the same plan, or between assets that make up a plan's surplus as opposed to those needed to fund the plan's benefits. ... [A]t all times, Hughes satisfied its continuing obligations under the provisions of the Plan and ERISA to ensure that the Plan was adequately funded. ... Hughes did not act impermissibly by using surplus assets from the contributory structure to add the noncontributory structure to the Plan. The act of amending a pre-existing plan cannot as a matter of law create two de facto plans if the obligations (both preamendment and postamendment) continue to draw from the same single, unsegregated pool or fund of assets. ... Because only one plan exists and respondents do not allege that Hughes used any of the assets

92. *Id.* at 893, 895.

93. 29 U.S.C. § 1103(c)(1). This issue has arisen with particular saliency in the "reducing plan benefit accruals" cases, see, e.g., *Stamper v. Total Petroleum, Inc. Retirement Plan*, 188 F.3d 1233 (10th Cir. 1999), and fund "spinoff" cases, see, e.g., *Systems Council EM–3 v. AT&T Corp.*, 159 F.3d 1376 (D.C. Cir. 1998), where employer-set-tlors in essence withdraw assets from "overfunded" defined-benefit pension plans. *See generally* Charles C. Shulman, *Qualified Plans in Mergers and Acquisitions*, 5 ERISA AND BENEFITS L.J. 297 (Spring 1999); Henry Talavera, *ERISA Plans at Risk: How to Take Control of Control Group Rules*, 12 BENEFITS L.J. 67 (no. 2, Summer 1999).

94. 525 U.S. 432 (1999).

for a purpose other than to pay its obligations to the Plan's beneficiaries, Hughes could not have violated the anti-inurement provision under ERISA § 403(c)(1).[95]

d. Promoting Employer Stock

The collapse of Enron, Global Crossing, and other companies has spawned significant "stock drop" litigation. On September 30, 2003, the district court in *In re Enron Corp. Securities, Derivative & ERISA Litigation* (Tittle v. Enron Corp.), No. 4:01–CV–3913, found that former Enron employees had stated a claim that Enron and its officers and directors breached their ERISA fiduciary duties by, inter alia, (i) initiating a "lockdown" in October 2001 that prevented employees from moving their pension assets out of Enron at a time when Enron's stock price was plummeting; and (ii) heavily promoting Enron stock and encouraging employees to invest their retirement funds in company stock, despite knowledge that Enron stock was an imprudent investment choice.[96] (The Enron litigation ultimately settled without producing any substantive law of the case.)

Note on Retiree Health Care Benefits

In part because of changing accounting rules that require companies to report the anticipated cost of post-retirement medical expenses and other non-pension benefits,[97] many employers have terminated or substantially reduced programs that had provided for retiree health care benefits.[98] Challenges to these employer-sponsor decisions are difficult to mount because retiree health care benefits are "welfare benefits" not subject to the vesting requirement applicable to pension benefits. Contract-based claims are possible where employers have made unqualified promises of post-retirement benefits. These claims are adjudicated under a "federal common law" that has developed pursuant to ERISA, not state contract

95. *Id.* at 442.

96. See generally Susan J. Stabile, *Enron, Global Crossing and Beyond: Implications for Workers,* 76 ST. JOHN'S L. REV. 815 (2002). The Enron litigation also raised the issue whether ERISA fiduciaries have a duty to disclose non-public information to plan participants. See also *Rankin v. Rots,* 278 F.Supp.2d 853 (E.D. Mich. 2003).

97. See Employers' Accounting for Postretirement Benefits Other than Pensions, *Financial Accounting Standard No. 106* (Fin. Accounting Standards Bd., 1990).

98. See Marilyn J. Ward Ford, *Broken Promises: Implementation of Financial Accounting Standards Board Rule 106, ERISA, and Legal Challenges to Modification and Termination of Postretirement Health Care Benefit Plans,* 68 ST. JOHN'S L. REV. 427 (1994).

law. Courts disagree over whether retiree benefits are a kind of "status" benefit that is presumed to continue as long as the prerequisite status is maintained.[99]

In *Curtiss–Wright Corp. v. Schoonejongen*,[100] the company amended its employee benefit plan to provide that post-retirement health care coverage would cease for retirees upon the termination of business operations in the facility from which they retired. The lower courts held that Curtiss–Wright had not reserved the authority to amend the plan because the plan's reservation clause—which stated that "[t]he Company reserves the right ... to modify or amend" the plan—was too vague to be a valid amendment procedure under § 402(b)(3) of ERISA, 29 U.S.C. § 1102(b)(3). The Supreme Court unanimously reversed:

> The text of § 402(b)(3) actually requires *two* things: a "procedure for amending (the) plan" *and* "(a procedure) for identifying the persons who have authority to amend the plan." With respect to the second requirement, the general "Definitions" section of ERISA makes quite clear that the term "person," wherever it appears in the statute, includes companies. See 29 U.S.C. § 1002(9). ...
>
> The text of § 402(b)(3) speaks, somewhat awkwardly, of requiring a *procedure* for identifying the persons with amendment authority, rather than requiring identification of those persons outright. Be that as it may, a plan that simply identifies the persons outright necessarily indicates a procedure for identifying the persons as well. With respect to the Curtiss–Wright plan, for example, to identify "(t)he Company" as the person with amendment authority is to say, in effect, that the procedure for identifying the person with amendment authority is to look always to the "(t)he Company."

Curtiss-Wright appears, however, not to have dampened litigation over termination of retiree health care plans. Despite clear language in the reservation clause of a plan, plaintiffs have been able in some cases successfully to argue that such language was

---

99. Compare, e.g., *UAW v. Yard–Man, Inc.*, 716 F.2d 1476, 1482 (6th Cir. 1983) ("retiree benefits are in a sense 'status' benefits which, as such, carry with them an inference that they continue so long as the prerequisite status is maintained"), with *UAW v. Skinner Engine Co.*, 188 F.3d 130, 140–41 (3d Cir. 1999) ("We cannot agree with *Yard–Man* and its progeny that there exists a presumption of lifetime benefits in the context of employee welfare benefits";

"*Yard–Man's* inference may be contrary to Congress' intent in choosing specifically not to provide for the vesting of employee welfare benefits"); *United Paperworkers International Union v. Champion International Corp.*, 908 F.2d 1252 (5th Cir. 1990); *Anderson v. Alpha Portland Industries, Inc.*, 836 F.2d 1512, 1517 (8th Cir. 1988).

100. 514 U.S. 73, 78–79 (1995).

essentially negated by representations in summary plan descriptions to the effect that medical benefits would "be continued for the rest of your life." The Third Circuit in one case reasoned:

> [W]e hold that the district court did not err as a matter of law in concluding that the duty to convey complete and accurate information that was material to its employees' circumstance arose from these facts since the trustees had to know that their silence might cause harm. The district court's findings that the company actively misinformed its employees by affirmatively representing to them that their medical benefits were guaranteed once they retired, when in fact the company knew that this was not true and that employees were making important retirement decisions relying upon this information, clearly support a claim for breach of fiduciary duty under ERISA.[101]

3. Fiduciary Investing: Prudence

ERISA § 404(a)(1)(B) & (C) requires prudent investment of plan assets, 29 U.S.C. § 1104(a)(1)(B)–(C);—specifically insisting on diversification of investments in order to minimize "large losses, unless under the circumstances it would be clearly prudent not to do so." Not surprisingly, DB plans cannot invest more than 10 percent of plan assets in the stock of the sponsor-employer (§ 407(a)(2)). Whereas the law of trusts, at least as traditionally formulated, might have required conservative investment strategies, ERISA has been more flexibly interpreted. In line with modern portfolio theory, prudent investments need not avoid some risky investments provided that risk-adjusted returns and the overall mix of strategies for plan assets indicate prudence.[102]

---

101. *In re Unisys Corp. Retiree Medical Benefit "ERISA" Litigation*, 57 F.3d 1255, 1266 (3d Cir. 1995) (claim for breach of fiduciary duty under § 502(a)(3)(B) of ERISA, 29 U.S.C. § 1132(a)(3), may be maintained in such circumstances for failing to disclose to employees that they did not have a lifetime medical benefit before they retired).

102. See 29 C.F.R. § 2550.404a–1: "The Department is of the opinion that (1) generally, the relative riskiness of a specific investment or investment course of action does not render such investment or investment course of action either per se prudent or per se imprudent, and (2) the prudence of an investment decision should not be judged without regard to the role that the proposed investment or investment course of action plays in the overall plan portfolio." See, e.g., *Laborers National Pension Fund v. Northern Trust Quantitative Advisors*, 173 F.3d 313 (5th Cir. 1999).

Note on Fiduciary Duties in Participant–Directed DC Plans

As discussed above, employers increasingly have moved away from DB plans in favor of DC plans, which are defined as individual account plans where benefits are "based solely on the amounts contributed to the participant's account and any income, expenses, gains and losses . . . ." ERISA § 3 (34), 29 U.S.C. § 1002 (34). DC plans offer employers certain administrative efficiencies, shift the burden of market risk to participants, and pursuant to ERISA § 404(c) can remove a good deal of fiduciary responsibility when such plans take the form of "participant directed" plans. Because of a likely financial illiteracy on the part of most participants, these plans have come under criticism as poorly designed retirement vehicles.[103]

The Department of Labor has tried to create some incentives for employers to provide essential financial information. Its 1992 regulations provide that a plan will not be deemed to meet § 404(c)'s participant-control requirement unless the participant is provided with "an opportunity to choose, from a broad range of investment alternatives, the manner in which some or all of the investments in his account are invested."[104] At least three diversified investment alternatives, each with "materially different risk and return characteristics," must be provided. Plans may allow investment in employer securities but only as an option in addition to the minimum three diversified alternatives. The participant must also be "provided or ha[ve] the opportunity to obtain sufficient information to make informed decisions with regard to the investment alternatives available under the plan."[105] "Sufficient information" must include a "description of the investment alternatives available under the plan, and, with respect to each designated investment alternative, a general description of the investment objectives and risk and return characteristics of each alternative, including information relating to the type and diversification of assets comprising the portfolio of the designated investment alternative."[106] To address concerns of employers and financial institutions that any provision of information might trigger fiduciary

---

103. On participant-directed plans, see ERISA 404(c), 29 U.S.C. § 1104(c). For criticism, see Lorraine Schmall, *Defined Contribution Plans After Enron*, 41 BRANDEIS L.J. 891 (2003); Susan J. Stabile, *Paternalism Isn't Always a Dirty Word: Can the Law Better Protect Defined Contribution Plan Participants?*, 5 EMPLOYE RTS. & EMP. POL'Y J. 491 (2001); Colleen E. Medill, *The Individual Re-* *sponsibility Model of Retirement Plans Today: Conforming ERISA Policy to Reality*, 49 EMORY L.J. 1 (2000).

104. 29 C.F.R. § 2550.404(c)–1(b)(1)(ii).

105. 29 C.F.R. § 2550.404(c)–1(b)(2)(i)(B).

106. 29 C.F.R. § 2550.404(c)–1(b)(2)(i)(B)(ii).

status, DOL issued a 1996 bulletin specifying a range of financial information that will not be presumed to constitute investment advice possibly triggering fiduciary duties, including descriptions of "hypothetical" portfolio recommendations not tailored to the objectives of particular participants.[107]

DOL has also experimented under its ERISA § 408 authority in granting administrative exceptions to the prohibited-transaction rules of § 406 as a means of broadening the availability of financial information. For example, on December 14, 2001, the agency issued an advisory opinion endorsing SunAmerica's request for § 408 relief. SunAmerica proposed to hire an independent contractor to collect information about investment goals and risk tolerance from participants, and then send the information to an independent financial consultant who would produce computer-generated portfolio recommendations for each individual. The participant could then choose either the "Discretionary Asset Allocation" option, in which the computer-generated recommendations would be automatically implemented, or the "Recommended Asset Allocation Service," where the participant would be provided with a suggested portfolio which he could choose to implement or disregard. SunAmerica would collect customary fees from the purchase and holding of its mutual funds by the plan participants. The Department reasoned that although SunAmerica would be acting as a financial advisor, and thus an ERISA fiduciary, it would not be using its fiduciary authority to cause the plan to pay additional fees to SunAmerica because the participants' investment decisions would be guided not by SunAmerica's advice, but by the recommendations of an independent consultant.[108]

The Pension Protection Act of 2006 eases some of the restrictions on the provision of advice to participants and beneficiaries in DC plans. It does so by creating a new category of prohibited transaction exemption for the provision of investment advice through an "eligible investment advice arrangement" to participants and beneficiaries of a DC plan who direct the investment of their accounts under the plan and to beneficiaries of IRAs. Such arrangements must provide that fees received by the fiduciary adviser do not depend on which investment option is selected, or use a computer model containing prescribed objective criteria. Subject to certain requirements, an employer or plan fiduciary, other

---

107. See 29 C.F.R. § 2509.96–1.

108. See Advisory Opinion Letter 2001–09A from Louis Campagna, Chief Division of Fiduciary Interpretations, Pension & Welfare Benefits Admin. to William A. Schmid & Eric Berger, Kirkpatrick & Lockhart, LLP (U.S. Dept. of Labor, Dec. 14, 2001), available at http:/www.dol.gov/esba/regs/AOs/ao2001–09a.html.

than a fiduciary adviser, is treated as not failing to meet ERISA fiduciary requirements by contracting for the provision of advice under an eligible arrangement; the employer or plan fiduciary is still subject to fiduciary responsibility for the prudent selection and periodic review of the fiduciary adviser, but has no duty to monitor the specific advice given by the fiduciary adviser. Plan assets may be sued to pay for reasonable expenses in providing investment advice under an eligible arrangement.

4. Fiduciary Investing: Duty of Loyalty and "Exclusive Benefit" Rule

Under ERISA § 404(a)(1)(A) & (B), a fiduciary must discharge his duties "solely in the interests of the participants and beneficiaries" and "for the exclusive purpose" of providing benefits to them. In *Donovan v. Bierwirth*,[109] the trustees of the Grumman Corporation pension plan, who were also Grumman directors (permitted under § 408(c)(3)), declined to tender the plan's stock and indeed made substantial additional purchases (at an elevated stock price) to help thwart a hostile takeover bid in 1981 by LTV Corporation. The Second Circuit held that the trustees had not taken sufficient precautionary measures to insure that they were acting not in Grumman's interests but, rather, in the exclusive interest of plan participants and beneficiaries.[110]

Does the "exclusive benefit" rule preclude "social investing"? Is it, for example, consistent with ERISA fiduciary standards for pension funds to engage in "economically targeted investments" (ETIs) as a means of promoting, say, labor relations objectives of existing plan participants (who may or may not be ultimate plan beneficiaries)? The Labor Department in 1994 offered some qualified encouragement for investment of plan assets in an ETI—"if the ETI has an expected rate of return that is commensurate to rates of return of alternative investments with similar risk characteristics that are available to the plan, and if the ETI is otherwise an appropriate investment for the plan in terms of such factors as diversification and the investment policy of the plan."[111]

109. 680 F.2d 263 (2d Cir. 1982).

110. It has been suggested that since Grumman had a fully funded DB plan at the time, the trustees could safely advance the interests of active Grumman employees by resisting the hostile tender offer; only Grumman shareholders would lose by its defeat. See Daniel Fis-chel & John H. Langbein, *ERISA's Fundamental Contradiction: The Exclusive Benefit Rule*, 55 U. CHI. L.REV. 1105, 1139–40 (1988).

111. See DOL Interpretive Bull. 94–1 on Economically Targeted Investments, codified at 29 C.F.R. § 2509.94–1. For a defense of the "social investing" approach, see Teresa Ghilarducci, *Em-*

G.   Non-"Interference" Obligations

As previously discussed, ERISA § 510 prohibits an employer from discharging or otherwise disciplining an employee "for the purpose of interfering with the attainment of any right to which [an employee] may become entitled" under an employee pension or welfare benefit plan.[112] Although the principal purpose of § 510 was to ensure the integrity of the pension plan vesting rules by preventing discharges strategically timed to prevent vesting from occurring, the courts have held that even employees who are fully qualified for benefits may state a § 510 claim.[113]

1.   *Application to Welfare Benefit Plans*

Under the Supreme Court's decision in *Inter–Modal Rail Employees Assn. v. Atchison, Topeka & Santa Fe Ry. Co.*,[114] § 510 reaches discharge or other discipline motivated by a desire to stop paying welfare benefits which are neither vested nor capable of vesting under ERISA. As applied to welfare benefits, § 510 essentially requires employer-sponsors to honor the terms of pre-existing

ployee Investment on Pension Investment Boards: An Economic Model of the Pension Contract, in EMPLOYEE REPRESENTATION IN THE EMERGING WORKPLACE, supra note 22, at 703–24; Jayne Elizabeth Zanglein, *High Performance Investing: Harnessing the Power of Pension Funds to Promote Economic Growth and Workplace Integrity*, 11 LABOR LAWYER 59 (1995). For a critique, see Geoffrey P. Miller, *On the Advantages of Defined–Contribution Plans: Commentary on Ghilarducci*, in EMPLOYEE REPRESENTATION IN THE EMERGING WORKPLACE, supra, at 725–34. On the related phenomenon of shareholder activism by pension funds, see Stewart J. Schwab & Randall S. Thomas, *Realigning Corporate Governance: Shareholder Activism by Labor Unions*, 96 MICH. L.REV. 1018 (1998).

112. The Supreme Court has held that ERISA preempts state wrongful termination suits based on allegations that the employee was discharged in order to prevent his attainment of benefits under an ERISA-covered plan. See *Ingersoll–Rand Co. v. McClendon*, 498 U.S. 133 (1990). Some courts may be reluctant to find that § 510 applies in order to avoid ERISA preemption of a state law cause of action for wrongful discharge. See, e.g., *King v. Marriott Int'l, Inc.*, 337 F.3d 421 (4th Cir. 2003) (holding that intra-company complaints does not qualify as an "inquiry or proceeding" under § 510, and thus allowing state law claim to proceed). On retaliation issues, see Chapter 11, Part G, on ERISA preemption, see Part H below.

113. In *Hazen Paper Co. v. Biggins*, 507 U.S. 604 (1993), the Court held that an allegation that an employer engineered the discharge of an employee in order to prevent vesting of a pension benefit did not state a claim of intentional age discrimination in violation of ADEA, because reliance on a factor that merely correlated with age—here, length of service—could not be equated with reliance on age. The *Hazen* Court suggested, however, that the plaintiff in that case may have stated a claim under § 510 of ERISA. The Court also intimated that where eligibility for pension benefits is based on a combination of age and length of service, a similarly motivated discharge might also violate ADEA.

114. 520 U.S. 510 (1997).

plans until they are properly amended. As Justice O'Connor explained in *Inter-Modal*:

> An employer may, of course, retain the unfettered right to alter its promises, but to do so it must follow the formal procedures set forth in the plan ... Adherence to these formal procedures "increases the likelihood that proposed plan amendments, which are fairly serious events, are recognized as such and given the special consideration they deserve." The formal amendment process would be undermined if § 510 did not apply because employers could "informally" amend their plans one participant at a time. Thus, the power to amend or abolish a welfare benefit plan does not include the power to "discharge, fine, suspend, expel, discipline, or discriminate against" the plan's participants and beneficiaries "for the purpose of interfering with [their] attainment of ... rights ... under the plan." To be sure, when an employer acts without this purpose, as could be the case when making fundamental business decisions, such actions are not barred by § 510. But in the case where an employer acts with a purpose that triggers the protection of § 510, any tension that might exist between an employer's power to amend the plan and a participant's rights under § 510 is the product of a careful balance of competing interests [intended by Congress by enacting § 510].[115]

2. *Application to "Basic Organizational Decisions"*

Some courts have held that § 510 has only a limited role to play in cases where "basic organizational decisions," like the sale of a business, essentially wipe away long-expected eligibility for non-vested welfare benefits. In *Andes v. Ford Motor Co.*,[116] Ford saved $18.5 million in expected pension benefit costs by selling its subsidiary DCS, which provided computer services to Ford dealers, to Universal Computer Services (UCS). Former DCS employees were given the option of losing their jobs or working for UCS which had announced plans to reduce the workforce after an initial evaluation period. Ford had rejected proposals from its personnel department to allow former DCS employees to "grow into" early retirement

---

115. *Id.* at 515–16. The Court left open disposition of the employer's argument that once employees have crossed over the "threshold of eligibility" for welfare benefits, and hence have already retained their rights under their plan, "any subsequent actions taken by an employer cannot, by definition, 'interfere' with the 'attainment of ... rights' under the plan." *Id.* at 516.

116. 70 F.3d 1332, 1337–38 (D.C. Cir. 1995).

benefits under Ford's plan by crediting service with UCS for this purpose, or to keep these individuals on Ford's payroll and simply lease them to UCS. UCS made clear that it would not duplicate Ford retirement benefits, but would replicate Ford's severance benefits for one year and provide a periodic cash bonus equal to a portion of total value of the benefits that the former DCS employees lost. As part of the sale, UCS also agreed to allow Ford some continuing influence over UCS prices and technological developments. The D.C. Circuit agreed with the trial courts that these facts did not establish a § 510 claim:

> Examining the language of § 510 closely, one notes the word "discharge" is included along with the words "fine, suspend, expel, discipline, or discriminate," all words that connote actions aimed directly at individuals. . . . In this case, it seems rather clear to us that . . . an employer's decision to sell or close down an operation would not normally implicate § 510 merely because the action caused the termination of employees. If Congress had wished for § 510 to apply routinely to such decisions, which are virtually always based, at least in part, on labor costs, it would surely have included the terms "layoff" and "termination." . . .

> This is not to say that § 510 could never be implicated in a company's basic organizational decisions. If, for example, a plaintiff produced evidence that a particular company determined that 20 of its employees were soon to become eligible for a rich benefits package and noted that 19 of those employees were conveniently located in one subdivision with perhaps only a few other employees—a company shutdown might be only an indirect method of discharging those high benefit employees. In such a situation, the organization's decision merely masks a determination to interfere with the employees' attainment of benefit plan rights. . . .

> Of course, even after an organizational decision, determinations as to which individuals, if any, are to be retained by the selling company might implicate § 510. In this case, however, since Ford was selling a going business to UCS, Ford naturally wished all of the existing employees to go with the business; otherwise its value to the purchaser would be less.
> . . .

3. "Specific Intent" Requirement

Decisions like *Andes* help explain why some courts have engrafted a "specific intent" requirement onto § 510. To establish a

§ 510 violation, plaintiff must show that "an employer was at least in part motivated by the specific intent to engage in activity prohibited by Sec. 510"; "mere cost savings and proximity to benefits are [not] sufficient *per se* to create a genuine issue of fact requiring a trial."[117] An often-cited case is *Gavalik v. Continental Can Co.,*[118] where the company employed a "liability avoidance" scheme to minimize benefit costs by "shift[ing] business to plants that either had low unfunded pension liability or plants that needed the work in order to retain employees with vested 70/75 benefits."[119] *Gavalik* is cited with qualified approval in the *Andes* decision, as a case where the Third Circuit determined that pension eligibility was the "determinative" factor in each of Continental's challenged actions.[120]

Is the requisite "specific intent" shown by an employer's consideration of the level of pension and welfare benefits and other labor costs associated with a particular facility or department in deciding to close down that facility or department? Does it make sense to bar employers from considering benefit costs, provided they do not act strategically to deprive employees of vested benefits on the eve of entitlement?[121]

4.   Targeted Benefit Plan Changes

Decisions like *Gavalik* suggest that if an employer is specifically motivated by benefit-cost considerations in making a personnel decision, "specific intent" for § 510 purposes would seem to be

117. *Dister v. The Continental Group,* 859 F.2d 1108, & n. 1 (2d Cir. 1988); *Gavalik v. Continental Can Co.,* 812 F.2d 834, 851–52 (3d Cir. 1987).

118. 812 F.2d 834 (3d Cir. 1987).

119. *Id.* at 853. Compare the facts in a case like *Gavalik* with the situation that confronted the Massachusetts court in *Fortune,* discussed in Chapter 3, at 54–55. The implied-covenant approach may be available in cases involving compensation or non-ERISA benefits.

120. 70 F.3d at 1338. See also *Gitlitz v. Compagnie Nationale Air France,* 129 F.3d 554 (11th Cir. 1997) (questioning employer's motivation for converting outside sales employees to independent-contractor status).

121. Compare *McLendon v. Continental Can Co.,* 908 F.2d 1171 (3d Cir.

1990) (sustaining nationwide injunction against company's use of computerized system for identifying high-cost employees who had not yet qualified for pension benefits as possible targets for layoff, while requiring trial on a plant-by-plant basis of company's defense that layoffs at particular plants would have occurred because of legitimate economic factors irrespective of the computerized targeting scheme), with *Colizza v. United States Steel Corp.,* 116 F.R.D. 653 (W.D. Pa. 1987) (the fact that plaintiffs' termination was a few months shy of qualification for enhanced pension benefits was "a mere consequence of a termination of employment due to a total restructuring of USX'[s] steel operations" rather than the "motivating factor" behind the decision).

established.[122] Yet, courts also hold that such "benefit conscious-
ness" does not establish the requisite "specific intent" when employers make plan design decisions—whether establishing, modifying or withdrawing benefits. Thus, for example, in *McGann v. H &
H Music Company*,[123] the Fifth Circuit held that an employer did
not violate § 510 in amending its medical benefit plan by substantially reducing coverage from a previous $1 million lifetime cap for
medical expenses to a $5000 limit for treatment for acquired
immune deficiency syndrome (AIDS) and related illnesses, even
though this change did not apply to other catastrophic illnesses:

> McGann's claim cannot be reconciled with the well-settled
> principle that Congress did not intend that ERISA circum-
> scribe employers' control over the content of benefits plans
> they offered to their employees. McGann interprets section 510
> to prevent an employer from reducing or eliminating coverage
> for a particular illness in response to the escalating costs of
> covering an employee suffering from that illness. Such an
> interpretation would, in effect, change the terms of H & H
> Music's plan. Instead of making the $1,000,000 limit available
> for medical expenses on an as-incurred basis only as long as the
> limit remained in effect, the policy would make the limit
> permanently available for all medical expenses as they might
> thereafter be incurred because of a single event, such as the
> contracting of AIDS. Under McGann's theory, defendants
> would be effectively proscribed from reducing coverage for
> AIDS once McGann had contracted that illness and filed claims
> for AIDS-related expenses. If a federal court could prevent an
> employer from reducing an employee's coverage limits for
> AIDS treatment once that employee contracted AIDS, the
> boundaries of judicial involvement in the creation, alteration or
> termination of ERISA plans would be sorely tested. . . .

122. An employer's decision to take benefits into account in setting compensation may also raise § 510 issues. In *Garratt v. Walker*, 164 F.3d 1249 (10th Cir. 1998) (en banc) (reversing panel and finding violation), Garratt had been paid $10 an hour. Starting in January 1994 she was paid a monthly wage of $2000. Dr. Walker, her employer, had been contributing 15 percent of his wages to a "Simplified Employee Pension" (SEP) on his own behalf. An SEP, authorized by § 408(k) of the Code, is a form of independent retirement account funded by employer contributions. After increasing Garratt's salary to $2000 a month, Dr. Walker focused on the fact that an annual SEP contribution of 15% might be required for Garratt if Walker wanted to receive the 15% contribution he had been accustomed to, for § 408(k) requires that all employees meeting certain service and compensation requirements be eligible to participate in a SEP. Dr. Walker ultimately gave Garratt two choices: She could take a salary cut to $21,000 per year with a 15% contribution to the SEP, or maintain her salary with no SEP contribution. The latter option was not, however, legally available without disqualifying the SEP entirely.

123. 946 F.2d 401 (5th Cir. 1991).

... ERISA does not broadly prevent an employer from "discriminating" in the creation, alteration or termination of employee benefits plans; thus, evidence of such intentional discrimination cannot alone sustain a claim under section 510. That section does not prohibit welfare plan discrimination between or among categories of diseases. Section 510 does not mandate that if some, or most, or virtually all catastrophic illnesses are covered, AIDS (or any other particular catastrophic illness) must be among them. It does not prohibit an employer from electing not to cover or continue to cover AIDS, while covering or continuing to cover other catastrophic illnesses, even though the employer's decision in this respect may stem from some "prejudice" against AIDS or its victims generally. The same, of course, is true of any other disease and its victims. That sort of "discrimination" is simply not addressed by section 510. Under section 510, the asserted discrimination is illegal only if it is motivated by a desire to retaliate against an employee or to deprive an employee of an existing right to which he may become entitled. The district court's decision to grant summary judgment to defendants therefore was proper.[124]

The *McGann* decision indicates that the selective or discriminatory character of the employer's benefit design—targeting only one particular disease for disfavored treatment—does not implicate § 510. This sort of targeted decision, however, may violate antidiscrimination principles of state insurance law for those employers who purchase health insurance for their employees. Because of ERISA preemption, state insurance law would not apply to self-insured employers who insure their own risks although they may use carriers to administer their plans. For self-insured employers, discriminatory coverage decisions may raise questions under § 501(c) of the Americans with Disabilities Act of 1990.[125]

H.   ERISA Preemption of State Law

ERISA contains a broad preemption provision "supersed[ing] any and all States insofar as they may now or hereafter relate to any employee benefit plan described in § 1003(a) of this title and not exempt under § 1003(b) of this title."[126] As the Court stated in

---

124. *Id.* at 407–408.

125. 42 U.S.C. § 12201(c); see EEOC COMPLIANCE MANUAL, ch. 3, "Employee Benefits: ADA Issues" (Transmittal Date Oct. 2000), available at www.eeoc. gov/policy/compliance; see also 29 U.S.C.

§ 1182 (HIPAA provision prohibiting discrimination on account of "health status"). See Chapter 11, Part F.

126. 29 U.S.C. § 1144(a). ERISA § 4, 29 U.S.C. § 1003(a)–(b) sets out the statute's coverage.

Shaw v. Delta Air Lines, Inc.,[127] "[a] law 'relates to' an employee benefit plan, in the normal sense of the phrase, if it has a connection with or reference to such plan." Over two dozen decisions of the high court make clear that ERISA preempts virtually the entire field "relat[ing] to" employee benefit plans, not simply overriding state laws in direct conflict with its requirements. There are some limits, however, to ERISA's preemptive sweep.

1. State Mandates Not Requiring Ongoing Administration of a Plan

In *Fort Halifax Packing Co., Inc. v. Coyne*,[128] the Court upheld a Maine statute requiring employers to provide a one-time payment to employees in the event of a plant closing. Even though the law required the provision of an employee benefit, it was not a law "relating to" an employee benefit plan:

> The Maine statute neither establishes, nor requires an employer to maintain, an employee benefit plan. The requirement of a one-time lump-sum payment triggered by a single event requires no administrative scheme whatsoever to meet the employer's obligation. The employer assumes no responsibility to pay benefits on a regular basis, and thus faces no periodic demands on its assets that create a need for financial coordination and control. Rather, the employer's obligation is predicated on the occurrence of a single contingency that may never materialize.[129]

The Court insisted, however, that "if a State required a benefit whose regularity of payment necessarily required an ongoing benefit program, it cannot evade pre-emption by the simple expedient of somehow formally characterizing the obligation as a one-time lump-sum payment triggered by the occurrence of a certain contingency."[130]

2. State Mandates Regulating "Payroll Practices"

In *Massachusetts v. Morash*,[131] the Court held that a state criminal prosecution of a corporate officer for failing to pay discharged employees their unused vacation time was not preempted by ERISA. Relying on DOL regulations excluding from the sphere of ERISA preemption certain types of regular compensation and

127. 463 U.S. 85, 96–97 (1983).
128. 482 U.S. 1 (1987).
129. *Id.* at 11–12.

130. *Id.* at 19 n.12.
131. 490 U.S. 107 (1989).

"payroll practices," including the payment of vacation benefits from an employer's general assets, the Court explained:

> Congress' primary concern was with the mismanagement of funds accumulated to finance benefits and the failure to pay employees benefits from accumulated funds.... Because ordinary vacation payments are typically fixed, due at known times, and do not depend on contingencies outside the employee's control, they present none of the risks that ERISA is intended to address.[132]

3. State Regulation of Insurance

ERISA contains an express exclusion from preemption for state regulation of insurance:

> Except as provided in subparagraph (B) [the deemer clause], nothing in this subchapter shall be construed to exempt or relieve any person from any law of any State which regulates insurance, banking, or securities. (§ 514(b)(2)(A) (saving clause)).[133]

> Neither an employee benefit plan ... nor any trust established under such a plan, shall be deemed to be an insurance company or other insurer, bank, trust company, or investment company or to be engaged in the business of insurance or banking for purposes of any law of any State purporting to regulate insurance companies, insurance contracts, banks, trust companies, or investment companies. (§ 514(b)(2)(B) (deemer clause)).[134]

Under the savings clause, states can, for example, require insurers to offer specified minimum mental-health benefits in employee health-care plans they offer.[135] By virtue of the deemer clause, however, employers that self-insure can invoke ERISA preemption to block the application of state laws regulating insurance carriers: "State laws directed toward the plans are pre-empted because they relate to an employee benefit plan but are not 'saved' because they do not regulate insurance. State laws that directly regulate insurance are 'saved' but do not reach self-funded employee benefit plans because the plans may not be deemed to be insurance companies, other insurers, or engaged in the business of

---

132. *Id.* at 115. This approach was followed in *California Div. of Labor Standards Enforcement v. Dillingham Construction, N.A., Inc.,* 519 U.S. 316 (1997).

133. 29 U.S.C. § 1144(b)(2)(A).

134. 29 U.S.C. § 1144(b)(2)(B).

135. See *Metropolitan Life Ins. Co. v. Massachusetts,* 471 U.S. 724 (1985).

insurance for purposes of such state laws."[136] In effect, large employers able to self-insure are, by virtue of ERISA preemption and the deemer clause, free of state regulation of their benefits plans; and yet ERISA provides little in the way of substantive regulation of employee welfare benefit plans.

4. State Regulation of Practices Violative of Federal Discrimination Law

ERISA § 514(d) provides that the preemption provision shall not "be construed to alter, amend, modify, invalidate, impair, or supersede any law of the United States. . . ." 29 U.S.C. § 1144(d). This provision was interpreted in *Shaw v. Delta Air Lines, Inc.*[137] to exempt from preemption state anti-discrimination laws that assist the Title VII enforcement scheme by prohibiting practices that are unlawful under Title VII, but not to exempt state anti-discrimination laws relating to ERISA benefit plans that prohibit practices that are lawful under Title VII.

The *Shaw* Court also dealt with § 4(b)(3) which exempts from ERISA coverage plans that are "maintained solely for the purpose of complying with applicable workmen's compensation laws or unemployment compensation or disability insurance laws. . . ." 29 U.S.C. § 1003(b)(3). The Court held that only "separately administered . . . plans maintained solely to comply" with the kinds of state laws covered by § 4(b)(3) are exempt from ERISA coverage, but that states may require employers to maintain separate plans to make possible the enforcement of their disability insurance (or presumably workers' compensation or unemployment compensation) laws.

5. Arguable Shift Towards Narrower Scope of ERISA Preemption

The Court arguably has begun to signal a less sweeping approach to ERISA preemption in a number of cases dealing with state regulation of health maintenance organizations (HMOs). In *Rush Prudential HMO, Inc. v. Moran,*[138] ERISA was held not to preempt a state law providing for an independent medical review of an HMO's denial of a claim for benefits; the law came within the saving clause for insurance-industry regulation even though the HMO provided both health care as well as insurance and regulated

---

136. *FMC Corporation v. Holliday,* 498 U.S. 52, 61 (1990).

137. 463 U.S. 85 (1983).

138. 536 U.S. 355 (2002).

an "integral part of the policy relationship between the insurer and the insured."[139] On similar grounds, in *Kentucky Assn. of Health Plans, Inc. v. Miller,*[140] the Court rejected an ERISA preemption challenge to a state law requiring HMOs to include "any willing provider" within their provider network.

HMOs also raise nettlesome questions over the status of health care providers whose treatment decisions may be influenced by the eligibility/coverage provisions of the HMO plan. The Court in *Pegram v. Herdrich*[141] held that "mixed eligibility" decisions by HMO-employed physicians—treatment decisions involving consideration of whether the particular condition was covered by the plan—are not fiduciary decisions under ERISA. In *Aetna Health Inc. v. Davila,*[142] the Court further held that ERISA broadly preempted state laws providing tort remedies for HMO decisions denying coverage or authorizing payment only for particular treatments of services because ERISA provided an exclusive remedy for such decisions in § 502(a).

In another group of cases, the Supreme Court has begun to question the reach of its "have a connection with or reference to" in any way employee benefit plans. In *New York State Conference of Blue Cross & Blue Shield Plans v. Travelers Insurance Co.,*[143] the Court upheld as non-preempted a New York statute that required hospitals to collect surcharges from patients covered by commercial insurers, plans maintained by self-insured employers or HMOs, but not from patients insured by a state-subsidized Red Cross & Blue Shield plan (the Blues). The Court (per Justice Stevens) explained that the *Shaw* formulation was so broad as to be unhelpful. Here, the state's purpose was to provide an implicit subsidy for the Blues which tended to provide coverage for subscribers whom the commercial insurers would regard as an unacceptable risk. The fact that there was an "indirect economic influence" on ERISA plans because the state surcharge made the Blues a more attractive option did not drive commercial insurers, self-insured plans or HMOS from the market or implicate the Congressional concern

139. *Union Labor Life Ins. Co. v. Pireno,* 458 U.S. 119, 129 (1982).

140. 538 U.S. 329 (2003).

141. 530 U.S. 211 (2000).

142. 542 U.S. 200 (2004).

143. 514 U.S. 645 (1995). For other decisions in a similar vein, see *De Buono v. NYSA–ILA Medical and Clinical Services Fund,* 520 U.S. 806 (1997) (upholding state tax on gross receipts for patient services at hospitals and similar facilities even though the tax was applied to medical centers owned and operated by an ERISA plan); *California Division of Labor Standards Enforcement v. Dillingham Construction, N.A., Inc.,* 519 U.S. 316 (1997) (upholding a state prevailing wage for public construction projects but allowing payment of lower wages for state-approved apprentice programs even though separately-funded apprenticeship plans are covered by ERISA § 3(1)).

with uniformity: "commercial insurers and HMOs may still offer more attractive packages than the Blues," and employer-sponsors could still maintain a "uniform administrative practice" or provide "a uniform interstate benefit" for its employees.[144]

The movement in some states and local governments to require certain companies within their jurisdiction to pay "living wages" (well above federal and state minimum wages) and provide for health insurance coverage for employees implicates the question of ERISA jurisdiction. Given the Court's jurisprudence and the long-standing view that ERISA does not deal with "pay practices,"[145] the state law requirement to pay "living" or "prevailing" wages would seem not to be preempted by ERISA. On the other hand, a law requiring employers to establish a plan to provide particular benefits would seem problematic. Can a state avoid ERISA preemption by using its taxing power—requiring employers to pay a tax if they fail to provide a certain level of health insurance coverage?[146]

Note on Other Federal Regulation of Employee Benefits[147]

a. *Consolidated Omnibus Budget Reconciliation Act of 1986– Health Care Continuation Coverage.* Under the Consolidated Omnibus Budget Reconciliation Act (COBRA) of 1986,[148] all employees and their qualified beneficiaries under group health plans subject to COBRA have the right to continue their coverage for certain periods of time (up to 18 or 36 months) if they would otherwise lose their coverage due to certain "qualifying events". These events include the employee's death or voluntary or involuntary termination (except for gross misconduct), reduction in hours of employment, divorce or legal separation, or entitlement to Medicare benefits. Once a qualifying event occurs, employers must notify plan administrators of the occurrence of these events, generally within 30 days, and plan administrators then have 14 days to notify all

---

144. 514 U.S. at 659.

145. See pp. 227 n.5 & 234–36 supra.

146. Maryland's FAIR SHARE HEALTH CARE FUND ACT, MD. CODE ANN. LAB. & EMPL. §§ 8.5–101 *et seq.* takes this form:

An employer that is not organized as a nonprofit organization and does not spend up to 8 percent of the total wages paid to employees in the state on health insurance costs shall pay to the [Maryland Secretary of Labor] an amount equal to the difference between what the employer spends for health insurance costs and an amount equal to 8 percent of the total wages paid to employees in the state.

See *Retail Industry Leaders Assn. v. Fielder*, 435 F.Supp.2d 481 (D. Md. 2006) (held preempted).

147. The Family and Medical Leave Act of 1993, 29 U.S.C. § 2601 *et seq.*, is the subject of Chapter 14.

148. COBRA's requirements can be found at ERISA §§ 601–608, Internal Revenue Code of 1986 § 4980B, and the Public Health Service Act, 42 U.S.C. §§ 300bb–1 *et seq.*

affected qualified beneficiaries of their COBRA election rights. Qualified beneficiaries generally have at least 60 days to notify the plan administrator whether they wish to elect COBRA coverage. The employee-beneficiaries ordinarily pay for the continuation of coverage, although employers sometimes pick up the tab.

b. *1986 Amendments to Age Discrimination in Employment Act.* In 1979, the Department of Labor, acting pursuant to § 4(f)(2) of the Age Discrimination in Employment Act (ADEA),[149] issued an "Interpretative Bulletin"[150] which permitted employers to cease contributions and accruals for employees working beyond normal retirement age. Responding to pressure from the courts,[151] the EEOC initiated a rulemaking proceeding to reverse this policy. Then in 1986, by adding a new section § 4(i) to ADEA (as well as amending the Code and ERISA), Congress required all pension plans to continue contributions and accruals regardless of an employee's age, for plan years commencing on or after January 1, 1988.[152] Congress expressly provided, however, that employers may limit the "amount of benefits that [a] plan provides" or limit "the number of years which are taken into account for purposes of determining benefit accrual under the plan."[153]

Can employers lawfully reduce health care benefits for retirees who become Medicare-eligible? The Third Circuit in *Erie County Retirees Assn. v. County of Erie*[154] held that an employer violates ADEA by providing Medicare-eligible retirees with lesser health benefits than those offered to retirees not old enough to receive Medicare. The court reasoned that ADEA § 4(a) prohibits age discrimination in benefits "against any individual," even retirees, unless the difference could be justified under the equal-cost or benefit rule of ADEA § 4(f)(2). The EEOC initially embraced this ruling but encountered criticism from employers arguing that it would have the effect of discouraging the offer of retiree health benefits in the first place, for presumably there would have been no ADEA claim in such a case. In April 2004, the agency promulgated

149. 29 U.S.C. § 623(f)(2).

150. 29 C.F.R. § 660.120, 44 Fed. Reg. 30648 (May 25, 1979).

151. See *American Ass'n of Retired Persons v. EEOC*, 823 F.2d 600 (D.C. Cir. 1987).

152. See Oᴍɴɪʙᴜꜱ Bᴜᴅɢᴇᴛ Rᴇᴄᴏɴᴄɪʟɪᴀᴛɪᴏɴ Aᴄᴛ ᴏꜰ 1986 (OBRA), Pub.L. 99–509, 100 Stat. 1973–80.

153. 29 U.S.C. § 623(i)(2).

154. 220 F.3d 193 (3d Cir. 2000).

a regulatory exception[155] to the statute, which has ignited its own controversy and litigation.[156] In December 2007, the EEOC issued its final rule codifying the exception.[157]

155. See 29 U.S.C. § 628.

156. See *AARP v. EEOC*, 383 F.Supp.2d 705 (E.D.Pa. 2005), on remand, 390 F.Supp 437 (E.D. Pa. 2005).

157. 72 Fed.Reg. 72938–45 (Dec. 26, 2007).

Chapter 14

PERSONAL LEAVE LAW

A. Introduction

The Family and Medical Leave Act (FMLA) of 1993 protects the job security of workers who need time away from work because of family caregiving obligations or illness. The purpose of the legislation is to help employees meet their personal and family obligations without losing their jobs.[1] Gender equality is also a central theme. The opening paragraphs state that "due to the nature of the roles of men and women in our society, the primary responsibility for family caretaking often falls on women, and such responsibility affects the working lives of women more than it affects the working lives of men".[2] Congress also declared that the protections of the statute are available on a gender-neutral basis in order to minimize the potential for employment discrimination and to promote the goal of equal employment opportunity for men and women.[3]

In Chapter 1, we discussed a number of reasons why the state might intervene in the provision of workplace benefits, some of which are applicable here: a variety of information-based bargaining failures and collective action problems may mean that private bargaining fails to produce optimal leave policies. Employees, even if they had the resources, would have difficulty purchasing in the private market leave benefits that would allow them to care for ill family members or attend to childbearing and adoption. Insurers would find it difficult to underwrite leave policies given the relatively high likelihood of job interruption (when we include not only the worker's own health conditions, but also those of his spouse, parents, and children) and the risk that employees might not be fully forthcoming with the information not only about their own health conditions but also those of their spouse, parents and children. Private insurance is also difficult to obtain for actions that potential insureds may affirmatively want to engage in (what is sometimes a "moral hazard" problem). Unlike illness, which workers generally seek to avoid, pregnancy and the decision to adopt are often desirable events, and made even easier by the availability of protection against job loss. None of this is to say that we ought not

---

1. 29 U.S.C. § 2601 (a) (2) and (3).

2. 29 U.S.C. § 2601 (a) (5).

3. 29 U.S.C. § 2601 (b) (4) and (5).

make leave available for these purposes; it is only to say that private insurers may find it unprofitable to underwrite the kinds of benefits provided by the FMLA, thus arguably creating a role for the state.

B. Basic Requirements

The FMLA allows eligible employees to take up to 12 weeks of job-protected leave during any 12–month period for any of the following reasons:[4] (1) the birth or adoption of a child of the employee, or foster care placement of a child with the employee;[5] (2) to care for a spouse, son, daughter, or parent who has a serious health condition; or (3) if the employee has a serious health condition that makes him or her unable to perform the functions of the job. A "serious health condition" is an illness, injury, impairment, or physical or mental condition that involves inpatient care in a medical facility or continuing treatment by a health care provider.[6] An employer may not interfere with an employee's rights under the FMLA or retaliate against an employee for exercising rights protected by the FMLA.[7]

Employers must continue to provide health insurance coverage while an employee is on FMLA leave.[8] When the employee returns, the employer must restore the employee to his or her original position, or an equivalent position in terms of pay, benefits, and other terms and conditions of employment.[9] For key employees (those in the top 10% of the payroll) the employer may deny reinstatement if necessary to prevent "substantial and grievous economic injury to its operations."[10]

To be eligible for leave, the worker must be an employee (as defined under the Fair Labor Standards Act)[11] who has worked for the employer for at least 1,250 hours during the previous 12–month period and is employed at a worksite where the employer employs at least 50 employees within a 75–mile radius.[12] The FMLA covers only employers that employ 50 or more employees for each working day during each of 20 or more calendar workweeks in the current or preceding calendar year.[13]

---

4. 29 U.S.C. § 2612 (a) (1).

5. This entitlement expires one year after the birth, adoption and foster care placement. 29 U.S.C. § 2612(a)(2).

6. 29 U.S.C. § 2611 (11).

7. 29 U.S.C. § 2615 (a).

8. 29 U.S.C. § 2614 (c) (1).

9. 29 U.S.C. § 2614 (a) (1) (A)–(B).

10. 29 U.S.C. § 2614 (b).

11. Fair Labor Standards Act of 1938, 29 U.S.C. § 207 (e).

12. 29 U.S.C. § 2611(2).

13. 29 U.S.C. § 2611(2)(B)(ii).

An employee may sue the employer directly under the FLMA.[14] However, the private right of action terminates if the Secretary of Labor files a complaint.[15] Available remedies include reinstatement and damages for lost wages, benefits, or other losses, such as childcare expenses, caused by a violation. In addition, liquidated damages in an amount equaling monetary damages are awarded unless the employer can show its violation was in good faith and based on a reasonable belief that it was not violating the Act.[16]

The definition of "employer" under the FMLA includes public agencies, including state governments. Whether a claimant could actually sue a state was the issue in *Nevada Dept. of Human Resources v. Hibbs*.[17] The Supreme Court found that Congress acted within its authority under § 5 of the Fourteenth Amendment when it sought to abrogate the states' immunity for purposes of the FMLA's family-leave provision. In the proper exercise of its § 5 power, said the Court, "Congress may enact so-called prophylactic legislation that proscribes facially constitutional conduct."[18] The Court found "the States' record of unconstitutional participation in, and fostering of, gender-based discrimination in the administration of leave benefits" was weighty enough to justify the legislation.[19] Chief Justice Rehnquist reasoned for the Court:

> By creating an across-the-board, routine employment benefit for all eligible employees, Congress sought to ensure that family-care leave would no longer be stigmatized as an inordinate drain on the workplace caused by female employees, and that employers could not evade leave obligations simply by hiring men. By setting a minimum standard of family leave for all eligible employees, irrespective of gender, the FMLA attacks the formerly state-sanctioned stereotype that only women are responsible for family caregiving, thereby reducing employers' incentives to engage in discrimination by basing hiring and promotion decisions on stereotypes.[20]

C. Notice and Designation of Leaves

An employee who wants to take leave must give 30 days' notice to the employer if the need for leave is foreseeable (e.g., if parents know the due date of their child, or an employee has a scheduled

---

14. 29 U.S.C. § 2617(a)(2). There is no requirement that an individual first exhaust administrative remedies or file a complaint with the Secretary of Labor.

15. 29 U.S.C. § 2617(4).

16. 29 U.S.C. § 2617(a)(1), (a)(3), (d).

17. 538 U.S. 721 (2003).

18. 538 U.S. 721, 727 (2003).

19. *Id*. at 735.

20. *Id*. at 737.

date for surgery), or else "such notice as is practicable."[21] The employer may request certification by a health care provider as to the need for FMLA leave for the serious health condition of the eligible employee or of the son, daughter, spouse or parent of the employee.[22]

The employer must also give notice to employees of their right to leave under the FMLA. The statute requires employers to prominently post a notice of employees' FMLA rights in the workplace.[23] In addition, the Department of Labor's regulations require that similar information be incorporated in employee handbooks and that employees be informed of their FMLA rights when they request personal or medical leave. Most importantly, an employer must specifically designate a leave as FLMA-qualifying and notify the employee of this designation, if it wants the leave to count towards the employee's 12–week entitlement.[24] The Secretary of Labor's designation requirement suffered a partial set back in *Ragsdale v. Wolverine World Wide, Inc.*[25] In that case, the Supreme Court struck down the portion of the Secretary's regulations that provide that the consequence of an employer's failure to satisfy the designation requirement was that any leave taken by an employee would not count against the 12–week statutory guarantee. Ragsdale had taken a 30-week leave—well beyond the FMLA entitlement. Because the regulation purported to entitle her to an additional 12 weeks' leave due to the employer's failure to designate the prior leave as FMLA leave, the Court found the regulation inconsistent with the enforcement provisions of the FMLA, which offer no relief unless the employee can prove she has suffered harm from a violation. In the Court's view, Ragsdale suffered no harm because she had taken a leave in excess of the maximum statutory entitlement.

The state of post-*Ragsdale* law on the designation requirement is illustrated by *Conoshenti v. Public Service Electric & Gas Co.*[26] In this case, the First Circuit reversed summary judgment in favor of the employer, finding a triable issue as to prejudice, where the employer failed to advise the employee of his right to twelve weeks of FMLA leave after the employee gave proper notice of a serious

21. 29 U.S.C. § 2612(e).

22. 29 U.S.C. § 2613(a).

23. 29 U.S.C. § 2619(a) provides that "Each employer shall post and keep posted, in conspicuous places on the premises of the employer where notices to employees and applicants for employment are customarily posted, a notice, to be prepared or approved by the Secretary, setting forth excerpts from, or summaries of, the pertinent provisions of this subchapter and information pertaining to the filing of a charge."

24. 29 C.F.R. § 825.208(a).

25. 535 U.S. 81 (2002).

26. 364 F.3d 135, 142 (3d Cir. 2004).

health condition and there was evidence that the employee might have postponed surgery in order to return to work before expiration of his leave if he had been aware of his rights.[27]

D.   Interaction of FMLA with the Americans with Disabilities Act

The FMLA and the Americans with Disabilities Act (ADA) operate concurrently, which can complicate the task of determining the injured or ill employee's rights.[28] The regulations to the FMLA specify that where an employee would be eligible for leave under both the ADA's reasonable-accommodation provisions and the FMLA, the employer must grant leave under the provision that is most generous.[29] Some examples will illustrate the interplay between the two statutes.

The ADA requires the employer to provide a reasonable accommodation to a qualified individual with a disability.[30] A reasonable accommodation could conceivably involve a leave of absence.[31] Unlike the FMLA's fixed maximum of twelve weeks' leave in one year, the rule for determining the appropriate duration of a leave under the ADA is a question of what a reasonable accommodation is required to allow the disabled employee to perform the essential features of the job without imposing an undue hardship on the employer.[32] Assume, then, that an employee has a disability that is both a "serious medical condition" under the FMLA and a "qualifying disability" under the ADA. The employer must grant up to 12 weeks' leave under the FMLA, but (if additional leave is considered a reasonable accommodation) may also be obligated to grant additional leave.[33]

In some cases, however, an employee's disability does not satisfy both the FMLA's "serious medical condition" and the ADA's "qualifying disability" standards. Indeed, in part because the statutory requirements are different, it may be easier for employees to prevail under the FMLA than under the ADA.[34] The decision of the

---

27. *Id.* at 145.

28. See generally, S. Elizabeth Wilborn Malloy, *The Interaction of the ADA, the FMLA and Workers' Compensation: Why Can't We Be Friends?* 41 BRANDEIS L.J. 821, 836–41 (2003).

29. 29 C.F.R. § 825.702 (a).

30. 42 U.S.C. § 12112 (5) (A).

31. 42 U.S.C. § 12111 (9) (B).

32. 42 U.S.C. § 12112 (b)(5)(A).

33. 29 C.F.R. § 825.702(b). See, also, *Boykin v. ATC/VanCom of Colorado L.P.,* 247 F.3d 1061, 1064 (10th Cir. 2001) (holding that the ADA does not require an employer to grant a disabled employee an indefinite leave as an accommodation).

34. David L. Hudson Jr., *Changing Act: Family Leave Law Taking Center Stage from Disabilities Act Litigation,* ABA J. 15 (Sept., 2003).

Seventh Circuit in *Byrne v. Avon Products Inc.*[35] illustrates this point. The plaintiff, Byrne, who suffered from depression, was fired for sleeping on the job and failing to attend a meeting. He filed claims under both the FMLA and the ADA, arguing that his disability caused these shortcomings and as a result his behavior should be excused. The court rejected his ADA claim on the basis that he did not meet the definition of a "qualified person with a disability": his inability to stay awake while working made him unable to perform the essential functions of the job and therefore he was not "qualified".[36] This precluded a right to accommodation. Judge Easterbrook, writing for the court, acknowledged that time off may be an apt accommodation for intermittent conditions such as arthritis or lupus, but asserted that the plaintiff's demand that he be excused from work for an extended period simply removed him from the class of "qualified individuals" protected by the ADA.[37] Although the ADA applies to those who *can* do the job, the FMLA, by contrast, gives relief to those who *cannot* work as a result of a "serious health condition". The court remanded the plaintiff's FMLA claim because a trier of fact could find that when the employer fired Byrne, it was either on notice that something was medically wrong (Byrne's behavior represented a sudden change after more than four years of model service), or notice was excused due to the unforeseeable nature of the need for leave. In essence, then, the very thing that disqualified Mr. Byrne from claiming a right to ADA accommodation potentially triggered his right to FMLA leave.[38]

E. Paid Leave and Other Policy Issues

The statute does not require employers to continue paying workers while they are on leave, although they may voluntarily do so. An employer may substitute paid leave accrued under an existing sick leave, personal leave, or family leave plan for any portion of the 12–week period.[39] A government survey of American workers who took leaves from work in 1999–2000 reported that about two-

---

35. 328 F.3d 379 (2003).

36. Id. at 380–81.

37. Id. at 381.

38. The FMLA interacts with other statutes as well, such as workers' compensation laws. For example, an employee injured in the workplace may be eligible for both workers compensation and an FMLA-protected leave. These state laws, of course, do not preempt the FMLA. Regardless of whether an injury is covered by workers' compensation, it if meets the FMLA's definition of a "serious health condition," the parties' rights and responsibilities under the FMLA will also apply. For example, the employee's time off work will count towards his twelve weeks of FMLA leave if the employer designates it as an FMLA leave, and the employee will have reinstatement rights under the FMLA.

39. 29 U.S.C. § 2612 (d).

thirds received full or partial wage replacement from their employer, mainly through sick leave benefits.[40]

In contrast to the American model of unpaid leave, many Western European nations require wage replacement during parental leave.[41] In recent years a number of states have considered bills for legislation that would add a wage replacement component to personal leaves through modification of existing unemployment insurance laws or disability insurance programs, or through the establishment of some other scheme of public insurance.[42] However, only California has passed a law to fund family leaves through partial wage replacement.[43] The law expands the state's existing temporary disability insurance program (which previously funded personal illness leaves) to also fund parental leaves and leaves to care for ill family members for up to six weeks per year. The expanded program is financed through a tax on employee wages.[44]

Some critics question whether the FMLA's gender-neutral provision of unpaid job-protection benefits does enough to advance Congress's articulated goal of promoting equal employment opportunity for men and women. Women are significantly more likely than men to take a leave from work to care for children or elders, and the average length of leave taken by men for a birth or adoption is only about five days.[45] Household decisions to have the woman decline or reduce paid work in order to care for family members are significantly influenced by the differential opportunity costs to men and women of staying home. Analysts who believe men need stronger incentives to take leave have made various proposals,[46] although these ideas have not translated into legislation.

40. U.S. Dept. of Labor, FMLA Survey: Balancing the Needs of Families and Employers Tbl. 4.4 (January 2001).

41. See Christopher J. Ruhm, *The Economic Consequences of Parental Leave Mandates: Lessons from Europe* 113 Q. J. Econ. 285 (1998).

42. *See generally*, National Partnership for Women and Families website at www.nationalpartnership.org (contains updates of state legislative developments in paid family leave).

43. S.B. 1661, 2001–02 Reg. Sess. (Ca. 2002).

44. Cal. Unemp. Ins. Code § 984(a)(2)(B) (2007).

45. Joseph H. Pleck, *Paternal Involvement by U.S. Residential Fathers: Levels, Source, and Consequences*, in The Role of the Father in Child Development 93–94 (Michael Lamb ed., 3d. 1997).

46. See, e.g., Ariel Meysam Ayanna, *Aggressive Parental Leave Incentivizing: A Statutory Proposal Toward Gender Equalization in the Workplace*, 9 U. Pa. J. Lab. Emp. L. 293 (2007) (proposing to compensate both men and women at rates above their salaries for parental leave in order to achieve greater gender parity in leave-taking); Martin H. Malin, *Fathers and Parental Leave*, 72 Tex. L. Rev. 1047, 1081–89 (1994) (advocating compensating men for taking leaves;

Michael Selmi, *Family Leave and the Gender Wage Gap*, 78 N. C. L. REV. 707, 770–71 (2000) (advocating six weeks' paid leave that can be used only on an all-or-nothing basis by each parent or mandating that men take leave).

*

TABLE OF CASES

References are to Pages.

*

Index

References are to Pages

DISCRIMINATION LAW—Cont'd
State and local laws—Cont'd
  ERISA preemption, 273
Stereotypes, 195
Supply side economic analysis of employment discrimination, 191
Title VII, 193

DISEASE, OCCUPATIONAL
Workers' compensation, 124, 127

DRUG TESTING
Privacy rights, 73

DUAL-CAPACITY WORKERS
Status questions, 25

ECONOMIC ESPIONAGE ACT (EEA)
Generally, 88

ECONOMIC REALITIES TEST
Wage and hour regulation, 183

ECONOMICS AND LABOR LAW
  Generally, 1 et seq.
At-will employment, 34
Bargaining disparities of employees, 6, 155
Collective action problems, 10
Competition inhibiting regulation, 11
Demand side analysis of employment discrimination, 191
Discrimination in workplace, economic analyses, 191
Employee status, economic dependency analysis, 15, 21
Hour and wage regulation, 175
Information disparities and wage setting, 8
Intellectual property rights, 82
Market failure, regulatory correction, 7
Mobility and labor markets, 9
Monopsonistic wage setting conditions, 8
Pension rights, contractual, 230
Regulation policy, 6, 155
Sunk costs and labor mobility, 9
Supply side analysis of employment discrimination, 191
Transaction costs of individual employment contracts, 10
Wage and hour regulation, 175
Wage takers and wage setters, 5, 8

ELECTRONIC COMMUNICATIONS PRIVACY ACT OF 1986 (ECPA)
Generally, 78

EQUILIBRIUM WAGE
Definition, 1

EXTERNALITIES OF EMPLOYMENT RELATIONSHIP
Generally, 5, 8

FAIR CREDIT REPORTING ACT (FCRA)
Privacy rights, 80

FAIR DEALING
At-will employment and duties of, 54

FAIR LABOR STANDARDS ACT (FLSA)
See Wage and Hour Regulation, this index

FAMILY AND MEDICAL LEAVE ACT (FMLA)
See Personal Leave Law, this index

FAMILY OBLIGATIONS
Benefits plans, 228
Unemployment insurance, terminations related to family-work conflicts, 148

FARM WORKERS
Child labor, 174
Unemployment insurance, 139
Wage and hour regulation, 184

FEDERAL PREEMPTION OF STATE LAW
Discrimination laws, state and federal, 199, 273
ERISA. See Benefits Law, this index
Insurance law conflicts, 272
Safety and health regulation, 205
Unemployment insurance mandates, 130, 133
Unions
  Generally, 154
  Pension plan management, 230
Wage and hour regulation, 271
Wrongful termination torts, 265

FIDUCIARY DUTIES
Employees, fiduciary, 84
Personal Leave Law, this index

FRANCHISES
Employees and franchisees distinguished, 14

FRAUD AND DECEIT
Wrongful termination claims, 64

FREE RIDERS
Definition, 10

GENDER DISCRIMINATION
See Discrimination Law, this index

GOOD FAITH
At-will employment and duties of, 54
Bad faith breach of contract, 56

HANDBOOKS AND MANUALS
At-will employment, representations affecting, 46
Disclaimers, 50
Modifications and rescission, 51

†